ECDL 3
The Complete Coursebook

ECDL 3
The Complete Coursebook

Brendan Munnelly
with Paul Holden

Gill & Macmillan

Gill & Macmillan Ltd
Hume Avenue
Park West
Dublin 12

with associated companies throughout the world

www.gillmacmillan.ie

© Rédacteurs Software Documentation Limited 2000
0 7171 3076 2
Print origination by Rédacteurs Software Documentation Limited and Typeform
Repro

The paper used in this book is made from the wood pulp of managed forests. For every tree felled, at least one tree is planted, thereby renewing natural resources.

A catalogue record is available for this book from the British Library.

Screen images reproduced by permission of Microsoft Corporation. All trademarks in this book are acknowledged as the property of their respective owners.

'European Computer Driving Licence' and ECDL and Stars device are registered trade marks of the European Computer Driving Licence Foundation Limited in Ireland and other countries. Rédacteurs Software Documentation Limited is an independent entity from the European Computer Driving Licence Foundation Limited, and not affiliated with the European Computer Driving Licence Foundation Limited in any manner. *ECDL 3: The Complete Coursebook* may be used in assisting students to prepare for the European Computer Driving Licence Examination. Neither the European Computer Driving Licence Foundation Limited nor Rédacteurs Software Documentation Limited warrants that the use of *ECDL 3: The Complete Coursebook* will ensure passing the relevant examination. Use of the ECDL-F approved Courseware Logo on this product signifies that it has been independently reviewed and approved in complying with the following standards:

Acceptable coverage of all courseware content related to ECDL Syllabus Version 3.0. This courseware material has not been reviewed for technical accuracy and does not guarantee that the end user will pass the associated ECDL examinations. Any and all assessment tests and/or performance-based exercises contained in *ECDL 3: The Complete Coursebook* relate solely to this book and do not constitute, or imply, certification by the European Driving Licence Foundation in respect of any ECDL examinations. For details on sitting ECDL examinations in your country, please contact the local ECDL licensee or visit the European Computer Driving Licence Foundation Limited web site at http://www.ecdl.com.

References to the European Computer Driving Licence (ECDL) include the International Computer Driving Licence (ICDL). ECDL Foundation Syllabus Version 3.0 is published as the official syllabus for use within the European Computer Driving Licence (ECDL) and International Computer Driving Licence (ICDL) certification programme.

ECDL Approved Courseware
Syllabus Version 3.0

Rédacteurs Software Documentation Limited is at www.redact.ie
Brendan Munnelly is at www.munnelly.com

Dedicated to Robert, Andrew and Catherine Munnelly

PREFACE

The European Computer Driving Licence (ECDL) is an internationally recognised qualification in end-user computer skills. It is designed to give employers and job seekers a standard against which they can measure competence - not in theory, but in practice. Its seven Modules cover the areas most frequently required in today's business environment.

In addition to its application in business, the ECDL has a social and cultural purpose. With the proliferation of computers into every aspect of modern life, there is a danger that society will break down into two groups - those who have access to computer power, and those who do not: the information 'haves', and the information 'have nots'. The seven modules of the ECDL are not difficult, but they equip anyone who passes them to participate actively and fully in the Information Society.

This book covers the entire ECDL syllabus. The ECDL is not product-specific - you can use any hardware or software to perform the tasks in the examinations. All the examples in this book are based on PCs (rather than Apple Macintoshes), and on Microsoft software, as follows:

- Microsoft Windows 95/98

- Microsoft Word 97

- Microsoft Excel 97

- Microsoft Access 97

- Microsoft PowerPoint 97

- Microsoft Internet Explorer 5.0

- Microsoft Outlook Express 5.0

If you use other hardware or software, you can use the principles discussed in this book, but the details of operation will differ.

Welcome to the world of computers!

CONTENTS

Module 1: Basic Concepts of Information Technology　　1

Section 1.1: A Short History of Computing 2

In This Section 2
   New Activities 2
A Long Line of Machines 2
Section Summary: So Now You Know. 4

Section 1.2: What Exactly Is a Computer? 5

In This Section 5
   New Activities 5
   New Words. 5
The Trouble with Definitions 5
   Types of Computer 7
Section Summary: So Now You Know. 8

Section 1.3: Computer Hardware. 9

In This Section 9
   New Activities 9
   New Words. 9
In the Box. 10
   Processor 10
   Memory 10
   Hard Disk 11
   Diskettes, CD-ROMs, DVDs, Zip Disks, Tapes 12
Out of the Box: The Essentials 13
   Keyboard 13
   Screen. 14
   Mouse. 14
Out of the Box: Optional Extras 15
   Printers 15
   Modem 16
   Multimedia 16
Looking after Your Hardware. 17
When Something Goes Wrong 18
Section Summary: So Now You Know. 19

Section 1.4: Software and Data. 20

In This Section 20
   New Activities 20
   New Words. 20

Software 21
    System Software 21
    Application Software 22
    How Software is Made 22
    Software Copyright 22
    Problems with Software 23
Data 23
    Looking After Your Data 24
    Data Copyright 25
    Data Protection 25
Networks 26
    The Advantages of Networking 26
    LANs and WANs 27
Making the Connection 27
The Telephone Network 27
    ISDN 29
E-mail 29
The Internet 30
E-commerce 31
Section Summary: So Now You Know 32

Section 1.5: What Computers Are Used For 34

In This Section 34
    New Activities 34
Business and Administration 34
Industry 34
Retailing 35
Home 35
Schools 35
Health Care 36
Government and Public Administration 36
Everyday Life 36
Information Technology and Society 37
Participation in the Information Society 38
Section Summary: So Now You Know 39

Section 1.6: Looking after Number One: Health and Safety 40

In This Section 40
    New Activities 40
    New Words 40
Health Warning! 40
    Repetitive Strain Injury 40
    Eyesight 40
    Posture 40
    Accidents 41
Section Summary: So Now You Know 42

Section 2.1: Starting Up, Clicking Around, Shutting Down . . . 44

In This Section 44
   New Skills 44
   New Words 44
Starting Your Computer 45
   The Windows Desktop 45
Starting Applications 46
   Using the Mouse 46
   The Start Button 46
Multi-tasking with Windows 47
   Switching Between Open Applications 47
The Control Buttons 48
Moving Windows with the Title Bar 50
Working with Desktop Windows 50
Changing the Shape and Size of a Window 51
Scrolling a Window 52
Right-Clicking and Pop-Up Menus 52
Shutting Down 53
Restarting Your Computer 53
When Your Computer Hangs 53
   Application Problems 54
   Windows Problems 54
   Improper Shutdowns and ScanDisk 54
Dialog Boxes 55
   Dialog Box Components 55
   Default Options 55
Section Summary: So Now You Know 56

Section 2.2: Exploring Your Computer 57

In This Section 57
   New Skills 57
   New Words. 57
How Computers Store Information 58
   Files 58
   Folders 58
   Drives 59
Using My Computer 59
   Exploring Drives with My Computer 59
   Exploring Folders and Files with My Computer 60
   Sorting Folders and Files 61
   Looking at a Folder's Properties 62
File Name Extensions and Icons 62
Searching for Folders and Files 63
   Wildcard Searches 63
   Date-Based Searches 64
   Content-Based Searches 64

The Recycle Bin 64

Viewing Your System Information 65

Online Help 65

Using Help Menu Options 65

Using Help from Dialog Boxes 66

Section Summary: So Now You Know 67

Section 2.3: Working with Folders and Files 68

In This Section 68

New Skills 68

New Words 68

About Windows Explorer 69

The Two Panes of Windows Explorer 69

Viewing Options 70

Explorer's Plus and Minus Signs 71

Working with Folders 71

Changing a Folder's Name 71

Deleting a Folder 72

Restoring a Folder's Files 72

Working with Files 72

Creating a File 72

Naming and Saving a File 73

Changing a File's Name 74

Deleting a File 74

Restoring a File 74

The Windows Clipboard 75

About the Clipboard 75

Copying and Moving Folders 75

Copying and Moving Files 76

Working with Multiple Files 76

Menu bars, Toolbars and Shortcuts 77

Menu bars 77

Toolbars 78

Keyboard Shortcuts 79

Section Summary: So Now You Know 79

Section 2.4: Mastering Windows 80

In This Section 80

New Skills 80

New Words 80

Managing Your Desktop 81

Creating Desktop Shortcuts 81

Setting the Time and Date 82

Adjusting the Sound Volume 82

Setting the Screen Saver 83

Customising Your Screen 84

Background Pattern 84

Wallpaper 84

Scheme 84

Changing Your Screen Resolution 85
Changing Your Regional Settings 85
Working with Diskettes 86
    Formatting a Diskette 86
    Copying a File to a Diskette 87
    Saving a File to a Diskette 87
Printing Files 87
The Print Queue 88
    Viewing the Print Queue 88
    Cancelling a Print Job in the Queue 88
    Changing the Order of Jobs in the Print Queue 88
    Deleting All Documents from the Print Queue 89
The Print Dialog Box 89
    Name 89
    Print Range 89
    Copies 89
    The Properties Button 90
    Print Preview 90
Changing the Default Printer 90
Section Summary: So Now You Know 91

Module 3: Word Processing   93

Section 3.1: Your First Letter in Word 94

In This Section 94
    New Skills 94
    New Words 94
Starting Word 95
    What? No New, Blank Document? 95
Text Cursor and Paragraph Mark 95
What? No Paragraph Mark? 95
Actions You Need to Know 96
Keys You Need to Know 97
Typing a Letter 97
Moving Text with the Tab Key 100
    Non-Printing Characters and Wavy Underlines 100
Printing Your Letter 100
Word's Toolbars 101
Word's Undo Feature 101
Working with Word Documents 101
    Saving Your Document 101
    Creating a New Document 102
    Opening an Existing Document 102
    Closing a Document 102
Quitting Word 103
Online Help 103
    Using Help Menu Options 103
    Using Help from Dialog Boxes 104

Section Summary: So Now You Know 105

Section 3.2: Formatting, Positioning and Copying Text 106

In This Section 106
   New Skills 106
   New Words 107
Selecting Text 107
Formatting Text 108
Copying and Pasting Text 109
   About the Clipboard 110
   Cutting and Pasting Text 110
   Keyboard Shortcuts 110
Formatted Documents 111
Left and Right Indents 111
Aligning Text 111
Bullets and Numbered Lists 112
Fonts 114
   Serif Fonts 115
   Sans Serif Fonts 115
Font Sizes 115
Font Properties 115
   Font Style 115
   Underline 115
   Font Colour 116
   Font Effects 116
   Font Spacing 116
Font Borders and Shading 117
Word's Zoom Views 121
   Zoom and Printing 121
Saving to a Diskette 121
Symbols and Special Characters 121
Format Painter 122
Section Summary: So Now You Know 123

Section 3.3: Long Documents, Little Details 124

In This Section 124
   New Skills 124
   New Words 124
Creating Your Long Document 125
Inter-Line Spacing 126
Inter-Paragraph Spacing 127
First Line Indents 128
Hanging Indents 129
Finding Text 129
   The Basics 129
   Special Options 130
   Formats 130
Finding and Replacing Text 130
   The Two Replace Methods 130

Special Options 131
Page Setup 133
The Margins Tab 133
Paper Size 134
Headers and Footers 134
Page Numbering 136
Page Numbering Options 137
Document Date and Author Name 138
Manual Line and Page Breaks 139
Checking Your Spelling 139
Spell Checking: The Automatic Option 139
The Spell-Check Dialog Box 140
Watch Your Language 141
Checking Your Grammar 141
Printing Options 141
Print Preview 141
Print Range Options 142
Modifying the Toolbar 142
Hiding and Displaying Toolbars 142
Hiding and Displaying Toolbar Buttons 143
Section Summary: So Now You Know 143

Section 3.4: Tables, Tabs and Graphics **144**

In This Section 144
New Skills 144
New Words 144
Using Tables in Word 145
Selecting Table Cells 146
Table Operations 146
Column Width, Spacing and Row Height 148
The Table AutoFormat Option 148
Introduction to Tabs 149
Using Tabs in Word 150
Tab Alignment 152
Using Tabs with the Ruler 153
Using Graphics in Word 154
Importing Graphics: Two Options 154
Graphics: Copy and Paste 154
Graphics: File Insert 154
Working With Graphics 155
Moving a Graphic 155
Changing the Shape and Size of a Graphic 155
Inserting AutoShapes 156
Hyphenating Justified Text 158
Automatic Hyphenation 158
Automatic Hyphenation Options 158
Manual Hyphenation 159
Running Manual Hyphenation 159
Section Summary: So Now You Know. 159

Section 3.5: Mail Merge and Templates 160

In This Section 160
    New Skills 160
    New Words 160
Mail Merge: the Components 161
    Form Letter 161
    Data Source 161
    Merge Fields 161
Mail Merge: the Procedure 162
    One: Prepare Your Form Letter 162
    Two: Prepare Your Data Source 162
    Three: Insert Merge Fields in Your Form Letter 162
    Four: Preview Your Merged Letters 163
    Five: Print Your Merged Letters 163
Your Mail Merge Exercises 163
    Viewing Your Word Data Source 166
    Using Non-Word Data Sources 167
Inserting Merge Codes in Your Form Letter 167
Merging Addresses to Labels 168
Word Templates 170
    A Template as a Document Model 170
    A Template as an Interface Controller 170
Templates and Documents 170
    The Normal.dot Template 171
    Templates and New Documents 171
Templates and Styles 172
    Why Use Styles? 173
Creating a New Template 174
Styles and Outline View 175
Other Document Views 175
    Normal View 175
    Page Layout View 176
Section Summary: So Now You Know 176

Section 3.6: File Formats and Importing Spreadsheet Data . . . 177

In This Section 177
    New Skills 177
    New Words 177
File Formats 178
    Different Applications, Different File Formats 178
    File Name Extensions 178
Word's File Format Options 179
    Previous Word Version 179
    Rich Text Format 179
    WordPerfect Format 179
    Text-Only Format 179
    HTML (Web) Format 181
Embedding or Pasting Spreadsheet Data 181

Pasting Special Options 181
Pasting from Excel 182
Embedding from Excel 182
Section Summary: So Now You Know 186

Module 4: Spreadsheets   187

Section 4.1: Your First Steps in Excel **188**

In This Section 188
   New Skills 188
   New Words 188
Starting Excel 189
Worksheets and Workbooks 189
Cell References and the Name Box 190
   Column Letters: Upper or Lower Case? 191
Entering Numbers in Cells 191
   Why Does Excel Right-Align Numbers? 192
Entering Text in a Cell 192
Entering a Cell Reference in a Cell 193
   The ARROW Keys 193
Editing the Content of a Cell 193
Dependent Cells 193
   F2: Excel's EDIT Key 194
Deleting the Content of a Cell 194
   Deleting and the ENTER Key 194
   Deleting Cell Content – Not the Cell 194
Standard and Formatting Toolbars 194
   Working with Toolbars 195
Excel's Undo 195
Working with Excel Workbooks 196
   Saving Your Workbook 196
   Creating a New Workbook 196
   Opening an Existing Workbook 197
   Closing a Workbook 197
Quitting Excel. 197
Online Help 197
Using Help Menu Options 198
   Using Help from Dialog Boxes. 198
Section Summary: So Now You Know. 199

Section 4.2: Arithmetic with Excel **200**

In This Section 200
   New Skills 200
   New Words. 200
Formulas in Excel. 201
   Formulas and Arguments 201
   Calculated Cells 202
Adding Down and Across. 203
   Adding Non-Adjacent Cells 204

Editing Formulas. 204
Combining Operators 205
Formulas: Using Constants 205
Formulas: The Rules of Arithmetic 206
Fixed Factor Calculations 207
Calculations and Recalculations 209
Error Messages: When Bad Things Happen 210
Excel's Zoom Views. 210
    Zoom and Printing. 211
Saving to a Diskette. 211
Section Summary: So Now You Know 212

Section 4.3: Functions, Formatting and Printing. 213

In This Section 213
    New Skills. 213
    New Words 213
Excel Functions. 214
The SUM Function 214
    Upper or Lower Case?. 214
    The AutoSum Button. 215
    SUM Tolerates Text and Spaces 216
The AVERAGE Function 217
Formatting and Aligning Single Cells 217
Formatting and Aligning Cell Groups 218
Cancelling a Selection. 218
Cell Ranges. 219
    Adjacent Cell Range 219
    Non-Adjacent Cell Range 219
    Selected Cells and the Active Cell. 220
    F8: Excel's SELECT Key 220
Selecting Columns and Rows 221
    Deleting Rows and Column Contents 221
Selecting the Entire Worksheet 221
Adjusting Column Width and Row Height 221
Vertical Alignment 222
Orientation 223
Fonts 224
Font Sizes 224
Font Colours 224
Cell Borders 225
Cell Colour Backgrounds 226
Finding Cell Content. 227
    Find Options 227
Replacing Cell Content 227
Spell-Checking 228
Page Setup. 229
    Paper Size 229
    Orientation. 229
    Scaling. 229

Margins. 230
   Gridlines and Headings. 230
Headers and Footers 230
Printing Options 232
   Print Preview 232
   Print Range Options 232
Section Summary: So Now You Know. 234

Section 4.4: Inserting, Sorting and Moving Cells 235

In This Section 235
   New Skills 235
   New Words. 235
Inserting and Deleting Rows. 236
   Deleting Rows 237
Inserting and Deleting Columns 237
   Deleting Columns. 238
Inserting and Deleting Cells 238
Copying and Pasting Cell Contents. 238
   About the Clipboard 240
   The Flashing Marquee 240
Cutting and Pasting Cell Contents 241
Copying between Worksheets and Workbooks. 242
Moving Calculations. 242
Cell References: The Two Kinds 243
Sorting: Reordering Cells by Content 245
Symbols and Special Characters 248
Section Summary: So Now You Know. 249

Section 4.5: More About Numbers, Text and Calculations . . . 250

In This Section 250
   New Activities 250
   New Words. 250
Numbers: The Different Formats 251
The General Format 251
   Zeros after the Decimal Point 251
   Trailing Zeros. 251
   Thousands Separators 252
   Currency Symbols 252
   Unsuitable for Financial Amounts. 252
The Comma Style. 252
The Currency Style. 252
The Percent Style 253
   Changing from the General Format. 254
The Number Format 254
   Toolbar Buttons 255
Excel and Dates 255
   Entering Dates 255
   Formatting Dates 256
Regional Settings 256

Excel and Text. 257
   Text across Multiple Columns. 257
   Entering Numbers as Text 257
Excel's AutoFill Feature 258
   AutoFill and Single Numbers, Text 259
   AutoFill and Number Series 259
   AutoFill and Months, Days, Times and Years 259
   AutoFill and Calculations 259
   AutoFill and Cell References. 259
   AutoFill Keyboard Shortcut. 261
Section Summary: So Now You Know 261

Section 4.6: Charting with Excel. 262

In This Section 262
   New Skills. 262
   New Words 262
Charting: The Two Steps. 263
   The Four Dialog Boxes of an Excel Chart 263
Creating Your First Chart in Excel 263
Charts: Two Ideas You Need to Know 265
   About Data Points. 265
   About Data Series 265
Single Data Series Charts 266
Creating a Multiple Data Series Chart 266
Editing Your Chart 268
   Changing Chart Data 268
   Resizing the Chart 268
   Changing the Chart Title 268
   Adding a Chart Title 268
   Adding Data Labels. 269
   Formatting Data Labels 270
   Changing the Scale 270
   Changing Chart Colours 271
Charts Types 272
Setting the Chart Type. 273
   Changing Chart Type. 273
   Working with Pie Charts 275
Section Summary: So Now You Know 277

Section 4.7: File Formats and Data Importing. 278

In This Section 278
   New Skills. 278
   New Words 278
File Formats 279
   Different Applications, Different File Formats 279
   File Name Extensions 279
Excel's File Format Options 280
   Excel Template 280
   Previous Excel Versions 280

dBASE and Quatro Pro Formats 281
Text-Only Format 281
HTML (Web) Format 282
Inserting from Other Applications 282
Inserting Images 282
Inserting Graphs 283
Inserting Text 283
Text Import Wizard 284
Section Summary: So Now You Know. 286

Module 5: Databases　　　　　　　　　　　　　　287

Section 5.1: What is a Database? **288**

In This Section 288
New Skills 288
New Words. 288
An Organised Collection of Information. 289
Records and Fields 289
Tables and Databases 290
Two Views: Datasheet and Forms 291
Starting Access. 292
Exploring a Sample Database 292
Access File Name Extension. 293
The Database Dialog Box. 293
Database Design Considerations. 293
Example 1: The Wine Buff's Database 294
Example 2: The CD Collector's Database. 294
Example 3: The Household Manager's Database 295
Example 4: The Bird Spotter's Database. 295
Thinking Hard about Fields 295
Closing a Database 296
Quitting Access 296
Section Summary: So Now You Know. 296

Section 5.2: Building Your Access Database **297**

In This Section 297
New Skills 297
New Words. 297
Overview of Database Creation 298
Step One: Starting the Database Wizard 299
Step Two: Selecting Your Sample Table. 299
Step Three: Selecting Your Fields. 300
Step Four: Renaming Your Fields. 301
Step Five: Setting Your Primary Key 302
Step Six: Entering Data into Your Table. 303
Step Seven: Changing the Width of Your Columns 304
Step Eight: Switching to Design View 304
Step Nine: Creating Your Index 305

Section Summary: So Now You Know 306

Section 5.3: Modifying Your Access Database **307**

In This Section 307
New Skills 307
New Words 307
Changing and Deleting Database Records 308
Changing a Field 308
Deleting a Record 308
The Different Data Types 308
Changing Data Types 310
Adding New Fields to Your Table 311
Reordering the Fields in a Table 312
Saving to a Diskette 312
Online Help 313
Using Help Menu Options 313
Using Help from the Screen 314
Access Toolbars 315
Section Summary: So Now You Know 315

Section 5.4: Making the Database Work for You **316**

In This Section 316
New Skills 316
New Words 316
Changing the Order of Records in the Table 317
Saving a Query 318
Restricting the Information Displayed 320
Filtering by Selection 321
Filtering Filtered Records 322
Find 322
Section Summary: So Now You Know 323

Section 5.5: Working with Forms **324**

In This Section 324
New Skills 324
New Words 324
Forms: What Are They For? 325
Creating Your Form with the Form Wizard 325
Using Your Form to View Records 326
Sorting in Form View 327
Filtering by Selection in Form View 327
Filtering by Form 327
Wildcards in Filters and Queries 328
Creating an All Fields Form 328
Using a Form to Create New Records 329
Using a Form to Modify Existing Records 329
Modifying Form Layout and Content 329
Section Summary: So Now You Know 332

Section 5.6: Working with Reports 333

    In This Section 333
        New Activities 333
        New Words.................................... 333
    Your First Report 333
    Modifying the Report Layout 337
    Section Summary: So Now You Know.................. 339

Module 6: Presentations   *341*

Section 6.1: Presentation Basics 342

    In This Section 342
        New Skills 342
        New Words.................................... 342
    Presentations and Presentation Software............... 342
    Starting PowerPoint 343
    Opening an Existing Presentation 343
    Working with PowerPoint Presentations................ 344
        Different Views 344
        Zoom 345
        Finding Your Way Around a Presentation 345
        Printing a Presentation 346
        Using Online Help 346
        Modifying the Toolbar Display.................... 347
    Closing a Presentation 347
    Quitting PowerPoint............................... 348
    Section Summary: So Now You Know.................. 348

Section 6.2: Creating Your First Slides 349

    In This Section 349
        New Skills 349
        New Words.................................... 349
    Creating a New Presentation......................... 349
        Landscape or Portrait? 351
    Adding Slides to Your Presentation 351
    Using Outline View 352
    Copying Text within PowerPoint 353
    Importing Text from Another Application 354
    Deleting a Slide 355
    PowerPoint's Undo Feature 355
    Saving Your Presentation 355
    Section Summary: So Now You Know.................. 356

Section 6.3: Adding Graphics and Pictures 357

    In This Section 357
        New Skills 357
        New Words.................................... 357

Using PowerPoint's Drawing Tools 357
   Line and Arrow Tools 358
   Rectangle Tool 358
   Ellipse Tool 358
   Line Colour and Style 358
   Fill Colour 358
   Text Box 358
   Editing Drawn Objects 358
Grouping and Ungrouping Objects 360
Inserting AutoShapes. 360
Inserting Organisation Charts 360
Presenting Quantitative Information 362
Importing Pictures 364
Standing Out from the Crowd 366
Section Summary: So Now You Know 367

Section 6.4: Projecting a Consistent Image. 368

In This Section 368
   New Skills. 368
   New Words 368
Using Presentation Designs 368
Making the Design Your Own. 369
   Modifying the Colour Scheme. 369
   Modifying the Background 370
The Slide Master 371
Formatting Text on Individual Slides 372
Adding Borders to Objects 373
Tips for Better Presentations 373
   How Much Should You Put on a Slide? 373
   What Font Size Should You Choose? 374
   What Font Should You Choose? 374
   What Colours Should You Choose? 374
Using the Same Style Again 374
Section Summary: So Now You Know 374

Section 6.5: Building a Presentation 376

In This Section 376
   New Skills. 376
Using Slide Sorter to Check Your Slides 376
Changing the Order of Slides. 376
   Reordering by Dragging 376
   Reordering with Cut and Paste. 377
Copying Slides between Presentations. 377
Deleting a Slide 378
Hiding a Slide 378
Using PowerPoint Slides in Other Applications. 378
Working with Earlier Versions of PowerPoint 379
Section Summary: So Now You Know 380

Section 6.6: Wowing the Audience **381**

 In This Section 381
  New Skills 381
  New Words.. 381
 Slide Transitions..................................... 381
  Automatic or Manual Advance 382
 Build Slides 382
 Music and Other Noises 385
 Preparing Handouts 386
  Numbering Your Slides 386
 Speaker Notes....................................... 386
  Notes View....................................... 387
  Check Your Spelling! 387
 Saving Your Presentation as a Slide Show 387
 Section Summary: So Now You Know................... 388

Module 7: Information and Communication   389

Section 7.1: Exploring the Web **390**

 In This Section 390
  New Skills 390
  New Words.. 390
 Starting Internet Explorer 391
  Your Browser's Start Page 391
 Visiting and Exploring a Website 392
  Internet Explorer Toolbar 393
  Moving Through a Series of Web Pages.............. 393
  Browsing with the Address Bar..................... 393
 Printing a Web Page.................................. 394
  Page Setup Options............................... 394
 Saving from the Web 395
  Saving an Image 395
  Image File Formats............................... 396
  Selecting and Saving Text......................... 396
  Saving All Text................................... 397
  Saving a Web Page............................... 397
  Copyright 398
 Opening Multiple Web Pages........................... 398
 Web Words... 398
  Web Servers and Web Browsers.................... 399
 Online Help 399
  Using Help from Dialog Boxes..................... 399
  Using Help Menu Options 400
 Section Summary: So Now You Know................... 401

Section 7.2: Finding Information within Websites **402**

 In This Section 402

New Skills 402
New Words 402
Finding Text within a Web Page 403
Finding Information within a Website 403
Website Index Pages 404
Website Search Engines 405
Interactive Forms. 406
About Web Addresses 408
Sample URLs 408
URLs and Files 409
URLs and Folders 410
Section Summary: So Now You Know 411

Section 7.3: Finding Information on the Web **412**

In This Section 412
New Skills 412
New Words 412
Finding Information on the Web 413
Web Directory Sites 413
Web Search Engines 414
Phrase Searches. 416
The Plus Operator 417
The Minus Operator 418
Logical Searches 419
Meta Search Engines 419
Natural Language Search Engines 420
Section Summary: So Now You Know 421

Section 7.4: Taking Control of Internet Explorer **422**

In This Section 422
New Skills 422
New Words 422
Switching Web Page Images Off and On 423
Favorites 423
Organising Your Favorites. 424
Revisiting a Saved Web Address 425
Changing Your Start Page. 426
Screen Elements 426
Standard Toolbar 427
Address Bar. 427
Explorer Bars. 427
Text Size Display 428
Section Summary: So Now You Know 428

Section 7.5: E-mail with Outlook Express **429**

In This Section 429
New Skills 429
New Words 429

Starting Outlook Express 430
Changing Outlook Layout 430
The Four Layout Elements 431
    Folders List. 431
    Message List. 432
    Preview Pane 433
    Outlook Express Toolbar 434
Composing and Sending an E-mail. 434
    Outgoing E-mail: Permanent Internet Connection. 435
    Outgoing E-mail: Dial-up Connection 435
Outgoing E-mail and the Sent Items Folder 435
Collecting and Reading Your E-mail 436
    E-mail Collection: Dial-up Connection. 436
    E-mail Collection at Startup 436
    Reading an E-mail 437
    Printing an E-mail. 437
    Deleting an E-mail 437
    Manual E-mail Deletion 438
    Automatic E-mail Deletion 438
Quitting Outlook Express 438
Using Online Help 438
    Using Help from Dialog Boxes. 438
    Using Help Menu Options 439
Section Summary: So Now You Know. 440

Section 7.6: More about Outgoing Mail. 441

In This Section 441
    New Skills 441
    New Words. 441
Copying Text into E-mails 442
Checking Your Spelling 442
Finding an E-mail Address 443
E-mailing Multiple Recipients 444
    Several Equal Recipients. 444
    One Main Recipient, with Copy to Another 444
    Blind Carbon Copying 445
    Mass E-mail and Blind Carbon Copying. 446
Attaching Files to E-mails. 446
E-mail Priority 447
Bounced Messages 448
Your E-mail Signature 448
    Creating a Signature 449
    Alternative Signature Files 449
    Renaming Your Signature File 450
    Editing a Signature File. 450
The Drafts Folder 450
    Saving E-mail to the Drafts Folder 450
Text Size Display 451
Section Summary: So Now You Know. 451

Section 7.7: More about Incoming Mail **452**

In This Section 452
    New Skills. 452
    New Words 452
Actions with Your Incoming Mail. 453
Forwarding on E-mail 453
Replying to Sender Only 454
Replying to All Recipients. 455
Copying and Moving the Text of a Message 455
Deleting Text. 456
Receiving File Attachments. 456
    Opening Attachments 456
    Saving Attachments. 457
    Careful: Attachments Can Be Dangerous. 457
Using E-mail Folders. 457
    Transferring E-mails between Folders 458
    Deleting a Mail Folder. 458
Searching for Specific E-mails 459
    Sorting Messages in a Folder. 459
Section Summary: So Now You Know 460

Section 7.8: Address Book and Contact Groups **461**

In This Section 461
    New Skills. 461
    New Words 461
Your Address Book. 462
    Entering Contacts 462
    Contacts: The Minimum Details 463
    Editing Contacts 463
    Deleting Contacts 463
    Adding Contact Details from E-mail Messages 463
Sorting Your Contacts. 464
Mailing Lists (Contact Groups). 464
    Groups Within Groups. 466
Section Summary: So Now You Know 466

Module

1

Basic Concepts of Information Technology

Learning about computers for the first time is rather like learning about a foreign country. A land where words like 'megabyte' and 'peripheral' are part of the everyday conversation. The only crop grown and harvested is something called 'data'. And it is important not only to be faster than your neighbour, but smaller too!

But you need to learn about this country. It was once an out-of-the-way place that attracted only handfuls of scientists to its shores. Now no other destination is more popular.

Like all good tourist guides, this Module introduces you gently to the more commonly spoken words of the computer dialect. It points out the major landmarks (the hard disk, memory and processor are all places you need to take in). And it steers you away from the pitfalls that most offend native computer speakers – such as confusing an 'operating system' with an 'application program'.

Have a pleasant trip. And good luck!

Section 1.1: A Short History of Computing

In This Section

This Section gives you a brief overview of the history of commercial computing, and paints a picture of the role of computers in the world today.

New Activities

At the end of this Section, you should know that computers:

- Have been developed relatively recently
- Become faster, more reliable, and cheaper every year
- Are being used widely in business and education

A Long Line of Machines

From earliest times, people have counted things, measured things, kept records of things, and told other people about things. The 'things' could have been the number of sheep in a flock, the weight of a child, the size of a field, the length of time since the last drought, or the intensity of an earthquake.

From earliest times, people used tools and techniques to help them count more reliably, measure more accurately, record more indelibly, transmit more clearly – they used, for example, measuring tapes, slide rules, sextants, weighing scales, and clocks.

The computer is simply the latest in this long line of calculating and recording machines. That's all it is. Everything we see computers doing today – and we see them doing a lot – they are doing because they can calculate and they can store the results of their calculations.

However, this principle is masked by one outstanding fact: what computers do may be simple, but they do an incredible amount of work, quickly and reliably. The speed of computers today is measured in millions of operations per second. The operations may be simple, but they can be combined in all sorts of ways to yield a vast array of useful functions.

This has almost all come about within the last thirty or forty years, which is the entire history of commercial computers.

In the 1960s, a commercial computer occupied a large air-conditioned room; it needed a team of specialists to operate it; it consumed vast amounts of electricity; and it frequently broke down.

Today's computers are typically much smaller and faster: what previously took up a full room fits into a small box. They can store more information; they consume less power; and they have become far easier to operate.

To give you some idea of the speed of advance, the first personal computers (PCs) were launched in 1979, with a clock speed (don't worry about it – it's just how we measure the speed of computers) of about 5 megahertz (MHz). Today, if you go out to buy a new PC, it is unlikely that you will be offered anything less than 400 MHz or even 500 MHz – eighty or one hundred times as fast. Similar progress has been made in the other main measure of computer power – storage capacity.

You don't need to understand how this has been achieved, and you don't need to know all the details. However, you should be aware of the speed of progress and the main ways in which it is measured. So, if you go out to buy a computer, you will at least know what questions to ask, and will understand the answers.

Every year, computers are becoming smaller, faster, cheaper, more reliable, and easier to use. They are being used in all sorts of situations where it would previously have been impossible to use them: not only in business and government, but also in education, entertainment, health care, sport, art and design. You see computers in homes, clubs, and restaurants; you don't see them (but they are there) in car engines, in bank automatic teller machines, in supermarket checkouts, in washing machines, in telephone systems, in video recorders. You are probably wearing one at this moment, on your wrist, buried inside your watch.

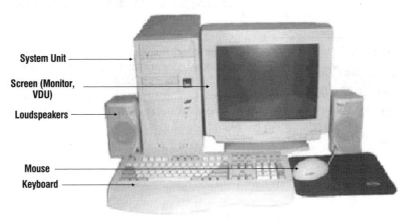

You're surrounded.

But you're *not* under threat: computers are machines, tools. They are designed by people to meet people's needs; they are operated by people. People turn them on. People turn them off.

People like you.

The ECDL is designed to take the fear out of computing, to give you the knowledge and the skills you need to use this technology. With this book, you will learn about the most common PC applications. You won't learn everything: it is not necessary to know everything – it's not even possible. What this book aims to do is to teach you *enough* – enough to perform most of the tasks that most people do most of the time, and to give you enough confidence to tackle the unknown, and to learn from experience.

Self-Test 1.1: History of Computing

1) Today's PCs are approximately how much faster than the first PCs?

   a) Five times as fast
   b) Ten times as fast
   c) A hundred times as fast
   d) A thousand times as fast

2) Which of the following devices may incorporate a computer? (Pick as many as you think, and for each, say what the computer might do.)

   a) A car engine
   b) A video recorder
   c) A bank cash machine
   d) A bicycle

3) True or false: In the 1960s, computers were built by hand from stronger materials. As a result, they were more reliable than today's computers, which are mass-produced, smaller and more delicate.

4) Because of the tiny size of modern computers, they are very hard to make, virtually impossible to repair, and as a result, very expensive.

Section Summary: So Now You Know

The computer is the latest in a long line of tools used to perform calculations and store the results. As they have developed, they have become faster, more reliable, and capable of storing more information. These developments have enabled them to be applied in many areas of commercial life, administration, education and entertainment.

Section 1.2: What Exactly Is a Computer?

In This Section

In this Section, you will learn what distinguishes a computer from other machines. You will also learn about the different types of computer in use today.

New Activities

At the end of this Section, you should know:

- What a computer is
- The difference between hardware and software
- The various categories of computers

New Words

At the end of this Section, you should be able to explain the following terms:

- Hardware
- Software
- PC
- Mainframe
- Dumb terminal
- Intelligent terminal

The Trouble with Definitions

It is relatively easy to define a washing machine, or a motor car, or a telephone: these devices may be complicated and technologically advanced, but we can talk about them in terms of what they do. They wash clothes, transport people from A to B, enable people to hold conversations with one another over a distance.

As we saw in the previous section, a computer can be used for almost anything – including controlling the different washing cycles in a washing machine.

In fact, the first part of our definition of a computer recognises this fact: computers are *general purpose* machines. The same computer can operate over a few hours as a typewriter, desktop publishing studio, sound editor, video editor, accounts tracker, e-mail sender, Internet browser, etc.

When you flick the light switch, the light comes on: you could say that the light has obeyed your instruction. Well, computers respond in the same way to instructions: these instructions are called *programs*. And programs are written to make computers behave in specific ways: to act as word processors or to control generating stations. Computers are *programmable*.

Different programs enable the same computer to operate under different guises. We could leave our definition at that, but it will help to add two other ideas: computers can *calculate*, and they can *store* the results of their calculations.

Computer

A computer is a general-purpose, programmable device that is capable of calculating and storing results.

One way of thinking about a computer is as a 'black box' that accepts input on one side, processes it in some way, and then produces output on the other side.

The input might be a mathematical problem, the supplier invoices for the month, a search for a good restaurant in Tullamore, or the temperature of a furnace. The output might be the answer to the mathematical problem, the cheques to pay the invoices, the name and address of the restaurant, or the instructions to shut the control valves on the fuel supply.

What goes on inside the black box is called *processing*: the manipulation of the input necessary to produce the output.

However, the black box is not magic: everything – *everything* – going into a computer is first converted into numbers, and all forms of output – including text on the page, graphics on the screen, music, even telephone conversations – have to be converted into their final form from numbers. In the middle – inside the black box – the numbers are added together in various ways and combinations, under a set of rules called a program. The only magic is the fact that these calculations take place at a rate of millions per second – and, of course, the human ingenuity in the design and the programming.

Computer systems consist of two very different types of elements: *hardware* and *software*.

- Hardware includes all the physical things that you can touch, feel, weigh, and, on rare occasions, kick.

- Software is the intangible information component – the instructions, or programs that tell the hardware how to behave.

Hardware

Hardware is the term used to describe the physical parts of a computer system.

Software
Software is the term used to describe the instructions that cause the computer system to behave in a given way.

Types of Computer

Computers fall into a number of different categories, although the dividing line between the categories is not always clear. At one end of the spectrum are *mainframes*. These are big, expensive machines, typically used by large corporations, governmental organisations and scientific research establishments. They are expected to run continuously, 24 hours a day, 365 days a year. They are capable of processing huge numbers of transactions, and performing extremely complex calculations.

At the other end of the spectrum are the computers most of us are familiar with – the *PC (personal computer)*, formerly known as the *microcomputer*. Today, PCs can be bought for less than £1,000. PCs come in various shapes and sizes. *Desktop* computers are the most common: they generally include a system unit, a screen, and a keyboard, as separate components. *Laptop* or *notebook* computers are more portable: the screen is a flat *liquid crystal display* (LCD), which forms a lid hinged to cover the keyboard and system unit. Laptops are somewhat more expensive than desktop PCs.

In between these two ends of the computer spectrum lie *minicomputers*, which are typically used by medium-sized enterprises, or by departments within larger organizations. Like mainframes, they offer greater processing power, storage capacity and reliability than PCs.

Network computers (*network servers*) are computers that administer, support, and protect the security of a computer network. Users on a network are able to use the resources (data, software, hardware) on the network server. In the past, such users mainly used *dumb terminals* – devices that simply accepted input from the user and displayed results. All the processing and storage was done by the server. Nowadays, most users have *intelligent terminals* – PCs that have their own 'local' processing and storage capacity.

Self-Test 1.2: A Computer Is...?

1) Distinguish between a computer and a pocket calculator.

    a) Because the calculator is purpose-built, it is more accurate.
    b) There is no difference: the calculator contains a computer.
    c) The computer includes a word processor; the calculator doesn't.
    d) The computer has a bigger screen.

2) Which of the following statements is/are true?

    a) Cables and other flexible parts of a computer are called software all the solid parts are called hardware.
    b) Hardware is the term used to describe the physical parts of a computer system.
    c) Diskettes and CDs are software the screen and keyboard are hardware.
    d) Software is another word for programs.

3) Which of the following statements is/are true?

    a) A mainframe is a large computer built in the 1960s or 1970s that is now obsolete.
    b) A mainframe is a large computer typically used by a big company or governmental organisation.
    c) A mainframe is a metal framework inside the plastic casing of a computer.
    d) A mainframe is another word for hardware.

4) A microcomputer is often called a PC. The abbreviation PC stands for:

    a) Personal Computer
    b) Portable Computer
    c) Politically Correct
    d) Personal Calculator
    e) Professional Capacity

5) Which of the following is/are portable computer(s)?

    a) Minicomputer
    b) Microcomputer
    c) Laptop
    d) Notebook

6) Which of the following statements is/are true?

    a) A network server is another name for a dumb terminal.
    b) A dumb terminal is useless without a network server.
    c) A network server is useless without a dumb terminal.
    d) A dumb terminal is a computer without any loudspeakers.
    e) An intelligent terminal is a computer used for military or industrial espionage.
    f) An intelligent terminal is another name for a bank cash machine.

Section Summary: So Now You Know

Computers are general-purpose machines. What distinguishes a computer calculating a payroll from one forecasting the weather is the program it is running. And in fact the *same* computer could be programmed to do both tasks.

Computers accept information from the outside (input), do something to it (processing), and display or print out the results (output). The two main elements in a computer system are *hardware*, which is the term used for the physical parts, and *software*, which describes the instructions or programs that cause the computer to behave in a given way.

The most familiar computers are called PCs or microcomputers. The biggest and most expensive – used by large organisations – are called mainframes. In between are minicomputers.

A computer network is controlled by a network computer, or network server. The devices connected to the server are called terminals. These may be dumb terminals – with no processing or storage power of their own – or intelligent terminals – with their own processing and storage capability.

Section 1.3: Computer Hardware

When you go out to buy a computer, you are immediately faced with a range of options that even experienced computer people find bewildering. To make a sensible choice, you need to know the function of the main components in a computer system, and the criteria upon which you should base your decision.

A typical PC system is made up of a number of components. Some of these are essential, and some optional. In some cases, a number of alternatives are available, from which you have to choose.

This Section takes you on a tour of the typical computer system, and identifies all the hardware components. We look first at the components that are normally inside the main '*system unit*' ('In the Box'), and then at the other components in a typical system ('Outside the Box').

New Activities

At the end of this Section, you should be able to:

- Name the hardware components in a computer system
- Say what each component is for
- Describe some of the 'optional extras'
- Describe how to look after your computer

New Words

At the end of this Section, you should be able to explain the following terms:

- Processor
- Memory
- Hard Disk
- Diskette
- Keyboard
- Screen
- Mouse
- Printer
- Modem
- Multimedia

Unfortunately, when talking about computer hardware, a certain amount of jargon is unavoidable. Other new terms in this Section are in *italics* and explained in their context.

In the Box

The system unit – usually a beige or grey box – is the most essential part of the computer. It houses the processor (the 'brain'), the various kinds of memory (described below), and the electronics to control all the other components. It also usually includes a fan, designed to keep the whole unit cool. The fan is responsible for the hum from the computer when you turn it on. The system unit may stand vertically on the floor (a *tower*), or horizontally on the desk, usually with the screen on top (a *desktop* unit). In a *laptop* or *notebook* computer, the system unit is usually built underneath the keyboard.

Processor

The length of time it takes a computer to perform a task depends on a number of factors. The first of these is the speed of the processor – the chip at the heart of the computer. This is measured in megahertz (MHz), and the bigger the number, the faster the processor (the more calculations it can perform per second). This measure of the computer's performance is so critical, that it is usually included in the name of the computer. So the Dell Dimension R450, for example, includes the Intel Pentium II 450 MHz processor.

The processor chip and the electronics that support it are referred to as the *Central Processing Unit* (CPU).

Memory

The definition of a computer includes the idea of storage: the computer has to be able to store the results of its calculations. In practice, a computer has to store a huge amount of information. It has a number of different kinds of memory, two of which are regularly cited in the advertisements for computers: RAM and disk space.

Random Access Memory
Random Access Memory (RAM) is used by the computer as a sort of working area while it is carrying out a given task. (It is often called *working storage*.) Here it holds the list of instructions that it is currently working on, the data on which it is working, and the interim results of its calculations. The 'R' in RAM is its main advantage. It can be accessed randomly, which means that the computer can get at any piece of data directly – it does not have to look through the storage area from the start until it finds the piece of interest. This makes it fast. In general, the more RAM the better, and a certain minimum is required for many programs. RAM is often called *main memory*.

Memory capacity is measured in *bytes*. One byte consists of eight *bits*. You can think of a bit in electrical terms as a switch: on or off, or in mathematical terms as a single binary number: 0 or 1. Eight of these – a byte – can represent a letter of the alphabet, or a single number. You are likely to be offered a new computer with at least 64 megabytes (64 MB – 64 million bytes) or possibly 128 MB of RAM. (This is twice as much as you would have been offered for the same price last year, and probably half as much as you will be offered this time next year.)

Read-Only Memory

RAM should not be confused with another kind of memory that you may occasionally hear of: ROM (Read-Only Memory). This is where the computer stores its low-level programs – the ones that tell it how to behave, how to check its own circuitry, how to treat various kinds of input devices, and so on. ROM differs from RAM in two ways: first, it is not changed after the computer is assembled (you can read it, but not write to it), and second, its contents remain unchanged even when the power is turned off. (RAM is *volatile* – its contents are erased if the power supply is cut off.)

It is relatively easy to upgrade the memory on your computer by buying additional memory chips. They are inexpensive and easy to install. Depending on what you are using your computer for, additional memory can make a huge difference to its performance. (Don't, however, attempt to install additional memory without expert guidance.)

Hard Disk

After processor speed and amount of RAM, the next major determinant of computer power is the amount of disk space. A disk is a device for storing information. It is very different from RAM, for a number of reasons:

- First, disks record information magnetically, in much the same way as music tapes or video tapes. They are not volatile: once the information is recorded, it remains on the disk until it is changed or deleted.

- Second, the process of getting information onto a disk or retrieving information from a disk involves mechanical movement. The disk revolves at a constant high speed, and a *read/write head* moves in and out just above the surface of the disk. The read/write head can change the polarisation of tiny magnetic particles on the surface of the disk, and can detect the polarisation of particles. Moving parts eventually wear out and as a result, disks are more likely to malfunction than non-moving RAM.

The moving parts also introduce delays into the processes of reading and writing, whereas reading from RAM is almost instantaneous.

Like memory capacity, disk capacity is measured in *bytes*. Disk capacity is bigger by several orders of magnitude: a new computer today will typically come with a 12-gigabyte disk (12 GB – 12 billion bytes) rising to 20 gigabytes.

Let's consider this slowly: 12,000,000,000 bytes. The 32 volumes of *Encyclopaedia Brittanica* contain approximately 44,000,000 words, or approximately 220,000,000 characters (bytes). A 12-GB disk could hold that text almost fifty-six times, yet it only weighs about 1 kilogram, and takes up less space than one of the encyclopaedia's volumes. The amount of information that a disk can hold is the third performance measure that you should consider when buying a computer.

The disks described on the previous page are built in to the computer. They are often called *hard disks*. They remain in the computer, and are not (generally) transferred between computers. There is, however, a wide range of removable storage devices that can be transferred easily from one computer to another, or used as security backups in case of loss, damage, or theft of the computer.

Diskettes (Floppy Disks)

Another kind of disk is the so-called '*floppy disk*' or *diskette*. (Early removable disks were housed in flexible envelopes, which earned them the name 'floppy'. The more recent design, with which you are probably familiar, uses a hard plastic shell with a sliding metal cover.)

The most common type of diskette holds 1.4 MB. This is enough to easily hold many typical word-processing documents, so that they can easily be passed from one person to another. You can use a diskette to transfer a document from your office computer to your home computer – simply copy the document to the diskette, and bring it home in your pocket. The entire text of this book (but not the graphics) fits onto a single diskette, with room to spare!

Just as RAM is often referred to as 'working storage' or 'main memory', disks and diskettes are often called 'backing storage', or 'secondary storage'.

CD-ROM and DVD

Until quite recently, diskettes were also the principal way of loading programs onto a computer. Nowadays, however, software is most often supplied on CD-ROM (Compact Disk Read-Only Memory). Physically, a CD-ROM is indistinguishable from a music CD, and in fact CD readers in computers are almost all capable of playing music CDs.

The move from diskette to CD-ROM as the favoured medium for distributing software has taken place mainly because of the size of modern software systems: they need more storage space. (More space is required because the programs have added functionality, because they are more graphic in design, and because they may include other multimedia elements.) A single CD-ROM can hold as much information as 460 diskettes – about 650 MB.

CD-ROM drives (the part of the computer that reads CD-ROMs) are now offered as standard on all new computers. The only performance measure to watch out for is the speed of the drive, always quoted as a multiple of the normal music CD-player speed: nowadays, 36x speed or 40x speed CD-ROM drives are normal.

CD-ROMs are now being overtaken by DVDs (Digital Versatile Disks), which look similar, but have a great deal more storage capacity – up to 3.9 gigabytes or GB.

To record information on a CD, you need a CD Writer (or 'burner'). Information is encoded on the surface of CDs as tiny holes, which are detected by a laser beam.

Remember, however, that CDs differ from magnetic disks (hard disks and diskettes) in that the holes burnt into the read/write surface of the CD are permanent: once burnt, they cannot be changed or erased (hence Read Only Memory). Magnetic media, on the other hand, can be changed at will. For this reason, hard disks will continue to be the favoured media for storing information in normal office applications.

Magnetic Tape
Magnetic tape – usually in cassettes not unlike music cassettes – is used for distributing software and for keeping backup copies of large volumes of data. It is less useful in normal everyday use, because it cannot be accessed randomly: the computer has to read it through from the beginning to find the part of interest.

Zip Disks, etc.
High-capacity removable diskettes are gaining favour for keeping backups and for transferring large files between computers. Some use magnetic technology, some laser technology. Among the most popular devices is the *Zip drive*, which attaches to any computer's parallel port (printer connection) and provides storage on 100-MB removable disks.

Medium	Typical Capacity	Typical Cost of Medium (Jan 2000)
Hard Disk (Fixed)	12 to 20 Gigabytes	£60 to £400
Diskette	1.4 Megabytes	Less than £1
CD	650 Megabytes	Less than £10
DVD	5.2 Gigabytes	£20 to £30
Zip	100 Megabytes	Less than £10
Tape	4 to 100 Gigabytes	£20 to £70

Out of the Box: The Essentials

Everything outside the grey box is peripheral, which is why all the other objects are called *peripherals*. (Here we're cheating a little: technically, all secondary storage, such as disks, CD-ROMs, etc. can be considered to be peripheral as well.) In most computer systems, the three *essential* peripherals are the keyboard and mouse (used for input), and the screen (used for output).

Keyboard

A keyboard is a set of typewriter-like keys that enables you, the user, to enter information and instructions into a computer. Keys on a computer keyboard are of three types:

- **Alphanumeric keys**: Letters and numbers

- **Punctuation keys**: Comma, full stop, semicolon, and so on

- **Special keys**: Function keys, control keys, arrow keys, Caps Lock key, and so on.

Screen

The screen looks somewhat like a television. It is also called the *monitor* (because you use it to monitor what is going on in the computer) or the *visual display unit (VDU)*. Most programs are designed in such a way that you appear to enter input directly from the keyboard onto the screen. In fact, you enter it into the processor, and the processor shows you what it has received by displaying it on the screen. Most programs also give you continuous feedback on their progress, and display their output on the screen.

Mouse

Many programs present themselves on the screen as *Graphical User Interfaces* (GUI – pronounced, believe it or not, 'gooey'). A GUI represents programs, files, and functions as pictures on the screen. The GUI includes a pointer that you can move around the screen until it is at the picture that represents what you want to do. You then indicate your intention, and the program responds accordingly.

The mouse is the tool that you use to move the pointer around the screen. The underside of the mouse houses a ball, and, as you move the mouse over your desk, this ball detects the movements, and converts them into movements of the pointer. Move the mouse left, the pointer moves left; right, and the pointer moves right; push the mouse away from you, and the pointer moves up the screen; pull it towards you, the pointer moves down. After a very short time it becomes second nature.

Note that the ball only moves (and therefore the pointer only moves) when the underside of the mouse is in contact with the desk. So you can move the pointer a long distance in one direction by making a series of short moves in that direction with the mouse, each time lifting the mouse so that the return journey does not affect the position of the pointer.

The mouse has two or three buttons on top: these are used to signal to the computer that the pointer has arrived where you want to go. You press one or other buttons once (called a *click*), or twice in quick succession (called a *double click*).

The mouse (or whatever pointing device you use – see *Other Pointing Devices*) makes operation of the computer easy, and even intuitive, but it is seldom absolutely necessary. Most programs allow you to move the pointer around the screen and choose your options using special keys or combinations of keys on the keyboard. Some users prefer this: it means they can do all their work from the keyboard – they don't have to switch back and forth between the keyboard and the mouse.

Other Pointing Devices

The mouse is by far the most common pointing device, but there are others.

Trackballs are like an upside-down mouse: you move the pointer by manipulating a ball in a special housing with your fingers. They are useful in situations where desk space is limited.

Joysticks and *Games Controllers* fulfil the same function, but are designed specially for games and simulation.

Most portable computers have a device built in to the keyboard for moving the pointer, either in the form of a miniature joystick, or a pressure-sensitive *touchpad* that detects movements of your finger.

Light Pens are pen-shaped devices that, when placed close to the screen, can be used both to draw and to control icons or choices shown on the screen.

Touch Screens are often seen in public information kiosks: the user simply touches the screen at the point of interest in order to exercise a choice from the options displayed.

Graphics Tablets are flat surfaces that detect the movement of a plastic stylus (pen) across them. They are typically used for art and design applications, but smaller versions are becoming common in 'pocket', 'hand-held' or 'palmtop' computers. These devices (known as *Personal Digital Assistants*, or *PDAs*) are too small to allow typing.

Out of the Box: Optional Extras

Without the components described in the previous section, it would be hard to get the computer to do anything useful. There are a number of other devices that, although they are not essential, are normal parts of the system in the home, school or office. These are a printer, a modem, and loudspeakers. Some others – scanners, digital cameras, microphones – would have been considered exotic a couple of years ago, but are increasingly considered 'normal'.

Printers

There are several kinds of printer on the market: the two most common are *laser printers* and *inkjet printers*.

Laser Printers
Laser printers use a technology similar to that used in photocopying to transfer the image of a page onto paper. The image is 'drawn' under instruction from the computer.

Inkjet Printers
Inkjet printers have a moving 'pen' (the *write head*) that holds an ink cartridge. This moves back and forth over the page and, under computer control, ejects a minute quantity of ink at the precise point where it is required on the page.

Other Kinds of Printer
You will occasionally come across a third category of printer: *impact printers*. These work like a typewriter: they hammer out the required characters onto the page through an ink-impregnated (or carbon-covered) ribbon. There are several kinds, using slightly different techniques for making the marks on the paper: dot matrix printers, daisy wheel printers, line printers. Nowadays their use is confined to specialist applications (printing receipts from cash registers, printing the time of arrival on a ticket in a car park), or high-volume printouts that do not use graphics (tax forms, electricity bills).

Plotters are used in specialist applications, such as producing architectural or engineering drawings. Most of them are designed to produce large drawings accurately. They are relatively expensive.

How to Choose a Printer
Some of the factors you should consider when buying a printer are:

- **Speed of output:** Most laser printers can print 8 or 12 pages a minute. This speed may depend on what you are printing: graphics, or text pages with a variety of different fonts, tend to be slower. If you need a faster printer, be prepared to pay a lot more.

  Inkjet printers are generally a lot slower than laser printers, but their speed doesn't depend on what you are printing. The quality of the print tends to vary, because they rely on a moving write head.

- **Colour:** If you want colour output, you have to buy a colour printer. It's that simple. Colour laser printers are expensive; colour inkjet printers are only slightly more expensive than black-and-white printers.

  Some colour printers use three different inks to produce their output, some four. Some use a combined three- or four-colour cartridge, some a separate cartridge for each colour. Your choice depends on what you are using the printer for. If you are only occasionally using colour output, make sure you have a separate black cartridge: the density of the black printout from a black cartridge is much higher than that from a combination of colours. If you get a combined four-colour cartridge, you will be throwing out the almost-full colour inks just because you have run out of black.

- **Cost of Consumables:** The initial cost of the printer is only one of the cost factors that you need to consider: ink cartridges (for inkjet printers) and toner cartridges (for laser printers) have to be replaced regularly, and it is worthwhile calculating the cost per page of output before making your final decision.

Modem

A *modem* is used to connect your computer to the telephone network, so that you can send e-mail, or use the Internet. Most computers sold today include a modem already installed in the system unit, but they can also be obtained as external devices that are connected to the computer by a cable. Most modems can enable your computer to function as a fax machine (although, unless you have a scanner, you are limited to sending text-only faxes).

Multimedia

Computers can manipulate any kind of data that can be converted into numbers, including music, pictures, animated drawings, video and speech. A range of applications has grown up around this capability, in which text, video, and sound are mixed to deliver instruction, information, or entertainment. These applications are called *multimedia applications*, and a computer that can run them is often called a *multimedia computer*. Most computers nowadays can run these applications. However, if this is your main interest, you may want to consider a computer with a larger screen, and more advanced sound generation and video display capabilities. In addition, a number of specialised peripherals are available.

Scanner

Think of a scanner as the first half of a photocopier – it copies a photograph, drawing, or page of text into the computer, where you can use a program to manipulate it, or print it out (like the second half of the photocopier). You can use the scanner to include a drawing or photograph in a newsletter, or use *Optical Character Recognition* software to decipher the text, and use all or part of it in a word-processing document (without having to re-type it).

Digital Camera

A digital camera works exactly like a standard camera, except that it does not use photographic film – the images are recorded digitally in the camera's memory. From there, you can transfer them to your computer and subsequently print them out, use graphics software to edit them, archive them for posterity, or e-mail them to your friends.

Loudspeakers

Loudspeakers are standard equipment on almost all new computers. They are used to play music and other sounds.

Sound Cards

Again, your system unit almost certainly includes a sound card, which is used to control all the audio output (music, speech, etc.). However, if the quality of music output is important to you, you may want to upgrade from the sound card supplied as standard equipment.

Microphone

Many software applications can be controlled by speech commands. These are spoken into a microphone.

Looking after Your Hardware

Modern computers are robust and reliable: once they start working, they tend to go on working. But remember that they are sensitive instruments, and avoid testing their tolerance.

DO give your computer room to breathe: it has to have access to fresh air so that the fan can keep the electronics cool.

DON'T block the air vents by stacking books or magazines or (worse) draping clothes over the back of the computer.

DO keep the computer dry. Excessive moisture can play havoc with electric circuitry.

DON'T eat or drink while using your computer: crumbs can clog up your keyboard. A spilt cup of coffee can wreck your computer and (probably worse) cause the loss of all your files stored on the computer.

DO keep your computer free of dust: you will notice that it tends to attract dust. Clean the air vents occasionally, and use an anti-static wipe on the screen.

DON'T expose your computer to extremes of temperature.

DO shut down the computer in an orderly fashion, by systematically closing the applications you have opened.

DON'T just switch it off or pull the plug from the socket.

DO keep diskettes away from the screen: the strong magnetic field generated by the screen may erase or change some of the data.

DON'T move the system unit while the computer is in operation – you risk damaging the hard disk drive.

When Something Goes Wrong

You are more likely to be a computer user than a computer engineer. Therefore respect your PC as a delicate instrument – if it seems to be malfunctioning, don't try to fix it. You risk destroying it or electrocuting yourself. Always call a person qualified to deal with the problem.

Self-Test 1.3: Hardware

1) Which of the following is/are essential pieces of hardware for a computer to work?

   a) Processor
   b) Scanner
   c) Hammer
   d) Word processor

2) The C in CPU stands for:

   a) Central
   b) Computer
   c) Complex
   d) Computing
   e) Commercial

3) What is a scanner used for?

4) What is a modem used for?

5) The speed of a computer is measured in:

   a) CPUs
   b) MHz
   c) MB
   d) K
   e) RAM
   f) GUIs

6) The R in ROM stands for:

   a) Random
   b) Read
   c) Regular
   d) Right

7) The R in RAM stands for:

    a) Random
    b) Read
    c) Regular
    d) Right

8) Correct any of the following statements that are wrong.

    a) There are exactly eight bytes in a bit.
    b) A megabyte is double the size of a normal byte.
    c) 100K bytes is equal to a GB.
    d) A gigabyte is approximately equal to 1,000,000,000 bytes.

9) Which of the following statements is/are true?

    a) Information stored in RAM is erased when the computer is turned off.
    b) Information stored in ROM is erased when the computer is turned off.
    c) The M in RAM stands for memory.
    d) The M in ROM stands for memory.
    e) Hard disks, diskettes, and CD-ROMs are all used to store computer programs.

10) Name three kinds of pointing device.

11) Name the two most common types of printer.

12) Which can store more information: a high-density diskette or a Zip disk?

Section Summary: So Now You Know

The basic PC consists of a system unit, a screen, and a keyboard. Virtually all PCs include a pointing device – most commonly a mouse.

Inside the system unit are the processor (CPU), main memory, hard disk, and some removable storage – usually a diskette drive.

Other items that are almost essential are a printer and a modem. A modem is used to connect the computer to the telephone network, so that you can send and receive e-mail or access the Internet.

Many – even most – PCs sold today are equipped for multimedia: they include loudspeakers, sound cards and microphones.

To capture images, drawings, or photographs and include them in newsletters, project reports, or e-mails, you need a scanner or a digital camera.

Finally, you learnt how to look after your computer, so that it gives a long life of good service.

Section 1.4: Software and Data

In This Section

In this Section, you will learn more about the different kinds of software and how they are made. You will also learn what the most valuable part of a computer system is – the data.

New Activities

At the end of this Section, you should be able to:

- Distinguish between system software and application software
- Describe the process of software development
- Discuss software licensing and the different types of licence
- Describe how to protect software and data from unauthorised access, loss or damage, and computer viruses
- State the principles of data copyright
- State the principles of data protection and the main provisions of the Data Protection Act
- Describe the advantages of computer networking
- Describe the use of the telephone network in computing
- Describe the uses of e-mail, the Internet, and the World Wide Web
- Describe how e-commerce is changing business practices

New Words

At the end of this Section, you should be able to explain the following terms:

- System software
- Application software
- Graphical user interface
- Systems analyst
- Programmer
- Backup
- Virus
- Copyright
- Data protection
- Network

- LAN
- WAN
- PSTN
- ISDN
- E-mail
- Internet
- World Wide Web
- Browser
- Search engine
- E-commerce

Software

Software is the intangible side of computing: it is the generic name given to all the programs – the sets of instructions – that determine how the computer behaves.

We distinguish between two kinds of software: *system software* and *applications software*.

- System software is concerned with the computer itself – what devices it can control, how it manages files and storage, and how it deals with exceptional conditions.
- Applications software is concerned with the world outside the computer – the world of business, entertainment or education.

System Software

The main piece of system software that we are concerned with is the *Operating System* (OS). This is the driving program of the PC: without it, the PC would be virtually unusable. All other programs depend on the operating system to communicate with and control the hardware. The operating system also controls the timing of different events to make sure they happen in the correct sequence, and manages access to data to ensure security and integrity.

When you add a new piece of hardware to your system, you might have to load a special piece of software called a *driver* to enable the operating system to control the hardware. Older PCs use an operating system called DOS (Disk Operating System). To use DOS, you have to type in commands such as DIR, COPY, or REN.

Graphical User Interface
More recent computers present their operating system through a *Graphical User Interface* (GUI). The GUI represents all the computer's resources – the hardware resources such as disks and printers, the software resources, including both system software and application programs, and the data files on which you can work – as small pictures or symbols called *icons*. You use the mouse to move the pointer to the icon representing the object you want to use, and press (or *click*) the mouse button to signal your

request. This is considerably easier than having to remember a command and typing it accurately. Examples of GUIs include Windows, MacOS, and SunOS.

Application Software

Nobody wants to use a lawnmower or a telephone or a satellite: what they want to do is cut the grass, talk to their friends, or predict the weather. Similarly, you don't really want to use a computer: you want to use a computer to do *something else*. That 'something else' is your application, and the program that enables you to do it is called the *application program*. By the time you have finished this book you will be able to use several application programs: word processing, spreadsheets, electronic mail, and so on. Some application programs are very common – it is hard to find an office that doesn't use Microsoft Word or Excel or various Internet browsers such as Netscape Navigator or Microsoft Explorer. Many computers are sold with these applications pre-loaded.

Other applications are developed for more specialised tasks. People and organisations purchase them in accordance with their particular needs. An architect might use a sophisticated drawing package to design houses; a submarine builder might purchase a piece of project management software to help keep track of the thousands of components. In Section 1.5, we will look in more detail at the types of applications in daily use in business, administration, education, entertainment, and communication.

How Software Is Made

The development of any software system involves a cycle of research, analysis, development, and testing, involving the following types of people:

- **Systems Analysts**: They study the business processes that the software is intended to support, and produce the design for the software. They decide what the software should do (but not necessarily how it should do it). You can think of the systems analyst as the software architect. Systems analysts are focused on the needs of the users and the application area.

- **Programmers**: They translate the design into a working program. They write instructions that tell the computer what to do in order to accomplish the task for which the system is intended. You can think of the programmer as the software builder. Programmers are focused on the computer, its capabilities and its limitations.

Software Copyright

In general, software is *licensed* rather than sold. When you buy a software package, you don't own the software: you gain the right to use it under specified conditions.

In general, software is easy to duplicate, so it is easy for unscrupulous people to make unauthorised copies: don't do it. It's piracy; it's illegal; and it deprives an individual developer or a company of their rightful income, which they need to produce the next version of that piece of software, or the next application that you will want to use.

Don't accept software from dubious sources, whether in person, by mail-order, or over the Internet. You are responsible for the legality of the software that you use.

Some software, called *freeware* is distributed without charge: you find it on disks given away with magazines, or download it from the Internet. Again, you should be clear about the terms of use: in most cases, you can use it, but you may not, for example, sell it for profit, change it in any way, or label it as if it was your own product.

Other software is called *shareware*. It is widely distributed in much the same way as freeware. You can try it out, but if you decide to use it, you are expected to send a licence fee to the developer. In some cases, this is based on honour; in other cases, the shareware version will not function after a time period (typically 30 days), or certain functions are disabled in some way. When you register with the developer and send the licence fee, you are given a fully working copy of the software, or a password to unlock the disabled functions.

Problems with Software

Software – even the smallest piece of application software – is complex. It is difficult to test thoroughly, because it is difficult to imagine every possible input in every possible combination. Sometimes mistakes are made, or unusual circumstances are not adequately catered for by the designers or programmers.

When the software produces incorrect or unexpected results, it is said to have a *bug*. Bugs can range from minor irritations, where, for example, the screen displays are inconsistent, through significant errors, such as incorrect totals on invoices, to total collapse.

An example of a problem caused by short-sighted programming practices was the so-called "Millennium Bug". Many programs stored dates as six digits — two each for day, month and year. For most purposes, this is fine, but when you use these dates in calculations, difficulties can arise. For example, if someone is born on 06 01 99, is he/she just over a year old or one hundred and one? Such ambiguities can be of critical importance in calculating interest payments, sell-by dates, eligibility for pensions, and so on. Although this problem may seem almost trivial, putting it right cost businesses around the world many millions of pounds.

When the computer 'freezes' – it ceases to function, refuses to accept any input, won't produce any output – we say that it *hangs*. When this happens, you may be able to resort to an old trick: press three of the keyboard keys simultaneously – CTRL, ALT, and DEL. Most of the time, this will enable you to shut down the offending program, and continue working on something else. Pressing this key combination *twice* generally causes your computer to restart.

Infrequently, a bug will cause the whole system to *crash*. The only solution is to turn off the power, wait a minute, and then turn it on again. A quicker way to achieve the same end is to press the Reset button on your system unit. Treat this as a last resort, you will lose any work since you last saved in all the applications that you have open at the time.

Data

We haven't yet dealt in any detail with data. Data is another intangible in a computer system, but it is not generally built by the software developer. It's built by users – people like you.

So to write a letter, you need a keyboard, a screen, and a printer (hardware), and you need a word-processing program (software). The letter itself, and the name and address of the recipient, are *data*.

Data is held on a computer system in *files*. Files are organised into *directories* (otherwise known as *folders*). Files and directories are given *names*, so that you can find them and recognise them when you need them, and so that the operating system can find them and work on them when it needs to.

Looking After Your Data

In most computer systems, the data is the most important element. Hardware and software are easily replaced if they break down, or are lost or stolen. Data, on the other hand, can represent years of work, and may be irreplaceable. So it makes sense to look after it. Data can be lost, corrupted, damaged, or abused in a variety of ways, accidentally or deliberately.

Security and Passwords

You can protect your data against theft, corruption, and prying eyes by using a system of *passwords*. Depending on the application, you can use passwords to decide who can see the data and who can change it.

Most applications allow you to choose your own password, and encourage you to change it frequently. Choose a password that is not too obvious – if it is easy to guess, its purpose may be defeated. However, choose a password that is easy to remember. If you forget it, you may not be able to get at your own data, and if you write it down, it may be discovered and used by someone else. The best passwords include both numbers and letters, so that unauthorised persons will find them less easy to guess.

Backups

Files can be lost or destroyed accidentally. The hard disk may develop problems, or the whole office may be destroyed by fire. You can protect yourself against these nightmare scenarios by keeping backup copies of all your data fles, on diskette or another removable medium, and storing it safely at home or at another location. That way, even in the worst situation, you can be up and running very quickly after a disaster.

Save Frequently

You should also save your work at regular intervals while you are working. Remember that the computer works on your data in working storage (RAM), which is volatile. If there is a power cut, or if someone accidentally unplugs your PC, everything you have done since you last saved will be lost. It is a good discipline to save after every paragraph of text, or after you have done any complex operation.

Viruses

Computer viruses are attempts at sabotage. They are clever but poisonous programs written by malicious software developers and amateur hacks who have nothing better to do. They attack the integrity of your files, and are designed to transfer easily and stealthily from one computer to another. Their effects vary from minor irritation (where a message is displayed on your screen, but no files are damaged), through inconvenience (where one or more files are affected), to total disaster (where the entire hard disk is rendered unusable).

Viruses are spread through e-mail attachments and the exchange of infected diskettes. So, never open an e-mail attachment if you are unsure of its origin, and always use virus scanning software to check any diskette that comes into your possession or organisation from outside.

Prevention is better than cure: make sure that you install reputable anti-virus software on your computer that will automatically scan your disks (hard drive and diskette), and detect and remove any viruses found. Anti-virus software must be kept up to date – new viruses are being concocted all the time, and the software used to detect them needs to be the very latest.

Data Copyright

Remember that computer data carries the same copyright rights and responsibilities as printed works or musical compositions: someone created it, and that person owns it. If you download information from the Internet, you may not have the right to include it in your own publications without the consent of the author or creator.

Data Protection

We all appear in numerous databases: banks, insurance companies, educational institutions, employers, and governments all hold files full of personal information. Our date of birth, address and marital status, our incomes, credit and educational records, our health, criminal and bill-paying histories are all known by various institutions. This information is sometimes general, sometimes special. It may be sensitive and, in the wrong hands, damaging or dangerous.

Marketing departments are willing to pay large sums of money for name and address databases of specific categories of people. This enables them to target products and services at precise sectors of the population.

It follows that the collection, maintenance, and protection of information is a responsibility that demands great respect. Wrong or misleading information could lead to a person being refused a mortgage, a job, an overseas work visa, or medical insurance. It could ruin their life. Holding personal information thus demands sensitivity and respect. This is reflected in the *data protection laws*.

Data Protection Legislation
The Data Protection Act entitles every person to request (in writing) any personal information pertaining to him or her which is contained in a computerised database. Such information can be deleted or corrected at the request of the individual concerned. This includes the right to have one's name taken off a mailing list or database.

Anyone who controls such data is also responsible for obtaining and using such personal information in a fair way. The information can be maintained only for specified lawful purposes, and cannot be disclosed for any illegal purpose. Appropriate security measures must be taken to ensure unauthorised persons do not have access to the data and to ensure the safe disposal of the information. Data must be up-to-date and accurate, and must not be kept longer than necessary.

Self-Test 1.4: Software

1) Is a word processor systems software or application software?

2) Is Windows systems software or application software?

3) What is the difference between freeware and shareware?

4) Which of the following statements is/are true?

   a) A folder is another name for a diskette.
   b) A file can contain any number of folders.
   c) Records have been made obsolete by CDs.
   d) Files contain records.

5) What is a computer virus?

6) State some of the ways to protect your data against loss or corruption.

7) You edit the newsletter for your local community. Are you entitled to sell the mailing list to a marketing company? Why/why not?

Networks

Computers can function quite happily on their own (*stand-alone computing*), but increasingly they are being connected together into *networks*.

The Advantages of Networking

When your computer is connected to other computers – whether they are in the same building or on the other side of the world – it is part of a computer network. You can still use it to do your own work as usual, but several new possibilities open up:

- **Sharing Hardware:** In a stand-alone world, people can print only if a printer is attached directly to their computer. By connecting one or more printers to a computer network, everyone whose computer is also attached to the same network can print their documents. Printer-sharing means that everyone can print (although not at the same time) without everyone having an individual printer. The same is true of other hardware resources, such as modems, scanners, and plotters.

- **File-sharing:** On a stand-alone computer, you can work with all the files stored on your computer's hard disk. On a network-connected computer, you may be able to work with files stored on other people's computers too. Rather than have network users rummaging through each other's hard disks, information that is needed by everyone in a particular department (in accounts, for example, or in a warehouse) is usually stored on a single, powerful, permanently switched-on computer called a *file server*.

- **E-mail:** Meetings, telephone conversations, letters and memos – typically, these are the ways in which people in an organisation communicate with one another. Computer networks make possible another form of communication called electronic mail, or e-mail for short. This is the exchange of (usually plain-text) messages between users of computers that are connected to a common network.

- **Data exchange:** Users connected to a computer network can exchange files: one person can write an article for the newsletter, another can edit it, a third can lay it out, while a fourth can contribute a drawing or a scanned photograph. This kind of co-operative work over a network is known as *workgroup computing*, or *groupwork*.

Computer Network

Two or more computers that are connected together by some means to provide their users with such services as printer-sharing, file-sharing and electronic mail.

LANs and WANs

Networks come in two sizes: big and small. A Local Area Network, or LAN, is the kind that connects the computers in a single office, building or group of adjoining buildings.

Local Area Network (LAN)

A network that connects computers located within a small area.

Large corporations operate computer networks that connect offices at locations within the same or different countries. Such Wide Area Networks, or WANs, can enable, for example:

- The Frankfurt office to exchange e-mails with the Sydney office

- The Tokyo office to read files that are stored on a computer in the New Orleans office

- The Cape Town office to print a report on a printer that is located in the Bombay office

Wide Area Network (WAN)

A network that connects computers over a wide area, typically across international boundaries.

In reality, most networks are bigger than LANs but smaller than WANs. But, for some reason, no one has thought up a name for them.

Computer networks can be open to everyone or restricted to the chosen few. An example of a *private access* network is one operated by a company or government agency for its own personnel only. An example of a *public access* network is the Internet.

Making the Connection

How do the computers in a network actually connect with one another? Well, in a LAN it's relatively simple: the computers (and printers) are connected together with a special cable. However, in a WAN, that isn't an option. It would be quite impractical to run cables from one side of the country to another, or from one continent to the next.

The Telephone Network

The solution is that WANs use cables already in place – the cables of the national and international telephone system (the PSTN, or Public Switched

Telephone Network). They also use all the other technology of the telephone network – satellites, microwaves, optic fibres, and so on. This has advantages, and one major disadvantage too:

- **Advantages:** It's already in place (so there is no need to run WAN cables across rivers and over mountains), and its connection points are never far away (the phone system reaches into every workplace and virtually every home).

- **Disadvantage:** Computer signals (the ones that travel around inside a computer) are a different 'shape' from the signals accepted by the phone system (ones resulting from the sound of the human voice). Computer signals are 'digital'; voice signals are 'analog'.

We therefore have a problem: a *signal shape* problem. To connect a computer to a phone line, we need a device than can do two jobs. Which job it does at any particular time depends on the direction of the information transfer:

- **Outgoing Information:** When your computer sends data (such as an e-mail) down the phone line, the device must 'shape' the signal – convert it from computer-shape to phone-shape (digital to analog).

- **Incoming Information:** When you receive data (such as a file from a distant computer), the device must 'deshape' the signal – reconvert it back from phone-shape to its original computer-shape (analog to digital).

Another, rather poetic, word for the act of shaping anything in this way is *modulation*. A device that shapes (*mod*ulates) and deshapes (*dem*odulates) a signal is called – guess what? – a modem.

> ### Modem
> *A device that enables computers to communicate over the telephone system. At the sending computer, the modem converts the outgoing data to the format acceptable to the phone system. At the receiving computer, another modem reconverts the data back to its original computer format.*

Most modern computers have built-in modems. To connect such a computer to the telephone system, you plug the phone line into the socket at the back of the computer. If your modem is a separate unit, you plug the telephone line into the modem and use another cable to connect the modem to the serial port on the computer. The modem may be battery-powered or may need to be plugged into the mains.

Modems are rated according to the speed at which they can transmit and receive data. The *baud rate* is the number of times the signal changes in one second. However, each change in the signal can carry more than one bit of data, so the measure more commonly used nowadays is *bits per second* or *bps*. The top speed of current modems is around 56 kbps (kilobits per second, or thousands of bits per second).

ISDN

An alternative to using modems and the normal telephone network (PSTN) is to use ISDN, or Integrated Services Digital Network. As its name suggests, this network is designed to carry digital signals. In the past it has been used mainly by businesses who need frequent high-volume communication with other offices, and has been relatively expensive for low-volume users. This is beginning to change – the cost of ISDN is now within the reach of small businesses and home users.

ISDN gives access to two 64 kbps channels; these can be used separately or combined to exchange data at 128 kbps.

E-mail

Networks enable users to exchange personal messages with one another: this is the idea behind *e-mail*.

To send someone an e-mail message, you need to have a computer connected to a network, and the recipient has to have a computer connected (directly or indirectly) to the same network. You also need e-mail software, and the unique 'address' of the recipient. That's the minimum. In practice, this means that both of you have:

- A PC
- A modem
- A telephone line
- A subscription to an Internet Service Provider (ISP)

The ISP maintains a continuous connection to the Internet, and stores on its computer all e-mail that is sent, from anywhere in the world, to your *mailbox*, until you collect it after submitting a password to prove your entitlement to it.

This system means that you can send a message to your friend even when their computer is turned off: it is stored for them, by their ISP, until they collect it.

Thus, you can carry on an electronic conversation over a period of time, during which neither you nor your friend are ever talking at the same time. This is particularly useful if you live in different time zones.

E-mail
The exchange of (usually plain-text) messages between users of computers that are connected to a common network.

E-mail has largely taken over from two earlier technologies that used the telephone network to send and receive written messages:

- **Fax** can be thought of as remote photocopying. The sender used a fax machine to scan a letter, drawing, map, or whatever. The fax machine encoded it so that it could be sent down the telephone line. The recipient's fax machine decoded the message and provided a printout.

- **Telex** was a much more primitive technology, which acted like a remote typewriter. It accepted only text typed on a special Telex machine (no pictures). At the receiving end, the Telex machine responded by typing out the same letters and numbers.

The Internet

The *Internet* – everyone's talking about it. It may even be one of the main reasons you decided to learn about computers.

> **Internet**
>
> *The Internet is a worldwide network of interconnected networks.*

If you connect to the Internet, you can:

- Send e-mail to other users
- Access information stored on computers all around the world

Millions of users have access to the Internet; hundreds of thousands of computers are permanently connected to it – computers owned by governments, universities, companies, retailers, voluntary organisations and private individuals. Any user, anywhere, can send a message to any other user, and can access files on the other computers. This rich resource can be used for research, news, entertainment, education, information, sports, current affairs, shopping and art.

The Internet has become by far the most popular network for carrying e-mail, for a number of reasons:

- The network is already in place: there is no need to create a new physical network connecting all the people you want to communicate with.
- It has a huge population of already-connected users: the chances are high that the person you want to communicate with has an Internet connection.
- It is very robust: it is designed so that there is no single point of failure – if one computer on the network breaks down, or one phone line fails, the message is routed a different way to avoid the problem.
- It uses common standards: messages sent from one computer system in one country can be received and interpreted correctly by a different computer system in a different country.

The term *World Wide Web* is used to describe documents made available over the Internet which are in a particular graphic format. The documents can be linked together, irrespective of where they are physically located, and users can follow the links from document to document. This enables you to pursue a research topic from the general to the specific, from detail to 'big picture', from graphic to text, from text to sound. These links are called *hyperlinks*, and documents constructed with hyperlinks are called *hypertext*, or *hypermedia* if sound, graphics, or video are involved.

The software used to display World Wide Web documents (or *web pages*) is called a *browser*. The two most frequently used browsers are Microsoft Internet Explorer, and Netscape Navigator.

> ### World Wide Web
> *The range of documents published on the Internet in a format that enables them to be displayed using a browser.*

> ### Browser
> *A program that enables you to display web pages and follow links from one web page to another.*

However, with hundreds of thousands of computers connected to the Internet, each with thousands of pages of information available to you, how do you find anything of value?

You use a *search engine*. A search engine is a program that trawls the Internet looking for documents that contain information of interest to you: the share price of a company, flight times from Rome to Athens, comparison of different brands of vacuum cleaner, the correct spelling of a word in German, the prognosis for a particular medical condition, tonight's TV listing ... it's all there somewhere.

> ### Search Engine
> *A program that searches the World Wide Web for documents that match your criteria.*

Another term used to describe the Internet and the World Wide Web is *Information Superhighway*.

E-commerce

Businesses around the world are beginning to use the Internet as a way of developing their markets. They use the Internet to advertise their goods, they take orders over the Internet, and, in many cases, they use the Internet to deliver their products and services. Obviously only certain kinds of goods can be delivered online, but this includes some that have traditionally been sold in shops, such as software, music, concert tickets and books. Businesses are also using the Internet to find the cheapest or most efficient source of supply of raw materials, to track orders and deliveries, and to communicate with customers.

This move of business to the Internet is known as *e-commerce* (or electronic commerce).

The Internet can change the way you shop. You can use the Internet to compare prices from different suppliers; you can buy direct from the manufacturer, instead of through a 'middle man'; you can buy anywhere in the world; you can communicate with other buyers to get their views on quality and suitability.

When you are planning a trip, you can plan your itinerary, find the cheapest flights, look at alternative hotels and compare their facilities and prices, check out special offers, look at maps, and check event listings. You can book flights, hire cars, hotel or guest-house accommodation, concerts, sporting events, even meals in your favourite restaurant.

Self-Test 1.5: Networks

1) Name two reasons you might connect your computer to a network.

2) The L in LAN stands for:

   a) Leading
   b) Local
   c) Long
   d) Linked

3) The A in WAN stands for:

   a) Access
   b) Attached
   c) Area
   d) Aerial

4) Comment on each of the following statements, indicating whether each is true or false.

   a) Computer networks will shortly make the telephone system obsolete.
   b) Modems are used to increase the speed at which computers can communicate.
   c) The telephone system is ideally suited for communication between computers.
   d) E-mail is another name for the Internet.

5) What is the Internet? State two of the most common uses of the Internet.

6) What is the World Wide Web? What kind of software do you need to use it?

7) What is a search engine?

8) Give some examples of e-commerce.

9) What kinds of goods and services are most easily traded over the Internet?

10) For *one* of the following businesses, state how its business could be changed by e-commerce: travel agent, record company, supermarket, restaurant, hairdresser.

Section Summary: So Now You Know

A computer *is* hardware, but it *does* software. Software determines how the computer behaves – the particular problems it solves at any given time.

System software is inward looking – it is software that controls the computer itself.

Application software is software that addresses a 'real world' problem – it does something that you or I want done.

Software is developed by systems analysts and programmers in a process that involves detailed research, analysis, program development and testing. Testing is almost never comprehensive, so that errors and problems sometimes occur (bugs).

Software belongs to the authors, and, in general, copying it is illegal.

Data is often the most valuable part of a computer system, because it is the least easily replaced. For that reason, you should protect your data against loss or damage by using passwords and anti-virus software. You should also save your work frequently and make backups at regular intervals.

You should be especially careful with personal information. The Data Protection Act imposes specific responsibilities on anyone who maintains databases of personal information.

Computer networking enables users to share resources such as hardware and data. They can also exchange messages. When the network covers a wide area (a Wide Area Network) the connection between the computers makes use of the telephone network. This requires the use of a modem.

To use e-mail, the sender and the receiver must each have a PC, a modem, access to a telephone line, and a subscription to an Internet Service Provider (or other e-mail carrier).

The Internet is a worldwide network of interconnected networks. It is by far the most common medium for e-mail, and also provides the infrastructure for the World Wide Web.

The World Wide Web is a vast array of documents that are available over the Internet in a particular format – a format that enables them to be displayed with a browser. The browser enables you to display the document of your choice, and to follow hyperlinks from one document to another.

The Internet is enabling many businesses to reach new markets and offer new services to customers around the world. This is known as e-commerce.

Section 1.5: What Computers Are Used For

In This Section

In this Section, we take a look at some of the ways in which computers are used, and the effects they have on our lives. This isn't comprehensive – it can't be, as new uses are being found every day. However, by the end of the Section, you should appreciate that the range of applications is very wide indeed.

New Activities

At the end of this Section, you should be able to:

- Discuss the widespread use of computers in modern society

- Offer examples of computer application in business, industry, schools, healthcare and the home

- Discuss appropriate and inappropriate uses of computers

- Discuss the Information Society

Business and Administration

Most offices today depend on computers. Computers are used to keep accounts, to send invoices, to maintain records of customers and suppliers, to hold details of stock, to calculate payroll, to write and edit letters, memos and reports, to design sales presentations, to communicate with other companies, to collect market intelligence, to collaborate with others in research activities.

Computers are also used in more complex business processes such as resource planning, scheduling, route planning, customer relationship management, sales analysis and simulation.

Computers are particularly useful where there are large volumes of data to be maintained, analysed, stored and filtered, or where complex or repetitive calculations have to be performed.

Industry

In the manufacturing industry, the range of applications includes all of the administrative functions mentioned above, and a whole lot more besides. Computers are used to schedule production, to monitor raw material usage and finished product quality, to control machine tools, to design new products, to minimise waste, to determine optimum stock levels.

In the most automated plants, computers are used to collect orders from customers, to issue instructions to build the required products to the customer's specifications, to automatically order the parts and materials from the relevant subsuppliers (having first checked that they can deliver on time), and to schedule the plant and personnel necessary for satisfying the customer's order.

Retailing

In supermarkets, and increasingly in smaller shops, computers are used at the checkout to scan the bar codes on your purchases, and to calculate your bill. In many stores, the information on your purchases is passed immediately to the warehouse, and orders for replacement stock are generated automatically when stock falls below a given point. Instructions can also be generated for the personnel responsible for stacking the shelves, so that the products are always available. This technology enables the supermarket to keep its stock to the minimum necessary to satisfy its customers, instead of having money tied up unnecessarily in stock and storage space.

Computers can also be used to control moving-message advertising panels. These displays are made up of hundreds of *Light-Emitting Diodes* (LEDs) that are turned on and off rapidly to create text and pictures.

Home

In the home, computers have found a wide variety of uses – for playing games (most often), for keeping household accounts, for getting information over the Internet (to research ancient history for a homework project or for checking the scores in the Italian football league), for sending e-mail to friends and relatives abroad. The list grows every day, and the only limit is imagination.

Many people have established professional design studios and desktop publishing businesses at home using PCs. Others have managed to use their PC to offer desktop video or sound editing comparable to that offered by expensive and sophisticated dedicated equipment. Book-keepers and accountants, journalists and writers and database designers are also able to work from home nowadays thanks to the PC and connectivity.

Schools

When you hear about young people using computers in schools, you may think they are doing something very technical, like programming, or electronics. They seldom are.

The main uses for computers in schools are in the traditional subject areas. There is a lot of educational software available that presents school subjects in a structured and entertaining way. Some students respond better to information presented this way. Computers also enable each student to progress at his or her own pace – the computer will repeat lessons as often as necessary, without losing patience!

In addition, the computer opens up the school to the outside world. Students can retrieve information from libraries, universities, government agencies, voluntary bodies, news organisations and other sources. They can communicate with students in other countries, and co-operate with them on research projects. They can take lessons from world experts without leaving their classroom.

In some science subjects, computers can be used to simulate experiments which are either dangerous or expensive. This enables the students to learn without exposing themselves to the dangers, or without incurring the costs of the materials of equipment involved in the experiment.

Students can also use the computer to write reports, produce school newsletters and design posters.

Health Care

The administration of hospitals depends more and more on computers. In fact, many of the applications are similar to manufacturing: scheduling expensive and scarce equipment, drawing up rosters, making appointments for patients, etc. In addition, computers are used for monitoring patients' conditions and alerting staff when abnormalities arise. Computers also allow doctors to keep comprehensive patient records, and to conduct research into the effectiveness of different treatments.

Research is also heavily dependent on computing power: most modern drugs are designed with the aid of computers and manufactured under computer control. The Human Genome Project, which promises major breakthroughs in the treatment of genetic disorders, would be impossible without powerful computers.

Computers and communications technology are also being used to deliver health services to remote regions: the patient can connect to a major centre (or a centre of specialist expertise) for diagnosis and, in some cases, for treatment. This development is expected to yield significant cost-savings and better treatment for patients in the coming years.

Government and Public Administration

Government agencies use computers for a wide range of purposes, in the same way as businesses – for accounting, stock control, project management, budgeting, forecasting, and so on. The main difference is one of scale: in general, governments need to maintain very large bodies of information e.g. registers of births, marriages and deaths; tax and social welfare records; census of population data; voting registers. It would be almost impossible to maintain these records in a usable condition without computers.

Everyday Life

You would recognise the computers used in the applications outlined so far. However, computer technology is also used in less visible ways. Computers control the cycles in your washing machine, the timer in your video recorder, the sequences of the traffic lights, the delivery of money through an Automatic Teller Machine, and the supply of fuel to your car engine. Almost anywhere you see something happening 'automatically', there is a computer at its heart, monitoring the outside world and responding to it.

Speech synthesizers are programs that produce computer-generated speech in imitation of the human voice. They are increasingly used in telephone applications such as in directory enquiries, in voicemail systems, in telephone banking, and in travel information systems. They are also used to enable blind or partially sighted people to use computers: the speech synthesizer 'reads' aloud any text that appears on the screen.

Information Technology and Society

Some people find this proliferation of computers somewhat disturbing. Is there no aspect of our lives that is untouched by computers? Are computers replacing people, creating unemployment? Are all uses of computers good, or are computers being used to manipulate and control us? Are all computer-assisted services, and all computer-manufactured goods better than their predecessors?

These questions don't have clear-cut answers.

From the discussion in this Section, you probably agree that the society we live in uses computers a lot, and that many of the goods we consume and many of the services we use would not be available without computers. Like it or not, we are living in the Computer Age, or the Information Age, or the Digital Age (take your pick), and our society can justifiably be called an *Information Society*. In essence this means that value in the society comes from information.

In the Age of Agriculture, most of the work, and most of the value, related to food production. In the Industrial Age, it was manufacturing that defined the society. The availability of food was almost taken for granted; proportionately less time and effort went into ensuring the food supply to the individual. Value, wealth and incomes depended more on manufactured goods.

In recent years, the balance has shifted again, this time towards service occupations, office-based occupations, in which information, knowledge, and intelligence play the key role. The emphasis has been transferred from brawn to brain. In this new economy, computers play a critical, central role.

It is worth asking, however, whether all uses of computers are good. We can see the benefit of using computers, for example, to process bank transactions. Would we be equally happy to let computers decide loan approvals? Routine administration of, say, parking fines could usefully be delegated to computers, but what about putting computer systems in the role of judges in court? In medicine and health care, there are many obvious useful applications, and there are other applications that make many people uncomfortable.

In the world of art, there are also difficulties: does computer-generated 'art' deserve the name? Can a computer write poetry, make paintings, compose music? Should we judge these 'creations' by the same criteria that we judge work made by humans?

As we said, these questions do not have clear-cut answers. But it is worth thinking about them, because they are becoming increasingly relevant to everyday life.

Participation in the Information Society

Computers and related technologies are touching our lives from the time the electronic alarm clock wakes us up to the time we use the remote control to turn off the television at night. We can respond as passive consumers of entertainment and advertising, or by becoming active participants in this society.

Participation means exercising choice: choice about what information we get, when we get it, in what form we get it and how we use it. It means analysing the information for relevance, salience, accuracy. It means deciding what to keep and what to discard. It means deciding what to produce: what to publish, to whom you publish it, in what form and at what time.

The idea of the ECDL – and the idea of this book – is to enable you to use some of the tools necessary for this kind of active participation in the Information Society.

However, you already have the most important tools, and you know how to use them: your natural intelligence, your critical faculties, the ability to judge whether or not something makes sense. No amount of technology can replace these, and you should never be blinded by technological wizardry so that you doubt these innate talents.

Self-Test 1.6: Computers in Society

1) Which of the following statements do you agree with, and why?

   a) Computers are faster than humans at mathematical calculations.
   b) Humans have more reliable long-term memory than computers.
   c) Computers can be programmed to write poetry.
   d) Computers can diagnose and treat medical conditions better than doctors.

2) Name some of the ways in which your local supermarket uses computers. State how each of these affects the management, staff, and customers.

3) What does the term *Information Society* mean?

4) Who benefits from the transition to an Information Society? What problems might arise?

5) 'The Information Society will involve gross invasions of personal privacy.' Discuss.

Section
Summary:
So Now You Know

Computers are used in business, in industry, in retailing, in the home, in schools and colleges, in health care, in public administration, and in almost every aspect of everyday life.

It is worthwhile pausing every so often to consider whether every possible application of computers is necessarily a good one. Some things are best left to human beings, exercising human judgement, and bringing human values to bear.

It is also worth considering what this proliferation of computers into every aspect of modern life means for society. There is a danger that society will be divided into those who have access to computers and know how to use them (the 'information rich'), and those that have no access to computers or don't know how to use them (the 'information poor').

The ECDL will equip you with the skills to participate in the Information Society, but you will increasingly need to exercise your critical faculties: remember that all the information available on the Internet, for example, was created and input by someone, somewhere. And that 'someone' could be biased, misguided, prejudiced or just plain wrong.

Section 1.6: Looking after Number One: Health and Safety

In This Section

This Section deals with something even more valuable than hardware, software, or data. Something irreplaceable – you.

Just as we have accustomed ourselves to using safety belts and child-proof locks in cars, we need to adopt safe computing practices. Problems can arise in a number of areas, but sensible precautions can help you avoid them.

New Activities

At the end of this Section, you should be able to:

- Describe some of the hazards associated with using a computer
- Describe sensible computing practices

New Words

At the end of this Section, you should be able to explain the following term:

- Repetitive strain injury

Health Warning!

In general, computers are clean, quiet, and safe to use. You should be aware, however, of a number of potential dangers, and how to avoid them.

Repetitive Strain Injury

If you do any physical activity for a long time without a break, you risk straining or injuring yourself. Using a keyboard or mouse for a prolonged period can lead to the computer user's equivalent of tennis elbow. It can affect the fingers, hands, wrists, elbows, or even the back. The best way to avoid this problem is to take a break every fifteen or twenty minutes to allow your muscles to rest and recuperate.

You should also make sure your desk and chair are at a suitable height, and that your keyboard is at a comfortable angle (see page 41).

Eyesight

Extended periods of staring at a PC screen can lead to fatigue and ultimately to eye-strain. Avoid locking your eyes in to a fixed screen stare. Look away frequently and focus your eyes on objects on the other side of the room, or out the window. Make sure that your work area is adequately lit and ventilated.

Posture

Simple ergonomics are often so obvious that they are overlooked. You should arrange the hardware elements of your PC in such a way as to provide the easiest and most physically comfortable access. Your desk should support your screen at the correct eye level. Your chair should be comfortable, adjustable, and provide adequate lumbar support.

46-61 cm

40° 15° 0°

0-20°

63-74 cm

41-51 cm

38-43 cm

Accidents

Your computer system includes a number of different physical devices. They are all connected together by cables. The system unit is plugged into the mains electricity socket. On some models, the screen takes its electricity supply from the system unit; in others it plugs directly into the mains. The loudspeakers are usually plugged into the mains. The modem is connected to the telephone socket.

That's a lot of cables and wires. Make sure that the cables connecting the components are kept tidy, secure, and out of the way, so that there is no danger of tripping over them. Also make sure that the mains electricity sockets you use are capable of handling the load safely: don't plug all the appliances into a single adaptor or you risk overloading the circuit.

Self-Test 1.7:

1) Which of the following is/are true?

   a) It is best to get all your data entry done in the morning, while you are fresh.
   b) You should sit as close to the screen as possible, so that you don't strain your eyes.
   c) If you sit too close to the screen, you can catch a computer virus.
   d) The best way to avoid Repetitive Strain Injury (RSI) is to continue working after you feel pain. That way, your arm muscles develop faster.

2) If you are using a computer for a long time, the best kind of chair is:

   a) An office chair that can be adjusted for height
   b) A dining chair with arm supports
   c) A comfortable sofa

3) True or false:

   In winter, it is a good idea to cover the system unit with a blanket, so that it doesn't get cold.

4) State some of the dangers associated with using a computer, and how to minimise them.

Section Summary: So Now You Know

While using a computer is generally safe, there are a number of hazards, and all of them are avoidable. Most of them – in particular repetitive strain injury and eye strain – arise only if you use the computer for long periods without a break. Others arise from bad posture or inappropriate positioning of equipment. Cabling also presents a potential source of accidents: you should make sure that cables are tidy and out of the way.

Module

2

Using a Computer and Managing Files

Module 1 was the tourist guidebook you used to prepare for your visit to computer land. Module 2 is where you now get to meet the natives in the flesh.

And what exotic creatures they are! The citizens are called files. They reside in houses called folders. And folders are built on areas called drives. (Files inside folders, and folders on top of drives – you have learnt quite a lot already!)

And such obedient citizens too! You can change their names, move them to a different location, alter their appearance, get rid of ones you don't want anymore – you can even create new ones out of nothing.

But remember this: files are delicate. So treat them with care. You do this by saving them regularly and by making copies of them every so often – just in case something bad happens to the originals. It's always the files you like and need most that seem to disappear the quickest. Better to learn this lesson from the book than from real life in computer land.

Section 2.1: Starting Up, Clicking Around, Shutting Down

Are you ready to take your first practical steps in computing?

This Section guides you through the basics. You will learn the correct ways of starting and shutting down a computer, discover the meaning of the various little pictures on the Windows screen, and find out how to start and close Word, Excel and other software applications that you will meet in later ECDL Modules.

New Skills

At the end of this Section you should be able to:

- Power up and power down a computer
- Use the Start menu to open software applications
- Switch between open applications
- Click, double-click, right-click and drag with the mouse
- Use the three control buttons at the top right of a window
- Move, resize and scroll windows
- Restart a computer when problems occur

New Words

At the end of this Section you should be able to explain the following terms:

Powering up/Booting	Cursor
Clicking	Menu
Taskbar	Close button
Restore button	Folder
Desktop window	Application window
Maximise button	Minimise button
Dragging	Double-clicking
Pop-up/Shortcut menu	Dialog box

Starting Your Computer

Before you start your computer, check that it is plugged into the electricity socket. Now, press the button to switch on the computer.

- On some computers, a *single button* switches on both the computer and the computer's screen.

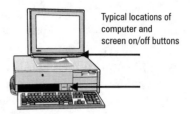

Typical locations of computer and screen on/off buttons

- Other computers have *two buttons*: one for the computer itself and a second for the screen.

Your computer will make some humming noises and some messages will flicker on your screen. Don't worry: this is just your computer warming up and checking that everything is in working order.

The Windows Desktop

The Windows desktop appears – little pictures set against a coloured background. These pictures are called *icons*. Along the bottom of your screen you will see a grey bar, with a button named **Start** in its left corner and a clock in its right. This is called the *Taskbar*.

You will learn more about icons and the Taskbar later. You will also discover how you can change the appearance of your Windows desktop to suit your working needs and personal taste.

A sample Windows desktop.

The little pictures are called *icons*.

The grey bar along the bottom of the screen is called the *Taskbar*.

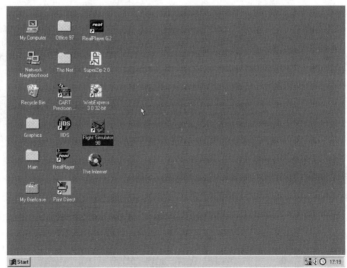

Congratulations. You have now powered up your computer.

> **Powering Up/Booting**
>
> *The technical terms for starting a computer and displaying the Windows desktop on the screen. You don't 'switch on' a computer; you 'power it up' or 'boot' the computer.*

Starting Applications

Software applications are useful programs such as Microsoft Word, Excel, Access and PowerPoint that enable you to create documents, spreadsheets, databases and presentations. You will learn a lot about these in Modules 3, 4, 5 and 6 of this ECDL course. Your first step in working with applications is to learn how to start them.

Using the Mouse

Place your hand over the mouse and move it around your (physical) desktop. As you move the mouse, the cursor moves around the Windows desktop, allowing you to point to the item you want to work with.

To move the cursor up the screen, move the mouse in the up direction.

To move the cursor down the screen, move the mouse in the down direction.

Cursor

A symbol, usually an arrow, that you move around the computer screen by moving the mouse across your (physical) desktop.

The Start Button

Move the cursor down to the bottom-left of your screen so that it is over the **Start** button. Now, press down the left mouse button and then release it. You don't need to hold down the button for more than a second. This is called clicking.

Clicking with the Mouse

Briefly holding down the left mouse button. By clicking on an item on the screen, you tell your computer: "I want to select this item".

Windows start-up menu

Your mouse-click causes the **Start** button to display the start-up *menu*. Move the cursor up over the item called **Programs**. As you do, another menu appears to its right. On this second menu or *submenu*, move the cursor over the item called **Microsoft Word** and click on it. This opens the Microsoft Word application.

Menu

A list of items displayed on the computer screen that allows you to work with applications and files, and get more information. Some menus offer submenus of further options.

Multi-tasking with Windows

You can open more than one application at one time – this is called *multi-tasking*. Move the cursor back down over the **Start** button and click on it. Next, move the cursor over the menu item called **Programs**. On the next menu displayed, move the cursor over the item called **Microsoft Excel** and click on it. You have now started a second application.

Why stop at two applications? Exercise 2.1 takes you through the steps of starting a third application, Notepad.

Exercise 2.1: Opening the Notepad Application

1) Click on the **Start** button.

2) Click **Start | Programs** to display the start-up menu.

3) Click **Start | Programs | Accessories** to display the Accessories submenu.

4) Click **Start | Programs | Accessories | Notepad** to open the Notepad application.

Congratulations. You have now three applications open on your screen.

Switching Between Open Applications

The expression **Start | Programs** is a shorthand way of saying 'Open the start-up menu and select the option named Programs'. And **Start | Programs | Accessories | Notepad** means: 'Open the start-up menu and select the option called Programs. Next, on the Programs menu, choose the option named Accessories, and the Accessories menu, choose Notepad'.

Although you can have lots of applications open at one time, only one can be in the *foreground*; the others wait behind it in the *background*. How do you tell Windows which application you want to bring to the foreground?

Take a look at the Taskbar along the bottom of your Windows desktop. Notice how it displays the names of all your open applications.

| Start | Microsoft Word | Microsoft Excel - Book1 | Untitled - Notepad | 17:19 |

Click on an application's name to display it in the foreground

To select one, for example Word, click on Word. Or, to select Excel, click on Excel. You use the Taskbar to switch between open applications and display a particular one in the foreground.

> ### Taskbar
> *A horizontal bar across the bottom of the Windows desktop that displays the Start button, plus the names of any open applications. Click an application's name to display it in the foreground.*

You will find Windows' ability to open several applications at one time very useful. For example, you could have the following open on your computer: a Word letter (see ECDL Module 3), an Excel spreadsheet (Module 4), and an e-mail (Module 7). As you will also learn, you can copy items from one application to another.

The Control Buttons

Using the Taskbar, switch to Notepad. Notice the three buttons at the top-right? These are called *control buttons*. You can use these to perform various actions, as the following Exercises show.

Exercise 2.2: Using the Close Button to Close a Notepad

1) Is Notepad in the foreground? If not, click its name on the Taskbar.

2) Move the mouse to the top-right of the Notepad screen, and click on the button that contains an X.

You have closed the Notepad application by clicking on one of the Control Buttons – the *Close button*.

Close button

In the next two Exercises you will learn how to use the Restore and Maximise Control Buttons.

Exercise 2.3: Using the Restore Button to Reduce a Window's Size

1) Is Excel in the foreground? If not, click its name on the Taskbar.

2) Move the mouse to the top-right of the Excel screen, and click on the Restore button.

Restore button

This reduces the size of the Excel screen, so that it no longer fills the entire Windows desktop.

3) Using the Taskbar, switch to Word. Click on Word's Restore button.

You should now be able to see both applications on your screen, with the currently selected application (Word) overlapping the other (Excel). Each application appears within its own *window*.

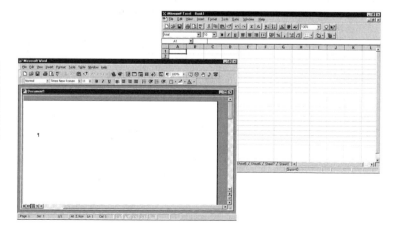

Overlapping application windows of Microsoft Word and Microsoft Excel

To bring Excel to the foreground, click on any part of its window. You do not need to click its name on the Taskbar. The Excel window now overlaps the Word window. To return the Word window to the foreground, click on any part of it.

Maximise button

When you click on a Restore button to reduce the size of a window, the Restore button disappears and is replaced by another button, called the Maximise button.

Clicking on this button reverses the effect of Restore: that is, it increases the size of the window so that it again fills the Windows desktop.

One Control Button remains: the Minimise button. Exercise 2.4 provides an example of the Minimise button in use.

Exercise 2.4: Shrinking a Window with the Minimise Button

Minimise button

1) Is Word in the foreground? If not, click on any part of its window.

2) Click on Word's Minimise button.

   This 'shrinks' Word so that it appears on the Taskbar and nowhere else.

3) Click on any part of the Excel window to select it, and then click its Minimise button.

   Both applications now appear only on the Taskbar.

To display Word and Excel again, click on their names on the Taskbar.

Your will find the Close, Restore, Maximise and Minimise buttons at the top-right corner of every window.

Moving Windows with the Title Bar

Another feature that every window shares is a *title bar* – the identifying bar that runs across the top of the window. You use the title bar to move a window to a different position on the desktop as follows:

- Click on the window's title bar – but do not release the mouse button.

- With your finger still on the mouse button, move the mouse to reposition the window.

- When you have positioned the window where you want it, release the mouse button.

Click on the title bar and drag to reposition a window

This series of click-move-release actions is called dragging.

> ### Dragging with the Mouse
> *Moving a selected item on the desktop by clicking on it with the left mouse button, and holding down the button as you move the item.*

Using the Close box, close Excel. You now have only the Word application open on your desktop.

Working with Desktop Windows

On the Windows desktop, move your cursor over the icon (little picture) named My Computer and click. Notice that the icon is highlighted. Your single click selected it – but does not perform any action on it.

Now, click anywhere on the desktop to deselect the My Computer icon.

Once again, move the cursor over the My Computer icon. Now, click once and then, very quickly, click a second time on My Computer. This two-click action (called *double-clicking*) opens the My Computer icon so that you can see its contents.

A sample My Computer desktop window

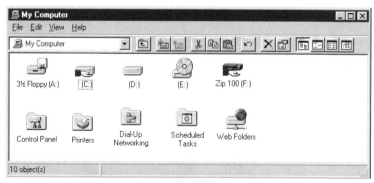

> ### Double-clicking with the Mouse
> *To tell Windows to perform an action on a selected item, press the left button quickly twice in succession.*

Click on the Close box at the top right of the My Computer window to close it. My Computer is an example of a desktop *folder* – an icon that represents a number of items grouped together.

Except for My Computer, every other folder on your desktop looks like a 'real' folder. Here are some examples.

Office 97   The Net   Graphics

> **Folder**
>
> *An icon on the Windows desktop that contains within it one or more icons representing applications, files or physical devices.*

A window opened when a folder is double-clicked is called a desktop window. Desktop windows look and can be used in a similar way to applications windows – so much so that the term 'window' is commonly used to describe either type.

> **Desktop Window**
>
> *A window opened when a folder is double-clicked. Desktop windows contain similar components and features to application windows.*

Practise opening folders on your desktop by double-clicking on them. Some folders, you may find, contain subfolders. (A subfolder is no different to a folder; it's just a folder that happens to be inside another folder.) Close any folders you open by using their Close box.

Changing the Shape and Size of a Window

You can change the shape and size of an application or desktop window by selecting it, and dragging any of its four sides.

To change the width of a window, click on its left or right edge. The cursor changes to a double-headed arrow. Then drag with the mouse. As you drag the window, its edges change to dashed lines.

To make a window taller or shorter, click on its top or bottom edge. Again, the cursor changes to a double-headed arrow. Drag the edge with the mouse.

To change both window height and width, click in the bottom right corner of the window. The cursor changes to a double-headed, diagonal arrow. Drag the corner with the mouse.

Practise your window resizing skills with the My Computer folder window.

Scrolling a Window

Sometimes a window may not be large enough to display all its contents. In such cases, scroll bars appear on the right and/or along the bottom of the window. To view a different part of the window:

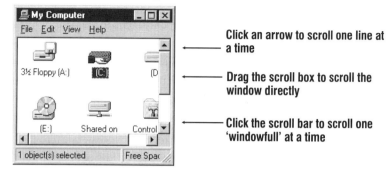

Click an arrow to scroll one line at a time

Drag the scroll box to scroll the window directly

Click the scroll bar to scroll one 'windowfull' at a time

- The *position* of the scroll box in relation to the scroll bar indicates which area of the window you are viewing. When the scroll box is in the middle of the scroll bar, for example, the window is positioned halfway through its contents.

- The *size* of the scroll box indicates how much of the window's contents you can see at one time. For example, if the scroll box is half the length of the scroll bar, you can see half the contents.

Right-Clicking and Pop-Up Menus

In addition to clicking (to select), dragging (to move) and double-clicking (to perform an action), Windows offers a fourth kind of mouse movement: right-clicking.

To right-click something is to click on it once with the *right* mouse button.

Right-clicking on anything – whether a folder, application or file icon, or even the desktop – displays a pop-up menu. The menu options shown depend on the item you right-click.

A pop-up menu displayed by right-clicking on an application icon

Right-Clicking with the Mouse
Briefly holding down the right mouse button. Windows responds by displaying a pop-up menu of options.

One option that a right-click always displays is called **Properties**. Select this option from the pop-up menu to view details about the item.

Practise right-clicking on icons and on the desktop background. In each case, click the **Properties** option on the pop-up menu.

Pop Up or Shortcut Menu
A small menu that appears temporarily, typically when you right-click on an item. When you select an option from a pop-up menu, the menu usually disappears.

Shutting Down

The opposite of powering up a computer is powering or shutting it down. *Never* just switch off your computer – you may lose unsaved information and damage your computer's hard disk drive (thereby losing saved information too!)

To shut down your computer properly, follow the steps in Exercise 2.5:

Exercise 2.5: Shutting Down Your Computer

1) Click the **Start** button.

2) Click **Shut Down**.

3) Select the Shut down the computer option by clicking on it.

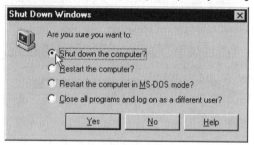

4) Click the **Yes** button to confirm your selection.

Some computers can switch themselves off automatically. On others, you need to press the on/off button after you see the message: 'It is now safe to turn off your computer'.

Now, power up your computer again – *but wait at least twenty seconds.* Otherwise, you may damage your computer's hard disk drive.

Restarting Your Computer

The Restart the Computer option has the same effect as powering down the computer and powering it up again very quickly – but without the risk of damage to the computer hardware.

Exercise 2.6: Restarting Your Computer

1) Click **Start | Shut Down**.

2) Select the Restart the Computer option.

3) Click the **Yes** button.

When Your Computer Hangs

Sometimes, an open application on a computer may 'hang' or 'freeze'. This means that it does not respond to the pressing of any keys or any clicking with the mouse.

On other occasions, Windows itself may fail to respond to any user action, with the result that the entire computer hangs. What do you do? This topic provides the answers.

Application Problems

When a particular application fails to respond to any action you take, press the following three keys simultaneously: CTRL, ALT and DELETE. Most computer users do this by holding down the CTRL and ALT keys with the fingers of their left hand, and then pressing the DELETE key with a finger of their right.

The shorthand way of writing 'Press the CTRL, ALT and DELETE keys simultaneously' is CTRL+ALT+DELETE.

You are then shown a window similar to the one below, which lists all the applications currently open on your computer. The frozen application is indicated by the message 'Not Responding'.

The Close Program dialog box showing a 'Not Responding' application

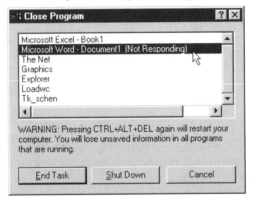

Click on the frozen application, and then click on the **End Task** button. The application closes, as does the Close Program window. You can then reopen the application in the usual way.

Windows Problems

If Windows hangs and your computer freezes, press CTRL+ALT+ DELETE *twice* in quick succession. This has the effect of powering down the computer and powering it up again very quickly – but without the risk of damage to the computer hardware. In fact, it has the same effect as selecting the Restart the Computer option from the Shut Down Windows window.

Improper Shutdowns and ScanDisk

If you power down your computer in any way other than using **Start | Shut Down**, Windows will typically suggest that you run a program called ScanDisk when you next power up the computer. This checks your hard disk drive(s) for errors. Windows starts when ScanDisk finishes.

Dialog Boxes

The Close Program window described in the previous topic is an example of a Windows *dialog box*. You will meet many such dialog boxes when you use Windows Explorer, Word, Excel and other applications.

Dialog Box
A rectangular box that Windows displays when it needs further information before it can carry out a command, or when it needs to provide you with more information.

Dialog Box Components

Dialog boxes typically contain some or all of the following components:

- **Command Button:** A button that performs or cancels an action. **OK** and **Cancel** are the two most common buttons. Here are some more:

- **Drop-Down List Box:** A list of options that you can select from. Click the arrow on its right to view all the choices available.

  The example below is from the Print dialog box. It shows the printer choices available to you. You click to select the one you require.

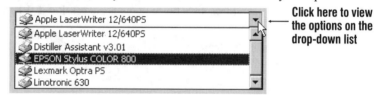

  Click here to view the options on the drop-down list

- **Option Buttons:** A group of *round buttons* indicating alternative choices. The example below is also from the Print dialog box.

- **Checkboxes:** A set of *square boxes* you can select or deselect to turn options on or off. More than one checkbox can be selected at one time.

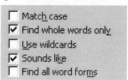

Default Options

Most dialog boxes offer preselected or *default* settings. Unless you choose otherwise, the default settings decide which options and actions are performed. When you choose **Start | Shut Down**, for example, the default option is Shut down the computer, and the default action is **Yes.** To accept the defaults offered by a dialog box, simply press the ENTER key.

Section Summary: So Now You Know

To power up a computer, switch on the system box. If the screen has a separate on/off switch, switch it on also. Windows starts and displays *icons* on the *desktop*.

Use the **Start | Programs** menu to start software applications such as Word or Excel, and the *Taskbar* to switch between open applications.

The *control buttons* at the top left of a window enable you to *restore* (decrease the size of), *maximise*, *minimise* and *close* that window. To *move* a window across the desktop, drag it by its *title bar*. To *resize* a window, drag its edges.

Icons on the desktop represent drives, applications, files and folders.

Clicking an item selects it. *Double-clicking* performs an action on it. And *right-clicking* displays a small, *pop-up menu* of relevant options.

Where a window is too small to display all its contents, *scroll* to view different parts of that window. When Windows needs further information before carrying out an action, it displays a *dialog box*.

Always use the *shut down* procedure when switching off your computer. To restart a 'hung' application, press CTRL+ALT+DELETE. Press the three keys twice in quick succession if Windows itself hangs.

Section 2.2: Exploring Your Computer

In This Section

Ever wondered what information was stored on your computer? Or on someone else's computer? After reading this Section, you will be able to answer such questions as: what drives are installed on a computer, what are the names of its folders and files, and what processor chip and how much memory does it have?

You will also discover how to find a particular file without knowing its name, and how to use the Windows online help system.

New Skills

At the end of this Section you should be able to:

- Distinguish between files, folders and drives
- Use My Computer to view drives, folders and files
- Change the order in which folders and files are displayed in My Computer
- Explain file name extensions and recognise the most common types
- Search for folders and files
- Use Windows online help

New Words

At the end of this Section you should be able to explain the following terms:

- File
- Folder
- Subfolder
- Drive
- My Computer
- Recycle Bin
- File name extension
- Windows Find
- Wildcard

How Computers Store Information

If you throw all your belongings in a heap together on the floor, you will have a difficult time finding anything. How much easier to sort your valuables beforehand, dividing them neatly between shelves or drawers. When you need to find something, you know exactly where it is.

As with your belongings, so with information stored on a computer. In this Section you will learn about files, folder and drives – the three levels at which information is organised on a computer.

Files

All the information and applications on your computer are stored in individual files. Think of a file as the computer's basic unit of storage.

File
The computer's basic unit of information storage. Everything on a computer is stored in a file of one type or another.

Folders

A computer may contain many thousands of files. To make it easier for you (and the computer) to find and keep track of files, you can group files together in folders.

Folder
A group of files. Files grouped into folders are easier to find and work with.

A folder can also contain one or more folders, thereby forming a tree-like hierarchy.

Subfolder
A folder located within another folder.

A sample hierarchy of folders and files

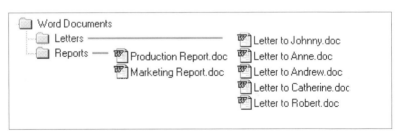

In the example above, the folder named Word Documents contains two subfolders: Letters and Reports.

Another advantage of placing files in a folder or subfolder is that you can work with the files as a group. For example, you can copy or delete all files in a folder in a single operation.

Drives

A drive is a device that stores folders and files. Typical PCs have a hard disk drive that is named the C: drive. On some computers, the hard disk is divided ('partitioned') into two – a C: drive and a D: drive.

The next available letter after the hard disk is given to the CD-ROM drive. This can be D: or E:, depending on whether your hard drive is partitioned or not. The floppy diskette drive is named the A: drive.

> **Drive**
> *A physical storage device for holding files and folders. Typically, A: is the floppy diskette drive, C: the hard disk, and D: is the CD-ROM drive.*

Where is the B: drive? Early personal computers had just two floppy diskette drives, A: and B:. The advent of hard disks, which were named as C: drives, eliminated the need for a second floppy drive.

Using My Computer

My Computer

Take a look at your Windows desktop. Can you see a folder named My Computer? If not, resize or minimise any open windows until the My Computer icon is visible.

My Computer displays icons showing the hard disk, floppy diskette and CD-ROM drives on your PC. You can also see folders called Control Panel (in which you can change your computer's settings), Printers (for changing printer's settings) and Dial-up Networking (for changing Internet connection settings).

> **My Computer**
> *A desktop folder in which you view almost everything on your computer, including drive contents, and computer, printer and Internet settings.*

Exploring Drives with My Computer

What disk drives does your computer contain? Find out in Exercise 2.7.

Exercise 2.7: Exploring Drives with My Computer

1) Double-click the My Computer icon on the Windows desktop. In the example below, you can see fives drives: a floppy diskette drive (A:), two hard disk drives (C: and D:), a CD-ROM drive (E:), and a Zip drive (F:).

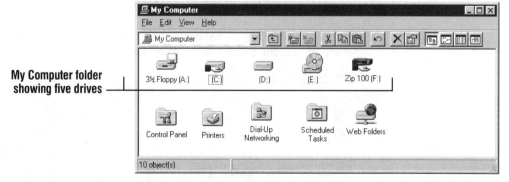

My Computer folder showing five drives

What drives are on your computer?

Now you know how to discover what drives are installed on your PC – or on any other PC you encounter. In Exercise 2.8, you will learn how to view basic information about an installed drive.

Exercise 2.8: Viewing Drive Properties

1) With the My Computer window open, right-click on the C: drive icon.

2) On the pop-up menu displayed, click the last option, **Properties**.

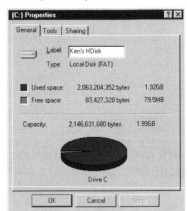

You are now shown a dialog box similar to the one on the right.

You can see how much space is occupied on your hard disk, and how much is still free.

You can also use this dialog box to give a name ('label') to your hard disk drive.

When finished, click **OK**.

As further practice, perform this Exercise on your other drives.

Leave the My Computer window open on your desktop. Note that an icon for the My Computer window is displayed on your Taskbar.

Exploring Folders and Files with My Computer

You can use My Computer to display the folders and files contained on any drive of your computer. Just double-click a drive icon – for example, the C: icon – and My Computer opens a second window showing the selected drive's contents.

My Computer can display folders and files within a drive in a number of ways. Click the **View** menu to display the options available. Here are the main ones:

- **Large icons:** Displays folders and files like this:

- **Small icons:** Displays folders and files in columns, with folders at the top of each column and files underneath.

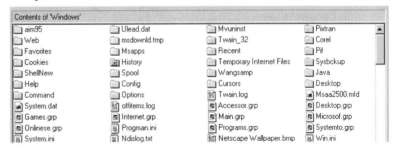

- **List:** Displays folders and files in columns, but lists all your folders before it shows the files.

- **Details**: Lists folders first and then files in a single column, and displays additional information about each item.

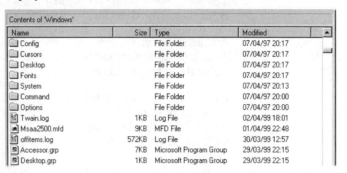

For the Exercises in this book, choose **View | Details**. This viewing option provides the most information about your drives' contents.

Along the bottom of the My Computer window, in the Status Bar, you can see the number of items in the window, and the disk space that they occupy. Can't see the Status Bar or Toolbar? Click the relevant options on the View menu to display them.

Sorting Folders and Files

You can change the order in which My Computer displays your folders and files. By default, folders and files are listed alphabetically by name. To view them in order of size, for example, click on Size in the bar across the top of the window. Alternatively, you can sort them by Type or (date) Modified.

Exercise 2.9: Sorting Folders and Files in My Computer
1) Use My Computer to display the contents of your C: drive.

2) Click on Name in the window heading. My Computer sorts the folders and files in reverse alphabetical order. Click again on Name to resort them in their original order.

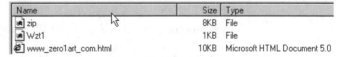

3) Click on Size in the window heading. My Computer sorts the folders and files in order of decreasing size, with the largest shown first. Click again on Size to resort them so that the smallest files are listed first.

4) Click on Modified in the window heading. My Computer sorts the folders and files so that the most recently created or changed are shown first. Click again on Modified to resort them so that the oldest are listed first.

You can make any column narrower or wider by clicking on the boundary line and holding down the mouse button. The cursor changes to a cross-wire. Next, drag the boundary left or right.

Looking at a Folder's Properties

To display information about a folder in My Computer – for example, the Windows folder – right-click on it. From the pop-up menu displayed, click the **Properties** option.

You are shown a dialog box similar to the one on the right.

Among other details, this tells you the number of folders and files within the Windows folder.

It also shows the drive where the folder is located (in this case, C:), and the size of the folder (in this case, 445 megabytes).

File Name Extensions and Icons

A file, as stated at the beginning of this Section, is the basic unit of information storage on a computer. When you look at files in My Computer windows, you can see that different files are represented by different icons.

The icon that Windows uses to represent a file depends on the file's three-letter *file name extension*. Application files have the extension .exe or .dll. A file name extension is separated from the remainder of the file name by a full stop.

When you name and save a file within an application (for example, a Word document within Microsoft Word), Windows automatically attaches the appropriate three-letter extension to that file.

> **File Name Extension**
> *A three-letter addition to a file name that indicates the type of information stored in the file. A full stop separates the extension from the remainder of the file name.*

Here are some common application file name extensions and their icons:

Application File Type	Extension	Icon
Microsoft Word document	.doc	
Microsoft Excel spreadsheet	.xls	
Microsoft Access database	.mdb	
Microsoft PowerPoint presentation	.ppt	
Plain text file	.txt	
Online help file	.hlp	
Web page file	.htm	

Searching for Folders and Files

The quickest way to locate a folder or file on your (or anyone else's) computer is to use the Windows Find feature. Most Find actions are based on all or part of the folder or file name. But Find also allows you perform sophisticated searches based on date ranges or content.

To find a folder or file on a drive, choose the **Start | Find | Files or Folders** command. This displays the dialog box below. Using the Look in: box, you can specify My Computer (all your drives), a particular drive or a folder within a drive. In the Named: box, type the file name. Next, click **Find Now**.

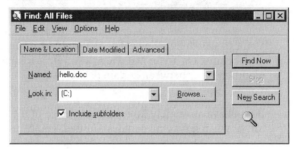

You can use the **Browse** button to display a My Computer-style view of the drives, folders and files of the computer that you are searching on.

Wildcard Searches

In folder and file names, an asterisk (*) is called a wildcard – it can represent one or several characters. If you cannot remember the full name of the item you want to search for, type the wildcard character in place of the missing letter(s).

For instance, report*.doc finds all files that begin with 'report' and have the .doc extension. Examples might be report3.doc, reportnew.doc and report-a.doc.

If you search for *.xls, Windows finds all files on your computer that have the Microsoft Excel file name extension. Try it and see!

> **Wildcard**
> *The asterisk symbol (*) that can stand for one or a combination of characters when performing a search for a folder or file.*

Exercise 2.10: Finding All Word Documents Using a Wildcard
1) Choose **Start | Find | Files or Folders**.

2) In the Named: box, type *.doc.

3) In the Look in: box, select the C: drive.

4) Click **Find Now**.

   Windows displays all files ending in .doc in a My Computer-style window. You can open any listed file by double-clicking on it. To close the Find dialog box, click the Close button in the top-right corner.

Date-Based Searches

If you click on the Date Modified tab of the File Find dialog box, you can limit your search to only those folders or files created or changed between certain dates, or during a specified number of days or months.

Limiting your search by date

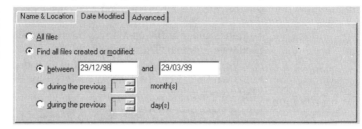

You can search by date or date range alone, if you don't know the file or folder name. Or if you just want to see what folders or files were created or modified on or between certain dates.

Content-Based Searches

If you have absolutely no idea of the name of the item that you are looking for, or when it was created or modified, you can search by content.

Click on the Advanced tab of the File Find dialog box and type one or more words you think are contained within the files you are searching for.

Searching by file content

Windows Find

A search feature that enables you to locate folders or files on any of the following bases: all or part of their name, date of creation or last modification, or their content.

The Recycle Bin

Windows stores files that you delete in an area it calls the Recycle Bin. Can you see its icon on your Windows desktop? If not, resize or minimise some open windows.

 Bin containing files marked for deletion

Recycle Bin

 Empty Bin

Recycle Bin

If you delete a file in error, double-click on the Recycle Bin icon, click the file to select it, and choose **File | Restore**. You can empty your Recycle Bin by choosing **File | Empty Recycle Bin**. Emptying your Bin increases the free space available on your C: drive.

Viewing Your System Information

System

What are your computer's specifications? To find out, follow these steps:

- Choose **Start | Settings | Control Panel** to display the Control Panel desktop folder.

  Alternatively, double-click the Control Panel icon within My Computer.

- Double-click the System icon.

You are now shown the System Properties dialog box. Its General tab displays your computer's operating system type, processor type, and amount of RAM.

System:
Microsoft Windows 95
4.00.950 B
IE 5 5.00.2314.1003

Registered to:
User 1
Rédacteurs
03697-OEM-0020372-54560

Dell Computer Corporation
Dell Windows 95 PC
Pentium(r)
32.0MB RAM

Online Help

Windows offers a searchable online help system:

- The 'help' means that the information is there to assist you understand and use the operating system.

- The 'online' means that the material is presented on the computer screen rather than as a traditional printed manual.

You can search through and read online help by choosing **Start | Help**. Alternatively, when using My Computer, choose **Help | Help Topics**.

You can search through and read online help in two ways: from the Help menu, or from dialog boxes.

Using Help Menu Options

Choose **Help | Contents and Index** to display the three tabs of the Help Topics dialog box. These are explained on the following page:

Contents Tab

This offers short descriptions of Windows' main features.

◆ Where you see a heading with a book symbol, double-click to view the related sub-headings.

❓ Double-click on a question mark symbol to read the help text.

◣ Click a Show me arrow for Windows to demonstrate how to perform a particular action.

≫ Click a double-arrow to view step-by-step instructions.

Index Tab

Reading the material displayed on this tab is like looking through the index of a printed book.

Just type the first letters of the word or phrase you are interested in.

Windows responds by displaying all matches from the online help in the lower half of the dialog box.

When you find the index entry that you are looking for, click the **Display** button.

Find Tab

Can't find what you are looking for in the Contents or Index tabs? Try this tab.

When you type a word or phrase, Windows performs a deeper search of the online help.

Windows also displays some related words to help you narrow your search.

When you find the item you are looking for, double-click on it to display it.

As you search through and read online help topics, you will see the following buttons at the top of the online help window:

- **Help Topics:** Click this to return to the Contents tab.

- **Back**: Click this to return to the previous help topic.

- **Options:** Click this to perform such actions as copying the online help text to a document, or printing it on your printer.

Using Help from Dialog Boxes

You can also access online help directly from a dialog box, as Exercise 2.11 demonstrates.

Exercise 2.11: Using Online Help in a Dialog Box

1) Choose **Start | Find | Files or Folders** to display the Find dialog box.

2) Click on the Advanced tab, and then in the Containing text: box.

3) Press **F1**. Windows displays online help text telling you about the purpose of the selected box.

> Provides a place for you to type some of the text a file contains. If you don't know a file's name, you may be able to find the file by typing some of its contents.

4) Click anywhere on the Find dialog box to remove the online help text.

Practise this Exercise with other dialog boxes in Windows.

Section Summary: So Now You Know

A *file* is the computer's basic unit of information storage. A *folder* is a group of files (and perhaps subfolders too). Grouping files into folders makes them easier to find and work with.

A *drive* is a physical storage device for holding files and folders. Typically, A: is the floppy drive, C: the hard disk, and D: is the CD-ROM drive.

Use *My Computer* to view the hierarchy of folders on your computer, and to see all the files and subfolders in any selected folder.

To display the details of a drive, folder or file, right-click on it and select the *Properties* option.

Windows adds a three-letter *file name extension* to every file, to indicate the file type. A full stop (.) separates the extension from the remainder of the file name. Common file name extensions are *.doc* (Word), *.xls* (Excel), *.mdb* (Access) and *.ppt* (PowerPoint).

To *find* a file on a drive, choose the **Start | Find | Files or Folders** command. Windows allows you to use *wildcards* to represent missing letters. You can also restrict your search to files of a certain date or date range, or that contain the specified keywords.

The Windows *online help* system provides a comprehensive and searchable guide to the system's features and procedures.

Section 2.3: Working with Folders and Files

In This Section

In the previous Section, you used My Computer to explore the folders and files on your PC. Now, you will learn how to perform actions on folders and files – how to create, name and rename, move and copy, and delete and undelete them – using the Windows Explorer application.

New Skills

At the end of this Section you should be able to:

- Create, save, rename and delete folders
- Create, save, rename and delete files
- Move and copy folders and files
- Select several folders or files, whether adjacent or non-adjacent

New Words

At the end of this Section you should be able to explain the following terms:

- Windows Explorer
- Clipboard
- Pull-down menu
- Toolbar

About Windows Explorer

Think of a Windows application and names such as Word, Excel and PowerPoint are probably the first to come to mind. Included with the Windows operating system is another powerful application. It's called Windows Explorer and you can use it to:

- *View* the folders on your computer, and the hierarchy of subfolders and files within any folder.

- *Perform operations* on various folders and files such as renaming, copying, moving and deleting.

You can open Windows Explorer in either of two ways:

- Choose **Start | Programs | Windows Explorer**

  or

- Right-click on the Start button, and click **Explore**.

The Two Panes of Windows Explorer

Windows Explorer differs from My Computer in that its window is divided into left and right subwindows called *panes*.

- You use the *left pane* to select a particular drive or folder. You cannot view files in the left pane.

- You use the *right pane* to view the folders and files in the drive or folder selected in the left pane.

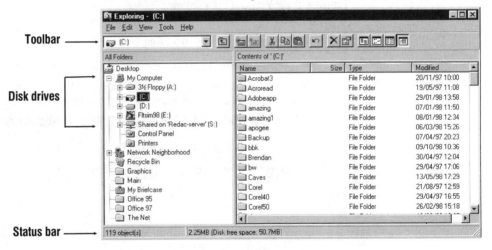

In the Windows Explorer left pane, you can see a hierarchical diagram of your computer's storage space:

- **Top Level:** The Windows Desktop.

- **Second Level:** System folders such as My Computer and Recycle Bin, and any user-created desktop folders.

- **Third Level:** Disk drives, Control Panel and Printers.

The right pane looks and works in a similar way to My Computer.

- Click on any drive in the left pane to display, in the right pane, the folders and files stored on that drive.

- Double click on any folder in the right pane to view any subfolders and files contained within that folder.

Windows Explorer

A Windows application for viewing the hierarchy of folders and files, and for performing such actions as renaming, moving and deleting.

Viewing Options

As with My Computer, Windows Explorer offers a number of options that let you control how you view your drives, folders and files. Choose **View | Details** – it's the option that provides the most information in the smallest screen space.

Along the bottom of the Windows Explorer window, in the Status Bar, you can see the number of items in the currently open folder (the one whose contents are shown in the right pane), the disk space occupied by the folder's contents, and the remaining free space on the drive.

Can't see the Status Bar or Toolbar? Click the relevant options on the View menu to display them.

Follow Exercise 2.12 to practise your Windows Explorer skills.

Exercise 2.12: Viewing the Windows Folder

1) If Windows Explorer is not already open, open it now.

2) In the left pane, click on the C: drive icon.

3) In the right pane, scroll down until you see the Windows folder. Double-click on it.

   You can now see the folders and files stored within it. Folders are listed first. Scroll down through the Windows folder to see what files are within it.

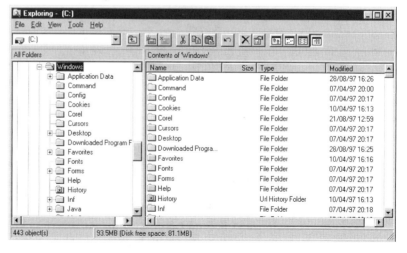

Explorer's Plus and Minus Signs

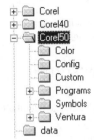

In Windows Explorer, a folder without a plus (+) or a minus (-) sign in front of it is either empty or has only files inside it.

A folder with a plus (+) sign has folders inside it, and perhaps files too. To open it, click on the folder name or the + sign.

A minus (-) sign in front of a folder indicates that the folder is open – its subfolders and files are currently displayed on the screen.

Click on a plus sign to display ('expand') or a minus sign to hide ('collapse') your view of a folder.

Working with Folders

In the next few Exercises you will use Windows Explorer to create folders and subfolders, and to rename, delete and restore (undelete) folders.

Exercise 2.13: Creating Two New Folders

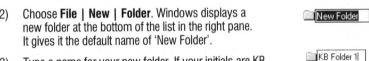

1) In the left pane of the Windows Explorer window, click on the C: drive.

2) Choose **File | New | Folder**. Windows displays a new folder at the bottom of the list in the right pane. It gives it the default name of 'New Folder'.

3) Type a name for your new folder. If your initials are KB, for example, call it KB Folder 1.

4) Repeat steps 1, 2 and 3. Name your second folder KB Folder 2.

Exercise 2.14: Creating a Subfolder

1) In the right pane of the Windows Explorer window, double-click on the first folder that you created in Exercise 2.13 – in this example, the folder named KB Folder 1.

2) Choose **File | New | Folder**. Windows displays a new subfolder.

3) Type a name for your new folder. If your initials are KB, for example, call it KB Sub Folder 1.

Changing a Folder's Name

You can change a folder's name at any stage. Exercise 2.15 shows you how.

Exercise 2.15: Changing a Folder's Name

1) Right-click on one of your new folders to display a pop-up menu.

2) Choose **Rename**.

3) Type a new folder name. For example, KB New Folder.

Well done! You have given your folder a new name.

Deleting a Folder

Suppose that you don't need a folder any more? Here is how to delete an unwanted folder.

Exercise 2.16: Deleting a Folder

1) In the left pane of the Windows Explorer window, click on the first folder that you created in Exercise 2.13. It should contain the subfolder you created in Exercise 2.14.

Delete button

2) In the left pane of the Windows Explorer window, right-click on the subfolder. From the pop-up menu, select **Delete**.

Alternatively, click once on the subfolder to select it, and click the Delete button on the Windows Explorer Toolbar.

3) Click **Yes** to confirm that you want to remove the folder.

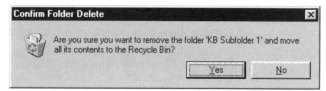

The folder is deleted, as are any subfolders and files it may have contained.

Restoring a Folder's Files

Where did your deleted folder go? If it contained no files, it has been deleted permanently by Windows. If it contained files, Windows moves the files to the Recycle Bin. Follow the steps in Exercise 2.17 to bring your deleted folder and files back to life.

Exercise 2.17: Restoring a Folder's Files

1) In the left pane of the Windows Explorer window, scroll down until you can see the Recycle Bin, and click on it.

Windows Explorer now displays the contents of the Recycle Bin in the right pane.

2) Choose **Edit | Undo Delete** to restore the files and the folder it contained.

Working with Files

A file, as you learnt in Section 2.2, is the basic unit of information storage on a computer. In the next few Exercises you will discover how to create, save and name, delete and restore a file.

Creating a File

Files are created by applications. For example, you can create a letter in Microsoft Word and a spreadsheet in Microsoft Excel.

The simplest type of file that you can create on a computer is a plain text file. A file of this kind contains just words, numbers and punctuation marks – and no fancy formatting or graphics of any kind.

The Windows application for creating plain text files is called Notepad.

Exercise 2.18: Creating a File

1) Choose **Start | Programs | Accessories | Notepad**. A blank Notepad window appears on your screen, ready to accept text.

2) Type the following words: Just testing

You have now created a file and entered content in that file. But your file is not saved on your hard disk. It exists only in the computer's memory. If the computer were to switch off for any reason, your file would be lost.

Naming and Saving a File

The first time that you save a file, Windows asks you to give that file a name. Follow the steps in Exercise 2.19 to discover how.

Exercise 2.19: Naming and Saving a File

1) Choose **File | Save** to view the Save As dialog box. By displaying this dialog box, Windows is asking:

– Which *drive* do you want to save your folder in?

– Which *folder* (or subfolder) do you want to save your file in?

– Which *name* do you want to give your new file?

2) Click on the arrow at the right of the Save to: drop-down list box.

Now, scroll up until you see the C: drive icon. Click on it.

The Save As dialog box now displays a list of the folders on your C: drive.

3) Locate the folder that you renamed in Exercise 2.15. Double-click on it.

You have now told Windows the drive and folder where you want to save your file. All that remains is for you to give your new file a name.

4) Click in the File name: box, delete any text there, and type a name for your new file. If your initials are KB, for example, name it KB New File.

When finished, click **Save**.

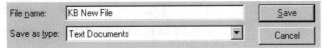

Windows automatically adds the three-letter file name extension of .txt to all plain-text files created with the Notepad application.

Well done! You have learnt how to name and save a file.

Move the mouse to the top-right of the Notepad window, and click on the Close box to close it.

Changing a File's Name

You can change a file's name at any stage. Exercise 2.20 shows you how.

Exercise 2.20: Changing a File's Name

1) Using Windows Explorer, open the folder containing the file you saved in Exercise 2.19.

2) Right-click on the file to display a pop-up menu.

3) Choose **Rename**.

4) Type a new file name. For example, KB Renamed File. Do not change or delete the file name extension (.txt).

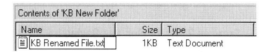

You have given your file a new name. Another Exercise completed!

Deleting a File

When you have been working on your computer for a while, you may find that its hard disk is taken up by files and folders you no longer use or need.

You can delete these files, but be careful not to delete any files that your computer needs to run programs! If in doubt, don't delete!

Exercise 2.21 shows you how to delete an unwanted file.

Exercise 2.21: Deleting a File

1) Using Windows Explorer, display and right-click on the file that you renamed in Exercise 2.20.

2) From the pop-up menu, select the **Delete** command.

3) Click **Yes** to confirm that you want to remove the file to the Recycle Bin.

Alternatively, click once on the file in Windows Explorer, and click the Delete button on the Toolbar.

Restoring a File

Follow the steps in Exercise 2.22 to restore your deleted file.

Exercise 2.22: Restoring a File

1) In the left pane of the Windows Explorer window, scroll until you can see the Recycle Bin, and click on it.

Windows Explorer now displays the contents of the Recycle Bin in the right pane.

2) Click the file to select it, and then choose **File | Restore**.

The Windows Clipboard

Suppose you want to place a folder or file in a different location on your computer. Or reproduce a folder or file so that two copies of it appear in different locations. Can you do it? Yes. This is a two-step process:

- **Copy**: You select and then *copy* the folder or file to the Clipboard, a temporary storage area. The selected folder or file remains in its original location.

  or

  Cut: You select and then *cut* the folder or file to the Clipboard. The selected folder or file is no longer in its original location.

- **Paste**: You *paste* the folder or file from the Clipboard into a different part of your computer – into a different folder, or even a different drive.

> **Clipboard**
>
> *A temporary storage area to which you can copy or cut folders or files. You can paste from the Clipboard to any location within the same or a different drive.*

About the Clipboard

Three points you should remember about the Windows Clipboard:

- The Clipboard is temporary. Turn off your computer and the Clipboard contents are deleted.

- The Clipboard can hold only a single, copied item at a time. If you copy or cut a second item, the second overwrites the first.

- Items stay in the Clipboard after you paste from it, so you can paste the same folder or file into as many locations as you need.

Copying and Moving Folders

To copy a folder means to make a copy of it, and to place that copy in a new location. Exercise 2.23 takes you through the steps.

Copy button

Paste button

Exercise 2.23: Copying a Folder

1) In the left pane of Windows Explorer, click the folder that you renamed in Exercise 2.15.

2) Choose **Edit | Copy** click the Copy button on the Windows Explorer Toolbar.

3) Scroll down the left pane until you can see the Windows folder. Click on it to display its contents in the right pane.

4) Choose **Edit | Paste** or click the Paste button on the Toolbar.

This places a copy of your folder within the Windows folder.

To move a folder means to place it in a new location – and to *remove* it from its original location. Exercise 2.24 shows you how.

Cut button

Exercise 2.24: Moving a Folder
1) In the right pane, display the folder that you copied to the Windows folder in Exercise 2.23. Click on it to select it.

2) Choose **Edit | Cut** or click the Cut button on the Toolbar.

3) Scroll back up the right pane to locate the folder named System.

4) Double-click on the System folder to open it.

5) Choose **Edit | Paste** or click the Paste button on the Toolbar.

This places your folder within the System folder of the Windows folder.

Copying and Moving Files

In Exercise 2.25 you will make a copy of your plain text file, and place that copy in a different folder on your hard disk. Following that, in Exercise 2.26, you will move the file from its current folder to a new one.

Exercise 2.25: Copying a File
1) In the left pane, display folder the containing the file that you created in Exercise 2.21. Double-click on the folder to display its contents in the right pane.

2) Choose **Edit | Copy** or click the Copy button on the Toolbar.

3) In the left pane, scroll down to locate the folder called Windows.

4) Click on the Windows folder to open it. Its contents are now listed in the right pane.

5) Choose **Edit | Paste** or click the Paste button on the Toolbar.

You have now placed a copy of your file within the Windows folder.

Exercise 2.26: Moving a File
1) In the right pane, display the file that you copied to the Windows folder in Exercise 2.16. Click on it to select it.

2) Choose **Edit | Cut** or click the Cut button on the Toolbar.

3) Scroll back up the right pane to locate the folder named System.

4) Double-click the System folder to open it

5) Choose **Edit | Paste** or click the Paste button on the Toolbar.

You have now moved the file to the System subfolder of the Windows folder.

Working with Multiple Files

Windows Explorer provides an easy method of copying or moving several files in a single operation. This method works only when:

- The files you want to copy or move are currently located in the *same* folder.

- The place you want to copy or move them to is also a single folder.

When you list the files to copy or move in Windows Explorer, two situations are possible:

- The files are *adjacent*. They are positioned immediately below or above one another.

- The files are *non-adjacent*. They are not positioned immediately below or above one another.

If the files are adjacent, follow these steps:

- Click on the first file

- Press and hold down the SHIFT key

- Click on the last file

All the files – the first, last and in-between – are now selected, and you can copy or cut them in a single operation.

If the files are non-adjacent, follow these steps:

- Click on the first file

- Press and hold down the CTRL key

- Click the relevant files, one after the other, to select them.

Again, all the files are now selected, and you can copy or cut them in a single operation.

When selecting several files, you can scroll down or up as you make your selection. This methods works for folders as well as files. Another operation that you can perform on selected folders or files is deletion. Simply select the adjacent or non-adjacent files or folders, and click the Delete button on the Toolbar.

Menu bars, Toolbars and Shortcuts

In the final part of this Section, you will discover the three ways that you perform actions in a Windows application: menu commands, toolbar buttons, and keyboard shortcuts.

Menu bars

Start the Microsoft Word application. Take a look at the line of words that runs just under the title bar. Each of these words represents a pull-down menu.

Word's menu bar ⟶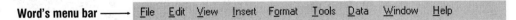

Word's pull-down File menu

Click the **File** menu name to display the commands (actions) available on this menu. You tell Word that you want to perform a particular action by clicking the action's name on the pull-down menu. Click the **Exit** command to close Word.

Pull-Down Menu

A list of options that appears when you click on a menu name. The menu name is generally on a menu bar along the top of the window, and the menu appears below that bar, as if you pulled it down.

Whenever you see an arrow to the right of a menu option, selecting that option displays a further submenu of choices.

All Windows applications share a number of common menus. Understand their general purpose and you will be able to use most applications. The common menus are:

- **File:** Use the commands on this menu to create a new (blank) file, open an existing file, save the current file, save the current file with a new name (**Save as**), print the current file, and quit the application.

- **Edit:** Use the commands on this menu to copy and move selected files, or items (such as text or graphics) within files.

- **View:** Use the commands on this menu to display your file in different ways, including a zoomed-in (up close) view or zoomed out (bird's eye) view.

- **Help:** Use the commands on this menu to display online help information about the application you are using.

Toolbars

A second way of performing an action is to click a button on a toolbar. Instead of choosing **File | Save** to save a file, for example, you could click the Save button on the toolbar. Not every menu command has a toolbar button equivalent, but the most commonly used commands do.

Toolbar

A collection of buttons that you can click to perform frequently used actions, such as creating, opening or saving files, and for Clipboard operations.

Here are the toolbar buttons that you will find on almost every Windows application:

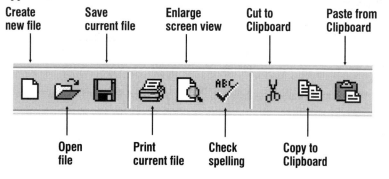

Keyboard Shortcuts

Keyboard shortcut for copying a selected item to the Clipboard

A third way of performing actions in Windows is to use keyboard shortcuts. You may find using these faster than either menu commands or toolbar buttons, as you need not take either hand away from the keyboard.

An example of a keyboard short cut is CTRL+c, which means 'Hold down the control key and press the letter c key'. This has the same effect as choosing **Edit | Copy** or clicking the Copy button on the toolbar.

Here are the most commonly used shortcut keys:

Keyboard Shortcut	Action Performed	Menu Command
CTRL+o	Opens an existing file	File | Open
CTRL+n	Opens a new file	File | New
CTRL+s	Saves the current file	File | Save
CTRL+c	Copies to the Clipboard	Edit | Copy
CTRL+x	Cuts to the Clipboard	Edit | Cut
CTRL+v	Pastes from the Clipboard	Edit | Paste

Section Summary: So Now You Know

Use *Windows Explorer* to view the hierarchy of folders on your computer, and to view and work with the drives, folders and files on your computer. Windows Explorer displays two subwindows or *panes*: you use the *left pane* to select a particular drive or folder. You use the *right pane* to view the folders and files in the drive or folder selected in the left pane.

Windows Explorer enables you to *copy*, *move*, *rename* and *delete* folders and files. You can also create folders with Windows Explorer. You create files with software applications. The *Clipboard* is a temporary storage area to which you can copy or cut folders or files. You can paste from the Clipboard to any location within the same or a different drive.

You can s*elect multiple files*, and then copy, cut, paste or delete them in a single operation. If the file are *adjacent*, click the first file, hold down the SHIFT key, and then click the last file. If *non-adjacent*, click the first file, hold down the CTRL key, and then click the individual files to select them.

A *pull-down menu* is a list of options that appears when you click a menu name on a menu bar. When you see an arrow to the right of a menu option, selecting that option displays a further *submenu* of choices. You tell Word that you want to perform a particular action by clicking the action's name on the pull-down menu.

A second way of performing an action is to click a button on a toolbar. Most applications have toolbar buttons for creating, opening or saving files, and for Clipboard operations.

A third option is to press the CTRL key in combination with a particular letter key. Examples of such *keyboard shortcuts* include CTRL+c to copy to the Clipboard and CTRL+v to paste from it.

Section 2.4: Mastering Windows

Now that you are familiar with Windows basics, you are ready to move on to the more advanced features.

You will discover how to take control of your Windows desktop, enabling you to customise it to reflect your working needs and your personal taste. You will also learn how to make backup copies of your files on diskettes.

New Skills

At the end of this Section you should be able to:

- Personalise your desktop by moving icons and creating folders to hold application and file icons

- Create shortcuts that take you directly to a particular application, file or folder

- Select a screen saver

- Customise your wallpaper, background pattern, scheme and screen resolution

- Change your computer's date and time settings

- Adjust your computer's sound volume

- Change your computer's regional settings

- Format a diskette

- Copy a file to a diskette

- Save a file to a diskette

- Use various print features and options

- View information about your computer's operating system, processor type, and amount of RAM.

New Words

At the end of this Section you should be able to explain the following terms:

- Desktop shortcut

- Screen saver

- Print queue

Managing Your Desktop

You can arrange your Windows desktop to suit your working needs and personal taste:

- To reposition your icons, simply drag them to where you want them.

- To make your screen look tidier, create desktop folders placing application and file icons in them.

You create a desktop folder as follows:

- Right-click on the desktop to display a pop-up menu.

- Choose **New | Folder**. Windows creates a desktop folder with the default name New Folder.

- Type your folder name and press ENTER.

Next, double-click the folder to open it, and drag icons into it, either from the desktop or from other desktop folders.

Creating Desktop Shortcuts

You will use some applications more frequently than others. You can save yourself time by creating a shortcut to these programs from your desktop (or from a folder on your desktop). As a result, you won't have to go the **Start | Programs** route every time you want to start that application.

Follow the steps in Exercise 2.27 to create a desktop shortcut for Notepad.

Exercise 2.27: Creating a Desktop Shortcut for Notepad

1) Choose **Start | Programs | Windows Explorer**. If the Explorer window occupies the full Windows desktop, click on the Restore button (top-right).

2) Display the application for which you want to create a shortcut. You will find Notepad in the Windows folder.

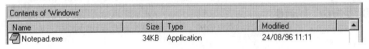

3) Right-click on the Notepad icon, drag it from Windows Explorer onto your desktop, and release the right mouse button.

4) On the pop-up menu displayed, choose **Select Create Shortcut(s) Here**.

If you don't like your shortcut's default name, right-click on it, choose **Rename**, type a new name, and press the ENTER key. You can also create shortcuts for frequently used folders and files. You can leave the Notepad icon on your desktop, or drag it to a desktop folder.

> **Desktop Shortcut**
> *A user-created icon that, when clicked on, takes you directly to an application, folder or file. It is a fast, convenient alternative to using the Start menu.*

In Exercise 2.28 you will create a desktop folder named Office 97, and create desktop shortcuts for three Office applications within it.

Exercise 2.28: Creating an Office 97 Desktop Folder Containing Shortcuts

1) Right-click on your desktop. On the pop-up menu displayed, choose **New | Folder**. Windows creates a folder with the default name New Folder.

2) Type the folder name Office 97 and press ENTER.

3) Double-click your new folder to open it. You are now ready to create desktop shortcuts and place them within the folder.

4) Let's start with a shortcut to Microsoft Word. Choose **Start | Find | Files or Folders** to display the Find dialog box.

5) In the Named: box, type winword.exe, and click **Find Now**.

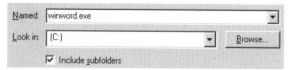

6) When winword.exe is found, right-click on its icon, and drag it from the Find dialog box into your Office 97 desktop folder.

7) Click on the Find dialog box again. Repeat steps 5 and 6 for the following other Office 97 application files: excel.exe, and powerpnt.exe.

    When finished, your Office 97 folder should look as shown.

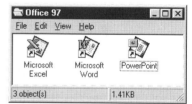

Setting the Time and Date

Date/Time

Is your computer set to the correct date and time? If not, the files you create and edit, and e-mails you send, will show misleading dates or times. Exercise 2.29 shows you how to set the date and time on your computer.

Exercise 2.29: Setting Your Computer's Date and Time

1) Choose **Start | Settings | Control Panel**.

2) On the folder displayed, double-click the Date/Time icon.

3) Make the changes you want. Click **Apply** and then **OK**.

A small battery inside your computer ensures that Windows remembers the date and time settings, even when your computer is turned off.

Adjusting the Sound Volume

Modern PCs have the ability to play sound files through attached loudspeakers or headphones. Follow Exercise 2.30 to discover how to adjust the playback volume setting on your computer.

Volume Control

Exercise 2.30: Changing the Playback Volume

1) Click the Volume Control icon displayed towards the right of the Taskbar. The icon's appearance depends on the type of sound card installed on your computer. Typically, it looks like a small loudspeaker.

   Unsure which Taskbar icon is the Volume Control? Position the cursor over each icon until you see a text box telling you the icon's purpose.

2) On the pop-up menu shown, drag the Volume Control slider up to raise the volume or down to lower it.

   You can switch off sound completely by selecting the Mute box.

3) When finished, click on any other part of your screen to close the Volume Control.

Setting the Screen Saver

A screen saver is a program that takes over the computer's display screen if there are no keystrokes or mouse movements for a specified amount of time.

They were developed originally to prevent damage to monitors that could arise if one fixed image was displayed continuously over a long period – such as a weekend, for example. Screen savers prevented this by either blanking out the screen entirely or by displaying a series of constantly moving images.

Today's monitors are less likely to suffer from the problem that screen savers were designed to prevent, and they are now mostly an adornment.

Exercise 2.31 shows you how to set up or change your computer's screen saver.

> **Screen Saver**
>
> *A program that takes over the computer's display screen if there are no keystrokes or mouse movements for a specified amount of time. They either blank out the screen entirely or display a series of continually moving images.*

Exercise 2.31: Setting Up or Changing Your Screen Saver

1) Right-click on the Windows desktop, choose **Properties** from the pop-up menu, and select the Screen Saver tab.

2) Click the arrow to the right of the Screen Saver drop-down list box to display a list of screen savers installed on your computer.

3) Click to select the screen saver you require from the list.

4) In the Wait: box enter the number of minutes before which the screen saver will activate, and click **OK**.

To clear the screen saver after it has started, move your mouse or press any key.

Customising Your Screen

The appearance of Windows on your computer is controlled by the setting of the following three items, each of which you can change to suit your working needs or personal taste:

- Background pattern
- Wallpaper
- Scheme

Background Pattern

By default, the Windows background is typically an area of one continuous colour. You can change this to one of a dozen or so patterns.

To view or adjust your background pattern setting:

- Right-click on the desktop, choose **Properties** from the pop-up menu, and select the Background tab.

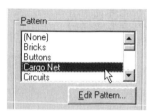

- Select your required pattern from the drop-down list box and click **OK**.

You can use the Edit Pattern button to edit an existing pattern or create a new one.

Wallpaper

You can insert an image, such as a scanned photograph or a picture downloaded from the Internet, on to your desktop background. Follow these steps to do so:

- Right-click on the desktop, choose **Properties** from the pop-up menu, and select the Background tab.

- Select your required wallpaper from the drop-down list box.

- Select Centre to position the image in the middle of your desktop, or Tile to repeat the image horizontally and vertically until it fills the entire screen, and click **OK**.

Scheme

This is the combination of colours, fonts and spacing that controls the appearance of such items as title bars, scroll bars and icons. To view or adjust your scheme:

- Right-click on the desktop, choose **Properties** from the pop-up menu, and select the Appearance tab.

- Select your required scheme from the drop-down list box and click **OK**.

You can change your background pattern, wallpaper and scheme as often as you wish. The relevant dialog boxes offer a preview area where you can view the effect of any changes before you apply them. Don't be afraid to experiment with different settings.

Changing Your Screen Resolution

Everything you view on your screen is composed of tiny square dots called *pixels*. The number of pixels displayed is determined by your screen resolution.

- Low resolution settings (e.g. 640x480) result in fewer, larger pixels, so that everything on your screen appears bigger and blockier.

- High resolution settings (e.g. 1024x768) use more, smaller pixels, so that everything appears smaller and more defined.

To change your screen resolution:

- Right-click on the desktop, choose **Properties** from the pop-up menu, and select the Settings tab.

- Drag the Desktop area slider left to decrease the resolution or right to increase it.

You can see the effect of a new screen resolution in the preview area. When finished, click **OK** to save your new settings and close the dialog box.

Changing Your Regional Settings

Regional Settings

The options you select in the Windows Regional Settings decide the default currency symbol shown in your applications, and which conventions Windows uses when displaying times, dates and numbers.

To change your regional settings:

- Choose **Start | Settings | Control Panel**, and click the Regional Settings icon.

- On the Regional Settings tab, select the relevant region from the drop-down list.

- To override the default conventions for your selected region, use the options on the Number, Currency, Time and Date tabs.

- When finished, click **OK** to save your new settings and to close the dialog box.

Working with Diskettes

You can copy files and folders from your hard disk to a floppy diskette to:

- Make a copy of your work that you can give to a colleague or friend.

- Have a second, backup copy of your work just in case your computer is somehow damaged and the files on it are 'lost'.

The more regularly you make backups, the more up-to-date your files will be if your computer fails.

Formatting a Diskette

You can only copy files to a diskette that is formatted. When Windows formats a floppy diskette it:

- Sets up a 'table of contents' on the diskette which it later uses to locate files stored on the disk.

- Checks for any damaged areas, and, when it finds them, marks those areas as off-limits for file storage.

Most new diskettes come already formatted. But it is cheaper to buy unformatted ones and format them yourself. The ECDL Syllabus also specifies that you must know how to format a diskette. Exercise 2.32 shows you how.

Exercise 2.32: Formatting a Floppy Diskette

1) Insert the floppy diskette you want to format into the diskette drive.

2) Chose **Start | Programs | Windows Explorer** and right-click the A: drive icon in the left-hand pane.

3) Choose **Format** and select the following two options on the dialog box displayed:

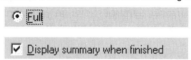

4) When Windows has formatted the disk, click **OK** to display the Format Results dialog box.

5) Click **Close**.

Formatting a disk overwrites any table of contents there may have been previously on the disk, so making it impossible for Windows to find files that were saved on the diskette before it was formatted.

For that reason, don't even think about formatting your computer's hard disk.

You cannot format a disk if there are files open on that disk.

Copying a File to a Diskette

You can copy a file to a diskette using the copy and paste option available with Windows Explorer. See Exercise 2.33.

Exercise 2.33: Copying a File to a Diskette

1) Place a formatted diskette in the A: drive of your computer.

2) Choose **Start | Programs | Windows Explorer** and, in the right-hand pane, display the file that you want to copy – for example, the Mouse.txt file from the Windows folder.

3) Click on the file and choose **Edit | Copy** or click the Copy button on the Toolbar.

Logfile.txt	50KB	Text Document	29/04/97 16:56
Modemdet.txt	1KB	Text Document	04/09/97 15:34
Mouse.txt	6KB	Text Document	24/08/96 11:11
Msdosdrv.txt	42KB	Text Document	24/08/96 11:11

4) In the left pane, click on the A: drive icon.

   If there are currently any files on the diskette, Windows Explorer lists them in its right pane.

5) Choose **Edit | Paste** or click the Paste button to copy the file to the diskette.

Saving a File to a Diskette

A second way to copy a file to a diskette is to use the **File | Save As** command of the application in which you created and work with the file. If you currently have the application open on your screen, this is faster than using Windows Explorer. See Exercise 2.34.

Exercise 2.34: Saving a File to a Diskette

1) Choose **Start | Programs | Accessories | Notepad**.

2) Choose **File | Open**, locate the file you saved in Exercise 2.32, and click **Open**.

3) Choose **File | Save As**, locate the A: drive, and click **Save** to save the file.

A copy of the Notepad file is now stored on the diskette.

Printing Files

Now that you can open and work with files, you will want to print copies of your work so you can see it on paper.

Exercise 2.35: Printing a File

1) Open the file, for example, a Word document.

2) Select **File | Print**.

If your printer is connected and set up correctly, your file should print.

The Print Queue

What happens to a file after you choose to print it with the **Print** command? The answer is that it goes to a file called a print queue, and is then taken from the print queue by the selected printer.

The print queue can store a number of files, which the printer then collects in turn as it becomes ready to print them. The time it takes to print a file depends on the number and size of the other print jobs in the print queue.

You can view your print queue to see what print jobs are waiting in it, delete print jobs from the queue, and reorder the sequence in which print jobs are listed.

> **Print Queue**
> A list of files (print jobs) that are waiting to be printed. The printer pulls the files off the queue one at a time.

Viewing the Print Queue

What jobs are currently in the print queue? See Exercise 2.36 to find out.

Exercise 2.36: Viewing the Print Queue
1) Choose **Start | Settings | Printers**.

2) Double-click on the icon for the printer you want to check.

Windows displays a list of all the print jobs in the queue.

Cancelling a Print Job in the Queue

There are many reasons why you may decide to cancel a print job – you may discover that the job is not printing correctly. You may realise that you already have a copy of the printout. Or you may simply change your mind about printing the file.

Follow the steps in Exercise 2.37 to cancel a job.

Exercise 2.37: Removing a Job from the Print Queue
1) Choose **Start | Settings | Printers**.

2) Double-click on the icon for the printer you want to look at. Windows displays a list of all the print jobs in the queue.

3) Select the document you want to cancel printing.

4) Choose **Document | Cancel Printing**.

Changing the Order of Jobs in the Print Queue

You can change the current sequence of jobs in the print queue. Here's how.

Exercise 2.38: Reordering the Jobs in a Print Queue
1) Choose **Start | Settings | Printers**.

2) Double-click on the icon for the printer you want to look at. Windows displays a list of all the print jobs in the queue.

3) Select the file you want to move, and drag it to the required place in the queue.

You can't move a file that is already in the process of printing.

Follow the steps in Exercise 2.39 to remove all pending print jobs from the print queue.

Exercise 2.39: Deleting All Jobs in the Print Queue
1) Choose **Start | Settings | Printers**.

2) Double-click on the icon for the printer you want to look at. Windows displays a list of all the print jobs in the queue.

3) Choose **Printer | Purge Jobs**.

The Print Dialog Box

When you choose the **File | Print** command within an application, you are shown a dialog box that typically offers the following options:

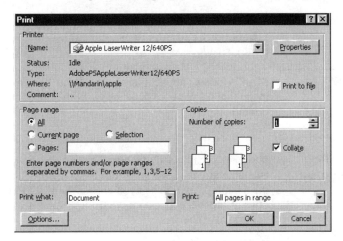

Name

To choose a different printer, click on the arrow on the right of the Name: drop-down list box, and then click the printer you require.

Print Range

You can choose to print all pages, the currently displayed page only or a range of pages.

To print a group of continuous pages, enter the first and last page number of the group, separated by a dash. For example, 2-6 or 12-13.

To print a non-continuous group of pages, enter their individual page numbers, separated by commas. For example, 3,5,9 or 12,17,34. You can combine continuous with non-continuous page selections.

Copies

You can specify how many copies of the file you want to print. For multiple copies, ensure that the Collate checkbox is selected.

The Properties Button

Clicking on the **Properties** button displays some further print choices that will vary with the type of printer selected – colour or black-and-white, inkjet or laser.

All printers offer choices about paper size (A4 is standard) and orientation (Portrait means 'standing up', Landscape means 'on its side').

When you have selected your options, click **OK** to print your file.

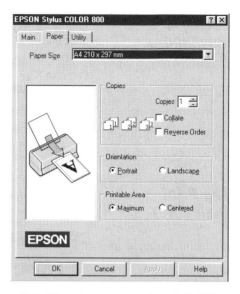

Print Preview

Most Windows applications have a **Print Preview** command on their **File** menu that lets you see on screen how the file contents will look when printed on paper.

Changing the Default Printer

If your PC is attached to a network, you may have a number of printers available to you. It's a good idea to set the printer you use most often as the default printer. When you choose the **File | Print** command in Word or other Windows application, your file outputs on the default printer unless you specify otherwise.

Follow this procedure to set a printer as the default printer:

- Choose **Start | Settings | Printers.**

- Right-click on the icon of the printer you want to set as the default.

- Select the **Set As Default** command from the pop-up menu.

If there is a check mark beside this command, the printer is already selected as the default printer.

Section Summary: So Now You Know

You can *personalise* your Windows desktop by repositioning icons, creating new folders, and placing application and file icons in them. You can create *desktop shortcuts* – icons that take you directly to a particular application, file or folder. You can also customise your *wallpaper*, *background pattern*, *scheme* and *screen saver*.

You can adjust the *date and time* settings on your computer so that Windows attaches the correct date and time to the files you create and edit, and to e-mails you send. You can also adjust the *sound volume*.

By either blanking out the screen or showing a series of continually moving images, a *screen saver* program takes over the computer's display screen if there are no keystrokes or mouse movements for a specified amount of time.

Your *Regional Settings* decide the default currency symbol shown in your applications, and which conventions Windows uses when displaying times, dates and numbers.

Your *screen resolution* is the number of pixels its displays. Low resolution settings make everything appear bigger and blockier. High resolution settings make everything appear smaller and more defined.

Before you can copy files to a floppy diskette, you must *format* the diskette. If you format a previously used diskette, any files that may have been on the disk are no longer accessible.

Anything you print goes first to a file called a *print queue* that can hold multiple print jobs. It is then taken from the print queue by the selected printer. You can view your print queue to see which jobs are waiting in it, delete jobs from the queue, and reorder the sequence in which jobs are listed.

Module

3

Word Processing

Back in the days when people thought they could predict the future, someone came up with the phrase 'paperless office'.

As computers found their way into more and more workplaces, the theory was that paper-based communication would disappear. Forever.

But alongside affordable computers came affordable printers. Result: computerisation has led to more rather than less paper usage. The office supplies people have never been busier.

In this Word Processing Module, you will learn how to add further to the world's output of computer-generated paperwork.

You will discover how to create formal business letters and reports, and produce stylish posters and restaurant menus. We will even share with you the secrets of generating personalised form letters, (un)popularly known as junk mail.

Good luck with it.

Section 3.1: Your First Letter in Word

In This Section

There is a lot more to word processing than just typing and editing words, but these are the two basics. Read the material and follow the examples in this Section and you will have the foundation skills to move on to more advanced tasks.

You will also learn how to access and search through Word's online help, which is a great place to find answers and advice on using any of the program's features.

New Skills

At the end of this Section you should be able to:

- Start and quit Word
- Enter and edit text
- Recognise Word's non-printing characters
- Use the SHIFT, BACKSPACE, DELETE, ARROW and TAB keys
- Type and print a standard letter
- Use Word's Insert Date feature
- Reverse typing and editing actions with Word's Undo feature
- Save, name, open, create and close Word documents
- Use online help to learn more about Word

New Words

At the end of this Section you should be able to explain the following terms:

- Document
- Paragraph mark
- Wrap around
- Non-printing characters

Starting Word

Microsoft
Word

Double click on the Microsoft Word icon or choose **Start | Programs | Microsoft Word**. Word starts and displays a new window containing a new, blank document ready for you to type into.

A blank Word document ready to accept your text

Word Document
A Microsoft Word file. For example, a letter or a report.

What? No New, Blank Document?

If starting Word did not automatically open a new, blank document, click on the New button at the top left of your screen.

New

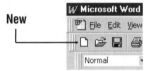

Text Cursor and Paragraph Mark

Text cursor

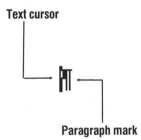

Paragraph mark

Near the top-left corner of your document you can see two items:

- **Text cursor**: A blinking vertical line. Whenever you type text, Word places the text at the text cursor's location. Think of the cursor as a 'you are here' indicator, telling you where you are in a document.

- **Paragraph mark**: Every new Word document contains one of these (it looks like a backwards letter P). Whenever you press the ENTER key to begin a new paragraph, Word inserts another one at that point. The paragraph mark appears on the screen only and not on printouts.

Paragraph Mark
Every document has at least one paragraph mark. Word displays another one each time you press the ENTER key.

What? No Paragraph Mark?

If Word does not display the paragraph mark in your document, click on the Show/Hide Paragraph Mark button at the top of the screen, near the top-right corner of your Word window.

Show/Hide Paragraph Mark

Actions You Need to Know

Here are the four basic operations in Word that you need to know:

- Typing text
- Editing (changing) text you previously typed
- Using the SHIFT key to type upper-case (capital) letters
- Using the ENTER key to type new paragraph marks

You will practise each one in the following four Exercises.

Exercise 3.1: Typing Text in Word

1) Type the following number: 7

2) Press the SPACEBAR. Word displays a dot on the screen. This is Word's way of telling that you have typed a space. Word will not print the dot.

3) Type the following six letters: dwarfs

That's it. Congratulations! You have typed your first text in Word.

Exercise 3.2: Editing Previously Typed Text

Often you will want to change – or, perhaps, remove completely – text that you have typed. This is called editing.

1) Using the mouse, click to the right of the 7.

2) Press the BACKSPACE key. (You will find it directly above the ENTER key.)

3) Type the following word: seven

You have completed the editing Exercise.

Exercise 3.3: Using the SHIFT Key

1) Click to the left of the letter s in seven.

2) Press the DELETE key to delete the letter s.

3) Hold down the SHIFT key and type the letter s. Word displays an upper-case S.

4) Move the cursor to the right of the letter d in dwarfs.

5) Press the BACKSPACE key to delete the letter d.

6) Hold down the SHIFT key and type the letter d. Word displays an upper-case D.

Well done! Another Exercise completed.

Exercise 3.4: Using ENTER to Type New Paragraph Marks

Now you will use the ENTER key to end one paragraph and begin another.

1) Click to the right of the word Dwarfs, and press ENTER. This creates a new paragraph. Word places the cursor at the start of a new line.

2) Type: John

3) Press ENTER.

4) Type: Paul

5) Press ENTER.

6) Type: George

7) Press ENTER.

8) Type: Ringo

You will not need this text for future Exercises. So delete it as follows:

9) Click to the right of the word Ringo.

10) Press and hold down the BACKSPACE key until Word has removed all the text from the document.

Keys You Need to Know

Now is a good time to summarise the role of these important keys:

SHIFT: Pressed in combination with a letter, this creates an upper-case letter. Pressed in combination with a number or symbol key, it creates the upper symbol. You will find a SHIFT key at both sides of the keyboard.

BACKSPACE: Deletes the character to the *left* of the cursor. You will find the BACKSPACE key at the top-right of the keyboard, just above the ENTER key.

DELETE: Deletes the character to the *right* of the cursor. You will find the DELETE key in a group of six keys to the right of the ENTER key.

ARROW: Rather than use the mouse to move the cursor around your document, you can press any of the four ARROW keys, located to the right of the ENTER key. You may find this method faster than moving and clicking the mouse, because you need not take either hand away from the keyboard.

Typing a Letter

Now you are ready to type a longer piece of text, a letter.

Exercise 3.5: Typing a Paragraph of a Letter
1) Type the following text:

I am writing to you in relation to our annual Sale of Work which will take place in our local Scout Den on 17 October next.

Your screen should look as follows.

I·am·writing·to·you·in·relation·to·our·annual·Sale·of·Work·which·will·take·place·in·our·local·
Scout·Den·on·17·October·next.¶

Notice how Word moved the cursor to the beginning of the next line when the text you were typing reached the right-hand edge of the page.

On an old-style typewriter, you would have needed to press the ENTER (also called RETURN) key to move down to the next line. Word does this for you automatically. This feature is called wrap around, and Word is said to 'wrap' the text to a new line once the previous line is full.

Word's automatic moving of the cursor to the beginning of a new line when the text reaches the end of the previous one.

Exercise 3.6: Typing More Text in Your Letter

In this Exercise, you will type your address at the top of the letter, type more text in the letter, and type your name at the bottom.

1) Click at the beginning of the first line, so that the cursor is just to the left of the letter I.

Click here ———

I·am·writing·to·you·in·relation·to·our·annual·Sale·of·Work·which·will·take·place·in·our·local· Scout·Hall·on·17·October·next.¶

2) Press the ENTER key to create a new line, and then the UP ARROW key to position the cursor at the start of the new line.

3) Type the following and press ENTER:

   24 Main Street,

4) Type the following and press ENTER:

   Anytown.

5) Type the following and press ENTER three times:

   333444

6) Type the following and press ENTER:

   Dear Ms Smith,

7) Click at the end of the last line, so that the cursor is just to the right of the full stop and to the left of the paragraph mark. Press ENTER twice.

I·am·writing·to·you·in·relation·to·our·annual·Sale·of·Work·which·will·take·place·in·our·local· Scout·Hall·on·17·October·next.¶

———— **Click here**

8) Type the following and press ENTER twice:

   In previous years your company was kind enough to donate a prize for our wheel of fortune.

9) Type the following and press ENTER twice:

   Could we ask you to be as generous again this year?

10) Hold down the SHIFT key and press the hyphen key about twenty times. (The hyphen key is the second key to the left of the BACKSPACE key.)

   Release the SHIFT key. When you print the letter, you can write your signature on the line created by the repeated pressing of the hyphen.

11) Press ENTER and type the following:

   Ken Bloggs

That's it. You have completed the Exercise.

The Hyphen key (to the left of the Equal To key)

No letter is complete with a date. In Exercise 3.7 you will discover how you can use Word to insert today's date in a letter or other document.

Click here

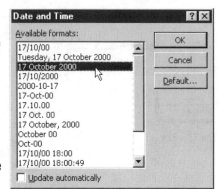

Dear·Ms·Smith,¶

Exercise 3.7: Entering a Date

1) Click the paragraph mark on the empty line above 'Dear Ms Smith'.

2) Choose **Insert | Date and Time**.

3) Word displays a dialog box that shows today's date in a variety of formats.

    Select the date format you want and click **OK**.

    This inserts the date in your letter and closes the dialog box.

4) Press ENTER twice to create two empty lines after the inserted date and before the 'Dear Ms Smith'.

Well done. You have typed your first letter in Word. It should look as shown below.

Your first letter in Microsoft Word

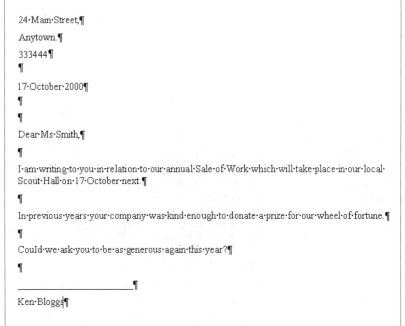

24·Main·Street,¶

Anytown.¶

333444¶

¶

17·October·2000¶

¶

¶

Dear·Ms·Smith,¶

¶

I·am·writing·to·you·in·relation·to·our·annual·Sale·of·Work·which·will·take·place·in·our·local·Scout·Hall·on·17·October·next.¶

¶

In·previous·years·your·company·was·kind·enough·to·donate·a·prize·for·our·wheel·of·fortune.¶

¶

Could·we·ask·you·to·be·as·generous·again·this·year?¶

¶

_____¶

Ken·Bloggs¶¶

Moving Text with the Tab Key

There is a problem with your letter. The address, phone number and date at the top are in the wrong position. You need to move them to the right.

In Exercise 3.8 you learn how to use the TAB key to change the position of text on the page.

Exercise 3.8: Using the Tab Key

1) Position the cursor at the top left of the page, just to the left of the 2.

Click here ———

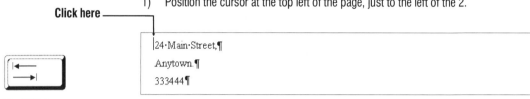

The TAB key

2) Press the TAB key eight times. Word moves all text between the cursor and the paragraph mark to the right.

3) Repeat step 2 for the second address line, the phone number line, and the date line. Your screen should look as shown below.

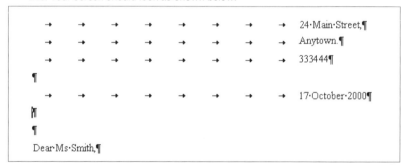

Non-Printing Characters and Wavy Underlines

Each time you press the TAB key, Word inserts an arrow symbol on the screen. Like the paragraph mark that indicates a paragraph ending, and the dot between words that represents a blank space, the tab symbol is a non-printing character.

> **Non-Printing Characters**
>
> *Symbols that Word displays on the screen to help you type and edit your document, but that are not printed.*

Ken·Bloggs¶

Depending on how Word is set up on your computer, you may see green and/or red wavy underlines beneath certain words or phrases. These have to do with Word's spell- and grammar-checking features, which are explained in Section 4.4, until then, ignore them.

Printing Your Letter

Your letter is ready to be printed out. Choose **File | Print**. If your printer is set up correctly all you need to do is click **OK** on the Print dialog box. You will learn more about printing in Section 3.3.

Word's Toolbars

Above the document window you can see Word's two main toolbars: the Standard Toolbar and the Formatting Toolbar.

The Standard Toolbar includes buttons for managing files – that is, Word documents – and for working with tables.

Word's Standard Toolbar

The Formatting Toolbar includes buttons for changing the appearance of text, and for inserting bullets.

Word's Formatting Toolbar

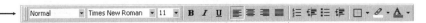

Rather than introduce all these buttons at once, we will explain each one as it becomes relevant through this ECDL Word Processing Module.

Word's Undo Feature

Click the arrow to view actions that you can Undo.

Enter the wrong text? Press the wrong key? Word's Undo feature enables you to reverse your most recent typing or editing action if it has produced unwanted results:

- Choose **Edit | Undo** or click the Undo ↶ button on the Standard Toolbar.

Pressing Undo repeatedly reverses your last series of actions. To view a list of recent actions that you can undo, click the arrow at the right of the Undo button. If you undo an action and then change your mind, click the Redo ↷ button (to the right of the Undo button).

Working with Word Documents

A Word document is a file containing text (and sometimes graphics too). The file names of Word documents end in .doc. This helps you to distinguish Word files from other file types.

Saving Your Document

In Word, as in other applications, always save your work as you go along. Don't wait until you are finished! To save a document:

- Choose **File | Save** or click the Save 🖫 button on the Standard Toolbar.

The first time you save a document file, Word asks you to give the file a name. The following Exercise shows you how.

Exercise 3.9: Saving and Naming a New Document

1) Choose **File | Save**. Word displays a dialog box similar to the one shown.

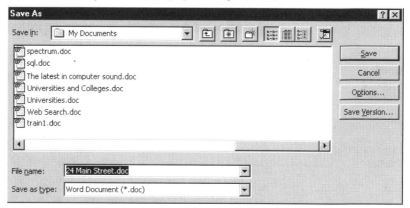

2) By default, Word suggests the first words of your document as the file name. Replace this file name with something that you will find easier to remember and recognise – such as your initials. If your name is Ken Bloggs, for example, name the document KBletter.doc. Click the **Save** button.

Word adds the file name extension of .doc automatically. You need not type it.

Creating a New Document

To create a new Word file:

- Choose **File | New** or click the New  button on the Standard Toolbar.

Opening an Existing Document

To open an existing Word file:

- Choose **File | Open** or click the Open button on the Standard Toolbar. Select the file you want from the dialog box.

Closing a Document

To close a Word document:

- Choose **File | Close** or click the Close button on the document window.

Document Close button

If you have made changes to your document since you last saved it, Word prompts you to save the changes before it closes the file.

Quitting Word

To leave Word:

- Choose **File | Exit** or click the Close button on the Word window.

 ◄──────── **Word Close button**

If you have left open any files containing unsaved work, Word prompts you to save them.

Online Help

Like Excel, Access, PowerPoint and other Microsoft applications, Word offers a searchable online help system.

- The word 'help' means that the information is there to assist you understand and use the application.

- The word 'online' means that the material is presented on the computer screen rather than as a traditional printed manual.

You can search through and read online help in two ways: from the Help menu, or from dialog boxes.

Using Help Menu Options

Choose **Help | Contents and Index** to display the three tabs of the Help Topics dialog box. These are explained below.

Contents Tab

This offers short descriptions of Word's main features.

📖 Where you see a heading with a book symbol, double-click to view the related sub-headings.

❓ Double-click on a question mark symbol to read the help text.

🔲 Click a Show me arrow for Word to demonstrate how to perform a particular action.

⏩ Click a double-arrow to view step-by-step instructions.

Index Tab

Reading the material displayed on this tab is like looking through the index of a printed book.

Just type the first letters of the word or phrase you are interested in.

Word responds by displaying all matches from the online help in the lower half of the dialog box.

When you find the index entry that you are looking for, click the **Display** button.

Find Tab

Can't find what you are looking for in the Contents or Index tabs? Try this tab.

When you type a word or phrase, Word performs a deeper search of the online help.

Word also displays some related words to help you narrow your search.

When you find the item you are looking for, double-click on it to display it.

As you search through and read online help topics, you will see the following buttons at the top of the online help window:

- **Help Topics**: Click this to return to the Contents tab.

- **Back**: Click this to return to the previous help topic.

- **Options**: Click this to perform such actions as copying the online help text to a document, or printing it on your printer.

Using Help from Dialog Boxes

You can also access online help directly from a dialog box, as Exercise 3.10 demonstrates.

Exercise 3.10: Using Online Help in a Dialog Box

1) Choose **Edit | Find** to display the Find and Replace dialog box.

2) Click on the question mark symbol near the top-right of the dialog box. Word displays a question mark to the right of the cursor.

3) Move the mouse down and right, and click anywhere in the Find what: box.

4) Word displays online help text telling you about the purpose of the Find what: box.

5) Click anywhere on the Word window to remove the online help text.

Practise this Exercise with other dialog boxes in Word.

When finished, you can close your letter document and close Microsoft Word. You have now completed Section 3.1 of the ECDL Word Processing Module.

Section Summary: So Now You Know

A *Word document* is a file containing text (and sometimes graphics too). Every new Word document contains a *text cursor*. Whenever you type text, Word places the text at the text cursor's location. You can move the text cursor with the mouse or with the ARROW keys.

Every new document also contains a *paragraph mark*. Whenever you press the ENTER key to type a new paragraph of text or insert a blank line, Word inserts another paragraph mark at that point.

You can edit text with the following two keys:

- BACKSPACE: Removes text to the *left* of the text cursor
- DELETE: Removes text to the *right* of the text cursor

Press the SHIFT key in combination with a letter, number or symbol key to type an *upper-case* (capital) character or symbol.

Press the TAB key repeatedly to move text to the right. When typing a letter, for example, use TAB to position the address and related details at the top-right of the letter.

Word's *Insert Date* feature inserts the current date in a document. You can choose from a wide range of date formats.

Word's *non-printing characters*, such as a single dot to represent a space, do not appear on printouts. They are displayed on the screen only as a guide to typing and editing.

Word's *Undo* feature enables you to reverse your most recent typing or editing actions if they have produced unwanted results.

In Word, as in other applications, always *save* your work as you go along. The first time you save a document file, Word prompts you to give it a *file name*. Word automatically adds the file name extension *.doc* to all saved documents.

Word offers a searchable *online help* system that you can access in two ways: from the Help menu, and from the question mark button at the top-right of individual dialog boxes.

Section 3.2: Formatting, Positioning and Copying Text

In addition to typing and editing text, you can use a word processor to:

- Change the *appearance* of the text. This is called formatting. It includes such actions as making text bolder (heavier), placing a line under it, and putting it in italics. You can also change the text font and font size, format text as bullets, and apply shading (coloured backgrounds) and borders to text.

- Change the *position* of text on the page. You have already learnt how to reposition text using the TAB key. Now you will discover two other methods: alignment and indenting.

Also in this Section you will learn how to copy text within and between documents, how to insert symbols and special characters.

New Skills

At the end of this Section you should be able to:

- Select text

- Format text (bold, italic and underline)

- Copy, cut and paste text

- Indent text from the left and right page margins

- Align text (left, right, centre and justified)

- Create text bullets

- Explain fonts and font sizes, and super- and subscripts

- Add borders and shading to text

- Use Word's Zoom feature to enlarge and reduce the document display

- Save a Word document to a diskette

- Insert symbols and special characters

- Use Word's Format Painter feature to copy formatting

At the end of this Section you should be able to explain the following terms:

■ Select	■ Bulleted text
■ Clipboard	■ Font
■ Indent	■ Superscript
■ Alignment	■ Subscript
■ Format Painter	

Selecting Text

Typically, when you want to format or position some text, it is only a particular character, word, group of words or paragraph that you want to change.

You tell Word which part of the document you want to change by first *selecting* that text. Selecting a piece of text is sometimes called highlighting that text.

Selected text ─────────────

In █previous·years█ your·company·was·kind·enough·to·donate·a·prize·for·our·wheel·of·fortune. ¶

When you select text, Word displays that text in reverse (white text on black background), rather like the negative of a photograph.

> **Selecting Text**
> *Highlighting a piece of text in order to perform an action on it such as formatting or alignment.*

Formatting and alignment are just two of the actions that you will learn how to perform on selected text. In later Sections, you will learn how to find and replace, and spell-check selected text.

To select text within a Word document, first position the mouse at the beginning of the text that you want to select:

- To select text on a single line, drag the mouse to the right until you have selected the characters or words.

Ctrl

CTRL (Control) key

- To select a sentence or other piece of text that is on more than a single line, drag the mouse to the right and down the page.

- To select your whole document, hold down the CTRL key and click anywhere in the left margin.

Exercise 3.11: Selecting Text

In this Exercise you will learn how to select text – characters, words sentences and paragraphs.

1) Open Word, and open the letter you saved in Exercise 3.9 of Section 3.1.

2) Position the cursor to the left of the letter D in Dear Ms Smith.

3) Drag the mouse to the right until you have selected the letter D. Release the mouse button.

   You have learned how to select a single character. Now click anywhere on the page to deselect the letter D. Deselecting a piece of text does not remove the text it just means that it is no longer selected.

4) Again, position the mouse to the left of the letter D, but this time keep dragging with the mouse until you have selected the entire word Dear.

   Release the mouse button.

5) Finally, position the mouse to the left of the letter D. Now drag the mouse down and right until you have selected the first paragraph of the letter.

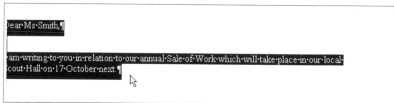

You have learned how to select several lines of text. Click anywhere outside the selected area to deselect it.

That completes the Exercise. But practise your text-selection skills by clicking at any point in your document, and dragging the mouse in various directions.

Formatting Text

Format buttons

Word's most commonly used formatting features are:

- **Bold**: Heavy black text, often used for headings

- *Italic*: Slanted text, often used for emphasis or foreign words

- <u>Underline</u>: A single line under the text, often used in legal documents and beneath signatures on letters

You will find the relevant buttons on the Formatting Toolbar. In the next Exercises you will learn how to apply the bold and italic formats.

Exercise 3.12: Applying the Bold Format

1) Place the cursor at the start of the first line of the address.

2) Drag right and down with the mouse until you have selected the two address lines and the phone number.

3) Click the Bold button or press CTRL+b (hold down CTRL and type b).

4) Deselect the lines by clicking on any other area of the document.

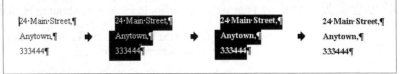

Exercise 3.13: Applying the Italic Format

1) Place the cursor at the start of the name, Ken Bloggs.

2) Drag right until you have selected the name.

3) Click the Italic button or press CTRL+i.

4) Deselect the name by clicking on any other area of the document.

Well done. Save your letter.

Copying and Pasting Text

Suppose you want to use the same text – words or paragraphs – more than once in a document. Do you need to retype it each time that you need it? No.

With Word, you can type the text just once, and then insert it as many times as you need. This is a two step process:

- **Copy**: You select and then *copy* the text to the Clipboard, a temporary holding area.

- **Paste**: You insert or *paste* the text from the Clipboard into a different part of the same document, or even a different document.

> **Clipboard**
>
> *A temporary storage area to which you can copy text (or graphics). You can paste to any location within the same or different documents.*

Exercise 3.14: Copying and Pasting Text within a Document

1) Select the second paragraph of your letter.

In·previous·years·your·company·was·kind·enough·to·donate·a·prize·for·our·wheel·of·fortune.¶

Copy button

2) Click the Copy button on the Standard Toolbar, or choose **Edit | Copy**.

3) Position the cursor at the left of the paragraph mark on the next line.

In·previous·years·your·company·was·kind·enough·to·donate·a·prize·for·our·wheel·of·fortune.¶
¶

Paste button

4) Click the Paste button on the Standard Toolbar, or choose **Edit | Paste**.

In·previous·years·your·company·was·kind·enough·to·donate·a·prize·for·our·wheel·of·fortune.¶
In·previous·years·your·company·was·kind·enough·to·donate·a·prize·for·our·wheel·of·fortune.¶

Select the line that you have pasted from the Clipboard, and press the DELETE key. You will not need it again.

Four points you should remember about the Clipboard:

- The Clipboard is temporary. Turn off your computer and the Clipboard contents are deleted.

- The same Clipboard is available to all Windows applications. For example, you can copy from Excel and paste into Word.

- The Clipboard can hold only a single, copied item at a time. If you copy a second piece of text, the second overwrites the first.

- Text stays in the Clipboard after you paste from it, so you can paste the same piece of text into as many locations as you need.

Exercise 3.15: Copying and Pasting Text between Documents
The line you copied in Exercise 3.14 is still in the Clipboard. In this Exercise you will copy it to a different document.

1) Click on the New File ▭ button to create a new, blank Word document.

   Word places the cursor at the beginning of the document.

2) Click the Paste button on the Standard Toolbar, or choose **Edit | Paste**.

3) Choose **File | Close** to close the new document. When Word asks you whether you want to save the new file, click **No**.

When you have more than one Word document open at a time, you can switch between them by choosing **Window | *<document name>*.**

Cutting and Pasting Text

Cut button

Sometimes, you may want to remove text from one part of a document and place it in a different part.

Rather than deleting the text and then retyping it elsewhere, Word allows you to move the text by cutting it from its current location and pasting it to the new location.

Cut-and-paste differs from copy-and-paste in that Word removes the cut text, whereas copied text remains in its original location. You can cut selected text using the Cut button on the Standard Toolbar by choosing **Edit | Cut**.

Keyboard Shortcuts

You may find it quicker to use Word's keyboard shortcuts for copy, cut and paste operations as you need not take either hand away from the keyboard:

- To copy, press CTRL+c.   • To cut, press CTRL+x.

- To paste, press CTRL+v.

You can also right-click on your document to get a pop-up menu displaying the available commands for copying, cutting or pasting.

Formatted Documents

All Word documents are formatted, but some are more formatted than others. In the remainder of this Section you will discover the Word tools that enable you to design a highly formatted poster: indents, alignment, bullets, fonts, borders and shading.

Left and Right Indents

The term indent means 'in from the margin'. Word's indenting feature lets you push a paragraph of text a specified distance in from the left margin, right margin, or both.

To indent a selected paragraph, choose **Format | Paragraph**, and enter the required left and/or right distances on the Indents and Spacing tab of the Paragraph dialog box.

In long documents, you may sometimes see indenting used as a way of attracting attention to a particular part of the text. Here is an example that combines a left and right indent with italics:

> *Another successful year has seen revenues rise by 35% and profits by 47.5%. Our company is well placed to face the challenges of the future.*

Indent

The positioning of a paragraph of text a specified distance in from the left and/or right margin.

Aligning Text

Alignment buttons

To align text means to 'line up' the text in a particular horizontal (left-right) way. Word gives you four choices:

- **Left**: The default, used for letters and business documents. Left-aligned text is generally the easiest to read.

- **Centre:** Places the text between the left and right margins. Used for headings.

- **Right**: Aligns the text against the right-hand margin of the page. Used by graphic designers for decorative purposes.

- **Justify:** Both left and right aligned at the same time! Used for narrow columns of text in newspapers and magazines.

Do not use justification when your text is in a single column across the width of the page (such as in letters), because it makes the text more difficult to read.

You can only align paragraphs. You cannot align selected characters or words within a paragraph.

To align a single paragraph, you don't need to select the text. You need only to position the cursor any place within the paragraph. You will find the four alignment buttons on the Formatting Toolbar.

Bullets and Numbered Lists

Lists are good ways to communicate a series of short statements or instructions. Lists are of two types:

- *Bulleted:* Used when the reading order is not critical. The bullet character is typically a dot, square, diamond, line or arrow.

  To make a bulleted list, select the paragraphs and click the Bullets button on the Formatting Toolbar.

- *Numbered:* Used when the order of reading is important. For example, in directions and instructions. Each item is assigned a sequentially increasing number.

  To make a numbered list, select the paragraphs and click the Numbering button on the Formatting Toolbar.

You can also make lists by choosing **Format | Bullets and Numbering**. Word offers you a wide range of options, such as the style of bullet or number character, and the distance between the bullet or number character and the bulleted or numbered text.

Exercises 3.16, 3.17 and 3.18 take you through the steps of applying numbering and bullets to selected text.

Exercise 3.16: Applying Numbering to Text

1) Open a new document, press the CAPS LOCK key once, type the following text, and press ENTER twice:

   MY FAVOURITE FRUIT

   (The CAPS LOCK key is to the left of the letter 'a' key. After you press it, every letter you type is displayed as a capital letter.)

2) Press the CAPS LOCK key again to turn off capitals.

3) Select the text by clicking in front of the 'M' in My, and dragging to the right with the mouse.

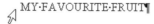

Caps Lock key

Click in front of the text...   **and drag to the right with the mouse.**

4) Click the Underline button on the Formatting Toolbar to underline the selected text.

5) Click the paragraph mark right of the text, and press ENTER twice to create two new lines.

6) Type the following six fruit names, pressing ENTER after each one: Apples, Bananas, Grapes, Kiwis, Oranges and Peaches.

Your text should look as shown on the right.

MY·FAVOURITE·FRUIT¶
¶
Apples¶
Bananas¶
Grapes¶
Kiwis¶
Oranges¶
Peaches¶

7) Select the six fruit names by clicking in front of the 'A' in Apples, and then dragging right and down with the mouse until you reach the final paragraph mark.

8) Click the Numbering button ⊟ on the Formatting Toolbar to applying numbering to the selected text.

9) Click anywhere in your document outside the selected area to deselect the text. Your text should now look as shown on the right.

(The arrows after the numbers are non-printing characters.)

MY·FAVOURITE·FRUIT¶
¶
1.→Apples¶
2.→Bananas¶
3.→Grapes¶
4.→Kiwis¶
5.→Oranges¶
6.→Peaches¶

10) Choose **File | Save** or press CTRL+s to save your document. If your initials are KB, for example, name it KBList.doc. Leave the document open.

In Exercise 3.17 you will replace the numbers in Exercise 3.16 with bullets.

Exercise 3.17: Applying Bullets to Text

1) Select the list of six fruit names that you entered in Exercise 3.16.

(Notice that you cannot select the numbers. Why? Because they are not entered text – they are generated automatically by Word.)

2) Click the Bullets button ⊟ on the Formatting Toolbar. Word replaces the numbers with bullets.

3) Choose **Format | Bullets and Numbering**, select the Bullets tab, and click **Customize**.

4) In the Text position area, increase the value in the Indent at: box from 0.63 cm (the default) to 1 cm, and click **OK**.

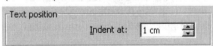

5) Click anywhere in your document outside the selected area to deselect the text.

Your text should now look as shown on the right.

(The arrows after the bullets are non-printing characters.)

MY·FAVOURITE·FRUIT¶
¶
• → Apples¶
• → Bananas¶
• → Grapes¶
• → Kiwis¶
• → Oranges¶
• → Peaches¶

Sometimes you want to apply bullets or numbering only to certain items in a list, and not to others. Exercise 3.18 provides an example.

Exercise 3.18: Applying Bullets to Selected Items in a List

1) Click at the paragraph mark after the words Kiwis, and press ENTER to create a new line. Notice that Word places a bullet in front of the line.

2) Type the following:

(my absolute favourite)

You don't want this new line to have a bullet character in front of it.

3) Select the new line and click the Bullets button on the Formatting Toolbar. Word removes the bullet format from the selected line.

4) Your final task is to align the new line with the other, bulleted lines.

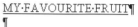

With the new line still selected, choose **Format | Paragraph**, type a Left: indent of 1 cm, and click **OK**.

Click anywhere in your document outside the selected line to deselect it. Your text should now look as shown on the right.

MY·FAVOURITE·FRUIT¶
¶
• → Apples¶
• → Bananas¶
• → Grapes¶
• → Kiwis¶
     (my·absolute·favourite)¶
• → Oranges¶
• → Peaches¶

This completes the bullets and numbering exercises. Save and close your document.

Fonts

A font or typeface is a particular style of text. What fonts are installed on your computer? Click the arrow on the drop-down Font box on the Formatting Toolbar to see.

Do you need to remember the names and characteristics of all these fonts? No. You need remember only two points about fonts:

Viewing the fonts on your computer

- There are really just two kinds (families) of fonts: *serif* and *sans serif*. Sans serif just means without serifs.

- Serif fonts are good for long paragraphs of text (what is called body text). Sans serif fonts are good for short pieces of text such as headlines, headers, captions and maybe bulleted text.

You can recognise which family a font belongs to by asking: do its characters have serifs (tails or squiggles) at their edges?

serif ⟶ NWI   NWI

A serif font   **A sans serif font**

Serif Fonts

Word's default font is a serif font called Times New Roman. It takes its name from *The Times* newspaper of London, where it was developed in the 1930s.

Other popular serif fonts include Garamond and Century Schoolbook:

- This text is written in a font named Garamond.
- This text is written in a font named New Century Schoolbook.

Sans Serif Fonts

Word's default sans serif font is Arial. It is based on another font, Helvetica, which was the world's widely used font in the 1970s.

Other common sans serif fonts include Futura and Avant Garde:

- **This text is written in a font named Futura.**
- This text is written in a font named Avant Garde.

> ### Font
> A typeface: a particular style of text. The two main font families are serif and sans serif.

Font Sizes

Font size is measured in a non-metric unit called the point, with approximately 72 points equal to one inch.

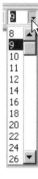

- For the body text of letters or longer business documents such as reports, 10, 11 or 12 points is a good choice. For headings, use larger font sizes in the range 14 to 28 points.

- Headers, footers, endnotes, footnotes and captions are often in 8 or 9 point font size.

To change the font size of selected text, click the required font size from the Font Size drop down list box on the Formatting Toolbar.

Font Properties

Word's **Format | Font** dialog box enables you to apply a number of properties to fonts: style, effects, colour and spacing.

Font Style

You have already applied these options using the Bold and Italic buttons on the Formatting Toolbar.

Underline

A lot of choices here. Single is both the simplest and most commonly used. It is also the type of underline applied with the Underline button on the Formatting Toolbar.

Font Colour

Have you a colour printer? Then you may want to select a text colour other than Auto. Even without a colour printer, you may want to print your headings in grey.

What colour is Auto? Auto is black, unless the background is black or a dark grey, in which case Auto switches to white.

Font Effects

You can experiment with the various font effects by selecting any of the Effects checkboxes and viewing the result in the Preview area at the bottom of the dialog box.

Effects
- ☐ Strikethrough
- ☐ Double strikethrough
- ☐ Superscript
- ☐ Subscript
- ☐ Shadow
- ☐ Outline
- ☐ Emboss
- ☐ Engrave
- ☐ Small caps
- ☐ All caps
- ☐ Hidden

One important effect you need to know about is superscript.

This raises the selected text above the other text on the same line, and reduces its font size. It is used most commonly for mathematical symbols. For example:

$2^2, x^8, 10^{-3}$

Superscript

Text that is raised above other text on the same line and is reduced in font size. Commonly used in maths texts for indices.

The opposite of superscript is subscript. You will find subscripts used in typing chemical formulas, for example:

H_2O and H_2SO_4

Subscript

Text that is lowered beneath other text on the same line and is reduced in font size. Commonly used in chemistry texts for formulas.

Font Spacing

You can expand or condense the space between characters by using the options on the Character Spacing tab of the Font dialog box.

Here is a line of text that is expanded by 1 point.

You may want to use this spacing effect for document headings.

Font Borders and Shading

You can brighten up your document with borders (decorative boxes) and shading (coloured backgrounds), using the options available with the **Format | Borders and Shading** command.

Word offers a range of border settings, with Box and Shadow the most common choices. Use the Preview section on the right of the dialog box to select the edges that you want bordered. The default is all four edges.

Pay attention to the Apply to: drop-down box at the bottom right. Your choice affects how Word draws the border. See the following example.

Sample·Text:·Apply·to·Text·Selected·¶

¶

Sample·Text:·Apply·to·Text·Paragraph¶

To apply shading, select the text, choose **Format | Borders and Shading**, and then select your required Fill, Style and Colour options from the Shading Tab of the dialog box:

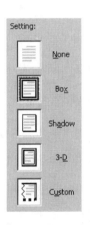

Border options

- **Fill**: This is the text background colour. If placing a grey shade behind black text, use 25% or less of grey. Otherwise, the text is difficult to read.

- **Style**: This allows you to apply tints (percentages of a colour) or patterns of a second colour (selected in the Colour box) on top of the selected Fill colour.

  Leave the Style: box at its default value of Clear if you do not want to apply a second colour.

- **Colour**: If you have selected a pattern in the Style box, select the colour of the lines and dots in the pattern here.

You can apply a border and shading to one or more characters, words or paragraphs. You need not apply both, but generally the border and shading features tend to be used together.

Exercise 3.19: Designing Your Poster

Practise makes perfect. In this Exercise you will apply the formatting (fonts, bullets, borders and shading) and text positioning (alignment and indenting) skills that you have learned in this Section. Your aim is to write and design a poster.

1) Open a new document and type the text shown.

2) Select the text: Annual Sale of Work. Using **Format | Font**, make it Times New Roman, 28 point.

3) Choose **Format | Borders and Shading**, select a Setting: of Box and select Text as the Apply to: option.

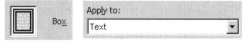

4) On the Shading tab, select a shading of 15% Grey.

When finished, click **OK**.

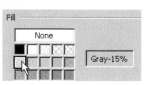

5) Select the text: In aid of Local Scout Troop. Use the options on the Formatting Toolbar to centre align it, and make it Arial Black, 14 point.

**Diamond style
bullet character**

6) Select the four attractions: Wheel of Fortune, Cakes, Books and Children's Play Area. Make them Arial, 20 point.

(Ensure the paragraph mark after Children's Play Area is included in your selection.)

Choose **Format | Bullets and Numbering**. On the Bullet tab, select the diamond bullet character style.

7) You want to place the bullets where they will get attention: in the centre of the page between the left and right page margins.

But *do not* apply centre alignment, as shown below, as the bullets are easier to read if they are left aligned.

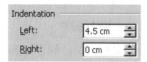

8) With the four attractions still selected, select **Format | Paragraph** and apply a left indent of 4.5 cm.

Your bulleted text remains left-aligned, but is now in the centre of the page.

9) Select the remainder of the text, and make it centre-aligned, Arial, Regular, 20 point.

10) Select each of the following words in turn and click the Bold button on the Formatting Toolbar:

Where:, When: and Admission Free.

11) Select the words All Welcome and click the Italics button on the Formatting Toolbar.

12) Finally, with the cursor positioned anywhere on the page, choose **Format | Borders and Shading**, and select the Page Border tab.

Select a Setting: of Box and, in the Apply to: field, select Whole Document, and click **OK**.

Your poster is now complete and should look like the sample shown. Save your poster with a name that you will find easy to remember and recognise. If your initials are KB, for example, save the poster document as KBposter.doc.

If you have a printer, print out your poster and inspect your work!

Annual Sale of Work

In aid of Local Scout Troop

- Wheel of Fortune
- Cakes
- Books
- Children's Play Area

Where:

Local Scout Hall, Main Street

When:

2pm,
Sunday, 17 October

Admission Free

All Welcome

Word's Zoom Views

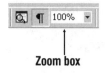

Zoom box

Word's Zoom feature enables you to magnify or reduce the document display. You can use Zoom in either of two ways:

- Click in the Zoom box on the Standard Toolbar, enter a number between 10% and 500%, and press ENTER.

- Choose **View | Zoom**, and select a magnification or reduction option from the Zoom dialog box.

To return from an enlarged or reduced view to normal view, select a magnification of 100% – or click the Undo button on the Standard Toolbar.

Zoom and Printing

The Zoom feature affects only the way that Word displays a document on-screen – and *not* how a document is printed. (You will learn about printing documents in Section 3.3.)

Saving to a Diskette

Have you been saving your documents as you went along? You should. It is also a good idea to save a copy of your document to a diskette. Follow the steps in Exercise 3.20 to learn how to save your poster to the A: drive.

Exercise 3.20: Saving a Word Document to a Diskette
1) Insert a diskette in the diskette drive of your computer:

- If it is a new diskette, ensure that it is formatted.

- If it is a previously used one, ensure that there is sufficient space on it to hold the Word document file. Your poster file should be around 60 KB in size.

2) Choose **File | Save As**, locate the A: drive, and click **Save** to save the file. Word suggests the default file name (in this example, KBposter.doc) for you to accept or amend.

When finished, use **File | Save As** again to resave the document to its original location on your computer. If you do not, saving the file in future (by clicking the Save button on the Standard Toolbar or choosing **File | Save**) will save the workbook to the diskette – and not to your computer.

Symbols and Special Characters

Word allows you to insert symbols and special characters in your documents:

- **Symbols:** Among the symbols are foreign language letters with accents (such as à, è, ä, and ë), fractions, and characters used in science and mathematics.

- **Special Characters:** These include the copyright ©, registered ® and trademark ™ signs, plus typographic characters such as the en dash (a short dash the width of the letter 'n'), the em dash (a longer dash the width of the letter 'm'), and various types of opening and closing quotes.

To insert a symbol or special character:

- Click where you want to insert the symbol.

- Choose **Insert | Symbol**, and then click the Symbols or Special Characters tab.

- Double-click the symbol or character you want to insert.

- Click **Close** to close the dialog box.

Format Painter

Format Painter button

Word's Format Painter provides a quick, convenient way to copy formatting from one piece of text to another. Follow these steps:

- Select the text that has the formatting you want to copy.

- Click the Format Painter button on the Standard Toolbar.

- Select the text to which you want to apply the formatting.

To copy the selected formatting to several locations, double-click Format Painter.

When finished copying the formatting, click the Format Painter button again or press the ESC key at the top-left of your keyboard.

Exercise 3.21: Copying Formatting
You begin this Exercise by removing the formatting from two lines of your Annual Sale of Work poster.

1) Is the poster document from Exercise 3.19 open? If not, open it now.

2) Select the text 'Where:', choose **Format | Font**, make it 10 point, Regular, Times New Roman, and click **OK**.

3) Select the text 'When:'. Also make it 10 point, Regular, Times New Roman.

In the next part of this Exercise, you will copy the formatting from another part of the poster to the two lines whose formatting you removed in steps 2 and 3 above.

4) Click anywhere within the words 'Admission Free'.

5) Double-click on the Format Painter button.

6) Select the text 'Where:', and click the Format Painter button.

7) Select the text 'When:', and click the Format Painter button.

8) Press the ESC key to switch off the Format Painter feature.

Your poster now looks as it did before this Exercise. Save the poster and close it. You can also close Microsoft Word. You have now completed Section 3.2 of the ECDL Word Processing Module.

Section Summary: So Now You Know

Before you format or align text, you must first *select* that text. You do so by clicking and then dragging with the mouse. Word displays selected text in reverse (white text on black background).

Bold, italic and underline are Word's most commonly used *formatting* features. Buttons for these options are provided on the Formatting Toolbar.

You can *copy* text from one part of a document and then *paste* it to another part (or even to a different document) using the *Clipboard*, a temporary storage area. You can also *cut* and paste text, in which case Word deletes the text from its original location.

Indenting is a way of moving text in a specified distance from the left or right margin of the page – or from both. *Alignment* is a way of positioning text in a paragraph so it lines up beside the left margin, beside the right margin, beside both left and right margins (justification) or away from both left and right margins (centering). Buttons for the alignment options are provided on the Formatting Toolbar.

Use lists to communicate short statements or instructions. *Bulleted lists*, in which each item is preceded by a symbol such as a square or diamond, are suitable when the reading order is not critical. *Numbered lists*, in which each item is preceded by a sequentially increasing number, are used for instructions and directions, where the order of reading is important.

Fonts (typefaces) are styles of text. Serif fonts are better for long paragraphs. Use sans serif fonts for shorter text items, such as headlines or captions. Two important font effects are *superscript* (used for writing mathematical indices) and *subscript* (used for writing chemical formulas).

You can brighten up your documents by adding decorative *borders* and background *shading*.

Word's *Zoom* feature enables you to magnify or reduce the document display – without affecting how the document is printed.

You can insert *symbols* and *special characters* in a document to represent such items as foreign language letters with accents, fractions, characters used in scientific and mathematical texts, and typographic characters such as dashes and quotes.

Word's *Format Painter* provides a quick, convenient way to copy formatting from one piece of text to another.

Section 3.3: Long Documents, Little Details

Both for the writer and reader, long documents present problems that shorter ones do not. Word offers features to make life easier for both.

To help you edit long documents, Word includes a spell-checker, grammar-checker, and a find and replace feature.

You can help readers navigate their way through long documents by inserting page numbers and other details in the header or footer.

Also in this Section, you will discover how to control vertical spacing between lines and paragraphs, how to create new types of indents to highlight breaks between paragraphs, and how to insert line and page breaks.

New Skills

At the end of this Section you should be able to:

- Change the spacing between lines and between paragraphs
- Apply a first line indent to a paragraph
- Apply a hanging indent to a paragraph
- Find and replace text, text with formatting, and special characters
- Adjust page margins and page orientation
- Create and format headers and footers
- Insert page numbers and document details in a header or footer
- Insert manual line breaks and page breaks
- Use Word's spell- and grammar-checkers
- Use Word's printing options

New Words

At the end of this Section you should be able to explain the following terms:

- Inter-line spacing
- Inter-paragraph spacing
- First line indent
- Hanging Indent
- Margin
- A4
- Header and footer

Creating Your Long Document

To learn how to work with long documents in Word, you need a sample long document to practise on. You begin this Section by copying some text from Word's online help.

Exercise 3.22: Copying Text from Word Online Help

1) Open Word and choose **Help | Contents and Index**. On the Contents tab of the Help Topics dialog box, double-click the topic: Working with Long Documents.

2) Word displays a list of sub-topics. Double-click on: Automatically summarising a document. You are shown a further sub-listing. Double-click on: Automatically summarise a document.

> 📖 Automatically Summarizing a Document
> [?] Automatically summarize a document
> [?] Troubleshoot automatically summarizing a document

3) On the help screen displayed, select the two paragraphs of text shown below by dragging the mouse over them.

> • If you want to read a summary of an online document, you can display the document in AutoSummarize view. In this view, you can switch between displaying only the key points in a document and highlighting them in the document. As you read, you can also change the level of detail at any time.
>
> How does AutoSummarize determine what the key points are? AutoSummarize analyzes the document and assigns a score to each sentence. (For example, it gives a higher score to sentences that contain words used frequently in the document.) You then choose a percentage of the highest-scoring sentences to display in the summary.
>
> Keep in mind that AutoSummarize works best on well-structured documents — for example, reports, articles, and scientific papers.
>
> **Note** For the best quality summaries, make sure that the Find All Word Forms tool is installed. For more information about installing this tool, click ».

4) Choose **Options | Copy**. Close the online help window by clicking on the close box in the top-right corner.

5) Click the New ▢ button on the Standard Toolbar to create a new Word document. The cursor is positioned at the start of the first line.

> ¶

6) Choose **Edit | Paste** to paste the online help text into the new document.

> How·does·AutoSummarize·determine·what·the·key·points·are?·AutoSummarize·analyzes·the· document·and·assigns·a·score·to·each·sentence.·(For·example,·it·gives·a·higher·score·to·sentences· that·contain·words·used·frequently·in·the·document.)·You·then·choose·a·percentage·of·the·highest- scoring·sentences·to·display·in·the·summary.¶
> ¶
> Keep·in·mind·that·AutoSummarize·works·best·on·well-structured·documents°‰·for·example,· reports,·articles,·and·scientific·papers.¶

7) Move the cursor to the start of the first line of the first paragraph. Press ENTER to create a new line, and move the cursor up to the start of that line.

> ¶
> How·does·AutoSummarize·determine·what·the·key·points·are?·AutoSummarize·analyzes·the·
> document·and·assigns·a·score·to·each·sentence.·(For·example,·it·gives·a·higher·score·to·sentences·

8) Type the following: Heading One

> Heading·One¶
> How·does·AutoSummarize·determine·what·the·key·points·are?·AutoSummarize·analyzes·the·
> document·and·assigns·a·score·to·each·sentence.·(For·example,·it·gives·a·higher·score·to·sentences·

9) Hold down the CTRL key and click in the left margin of the page where there is no text. This selects all the text in the document.

> Heading·One¶
> How·does·AutoSummarize·determine·what·the·key·points·are?·AutoSummarize·analyzes·the·
> document·and·assigns·a·score·to·each·sentence.·(For·example,·it·gives·a·higher·score·to·sentences·

10) Choose **Edit | Copy** to copy the text to the Clipboard. Deselect the text by clicking anywhere on the page outside the selected text.

11) Move the cursor down to the end of the second paragraph, and press ENTER twice to move down the cursor a further two lines.

> reports,·articles,·and·scientific·papers.¶
> ¶
> ¶

12) The text you copied from Word's online help in step 4) is still in the Clipboard. Choose **Edit | Paste** to paste it again.

13) Repeat steps 11 and 12 fifteen times to create three pages of sample text.

14) Choose **File | Save** to save the document with a name that you will find easy to remember. If your initials are KB, for example, call it KBlong.doc.

Inter-Line Spacing

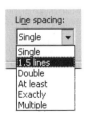

Inter-line spacing is the vertical space between lines within a paragraph of text. By default, Word applies single inter-line spacing. You can increase the inter-line spacing of a selected paragraph by choosing **Format | Paragraph**, and, in the Line Spacing: box, selecting 1.5 or Double.

Alternatively, enter a font size in the At: box, and select At Least: in the Line Spacing box. A good rule is to make inter-line spacing one point size larger than the font size. If your text is 10 points, for example, make inter-line spacing 11 points.

> **Inter-Line Spacing**
> *The vertical space between lines within a paragraph of text. Word's default is single line spacing.*

How·does·AutoS document·and·as that·contain·word scoring·sentence ¶ Keep·in·mind·tha reports,·articles,·: ¶ How·does·AutoS document·and·as that·contain·word scoring·sentence that·contain·word scoring·sentence	How·does·AutoSu document·and·assi that·contain·words scoring·sentences· ¶ Keep·in·mind·that· reports,·articles,·ar ¶ How·does·AutoSu	How·does·AutoS document·and·as that·contain·word scoring·sentence: ¶ Keep·in·mind·tha reports,·articles,·:

Inter-Paragraph Spacing

Pressing the ENTER key to add a blank line between paragraphs of text is a crude – if effective – way of controlling the inter-paragraph spacing (spacing between paragraphs) in your documents.

For longer documents, you may instead wish to use the **Format | Paragraph** command, and enter an inter-paragraph space value in the Space Before: and/or Space After: boxes:

- For body text, enter a Space After: (slightly larger than the text font size) to separate the next paragraph from the current one.

- For headings, enter a value in the Space Before: box to place an extra area of blank space above the headings. This helps your headings to stand out from the rest of the text.

How·does·AutoSι document·and·ass that·contain·word scoring·sentences ¶ Keep·in·mind·that reports,·articles,·a ¶ How·does·AutoSι document·and·ass that·contain·word scoring·sentences	How·does·AutoSι document·and·ass that·contain·word scoring·sentences Keep·in·mind·that reports,·articles,·a How·does·AutoSι document·and·ass that·contain·word scoring·sentences

> **Inter-Paragraph Spacing**
> *The spacing between successive paragraphs of text.*

Another option for long documents is to set inter-paragraph spacing for body text to zero, and to use instead first line indenting as a way of indicating where each new paragraph begins. See the next topic.

First Line Indents

In Section 3.2 you learned how to indent a selected paragraph from the left and/or right margins of the page. Word also lets you indent the first line of a paragraph only, so that it is in a greater distance from the left margin than the other lines of the same paragraph.

Exercise 3.23: Creating a First Line Indent

Here you will use a first line indent to separate two paragraphs of body text.

1)   Select the second paragraph of your sample text.

2)   Choose **Format | Paragraph**.

3)   On the Indents and Spacing tab, in the Special: box, select First Line. In the By: box, enter a value of 1 cm. Click **OK**.

4)   Delete the extra paragraph mark above the indented paragraph. Your text should now look as below.

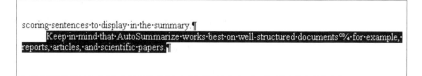

5)   Undo the first line indent change and paragraph mark deletion by choosing **Edit | Undo** twice. Word's Undo reverses formatting and text positioning operations as well as typing and editing. Also, replace the extra paragraph mark to separate the two paragraphs.

Your sample text should look as it was before this Exercise.

First Line Indent

The positioning of the first line of a paragraph a greater distance in from the left margin than the remaining lines of the same paragraph.

If using first line indents to separate paragraphs, set inter-paragraph spacing to zero or to just 1 or 2 points. Do not use first line indents for the first paragraph after a heading.

Hanging Indents

A hanging indent is where all the lines of a paragraph are indented – except the first one. Hanging indents are sometimes used for lists such as bibliographies. Below is an example.

> *The·Memoirs·of·James·II·*Translated·by·A.·Lytton·Sells·from·the·Bouillon· Manuscript.·Edited·and·collated·with·the·Clarke·Edition.·With·an· introduction·by·Sir·Arthur·Bryant.¶
>
> *The·History·of·England·from·the·Accession·of·James·II.*Lord·Macauley,·edited· by·Lady·Tevelyan.¶

Practise creating a hanging indent with the sample text by selecting a paragraph, choosing **Format | Paragraph**, selecting Hanging Indent from the Special: box, and entering a value in the By: box. Undo any changes that you make.

Hanging Indent

Where all the lines of a paragraph are indented – except the first one. Sometimes used for lists.

Finding Text

Need to locate quickly a particular word or phrase in a long document? Word's Find feature can take you straight to the text that you are looking for.

By default, Word searches the whole document. To limit the text that Word searches through, first select only that part of the document. When Word has finished searching the selected text, it asks whether you want to search the remainder of the document or not.

The Basics

Choose **Edit | Find** to display the Find and Replace dialog box.

In the Find what: box, type (or paste in from the Clipboard) the text you want to find, and choose **Find Next**.

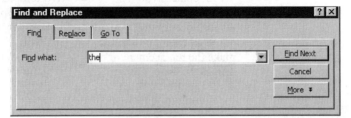

Word takes you to the first occurrence of the search text in your document. The dialog box stays open on your screen. Click **Find Next** to continue searching for further occurrences, or click **Cancel** to close the dialog box and end your search. Practise by searching for the word 'the' in your sample document.

Special Options

By default, Word finds parts of words as well as whole words. When you search for 'the', Word also finds 'then'. You can tell Word to find whole words only by clicking the **More** button, and then selecting the Find whole words only checkbox.

Another option is to select the Match case checkbox. So, for example, a search for 'The' does not find 'the' or 'THE'.

To find paragraph marks, tabs or other special or non-printing characters, choose the **Special** button and click on the relevant character.

Formats

You can tell Word to find only occurrences of text that is in a certain format. Click the **More** button, then the **Format** button, and select the formatting option that you require.

Finding and Replacing Text

Sometimes you will want to find and replace all occurrences of a word or phrase in a document with a different word or phrase. You might have misspelled a word consistently throughout a document, for example, or maybe you want to substitute 'person' for 'man' or 'woman'.

To replace text, choose **Edit | Replace**. On the Replace tab, enter the text you want to replace in the Find what: box, and the new text you want to substitute for the replaced text in the Replace with: box.

The Two Replace Methods

You are offered two options by the Replace tab of the Find and Replace dialog box.

- Word replaces your text one occurrence at a time. At each occurrence, you are asked whether you want to make the replacement or not. This is the 'safe' option.

- Word replaces all occurrences in a single operation. Use this option only if you are certain that you want to replace every instance of the text you are searching for!

Anything that you can locate with the Find command, you can replace with **Edit | Find and Replace** – including formatting, tabs and other special and non-printing characters.

Exercise 3.24: Finding and Replacing Text

In this Exercise you will practise finding and replacing text in your sample long document.

1) Look at the second of the two paragraphs that you pasted in from the online help text. Word pasted $^{o}\!\!\frac{3}{4}$ instead of a dash [-] after the word 'documents'.

2) Copy the following to the Clipboard: documents

3) Move the cursor to the start of the first line of the document. Choose **Edit | Replace**.

4) On the Replace tab, paste the copied text in the Find what: box.

5) Type this in the Replace with: box: documents -

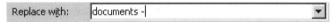

6) Choose the **Replace All** button.

Word performs the find-and-replace operation through the entire document. So much easier than correcting each occurrence of the error! Click **Close** to close the dialog box.

Exercise 3.25: Finding and Replacing Formatting

In this Exercise you will use Word's find and replace feature to reformat all occurrences of a heading in your sample long document.

1) Move the cursor to the start of the first line of the document. Choose **Edit | Replace**.

2) On the Replace tab, notice that the Find what: box still contains the text from Exercise 3.24. Click in the Find what: box, delete the previous text, and type the following: Heading One

3) Click in the Replace with: box, delete the text from the previous Exercise 3.24, and type the following: Heading One

4) Click the **More** button and then the **Format** button.

5) Select the **Font** option, and specify a Font of Arial, a Font Style of Bold, and a Font Size of 14. Then click **OK**.

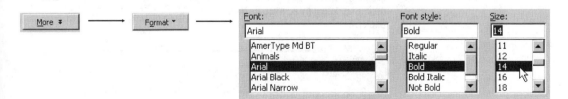

6) Click the **Replace All** button.

Word reformats every occurrence of the heading. Click **Close** to close the dialog box.

Exercise 3.26: Finding and Replacing Special Characters

In this Exercise you will remove the extra paragraph mark that separates the paragraphs of the sample text.

1) Move the cursor to the start of the first line of the document. Choose **Edit | Replace**.

2) On the Replace tab, click in the Find what: box and delete the text from Exercise 3.25.

3) With the cursor in the Find what: box, click the **Special** button and select Paragraph Mark from the pop-up menu. Click **Special** again and click Paragraph Mark.

   The Find what: box should contain Word's paragraph mark symbol twice (^ p ^ p).

4) Click in the Replace with box: and delete the text from Exercise 3.25. Also, click **No Formatting** to remove the formatting that you specified in Exercise 3.25.

5) With the cursor in the Replace with: box, click the **Special** button and select Paragraph Mark from the pop-up menu.

7) Click **Replace All**.

Word replaces all occurrences of two consecutive paragraph marks with a single paragraph mark. Click **Close** to close the dialog box.

Exercise 3.27: Finding and Replacing Text Positioning

In this Exercise you will apply a first line indent to all occurrences of the second paragraph of sample text.

1) Move the cursor to the start of the first line of the document. Choose **Edit | Replace**.

2) On the Replace tab, click in the Find what: box. Delete the text from Exercise 3.26 and type the first word of the second paragraph of the sample text: Keep

3) Click in the Replace with box:, delete the text from Exercise 3.26. and type the same word as in the Find what: box.

4) With the cursor still in the Replace with: box, click the **Format** button, then the **Paragraph** option, and specify a First Line Indent of 1 cm. Click **OK**.

5) Click **Replace All**.

Word indents the first line of every occurrence of the second paragraph. Click **Close** to close the dialog box. Your document should look like the sample shown below.

Heading·One¶
How·does·AutoSummarize·determine·what·the·key·points·are?·AutoSummarize·analyzes·the·
document·and·assigns·a·score·to·each·sentence.·(For·example,·it·gives·a·higher·score·to·sentences·
that·contain·words·used·frequently·in·the·document.)·You·then·choose·a·percentage·of·the·highest-
scoring·sentences·to·display·in·the·summary.¶
　　Keep·in·mind·that·AutoSummarize·works·best·on·well-structured·documents·-·for·example,·
reports,·articles,·and·scientific·papers.¶

You have completed the find-and-replace Exercises. Save your long document and leave it open.

Page Setup

You have learnt how to control where text appears on the printed page, using text alignment, indenting, inter-line spacing and inter-paragraph spacing.

But what about the page on which the text appears? What options does Word offer you?

Choose **File | Page Setup** to view the four tabs of page setup options. Only two of these tabs are relevant at this stage: Margins and Paper Size.

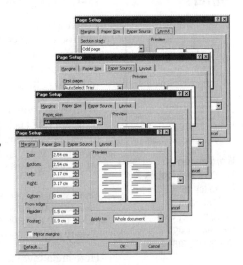

The four Page Setup tabs

The Margins Tab

Margins indicated by dashed lines

A margin is the distance that the text and graphics are positioned in from the edge of the printed page.

Word's default margin values – top and bottom, 1 inch (2.54 cm), left and right, 1.25 inches (3.17 cm) – are acceptable for most letters and business documents.

You can change the margins at any stage, and make your new values the new defaults by clicking the **Default** button.

Margin

The distance of the text and graphics from the edge of the printed page. Word lets you specify separate top, bottom, left and right margins.

For the Page size: box, accept the default of A4. This is the European standard paper size (21 cm wide and 29.7 cm high). A4 is used for almost all letters and other business documents.

> **A4**
>
> *The standard page size used for letters and most other business documents throughout Europe.*

Orientation is the direction in which the page is printed. Your options are Portrait ('standing up') and Landscape ('on its side'). Letters and most other business documents are printed in portrait.

Headers and Footers

Word places headers and footers in the top and bottom page margins, set with the File | Page Setup command

Headers and footers are pieces of text that appear on the top and bottom of every page of a document (except the title and contents pages).

Looking at examples of published documents, you will see that headers and footers typically contain such details as document title, organisation name, author name, and perhaps a version or draft number. Usually, headers and footers also contain page numbers. You will learn about page numbering in the next topic.

With Word, you need only type in header and/or footer text once, and the program repeats the text on every page. Any formatting that you can apply to text in your document – such as bold, italics, alignment, borders and shading – you can also apply to text in the headers and footers. You can also insert graphics, such as a company logo, in a header and footer.

> **Headers and Footers**
>
> *Standard text and graphics that are printed in the top and bottom margins of every page of a document.*

Here are a few facts about headers and footers in Word:

- You insert them with the **View | Headers and Footers** command.

- This command displays the header or footer area (surrounded by a dashed border), the document text (which you cannot edit when working with headers and footers), and a Header and Footer Toolbar (giving you quick access to the commonly used commands).

Word's header area with Toolbar

- Word positions the paragraph mark at the left of the header or footer area, ready for you to type text.

- Word inserts two preset tab stops to make it easy for you to centre-align or right-align headers or footers. Press TAB once to centre a header or footer, press TAB twice to line it up against the right margin.

Switch Between Header and Footer button

- Click the Switch between Header and Footer button to view the footer area when in the header area, and vice versa. The two areas are similar in appearance and operation.

- Place page numbers (discussed in the next topic) at the outside margin (left for left-hand side pages, right for right-hand pages) or at the centre of the header or footer area.

- Place text at the centre or at the inside margin of the header or footer area.

Exercise 3.28: Creating a Header
In this Exercise you will insert header text in your sample document.

1) Choose **File | Page Setup**, select the Layout tab, ensure that the Header and Footer checkboxes are as shown on the right, and click **OK**.

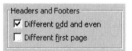

2) Choose **View | Header and Footer**. Word positions the paragraph mark at the left of the header area, ready for you to type text.

3) Type the following text: Annual Report

4) Click on the Show Next button on the Header and Footer Toolbar. Word takes you to the next page, the first even (left-hand) page of the document.

5) Press the TAB key twice to move the paragraph mark against the right-hand margin. Type the following text: ABC Limited

6) Click the **Close** button on the Header and Footer Toolbar.

Because you began this Exercise by selecting the Different odd and even: checkbox on **File | Setup**, Word allowed you to type separate headers for odd (right-hand) and even (left-hand) pages.

In the next Exercise you will place a border under the header text to help separate it from the main body of the document. You will also change the font and font size. Typically, the header font is 2 or 3 point sizes smaller than the body text. At that size, sans serif fonts such as Arial are easier to read than serif ones.

Apply a bottom border to the header text

Exercise 3.29: Formatting a Header

1) Choose **View | Header and Footer**.

2) Select the header text on the first page of your document.

3) Chose **Format | Font**, and select Arial, Regular, 8 point.

4) With the text still selected, choose **Format | Borders and Shading**.

5) On the Borders tab, select None for Setting:. Then, in the Preview area, select a bottom border. Select a Width: of 1 point, an Apply to: of Paragraph, and click **OK**.

6) Click on the Next page button on the Header and Footer Toolbar. Repeat steps 4 and 5 for the left-hand page.

7) Click the Close button on the Header and Footer Toolbar.

The top of your right-hand pages should now look as below.

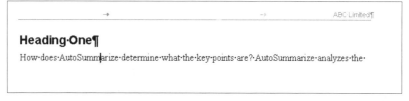

The top of your left-hand pages should now look as below.

Notice that the header text is 'greyed out', indicating that you cannot edit it when working with the main body of the document.

Page Numbering

You can insert a page number in the header or footer of a document. Word updates the page numbers as you add or remove document pages. The same formatting options are available for the page number as for header and footer text. You can align a page number at the left or right margin, or in the centre of the header or footer area.

Exercise 3.30: Inserting a Page Number

In this Exercise you will insert a centre-aligned page number in the footer of the document.

1) Choose **View | Headers and Footers**.

2) Display the footer area of the first page. Press TAB to move the cursor to the centre-aligned position.

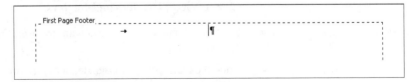

Insert Page Number button

3) Click the Insert Page Number Button on the Header and Footer Toolbar. Word inserts the page number and displays it against a grey background.

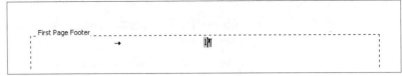

4) Click the Next button on the Header and Footer Toolbar to move to the second page, the first even (left-hand) page of your document.

5) Repeat steps 2 and 3 to insert the page number in the centre-aligned position.

6) Click the Close button on the Header and Footer Toolbar. Save the document.

Page Numbering Options

Format Page Number button

Click on the Format Page Number button on the Header and Footer Toolbar to display the page numbering options.

You can number the pages using numbers, letters, or Roman numerals. And you can start at a number other than one.

Document Date and Author Name

Word offers special features to make it easier for you to insert today's date and your name in a header or footer.

Document Creation Date

To insert today's date (as recorded on your computer) in a header or footer, follow these steps:

- Choose **View | Headers and Footers**.

- Position the cursor where you want to insert the current date.

- Click the Date button on the Header and Footer Toolbar.

Document Author Name

To insert the author's name (that is, your name), follow these steps:

- Choose **File | Properties**, and check that your name is displayed in the Author: box.

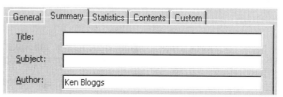

- Word displays in this box the user name entered when Windows was installed on your computer. If yours is not the name shown, delete the displayed name, type in your name and select **OK**.

- Choose **View | Headers and Footers**.

- Position the cursor in the header or footer area where you want to insert the author's name.

- Choose **Insert | Field** to display the Field dialog box.

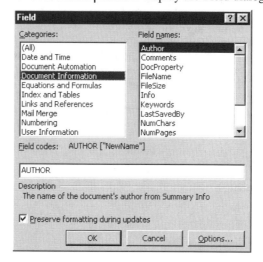

- In the Categories: list, select Document Information. In the Field names: list, select Author. Click **OK**.

Manual Line and Page Breaks

Pressing ENTER at any stage inserts a new paragraph mark, and causes Word to begin a new paragraph. To insert a line break within a paragraph, press SHIFT+ENTER.

Example of three line breaks

When text fills a page, Word automatically creates another page to hold the additional text.

You can insert a page break manually at any point in a document by pressing CTRL+ENTER. Alternatively, choose the **Insert | Breaks** command, select the Page break option, and click **OK**.

Word's Manual Page Break Indicator

¶

--Page Break--

Checking Your Spelling

How's your spelling? Word can check your spelling and suggest corrections to errors in two ways:

- As you type and edit your document (the automatic option).

- Whenever you choose the **Tools | Spelling and Grammar** command (the on-request option).

To turn the automatic spell-checking on or off, select or deselect the Check spelling as you type checkbox on the Spelling & Grammar tab of the Options dialog box. You display this dialog box with the **Tools | Options** command.

☑ Check spelling as you type

Spell Checking: The Automatic Option

As you type and edit, a wavy red line under words indicates possible spelling errors.

To correct an error, right-click the word with a wavy underline, and then select the correction you want on the pop-up menu.

Selecting the last menu option, Spelling, displays Word's Spelling dialog box.

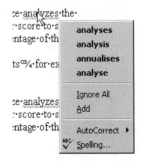

The Spell-Check Dialog Box

Whether automatic spell-checking is selected or not, you can spell check your document at any stage by choosing the **Tools | Spelling and Grammar** command.

If Word's spell-checker finds no errors, it displays a box telling you that the spell-check is complete.

If Word finds something it does not recognise, it displays the Spelling dialog box, and shows the relevant word in red.

The Spelling and Grammar dialog box includes a Suggestions area that offers likely alternatives to queried words. Click on any suggested word to substitute it for the incorrect one.

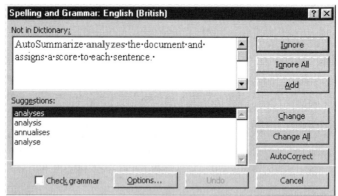

Whenever the spell-checker queries a word, your options include:

- **Ignore:** Leave this occurrence of the word unchanged.

- **Ignore All:** Leave this and all other occurrences of the word in the document unchanged.

- **Add:** Add the word to the spelling dictionary, so that Word will recognise it during future spell-checks of any document. Use this option for the names of people or places, or abbreviations or acronyms that you type regularly.

- **Change:** Correct this occurrence of the word, but prompt again on further occurrences.

- **Change All:** Correct this occurrence of the word – and all other occurrences without further prompting.

A word of caution: if the word that you have typed is correctly spelt but inappropriate – for example, 'their' instead of 'there'– your spell-checker will not detect it as an error. Therefore, you should always read over the final version of the document to ensure that it doesn't contain any errors.

Watch Your Language

Before spell-checking your documents, choose **Tools | Language | Set Language** to display the current dictionary language. If it is incorrect (perhaps US English instead of British), select your required language and choose **Default**.

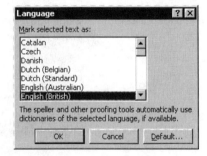

Checking Your Grammar

Word can check your grammar and suggest corrections to errors in two ways:

- As you type and edit your document (the automatic option).

- Whenever you choose the **Tools | Spelling and Grammar** command (the on-request option).

To turn automatic grammar-checking on or off, select or deselect the Check grammar as you type or the Check grammar with spelling checkbox on the Spelling & Grammar tab of the Options dialog box. You display this dialog box with the **Tools | Options** command.

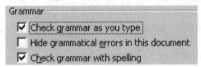

If automatic grammar-checking is turned on, a wavy green line under words indicates possible errors. You use Word's grammar checking features in the same way as its spell-checker.

Printing Options

Word offers a wide range of printing options. These include the ability to preview a document on your screen before you print it, and the choice of printing all your document, the current page, selected continuous or non-continuous pages, or the currently selected text.

Print Preview

This displays each page as it will appear when it is printed on paper. To preview your document:

- Choose **File | Print Preview** or click the Print Preview button on the Standard Toolbar. Click **Close** to return to your document.

When you choose **File | Print**, you have the following options regarding which pages of your document you may print:

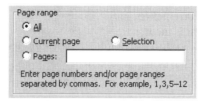

- **All:** Prints every page of your document.

- **Current Page:** Prints only the currently displayed page.

- **Selection:** Prints only the currently selected text (and/or graphic).

- **Pages:** To print any single page of your document, enter its page number here.

To print a group of continuous pages, enter the first and last page number of the group, separated by a dash. For example, 2-6 or 12-13.

To print a non-continuous group of pages, enter their individual page numbers, separated by commas. For example, 3,5,9 or 12,17,34. You can combine continuous with non-continuous page selections.

Other options on the Print dialog box allow you to specify how many copies you want to print of your selected pages, and indicate whether you want to print left or right pages only.

Save and close your long document, and close Microsoft Word. You have now completed Section 3.3 of the ECDL Word Processing Module.

Modifying the Toolbar

Word toolbars give you convenient, one-click access to the commands that you use most often. Too many toolbars, however, reduce the area on your screen in which you write and edit.

Hiding and Displaying Toolbars

You can display or hide any Word toolbars, according to your personal preference.

- To display a particular toolbar, choose **View | Toolbars** and select the toolbar that you want to display. On the toolbar sub-menu, Word displays a check mark against the toolbar that you have selected.

- To hide a particular toolbar, choose **View | Toolbars** and select the toolbar that you want to hide. On the toolbar sub-menu, Word removes the check mark from the toolbar.

The check marks beside the Standard and Formatting toolbars indicate that they are already selected for display on screen.

Hiding and Displaying Toolbar Buttons

You can remove one or more buttons from a toolbar. Follow these steps:

- Display the toolbar that you want to change.

- Hold down ALT key, and drag the button off the toolbar.

  Word removes the selected button from the toolbar.

Want the button back again? Follow this procedure:

- Display the toolbar.

- Choose **Tools | Customize.**

  Word displays the Customize dialog box. You do not need to use this dialog box, but it must remain open on your screen.

  Notice that any deleted buttons are again displayed on the toolbar.

- Right-click the button that you want to display again.

- From the pop-up menu displayed, choose **Reset.**

Word closes the Customize dialog box, and redisplays the button on the toolbar.

Section Summary: So Now You Know

You can increase or decrease Word's default *inter-line spacing* and *inter-paragraph spacing.*

You can highlight the start of each new paragraph by typing an extra paragraph mark (crude, but effective), by increasing inter-paragraph spacing, or by applying a *first line indent.* The opposite of a first-line indent is a *hanging indent,* which is sometimes used for lists.

Word's *find and replace* feature enables you quickly to locate a particular piece of text, and replace it with an alternative piece of text. You can also find and replace text with specific formatting, and special characters such as paragraph marks and tabs.

The standard page size is *A4,* and pages can be oriented in *portrait* or *landscape.* A *margin* is the distance of the text (and graphics) from a particular edge of the page.

Headers and footers are small text items that reoccur on every (or every second) page, and typically contain such details as the *document title* and *author name.* Either can also contain the automatically generated *page number.*

Word contains a *spell-checker* and a *grammar-checker.* You can set up these checkers so that they are permanently switched on, or you can run them only as you require.

Word's *print options* include a print preview feature and the ability to print one or a range of pages.

Section 3.4: Tables, Tabs and Graphics

On most Word documents, you want text to flow left to right across the width of the page. Sometimes, however, you may want to create narrow, side-by-side columns of text, numbers and graphics.

In this Section you will learn about Word's two options for creating such side-by-side columns: tables and tabs.

You will also discover how to insert and manipulate graphics and AutoShapes in Word.

Finally, you are introduced to hyphenation – a way of splitting long words across lines to improve the appearance of text.

New Skills

At the end of this Section you should be able to:

- Create and format tables

- Insert and edit tabs

- Paste and insert graphics

- Create AutoShapes

- Move, reshape and resize graphics and AutoShapes

- Apply automatic and manual hyphenation to text

New Words

At the end of this Section you should be able to explain the following terms:

- Table

- Tab

- AutoShape

- Hyphenation

Using Tables in Word

A table consists of rectangular cells, arranged in rows and columns. Inside cells, text wraps just as it does on a page. As you type text into a cell, the cell expands vertically to hold each new line.

You can create a new, blank table, and enter text and graphics in its empty cells. Or you can convert existing paragraphs of text to a table.

> **Table**
>
> *An array of cells arranged in rows and columns that can hold text and graphics.*

Exercise 3.31: Creating a New Table
In this Exercise you create a table, and enter text in it.

1) Open Word and click on the New button on the Standard Toolbar to create a new document. Click the Save button to save it. Give your new document a name that you will find easy to remember. If your initials are KB, for example, name it KBtable.doc.

2) Choose **Table | Insert Table**. In the Insert Table dialog box, select 2 columns and 4 rows, and click **OK**. You can add or remove columns and rows later, as required.

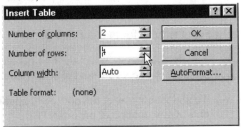

Accept the Column width default of Auto. This creates columns of equal size across the width of your page. Word displays a blank table as shown below.

¤	¤	¤
¤	¤	¤
¤	¤	¤
¤	¤	¤

3) Click in the top-left cell, and type: Sales Region

4) Press the TAB key. In a table, pressing TAB does not insert a tab stop. Instead, it moves the cursor to the next cell. SHIFT+TAB moves the cursor back to the previous cell. You can also use the ARROW keys or the mouse to move the cursor between different cells. (To insert a tab in a table, press CTRL+TAB.)

   With the cursor in the top-right cell, type the text: Number of Units Sold

5) Continue moving the cursor and typing text until your table looks like the one below.

Sales·Region¤	Number·of·Units·Sold¤	¤
Europe¤	1234¤	¤
Latin·America¤	5678¤	¤
China¤	4321¤	¤

Congratulations. You have created your first table in Word. Save your table document and leave it open.

Selecting Table Cells

You can format and align table text in the same way as text outside a table. Here are the rules on selecting table text:

- To select text in a cell, drag the mouse across the text.

- To select a single cell, click at the left edge of the cell.

- To select a row, double-click at the left edge of the leftmost cell.

- To select a column, use the mouse to move the cursor to the top edge of the column, wait for the cursor to change to a thick, downward arrow, and then click to select the column.

Number·of·Units·Sold¤	¤
1234¤	¤
5678¤	¤
4321¤	¤

- To select the entire table, click in any cell and choose **Table | Select Table**.

Table Operations

Here are the rules for making changes to a table:

- To add a new row, select the row *beneath* the position where you want to insert the new row, and choose **Table | Insert Rows**.

- To add a new row at the bottom of a table, select the last end-of-row mark and press ENTER.

- To add a new column, select the column to the *right* of where you want to insert the new column, and choose **Table | Insert Columns**.

- To add a new column at the right of a table, select all the end-of-row marks and choose **Table | Insert Column**.

- To delete a row or column, select it, and choose **Table | Delete Rows** or **Table | Delete Columns**.

- To merge two or more selected cells from the same row into a single cell, choose **Table | Merge Cells**.

- To split a single, selected cell into two cells on the same row, choose **Table | Split Cells**.

- To apply borders and shading, select the cells, rows, columns or entire table, and apply the **Format | Borders and Shading** command.

- To turn off a table's default borders (called *gridlines*) so that they appear only on the screen and not on the printout, select the table and choose **Table | Hide Gridlines**.

Exercise 3.32: Formatting and Changing Your Table

1) Select the top row of the table your created in Exercise 3.31, choose **Format | Font**, select Arial, 12 pt, Bold, and click **OK**.

2) With the top row still selected, click on the Centre Align button on the Formatting Toolbar.

Sales·Region¤	Number·of·Units·Sold¤	¤
Europe¤	1234¤	¤

3) Place the cursor in the cell that contains Latin America. Choose **Table | Insert Row**. Type the following text into the new row.

South·Africa¤	581¤	¤

4) Select the top row of the table, and choose **Table | Insert Row**.

5) With the new, inserted top row still selected, choose **Table | Merge Cells**.

6) Type the following text in the merged row: Sales Figures.

7) Select the top, merged row, choose **Format | Font**, select Arial, 14 pt, Bold and Italic, and click **OK**.

8) By default, Word places a 1/2 pt black, single solid-line border around each cell. Select the top row, choose **Format | Borders and Shading** and place a double-line border under the first row.

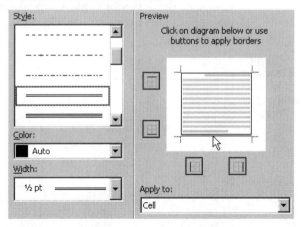

9) Select all rows except the top one, choose **Format | Borders and Shading**, click on the Shading tab, and select a 15% grey background.

Your table should look as shown.

Save your table document again and leave it open.

Sales·Figures¤	¤
Sales·Region¤	Number·of·Units·Sold¤
Europe¤	1234¤
South·Africa¤	581¤
Latin·America¤	5678¤
China¤	4321¤

Column Width, Spacing and Row Height

To change the width of a column, use the mouse to position the cursor over the left or right vertical edge of the column. Then drag with the mouse until the column is the width that you require.

As you make a column wider or narrower, Word adjusts the width of the other columns so that the overall table width stays the same. If you hold down the SHIFT key while dragging a column edge, Word changes the width of the whole table accordingly.

You can change the height of cells in a similar way.

The Table AutoFormat Option

Word's AutoFormat option offers a range of predefined formats for your table, including borders and shading. To apply AutoFormat, select your table and choose **Table | Table AutoFormat**. The Table AutoFormat dialog box offers a preview area where you can view the formatting effects on your table.

Some examples of Word's AutoFormat options

Practise by selecting your table and applying a series of AutoFormats. When finished, save and close your table document.

Introduction to Tabs

Old-style typewriters had a key called TAB that, when pressed, changed the position at which the letter keys struck the page and printed text. Typically, there were about ten tab positions – called tab stops – usually about half-an-inch apart.

Pressing the TAB key once advanced the text position to the first tab stop, pressing TAB again moved it to the second tab stop, and so on.

By typing text at the same tab position on successive lines, the typist could create vertical columns of text.

Tab stops used to position text in columns

1	2	3	4	5	6	7	8	9	10
	Cajun·Heat·Fries				£1.45				
	Onion·Rings				£1.65				
	Bread·Sticks				£1.25				
	Fried·Cheese·Ravioli				£2.75				
	Primo·Mozzarella·Poppers				£3.25				
	Cream·Cheese·Poppers				£3.95				
	Breaded·Mushrooms				£2.95				
	Breaded·Zucchini·Sticks				£2.75				

The example above shows the second tab stop used to position menu items, and the sixth tab stop used to position menu prices.

As computers and word-processing software replaced the typewriter, the idea of tabs continued. Computer keyboards include a TAB key, and Word, like other word-processing applications, offers a tab feature.

The effect of using tabs is similar to using tables: text appears in side-by-side columns rather than running continuously from the left to the right margin on the page.

Tabs
Predefined horizontal locations between the left and right page margins that determine where typed text is positioned. Using tabs on successive lines gives the effect of side-by-side columns of text.

If you want to position small amounts of text such as the address lines at the top of a letter, tabs are quicker to use than tables. Also, tabs have a feature called *leaders* that tables do not have, which can make it easier to read text that is separated into different columns.

Using Tabs in Word

To view the tab stops set up on your copy of Word, choose **Format | Tabs** to display the Tabs dialog box. By default, Word has 10 preset tab stops, each one of which is a half-inch apart.

Word's
default
tab stops in
centimetres
and inches

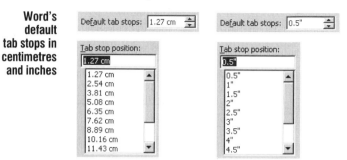

Exercise 3.33: Using Tab Stops

1) Open the letter that you created and saved in Section 3.1.

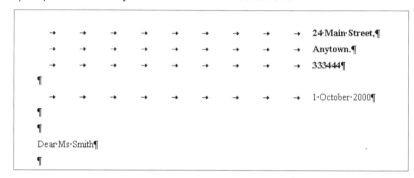

2) Move the cursor to the start of the first line and type: ABC Limited,

3) Move the cursor to the start of the second line and type: Unit 32A,

4) Move the cursor to the start of the third line and type: Smithstown Business Park.

   If your new text pushes any of the sender's address lines to the right or on to the next line, use the DELETE key to remove the tab stops from the line until that address line returns to its original position.

5) Your new text picks up the bold formatting of the sender's address. Change its formatting back to normal. Your letter should now look as below.

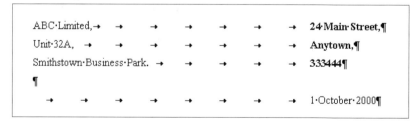

Save and close your letter document.

In the next Exercise you will use Word's tabs to create a restaurant menu.

Exercise 3.34: Creating a Restaurant Menu with Tabs

1) Open a new document and enter the following text:

> Cajun·Heat·Fries·£1.45·Primo·Mozzarella·Poppers·£3.25¶
> Onion·Rings·£1.65·Breaded·Zucchini·Sticks·£2.75¶
> Bread·Sticks·£1.25·Fried·Cheese·Ravioli·£2.75¶
> Cream·Cheese·Poppers·£3.95·Breaded·Mushrooms·£2.95¶

2) Are Word's tabs measured in centimetres or inches? Find out by choosing **Format | Tabs** to display the Tabs dialog box. Click **OK** to close the box.

   If inches, change the tabs to centimetres by choosing **Tools | Options**, selecting the General tab, and selecting centimetres.

3) On the first line of your document, position the cursor at the end of the word Fries, and press DELETE to remove the space between Fries and £1.45. Press TAB repeatedly to move the £1.45 rightwards to the 5.08 cm default tab stop.

4) Repeat step 3 for the remaining three lines. Your text should look as below.

> Cajun·Heat·Fries →   →   £1.45·Primo·Mozzarella·Poppers·£3.25¶
> Onion·Rings →   →   →   £1.65·Breaded·Zucchini·Sticks·£2.75¶
> Bread·Sticks →   →   →   £1.25·Fried·Cheese·Ravioli·£2.75¶
> Cream·Cheese·Poppers→   →   £3.95·Breaded·Mushrooms·£2.95¶

5) On the first line, position the cursor after £1.45, and press DELETE to remove the space before Primo. Press TAB twice to move the Primo Mozzarella Poppers rightwards to the 7.62 cm default tab stop.

6) Repeat step 5 for the remaining three lines.

7) On the first line, position the cursor after Poppers, and press DELETE to remove the space between Poppers and £3.25. Press TAB repeatedly to move the £3.25 rightwards to the 13.65 cm default tab stop.

8) Repeat step 7 for the remaining three lines. Your text should look as below.

> Cajun·Heat·Fries· →   →   £1.45→   →   Primo·Mozzarella·Poppers →   → £3.25¶
> Onion·Rings →   →   →   £1.65→   →   Breaded·Zucchini·Sticks   →   → £2.75¶
> Bread·Sticks →   →   →   £1.25→   →   Fried·Cheese·Ravioli →   →   → £2.75¶
> Cream·Cheese·Poppers→   →   £3.95→   →   Breaded·Mushrooms →   →   → £2.95¶

Save your document with a memorable name, and close it. If your initials are KB, for example, call it KBtabsmenu.doc.

Tab Alignment

The tabs you have used so far have all been left-aligned; that is, a tab stop of 5 cm means that the relevant text or number is positioned so that it begins 5 cm in from the left margin. Word offers three other tab alignment options:

- **Centred:** The tabbed text or number is positioned so that its centre is (say) 5 cm from the left margin.

- **Right-aligned:** The tabbed text or number is positioned so that it ends (say) 5 cm from the left margin.

- **Decimal:** If the tabbed item is a number that contains a decimal point, the number is positioned so that the decimal point is (say) 5 cm from the left margin.

  If the tabbed item is a number that does not contain a decimal point, or is text, a decimal tab stop has the same effect as a right-aligned tab.

In the next Exercise you will practise using all four tab stop types – left, right, centre and decimal.

Exercise 3.35: Using All Four Tab Alignment Types

1) Create a new document, and type the text and numbers as shown. Make the text 'Unit Cost' bold.

> Unit·Cost¶
> .853 ¶
> 621¶
> 45¶
> 26.82¶

2) In turn, select each of the five lines (but not the paragraph mark), and copy and paste it three times to its right. Your document should now look as shown below.

> Unit·CostUnit·CostUnit·CostUnit·Cost¶
> .853.853.853.853¶
> 621621621621¶
> 45454545¶
> 26.8226.8226.8226.82¶

3) Insert four tab stops on each line as shown below. (The tab positions are Word's default ones.)

> → Unit·Cost → Unit·Cost → Unit·Cost → Unit·Cost¶
> → .853 → .853 → .853 → .853¶
> → 621 → 621 → 621 → 621¶
> → 45 → 45 → 45 → 45¶
> → 26.82 → 26.82 → 26.82→26.82¶

4) Select the five lines of text, choose **Format | Tab**, and click **Clear All** to remove all the default tabs.

5) Set the following tab positions and alignments:

Tab stop position:	Alignment:
2 cm	Left
6 cm	Centre
10 cm	Right
13 cm	Decimal

In each case, type the
tab position, select the alignment, and click **Set**.

6) When finished, click **OK**. Your document should now look as shown.

→	Unit Cost	→	Unit Cost	→	Unit Cost	→	Unit Cost¶
→	.853	→	.853	→	.853	→	.853¶
→	621	→	621	→	621	→	621¶
→	45	→	45	→	45	→	45¶
→	26.82	→	26.82	→	26.82	→	26.82¶

Save your document with a memorable name, and close it. If your initials
are KB, for example, call it KBunitcost.doc.

Using Tabs with the Ruler

You can display and amend Word's default tab stops by choosing **View |
Ruler**. The ruler appears along the top of the document window. You can
see the default tab stops at evenly spaced positions along the base of the
ruler.

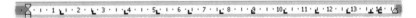

You can change the position of a tab stop by dragging it left or rightwards
to a new location on the ruler.

The space between all default tab stop changes proportionally. As you
drag a tab stop, Word displays a vertical, dashed line stretching down from
the tab ruler to the document itself.

L Left

⊥ Centre

⅃ Right

⅃. Decimal point types

At the left of the ruler you can
see the Tab Alignment button.
As you successively click this
button, it cycles through the four
possible tab alignment values:
left-aligned (default), centre-aligned,
right-aligned, and decimal
point-aligned.

**Tab Alignment
button**

To add a new tab stop, click the tab button to display the type of tab you
want, and then click the ruler where you want to place the tab. To remove
a tab stop, click on it and drag it to the right off the ruler.

Using Graphics in Word

You can illustrate your Word documents with graphics of various kinds. For example:

- Charts (graphs) created in a spreadsheet application such as Excel.

- Drawings and photographs created or manipulated in graphic applications such as Paint Shop Pro or Adobe Photoshop.

Also, Word contains sixteen categories of standard or so-called clip art images that you can use and reuse in a wide range of documents. Examples of clip art would be Man Answering Phone, Woman Sitting at Desk, Handshake, Sunset and so on. Clip art is available on CD-ROMs and on the Internet.

Clip Art
Standard or stock images that can be used and reused in a wide range of documents.

Importing Graphics: Two Options

You have two options for inserting graphics: copy-and-paste, and file insert. Let's look at these two in detail.

Graphics: Copy and Paste

This option is possible only if you can open the file containing the relevant graphic. To do so, you need to have installed on your computer a software application that can read that graphic format.

For example, to copy into Word a graphic created in Adobe Photoshop, you need Adobe Photoshop installed and open on your computer. Or, failing that, another graphics program capable of opening Adobe Photoshop (.psd) files.

When you have the graphic open in your graphics program, select it (or part of it, as you require), and choose **Edit | Copy** to copy it to the Clipboard. Then, switch to Word, position the cursor where you want the graphic to appear in your document, and choose **Edit | Paste**.

Graphics: File Insert

This option enables you to include a graphic in a Word document – even if you do not have installed the software package in which the graphic was created.

Position the cursor where you want the graphic to appear in your document, and choose **Insert | Picture | From File**. Locate the relevant graphic – it may be on your hard disk, on a diskette in the A: drive, or on a CD-ROM – and click **OK** to insert the image.

To include any of Word's own set of clip art images, choose the **Insert | File | Clip Art** command, select the clip art category, then the individual image, and click **Insert**.

Working With Graphics

There are a number of common operations that you can perform on imported graphics, regardless of their type.

Moving a Graphic

To move a graphic, first select it by clicking anywhere inside it. Next, hold down the mouse button. Word changes the cursor to a cross. Then drag the graphic to its new location.

To move a graphic between documents, use the **Cut** and **Paste** commands on the **Edit** menu.

Changing the Shape and Size of a Graphic

You can change the shape and size of a graphic by selecting it and clicking on any of its six handles.

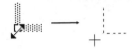

Hold down the mouse button and drag the edge of the graphic to change its shape. As you drag the object, Word changes its border to a dashed line.

To change a graphic's size but not its shape, hold down the SHIFT key as you drag with the mouse.

Exercise 3.36: Inserting a Word Clip Art Image

1) Open the poster document that you created in Section 3.2.

2) Position the cursor at the end of the last line, All Welcome. Press ENTER to insert a new paragraph mark.

3) With the cursor positioned at the new paragraph mark, choose **Insert | Picture | Clip Art**, select the Pictures tab, scroll down to display the Signs category, and click on it.

4) Click on the No Smoking symbol, and click **OK**. Word creates a new, second page, and inserts the clip art image on it.

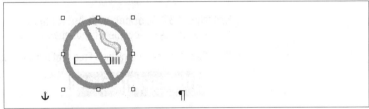

5) Select the graphic, reduce its size by a half, and drag it until it is under the All Welcome line. Delete the paragraph mark that you typed in step 2. The bottom of your poster should now look as shown below. Save your poster.

Inserting AutoShapes

AutoShapes are categories of ready-made shapes that you can insert in your Word documents. They include lines, basic shapes, flow-chart elements, stars and banners, and callouts.

When you insert an AutoShape in a document, you can reposition it, and change its size and colour, as required.

To select an AutoShape:

- Display Word's Drawing Toolbar by choosing **View | Toolbars | Drawing**.

- Click the AutoShapes button on the Drawing Toolbar.

You can then choose from the options offered by the pop-up menu.

AutoShapes

Categories of ready-made shapes, including lines, geometric shapes and flow-chart elements, which you can use in your Word documents.

When you right-click on an AutoShape, Word offers a number of options including:

- **Add Text:** This enables you to type characters inside the circle, square, oval or other AutoShape. You can also paste text from the Clipboard into an AutoShape.

- **Format AutoShape:** This enables you to change the border (edge) and fill (background) colours of the AutoShape.

- You move and resize AutoShapes in the same way that you can graphics.

Exercise 3.37 provides examples of creating AutoShapes and applying AutoShape features.

Exercise 3.37: Working with AutoShapes

1) If your poster document is not open after Exercise 3.36, open it now.

2) Select the text Admission Free (but not its accompanying paragraph mark).

Admission·Free¶

3) Cut the selected text from the poster to the Clipboard.

4) With the cursor positioned at the paragraph mark of the cut text, press ENTER to insert a second paragraph mark.

5) With the cursor positioned at the first of the two paragraph marks, choose **View | Toolbars**, and select the Drawing Toolbar option.

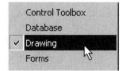

6) Click the AutoShapes button on the Drawing Toolbar. From the pop-up menu displayed, select Basic Shapes. Finally, select the Rounded Rectangle AutoShape.

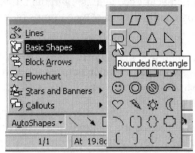

7) Draw the AutoShape so that it is big enough to hold the text in the Clipboard. Position it so that it is centered between the left and right page margins.

8) Right-click on the AutoShape, choose Add Text, and paste the text from the Clipboard to the AutoShape. Select the pasted text, and choose Centre-Align to centre it within the AutoShape. Make the text to Arial, 20 point, Bold.

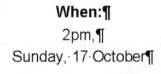

9) Click any edge of the AutoShape to select it, right-click to display the pop-up menu, and choose **Format AutoShape**.

On the Colours and Lines tab, select a Fill colour of Yellow.
Also, change the Line Weight to 1.5 pt.

10) Select the text within the AutoShape, and, using the **Format | Paragraph** command, change the Spacing Before until the text is centered vertically between the top and bottom edges of the AutoShape. The new poster layout should now look as below. Save and close your poster.

When:¶

2pm,¶

Sunday, 17 October¶

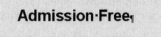

All Welcome¶

Save and close your poster document.

Hyphenating Justified Text

In Section 3.2 you learned about an alignment option called justification, whereby text is aligned against both the left and right margins. Justification is typically used for the narrow columns of text found in newspapers and magazines.

Justified columns can contain a lot of white (that is, blank) space, because Word spreads out the text in order to align it with both margins simultaneously. This is particularly true when the text contains a lot of long words.

Hyphenation – the process of breaking up long words and splitting them across two lines – gives justified text a more professional appearance. Consider the following two examples:

Hyphenation Off | Word spreads out the text in order to align it with both margins simultaneously. This is particularly true when the text contains a lot of long words.

Hyphenation On | Word spreads out the text in order to align it with both margins simultaneously. This is particularly true when the text contains a lot of long words.

Word applies two rules when hyphenating text: certain words are never hyphenated, and words that are hyphenated are split only in certain places. Word allows you to hyphenate both justified and unjustified text.

Hyphenation

The process of splitting a long word across two successive lines to avoid unsightly amounts of white space. Used mostly in narrow, justified columns of text.

You can hyphenate text in two ways: automatically or manually.

Automatic Hyphenation

Word can hyphenate your document automatically as you type. To use this option, choose **Tools | Language | Hyphenation**, select the Automatically hyphenate document checkbox, and click **OK**.

☑ Automatically hyphenate document

Automatic Hyphenation Options

If you select automatic hyphenation, Word offers you a number of options that let you control how it applies hyphenation to your document.

- **Text in Capitals:** Typically, only headings are in capitals, so you can decide to turn automatic hyphenation off for capitalised text.

- **Hyphenation Zone:** The amount of space that Word leaves between the end of the last word in a line and the right margin. It applies only to unjustified text. Make the zone wider to reduce the number of hyphens, or narrower to reduce the raggedness of the right margin.

- **Consecutive Hyphens:** The number of consecutive lines that Word hyphenates.

Manual Hyphenation

If you don't want Word to insert hyphens in your text automatically, ensure that the Automatically hyphenate document checkbox is deselected.

The better option is to turn automatic hyphenation off, and run manual hyphenation after you have finished writing, editing, adding and removing text.

Running Manual Hyphenation

To hyphenate your document (or a selected part of it) manually, choose **Tools | Language | Hyphenation** and click **Manual**.

Word scans through your text, and when it finds a word it thinks it should hyphenate, it displays a dialog box similar to the one below.

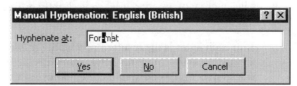

Click **Yes** if you want Word to insert a hyphen in the suggested location. If you prefer Word to insert the hyphen at a different location, move the cursor to that location, and then click **Yes**. Alternatively, click **No** to leave the word unbroken.

You can close any open documents and exit Microsoft Word. You have now completed Section 3.4 of the ECDL Word Processing Module.

Section Summary: So Now You Know

A Word *table* consists of rectangular cells arranged in rows and columns. As required, you can insert and delete rows and columns in a table, split a single cell into two cells, or merge multiple cells into a single cell.

You can also change row and column height and width, apply formatting, add borders and shading. Word's *AutoFormat* option provides a quick way to improve the appearance of any table.

Tabs are predefined horizontal locations that, when used on successive lines, give the appearance of columns. *Tab leaders* are dashed, dotted or continuous lines that draw the reader's eye from one tabbed column to the next.

You can add *graphics* to a Word document in two ways: by copy and paste, or by inserting the graphic as a file. You can move, reposition, resize or change the shape of any graphic.

AutoShapes are ready-made shapes that you can insert in your Word documents. They include lines, basic shapes, flow-chart elements, stars and banners, and callouts. You can manipulate AutoShapes in a similar way to graphics.

You can use Word's *hyphenation* feature to remove unsightly amounts of white space by splitting long words across successive lines. Hyphenation is applied mostly to narrow columns of justified text.

Section 3.5: Mail Merge and Templates

In This Section

Bulk mail is the name given to mass-produced letters that contain individual names and addresses (as in 'Dear Ms Murray') but have the same basic text (as in 'Allow us to introduce our Spring Promotion...'). A more commonly used term might be junk mail.

How is it done? Each letter is basically the same, but clearly no one letter is just a copy of another, as each is slightly different. Read this Section to find out.

Hint: each letter is the result of combining or *merging* two separate documents: one – the form letter – contains the basic text; the other – the data source – holds a list of names, addresses and other details.

Also in this Section you will learn about templates and styles. These are quick, convenient ways to create documents that can contain ready-made text, images, formatting and page settings.

New Skills

At the end of this Section you should be able to:

- Create the two components of a merged letter: the form letter and the data source

- Select the appropriate merge fields and insert them in a form letter

- Merge a form letter with a data source to produce a mail merge

- Explain the two possible roles of a Word template: document model, and interface controller

- Choose an appropriate Word template for a document type

- Explain the relationship between styles and templates, and apply styles to selected text

- Attach a different template to a document, and create a new template

- Apply Word's document views – normal, page layout and outline

New Words

At the end of this section you should be able to explain the following terms:

■ Form letter	■ Template
■ Data source	■ Style
■ Merge field	■ Normal view
■ Page layout view	■ Outline view

Mail Merge: the Components

Think of a mail merge as composed of two components: a *form letter* and a *data source*. And think of *merge fields* as the glue that binds the two together. Read on to discover what these three terms mean.

Form Letter

The form letter holds the text that *remains the same* in every letter – plus punctuation, spaces and perhaps graphics.

You never type the names or addresses in the form letter, because these will be different on each copy of the final, merged letter.

> **Form Letter**
> *A Word document containing information (text, spaces, punctuation and graphics) that remains the same in each copy of the merged letter.*

Data Source

The data source holds the information that *changes* for each copy of the final, merged letter – the names and addresses of the people that you want to send the merged letters to.

You can create a data source in Word, or in a spreadsheet (such as Excel) or database (such as Access). Whichever file type you use, its contents must be arranged in a table. Along the top row must be the titles identifying the information categories in the columns underneath, such as Title or Last Name.

> **Data Source**
> *A file containing information (such as names and addresses) that will be different in each merged copy of the final letter.*

Merge Fields

«FirstName»¶

«Title»·«LastName»,¶

«Company».¶

Merge fields are enclosed within double angle brackets.

In the merged letter, Word replaces the merge fields with the associated details from the data source.

The merge fields are special instructions that you insert in your form letter. They tell Word which details you want to merge from your data source, and where Word is to position them in your merged letter.

Merge fields have names such as Job Title, First Name and Town. When you merge the form letter and the data source, Word replaces the merge fields in the form letter with the associated details from the data source. For example, Word might replace the merge field called Town with Bristol, Carlisle or Derby on different copies of the merged letter.

> **Merge Field**
> *An instruction to Word to insert a particular type of information, such as job title or a line of an address, in a specified location on the form letter.*

Mail Merge: the Procedure

You can think of a mail merge as a five-step process. Steps one and two are about preparing the ingredients: the form letter and the data source.

In step three, you make the connection between the two by inserting the merge fields in your form letter – one merge field for every item of information that you want to merge to the form letter from the data source.

Step four is optional, but recommended. Before you produce your merged letters, take a preview of the first one or two to check that the merge worked successfully.

Finally in step five, print your merged letters.

One: Prepare Your Form Letter

This is simply a Word document. Using the **Tools | Mail Merge** command, you can do one of the following:

- Create a new letter specially for the merge operation.

- Select a letter you have already typed as the form letter.

Exercises 3.38 and 3.39 show you how to perform these steps.

Two: Prepare Your Data Source

Again, using the **Tools | Mail Merge** command, you can do one of the following:

- Create a new Word file and enter the names, addresses and other details of the people you plan to send the merged letter to

- Select a file created in another software application.

You will learn how to create a Word data source in Exercise 3.40.

Three: Insert Merge Fields in Your Form Letter

When you open your form letter on screen, Word displays a special Mail Merge Toolbar. One of its buttons is called Insert Merge Field. This is the one you use to select and then position the merge fields in your form letter. Exercise 3.41 shows you how to insert the merge field codes.

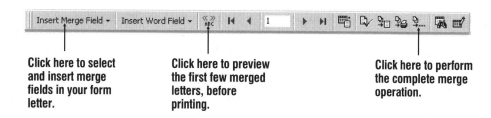

Click here to select and insert merge fields in your form letter.

Click here to preview the first few merged letters, before printing.

Click here to perform the complete merge operation.

Four: Preview Your Merged Letters

Before you produce your (perhaps hundreds or thousands!) of merged letters, click on the Toolbar's View Merged Data button to preview the first one or two merged letters.

You will learn how to preview your merged letters in Exercise 3.42.

Five: Print Your Merged Letters

If you are happy with the preview, click on the Mail Merge button to perform the complete merge operation. Select the **Merge to Printer** option to output copies of your merged letters.

You will learn how to print your merged letters in Exercise 3.43.

Word gives you the option of saving all the merged letters in a single file. You don't need to do this, because you can quickly recreate them at any stage by rerunning the merge operation.

Your Mail Merge Exercises

Exercises 3.38 to 3.43 take you, step-by-step, through a complete, worked example of a mail merge operation.

For these Exercises, we will assume that the merged letters are produced on pre-printed paper that already contains the sender's name and address. Only the recipients' names and addresses need therefore be inserted.

Exercise 3.38: Using an Existing Document as a Form Letter

Do you still have the letter you saved from Exercise 3.33? If so, this Exercise shows you how to use that text as a basis for your form letter.

If not, proceed to Exercise 3.39 to create a new form letter from scratch.

1) Open the file that you saved in Exercise 3.33 of Section 3.4.

2) Remove the recipient's name and address from the top left of the letter, and remove the sender's address from the top right. Also delete the 'Ms Smith' after the word 'Dear'.

3) At the top left, type 'To:' and press TAB. Insert three new lines, each with a tab stop, under the 'To:'. Your letter should look like that shown on the opposite page.

4) Choose **Tools | Mail Merge** to display the Mail Merge Helper dialog box.

5) In the Main document area, click the **Create** button to display a drop-down list of options.

From this list, select the option named **Form Letters**.

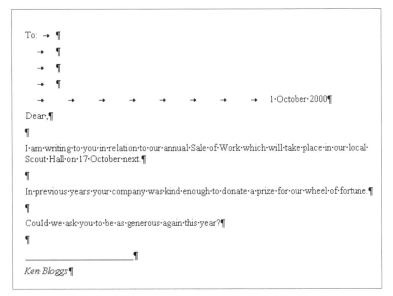

6) On the next dialog box displayed, click the **Active Window** button.

7) Word next displays a dialog box that asks you to select or create a data source. Proceed to Exercise 3.40.

Exercise 3.39: Creating a New Form Letter

Follow this Exercise to create a new form letter for a mail merge operation.

1) Choose **Tools | Mail Merge** to display the Mail Merge Helper dialog box.

2) In the Main Document area, choose the **Create** button to display a drop-down list of options.

From this list select the option called **Form Letters**.

3) On the next dialog box displayed, click the **New Main Document** button, and click **Cancel**.

4) Word leaves a new document open on your screen for you to enter the text of your form letter. Type the text as shown in Exercise 3.38.

5) Click the File Save button and give your new document a name that you will find easy to remember. If your initials are KB, for example, name it KBformlet.doc.

Proceed to Exercise 3.40.

Exercise 3.40: Creating a Data Source

In this Exercise you create your data source to contain the names, addresses and other information that will vary on each copy of the final, merged letter.

Do not begin this Exercise until you have completed either Exercise 3.38 or 3.39.

1) If the Mail Merge Helper dialog box is not already open, choose **Tools | Mail Merge** to display it.

2) In the Data source area, choose the **Get Data** button to display a drop-down list of options.

From this list, select the option called **Create Data Source**.

3) Word now displays the Create Data Source dialog box.

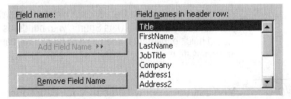

4) In the case of each of the following merge fields, click the field name in the list displayed then click the **Remove Field Name** button to delete them: JobTitle, City, State, PostalCode, Country, HomePhone and WorkPhone.

5) You now have all the merge fields that you need. Click **OK**.

6) Word next asks you to name and save your Data Source file. If your initials are KB, for example, name it KBDataSource and click **Save**.

7) You are now shown the dialog box below. Click **Edit Data Source**.

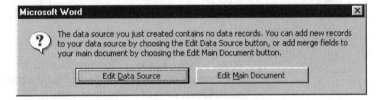

8) Word displays a Data Form dialog box. Enter the information as shown and click **Add New**.

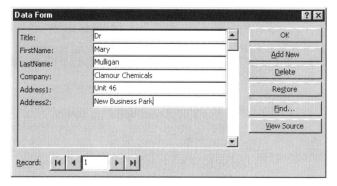

9) Enter a second set of details in the Data Form dialog box as shown below. Click **Add New** and then click **OK**.

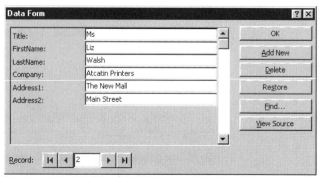

You have now created a Data Source with two records – enough for this Exercise. But you can easily imagine a Data Source with hundreds or thousands of records, each record holding the name, address and other information regarding a particular person or organisation.

Viewing Your Word Data Source

You can open, view and edit your data source file just as you can any other Word document. Open the data source you created in Exercise 3.40. It should look like the following:

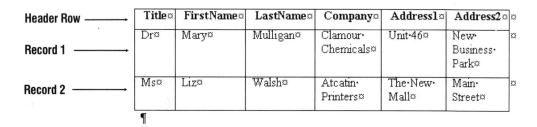

Title¤	FirstName¤	LastName¤	Company¤	Address1¤	Address2¤	¤
Dr¤	Mary¤	Mulligan¤	Clamour· Chemicals¤	Unit·46¤	New· Business· Park¤	¤
Ms¤	Liz¤	Walsh¤	Atcatin· Printers¤	The·New· Mall¤	Main· Street¤	¤

Header Row → (points to header row)
Record 1 → (points to Dr Mary row)
Record 2 → (points to Ms Liz row)

You can see a header row containing the merge field names such as FirstName and LastName. And under the header row are the records themselves, each in a row of its own.

Using Non-Word Data Sources

Does your data source have to be a Word document? No. You can also use files created in a spreadsheet such as Excel or a database such as Access. The only requirement is that the information is arranged in the same type of table format: a single, top row of merge field titles, followed by other rows holding individual records.

Inserting Merge Codes in Your Form Letter

Before you move on to the mail merge operation, you need to perform one more step. You must insert the merge field codes in your form letter. Exercise 3.41 shows you how.

Exercise 3.41: Inserting the Merge Field Codes

1) Open your form letter document.

2) For each merge field:

- Place the cursor in the appropriate position in your form letter

- Click the **Insert Merge Field** button on the Mail Merge Toolbar, and

- Click the relevant field title from the drop-down list.

Continue until your form letter looks like the sample shown.

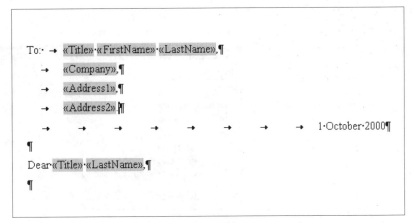

Do not forget to type spaces between merge fields just as you would between ordinary text. Also, type commas or full stops at the end of lines.

Save and name your form letter when finished.

Now everything is in place for the mail merge operation.

**View Merged
Data button**

Exercise 3.42: Previewing the Mail Merge

1) If your form letter is not already open, open it now and make it the active window.

2) Click the View Merged Data button on the Mail Merge Toolbar. Word displays the first merged letter. It should look as shown below.

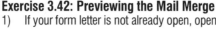

To: → Dr·Mary·Mulligan,¶

→ Clamour·Chemicals,¶

→ Unit·46,¶

→ New·Business·Park.¶

→   →   →   →   →   →   →   →   1·October·2000¶

¶

Dear·Dr·Mulligan,¶

¶

Arrow buttons

3) You can view the second merged letter by clicking the Forward Arrow button on the Mail Merge Toolbar.

You are now ready to perform the mail merge.

Exercise 3.43: Performing the Mail Merge

1) If your form letter is not already open, open it now and make it the active window.

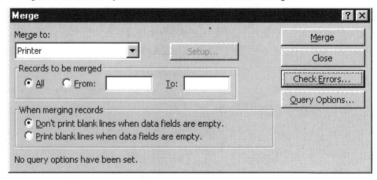

**Mail Merge
button**

2) Click on the Mail Merge button on the Mail Merge Toolbar to display the Merge dialog box. Select the options as shown below and click **Merge**.

3) Word now displays the Printer dialog box. Click **OK**. Your form letter and the two records from the data source are now merged to the printer.

Congratulations! You have performed your first mail merge in Word.

Merging Addresses to Labels

You can use Word's mail merge features to print a list of names and addresses (or any other list or structured information) on adhesive labels. Exercise 3.44 shows you how.

Exercise 3.44: Merging to Address Labels

1) Click New to open a new Word document.

2) Choose **Tools | Mail Merge.**

3) Click **Create**, select the Mailing Labels option, and then click the **Active Window** button.

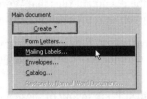

4) Click **Get Data** to select the source of the names and addresses that you want to use. Word offers the following options:

- **Create Data Source:** Select this to type the name and address information.

- **Open Data Source:** Select this to use an existing list of names and addresses that is contained in a Word document (or in a spreadsheet, database, or other list).

- **Use Address Book:** Select this to use names and addresses from an electronic address book such as that contained in Outlook Express.

For this Exercise, choose the **Open Data Source** option, and select the Word document that you created as a data source in Exercise 4.40.

5) Click **Set Up Main Document.**

In the Label Options dialog box, select the type of printer and the type of labels you want to use, and click **OK.**

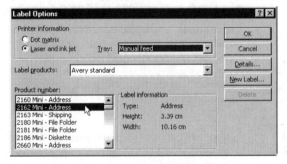

6) In the Create Labels dialog box, insert the merge fields for the address information.

7) In the Mail Merge Helper dialog box, click **Merge.**

8) In the Merge to box, click **Printer** to merge to the selected printer.

Well done! That completes your mail merge exercises.

Word Templates

Microsoft Word is made up of three components: the Word software application itself, the document files that Word produces, and a third component, which you now meet for the first time: templates.

- **Word Application:** This provides the standard Word menus, commands and toolbars – the things you use to create and work with documents.

- **Document Files:** Look in any of these and you will find the text, graphics, formatting, and settings such as margins and page layout for that particular document.

- **Word Templates:** These have two main purposes. They can:
    - Provide a model for creating documents
    - Control Word's interface: the menus, commands and toolbars available to the user.

A Template as a Document Model

A template can act as a document model by storing:

- Built-in text and graphics such as your company's name and logo. These are sometimes called 'boilerplate' text and graphics.

- Preset formatting (such as font settings) and text positioning (such as alignment, indents, tab stops, and inter-line and inter-paragraph spacing settings).

- Preset page settings (such as margins and page orientation).

For example, you could save everyone in your organisation time by creating a memo template that contained preset margins, the company logo, and text for standard headings such as 'Memo', 'To:' and 'From:'.

With much of the formatting and typing already done, users simply fill in the additional text.

A Template as an Interface Controller

A template can also store customised Word commands, menus and toolbar settings. This allows managers to remove unused and unnecessary features, and adapt Word to meet the needs of different levels of users.

For example, you could create a template that helped new Word users by displaying a customised toolbar with buttons and menus to lead them through everyday tasks.

Templates and Documents

Whether you realised it or not, every new Word document that you have created has been based on a template.

A single template can provide the basis for lots of documents. But each document can be based on only a single template at a time.

A template, like a document, is a Word file. Whereas document file names end in .doc template file names end in .dot.

The Normal.dot Template

Unless you choose otherwise, every new Word document you create is based on a template called Normal.dot.

In addition to this standard, all-purpose template, Word provides templates for specific document types such as letters, memos and reports.

> **Word Template**
>
> *A file that can contain ready-made text, formatting, page settings and interface controls. Every Word document is based on, and takes its characteristics from, a template of one kind or another.*

Templates and New Documents

In Section 3.1, you learned two ways to create a new document:

- Clicking on the New ⬜ button on the Standard Toolbar

- Choosing the **File | New** command.

If you click the New button, Word automatically bases your new document on the Normal.dot template.

Choose **File | New**, however, and Word presents you with a wide range of templates to choose from. You will find the various templates on different tabs of the New dialog box.

Exercise 3.45: Previewing Word's Templates

1) Choose **File | New** to display the New dialog box.

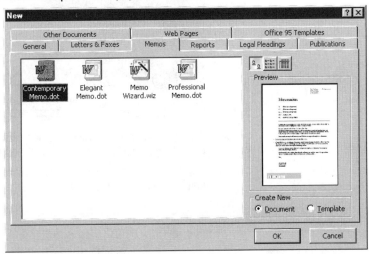

2) Click on the various tabs to view the available templates.

3) Click on the various templates to view a miniature of them in the Preview area on the right of the dialog box.

Templates and Styles

Style drop-down list box

At the top-left of the Standard Toolbar is a drop-down list box containing items called Normal, Heading 1, Heading 2 and so on. These items are termed styles.

For ECDL, you need to know only four things about *styles*:

- A style is a bundle of formatting and text positioning settings.

- You apply a style by first positioning the cursor in the text, and then clicking on that style from the drop-down list.

- Unless you choose otherwise, Word applies the style called Normal to all text you type in a document.

- Styles are linked to templates. For example, in one template the style called Heading 3 might be centre-aligned, Times, 10 point, italic. In another, Heading 3 might be left-aligned, Arial, 12 point, bold.

Exercise 3.46: Applying a Style to Text

In this Exercise you will open a document that you previously created and saved, and apply a style to its headings.

1) Open the document that you saved in Exercise 3.30 of Section 3.3.

2) Choose **Edit | Replace**, and on the Replace tab, type the text Heading One in both the Find what: and Replace with: boxes.

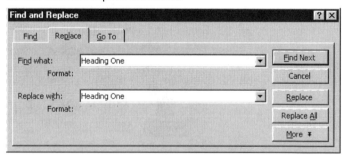

3) With the cursor in the Replace with: box, click the **More** button. Next, click the **No Formatting** button to remove the formatting left over from previous exercises.

4) Select the option **Style** from the pop-up menu, and then select the style Heading 1 from the list displayed. Click **OK**.

5) You are returned to the Find and Replace dialog box. Click **Replace All**.

Word now applies the style called Heading 1 to all the headings in your document. Unless you have at some stage changed the Heading 1 style that comes with Normal.dot, the Heading 1 font should be Arial 14 point, bold. Save the document.

Why Use Styles?

Using styles to control the appearance of a document has three advantages:

- You can apply a bundle of formatting and text positioning settings to a piece of selected text in a single, quick operation.

- By changing the settings of a particular style, Word can automatically apply your new settings to all occurrences of text in that style throughout the entire document.

  For example, by changing the Heading 1 style from bold to italic, all text with the Heading 1 style changes from bold to italic. This is so much faster than individually selecting and then changing every heading.

- If you change the template on which a document is based, the document takes its style settings from the new template.

You can therefore change the entire appearance of a document by linking it with a different template. Exercise 3.47 illustrates this point.

Style

A collection of formatting and positioning settings that you can apply to selected text in a single operation. Styles are linked to templates, and can have different settings in different templates.

Exercise 3.47: Attaching a Different Template to a Document

Professional Report.dot

1) If the document you worked with in Exercise 3.45 is not already open, open it now. Select all the text in the document, and chose **Edit | Copy** (or CTRL+c). You can now close that document.

2) Choose **File | New** to display the New dialog box. Click the Reports tab, and then click the template called Professional Report.dot. Finally, click **OK**.

3) Word opens a new document that is based on Professional Report.dot.

   This contains instructions which you can ignore. Hold down the CTRL key and click in the left margin to select everything in the new document, and then press DELETE to delete the new document's contents.

4) Choose **Edit | Paste** (or press CTRL+v) to paste the text copied from your document into the new document. Save and name your new document.

Heading·One¶

How·does·AutoSummarize·determine·what·the·key·points·are?·AutoSummarize· analyzes·the·document·and·assigns·a·score·to·each·sentence.·(For·example,·it·gives· a·higher·score·to·sentences·that·contain·words·used·frequently·in·the·document.)·You· then·choose·a·percentage·of·the·highest-scoring·sentences·to·display·in·the·summary.¶
Keep·in·mind·that·AutoSummarize·works·best·on·well-structured·documents·- for·example,·reports,·articles,·and·scientific·papers.¶

Notice how all text in your document with the Normal and Heading 1 styles changes in appearance. This is because such text is now taking its settings from the Professional

Report.dot template – and not from the Normal.dot template on which the document was originally based.

You can now close the document.

Creating a New Template

Word offers a number of ways of creating a new template. Here is the easiest way:

- Create a document that has the features you want in your template – some boilerplate text, perhaps, or a particular margin setting.

- With the document open on your screen, save it, not as a document, but as a template.

In future, whenever you use the **File | New** command to create a document, your new template appears as an option on the General tab of the New dialog box.

Exercise 3.48 takes you through an example of this procedure.

Exercise 3.48: Creating a New Template
1)   Create a new document and enter the following:

Bloggs·Limited·Monthly·Expenses·Report¶

Item		Amount	

Apply the following settings:

- Page Orientation: Use the Paper Size tab displayed by the **File | Page Setup** command to change the page orientation to Landscape.

- Heading: Centre-align the heading, and make it Times New Roman, 20 point.

- Table: Create a two-column, 19-row table. Select the table and, using the Row tab displayed by the **Table | Cell Height and Width** command, set the row height to 20 points.

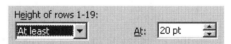

2) Choose **File | Save As**, and save the file as a template.

3) Choose **File | Close** to close your new template.

4) Choose File | New to display the General tab of the New dialog box, where you can see your new template as an option. Select your new template and then click OK.

   Word creates a new document based on your template. You can close the template.

Styles and Outline View

Using styles in your Word documents offers another advantage: it allows you to display documents in a way that reflects their structure. Such a structured view of a document is called an Outline view.

To switch to an Outline view, choose **Views | Outline**. An Outline view of a document that is formatted using styles would typically look as follows:

⊕ **This·is·Heading·One·Style¶**
    ▫ This·is·body·text·(in·Normal)¶
    ⊕ **This·is·a·Heading·Two·Style¶**
       ▫ This·is·body·text·(in·Normal)¶
⊕ **This·is·Heading·One·Style¶**
    ▫ This·is·body·text·(in·Normal)¶

In the above example, three styles are applied: Heading 1, Heading 2 and Normal (the default, used for body text).

Notice that Word progressively indents styled text according to its level of importance in the document, starting with Heading 1.

To change from the Outline view, choose the **Views** command and select the option **Normal** view or **Page Layout** view. These are explained in the next topic.

> **Outline View**
>
> *A view of a Word document that is formatted using styles. Outline view displays the structure of a document, with text indented progressively to reflect its level of importance.*

Other Document Views

The two most common document views in Word are Normal and Page Layout.

Normal View

Normal view is Word's default view for all new documents. It is the fastest view for typing, editing and scrolling. Any graphics or AutoShapes in the document are not displayed in this view. To switch to Normal view, choose **Views | Normal**.

> **Normal View**
>
> *A view of a Word document that displays only text.*

If you insert a graphic or an AutoShape in a document, Word automatically switches to Page Layout view. While it is necessary for manipulating graphics and AutoShapes, Page Layout view may slow down such tasks as typing, editing and scrolling. To switch to Page Layout view, choose **Views | Page Layout**.

If you are working with a long document that contains a small number of graphics or AutoShapes, you may want to switch to Normal view.

Page Layout View
A view of a Word document that displays any graphics or AutoShapes in that document.

You can close any open documents and exit Microsoft Word. You have now completed this Section 3.5 of the ECDL Word Processing Module.

Section Summary: So Now You Know

Mail merge is the process of combining a *form letter* (which holds the unchanging letter text) and a *data source* (which holds the names, addresses and other details that are different in every merged letter).

The *data source* can be created in Word, or in a spreadsheet (such as Excel) or database (such as Access). Whichever the file type, the data source contents must be arranged in a table. Along the top row must be the titles identifying the information categories in the columns underneath such as Title or Last Name.

Merge fields in the form letter indicate which details are taken from the data source, and where they are positioned on the final, merged letter.

A *template* can act as a *document model* by storing built-in text and graphics such as your company's name and logo, preset formatting, text positioning and page settings. A template can also act as an *interface controller* by specifying which of Word's menus, commands and toolbars are available to the user.

A *template,* like a document, is a Word file. Whereas document file names end in .doc, template file names end in .dot.

Unless you choose otherwise, every new Word document you create is based on a template called *Normal.dot*. Word also provides templates for specific document types. You can create new templates, and change the template on which a document is based.

Styles, which are linked to templates, enable you to apply a bundle of formatting and text positioning settings to selected text in a single, quick operation.

In *Outline* view, you can display the structure of a document that has been formatted using styles. Use *Normal* view to display only the text in a document, and *Page Layout* view to display both text and any graphics or AutoShapes that it may contain.

Section 3.6: File Formats and Importing Spreadsheet Data

In This Section

In this Section you will learn how Word 97, as with all other applications, uses a particular file format. You will also discover how to convert your documents into other, non-Word 97 file formats, so that they can be opened and read by people who work with applications other than Word 97.

Copying-and-pasting within and between Word documents was covered in previous Sections of this Word Processing Module. This Section takes you a step further, and shows you how to move data from a spreadsheet file to a word-processor document. As you will see, you can transfer the data in either of two ways: pasting or embedding.

New Skills

At the end of this Section you should be able to:

- Save Word 97 documents in the following file formats: earlier versions of Word, RTF, WordPerfect, Text-Only and HTML.

- Explain the difference between pasting and embedding spreadsheet data in Word.

- Paste spreadsheet data from Excel into a Word document.

- Embed spreadsheet data from Excel into a Word document.

New Words

At the end of this Section you should be able to explain the following term:

- File format

File Formats

In Section 3.2, you met the term *format*, where it referred to items that affect the appearance of text in a Word document – italics, colours, bullets, and so on. When used alongside the word 'file', however, format has another, different meaning.

In ECDL Module 1, you learnt how all information stored on a computer consists ultimately of just two characters: 1 and 0. This raises two questions:

- When you open a file, how are these 1s and 0s translated into the text and graphics you see on your computer screen?

- And, when you save a file, how are the text and graphics converted back to 1's and 0's on your computer?

The answer is that the application developers apply a set of rules that translate between the 1s and 0s and the displayed text and graphics. Such a set of rules is called a file format.

> **File Format**
> *A set of rules that translates 1s and 0s into text and graphics on computers screens and printouts, and vice versa.*

A Word file, for example, is said to be in Word file format, an Excel file in Excel file format, and so on.

Different Applications, Different File Formats

Different software companies, however, use different rules for translating 1s and 0s into the text and graphics on screens and printouts.

Moreover, different versions of the one application often use different file formats. The Microsoft Word 97 file format, for example, is different from the file format in the two previous versions of Word.

These different file formats, as you can imagine, can create problems.

- In one company's file format, for example, the characters 10101010 might translate as the letter 'w' in Arial, 12 point italics, positioned 5 cm from the left page margin.

- In another, the same characters of 10101010 might convert to a thick blue line running down the left-hand side of the page.

File Name Extensions

The format of a file is revealed by its three-letter file name extension, which the software application adds to the file name when the user saves the file.

The file name extension of .doc, for example, indicates a Word file, and .xls an Excel one. If you have worked with graphics files, you have probably met files with extensions such as .bmp, .gif and .jpg.

The file format used in pages on the World Wide Web is HTML, which stands for HyperText Markup Language. HTML file names typically end in .htm.

Word's File Format Options

Word 97 offers you the ability to save your documents in a format other than its own. This feature is very useful when you want to provide a file you have created to someone who uses a word processor other than Word 97.

To view the file formats in which you can save your Word 97 documents:

- Open a document.
- Choose **File | Save As**.
- Click on the arrow to the right of the Save as type: box.

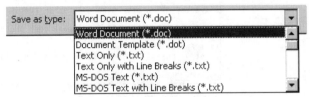

Only some of the listed options are relevant to this ECDL Word Processing Module.

Previous Word Version

To save your Word 97 document in a previous Word file format, select either Word 6.0/95 or Word 2.x for Windows. Both file formats have the same file name extension as Word 97 (.doc).

Saving a Word 97 file in an earlier file format may result in some adjustment or loss of formatting.

Rich Text Format

This is the common format of all Microsoft Office applications, including Word. A Word 97 document saved in this file format looks just like one saved in Word 97's own file format. The file name extension that is added is .rtf.

WordPerfect Format

Select from these options to save your document so that it can be opened and read within WordPerfect, another word processor application. Of the various WordPerfect options listed, the most commonly used is WordPerfect 5.x for Windows.

Converting a file from Word 97 to WordPerfect may result in some adjustment or loss of formatting. The file name extension of WordPerfect for Windows files is also .doc.

Text-Only Format

As its name suggests, this format saves only the text of a file. Any text formatting (such as bold or italics) or graphics contained in the Word 97 file are lost. The file name extension added is .txt. This format is also called plain-text or ASCII format.

Only two of the various plain-text options offered by Word are relevant:

- **Text-Only:** Each paragraph of the original Word document occupies a single line of the plain-text file, often resulting in very long lines of text that you can view only by scrolling horizontally.

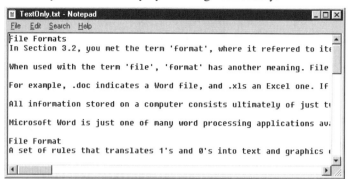

A Text-Only file, viewed in Notepad

- **Text-Only with Line Breaks:** A paragraph break is inserted everywhere a line ended in the original Word document, so that each line of the Word document becomes a separate paragraph in the plain-text file.

  The advantage of this file format is that line width remains the same as in the original Word document, so that the text is easier to read on screen.

  The disadvantage is that the plain-text file contains many more paragraph marks than the original Word file, and these can make editing the plain-text file awkward.

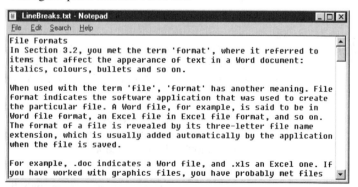

A Text-Only with Line Breaks file, viewed in Notepad

Because it is such a 'basic', no-frills format, plain-text files can be opened and read correctly by just about all software applications on virtually every type of computer. Plain-text is the file format most commonly used in electronic mail messages on the Internet.

HTML (Web) Format

Web pages are created using the HTML file format. The file name extension of this format is .htm (or, sometimes, .html).

You can save a Word 97 file in HTML format in either of two ways:

- Choose **File | Save As HTML**.

-or-

- Choose **File | Save As**, and select the HTML Document option.

You can display and print HTML format files with a Web browser application such as Microsoft Internet Explorer or Netscape Navigator.

Embedding or Pasting Spreadsheet Data

Microsoft Office applications (and most other Windows applications) allow you to transfer information between them. For this ECDL Module, you need only know how to insert data (text and numbers) into Word from the spreadsheet application, Microsoft Excel. In Excel, numbers and text are stored in little boxes called cells.

To transfer information from Excel to Word, follow these steps:

- Open the Excel file and select the required cells.
- Copy the selected Excel cells to the Clipboard.
- Open the Word file and insert the Excel cells in Word.

Pasting Special Options

The Word command you use for pasting Excel cells is **Edit | Paste Special**.

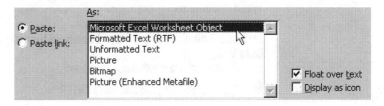

The Paste Special dialog box offers the following options:

- **Paste or Paste Link**: Leave this as the default of Paste.
- **Float Over Text/Display As Icon**: Leave this at its default of Float Over Text.
- **As:** Two options are relevant here: Formatted Text (RTF) and Microsoft Excel Worksheet Object. These options are explained in the next two topics.

When you insert with the Formatted Text (RTF) option, the inserted spreadsheet data:

- Becomes fully part of Word
- Is displayed as a Word table
- Can be edited within Word itself

Pasting Excel data into Word in this way is similar to pasting from another Word document.

Embedding from Excel

When you select with the Microsoft Excel Worksheet Object option, the inserted spreadsheet data:

- Is positioned within Word, but remains part of Excel
- Behaves like an imported graphic – it can be repositioned and resized by selecting and dragging
- Cannot be edited within Word

If you try to edit the spreadsheet data in any way, (to change a number, for example, or apply a different border style), Word's menu and toolbars disappear from your screen and are replaced by Excel's ones. Inserting data in this way brings with it the functionality of the application in which it was created. This is called *embedding*.

The following four Exercises demonstrate pasting and embedding from Excel to Word.

In Exercise 3.49, you create two copies of an identical Word document. In Exercise 3.50, you create the Excel data for inserting into Word. In Exercises 3.51 and 3.52 you embed and paste your Excel data in the two Word documents.

Exercise 3.49: Creating a Word Document that you can Embed and Paste Data into

1) Open Word and create a new document.

2) Type the following text and press ENTER twice:

First Quarter Sales Figures

3) Select the text and make it Arial, Bold Italic, 22 point. Centre-align the text.

4) Type the following text and press ENTER three times:

Congratulations Everyone!!!

5) Select the text you typed in step 4 and make it Times New Roman, Normal Italic, 24 point. Centre-align the text. Your document should now look as shown.

First·Quarter·Sales·Figures¶

¶

Congratulations·Everyone!!!¶

¶

6) Save and name the Word document. If your initials are KB, for example, save it as KBsalesfigures1.doc.

7) Choose **File | Save As** to resave your Word document – but this time save it under a different name. For example, KBsalesfigures2.doc.

8) Choose **File | Open** and re-open the first saved version of your Word document.

You now have two Word documents, with identical content, open on your screen.

Exercise 3.50: Creating an Excel Data Source File
1) Choose **Start | Programs | Microsoft Excel** to open a new Excel file on your screen.

2) Click on the cell at location C3, type the word January, and press ENTER.

	A	B	C	D	E
1					
2					
3			January		
4					
5					

3) Enter more text and numbers to Excel as shown below.

	A	B	C	D	E
1					
2			January	February	March
3		Product 1	213	345	698
4		Product 2	180	245	401
5		Product 3	270	389	528
6		Product 4	134	262	390
7		Product 5	90	145	310
8					

4) When finished, save the Excel file. If your initials are KB, for example, save it as KBsalesfigures.xls. Leave the Excel file open on your screen.

5) Click on cell B2 and hold down the mouse button. Drag rightwards and down to cell E8.

	A	B	C	D	E
1					
2			January	February	March
3		Product 1	213	345	698
4		Product 2	180	245	401
5		Product 3	270	389	528
6		Product 4	134	262	390
7		Product 5	90	145	310
8					

6) Choose **Edit | Copy** to copy the selected Excel cells to the Clipboard.

You may now close the Excel file, but, for Exercise 3.50 to work, you must *not* exit the Excel application.

Exercise 3.51: Embedding the Excel Data in Word

1) Use the **Windows | <Document Name>** command to display the first Word document that you saved (in this example, KBsalesfigures1.doc), and then click the last paragraph mark in that document.

2) Choose **Edit | Paste Special**, select the Microsoft Excel Worksheet Document option, and click **OK**.

   (The option is available *only* when the Excel application is open on your computer.)

   This embeds the Excel data from the Clipboard to the Word document.

3) Click on the bottom-right handle of the inserted data, and drag it until the inserted data is centered between the left and right page margins. Your Word document should now look like that shown.

You can work with the embedded data area just as you can with a graphic: you select it and reposition and resize it. You cannot edit it, however, at least not in Word.

To change the embedded data in any way – edit a number, delete a row, or add a coloured border – you must first double-click on it. This action causes Word's menus and toolbars to be replaced by Excel ones. Try it and see. Your screen should look as shown.

To return to Word, click anywhere on the Word document, outside the embedded spreadsheet area. Save your Word document.

You can now exit Excel. You do not need it open for Exercise 3.52.

Exercise 3.52: Pasting the Excel Data in Word

1) Use the **Windows | <Document Name>** command to display the second Word document that you saved (in this example, KBsalesfigures2.doc), and then click the last paragraph mark in that document.

2) Choose **Edit | Paste Special**, select the Formatted Text (RTF) option, and click **OK**.

   (The option is available whether Excel is open or not.)

   This pastes the Excel data from the Clipboard to the Word document. The spreadsheet cells have the format of a Word table.

3) Click anywhere in the table, choose **Table | Table Autoformat**, select the Classic 2 option, and click **OK**.

4) Drag the vertical edges of the column borders until the table is centered evenly between the left and right margins of the page.

5) With the cursor anywhere in the table, choose **Select | Table**. On the Formatting Toolbar, change the font size to 14 point.

   Your Word document should now look like that shown.

First·Quarter·Sales·Figures¶

¶

Congratulations·Everyone!!!¶

¶

	January¤	February¤	March¤
Product·1¤	213	345	698¤
Product·2¤	180	245	401¤
Product·3¤	270	389	528¤
Product·4¤	134	262	390¤
Product·5¤	90	145	310¤

Save your Word document. You have finished the embedding and pasting Exercises, and you can close both Word documents.

You have now completed the final Section of the ECDL Word Processing Module. Congratulations.

Section Summary: So Now You Know

A *file format* is a set of rules that translates between the 1s and 0s used by the computer to store information and the text and graphics displayed on screens and on printouts. Different applications – even different versions of the same application – can use different and incompatible file formats.

To help you share your files with others, Word 97 allows you to save your documents in a file format other than its own. The options include: earlier versions of Microsoft Word, RTF (the common Microsoft Office file format), WordPerfect (another word processor), and HTML (the Web page file format).

You can also save a Word document as a *text-only* file, so that it can be opened and read by virtually all applications on all types of computers. Any formatting or graphics in the Word document are lost, however.

You can insert spreadsheet data from Excel to Word in either of two ways: pasting or embedding.

Pasted data becomes fully part of the Word document: it is displayed as a Word table, and can be edited within Word itself. Inserting Excel data into Word in this way is similar to pasting from another Word document.

Embedded spreadsheet data, while positioned within the Word document, remains part of Excel: it behaves like an imported graphic and cannot be edited within Word. If you try to edit the spreadsheet data in any way, Word's menu and toolbars are replaced on screen by Excel's ones. Embedded data brings with it the functionality of the application in which it was created.

Module

4

Spreadsheets

Some things are easy to explain or describe – but difficult to use or operate. A spreadsheet is not one of those things. In fact, it's the very opposite.

At the end of this Module you will be able to build number-crunching, ECDL-exam-passing spreadsheets for recording, analysing and graphing just about any kind of numbers you can think of.

Quarterly sales commission, annual rainfall, or the monthly household budget: if you can count it now, you will be able to spreadsheet it later.

Along the way we will show you the shortcuts that will help you to get a lot of work done on long numbers, but with little typing, and in a very short time. But you will be no closer to being able to give a one-sentence definition of what exactly a spreadsheet is. Perhaps it's because spreadsheets are about processing numbers rather than words that makes them so hard to define.

Think of this Module as your chance to count rather than be counted. Good luck with it.

Section 4.1: Your First Steps in Excel

In This Section

'Why do I need to know all this ... What is the point ?' You may find yourself asking such questions when reading this Section.

But first lessons are like that – whether you are learning the guitar, karate or spreadsheets.

In your first hour you usually have the hard work of remembering new activities and words – but rarely the pleasure of putting your new knowledge into practice.

There is nothing in this Section that you will find difficult or complex. We have included only the material that you absolutely need to know, and we have introduced it as gently as possible.

Half-way through Section 4.2, when you discover the power and convenience of spreadsheets, you will be asking a very different question: 'How did I ever manage to organise my work or life without Microsoft Excel!'

New Skills

At the end of this Section you should be able to:

- Start and quit Excel

- Explain the difference between a worksheet and a workbook

- Create and name Excel worksheets

- Enter numbers, text and cell references in a worksheet

- Edit and delete the contents of a cell

- Use Excel's Undo feature to reverse commands and cell entries

- Save, name, open, create and close Excel workbooks

- Use Excel's online help

New Words

At the end of this Section you should be able to explain the following terms:

- Worksheet
- Workbook
- Cell
- Active Cell
- Row

- Column
- Cell Reference
- Name Box
- Dependent Cell

Starting Excel

To start Excel you can:

Double click on the Microsoft Excel icon
-or-
Choose **Start | Programs | Microsoft Excel**

Microsoft
Excel

Excel starts and displays a new workbook with three worksheets ready for you to use.

Worksheets and Workbooks

This ECDL Module is about spreadsheets. But Excel does not use the word spreadsheet. Instead, it uses two other words – worksheet and workbook. Let's explain what these mean.

Worksheet

A page that is made up of little boxes arranged in rows and columns. Relationships can be created between the cells so that changing the contents of one cell affects the contents of the related cells.

In Excel, a worksheet is a spreadsheet. A worksheet is much larger than your screen. You can see only a very small part of it at one time.

Workbook

A file containing worksheets.

When you create a new workbook, Excel creates three blank worksheets inside that workbook. Excel calls the worksheets Sheet1, Sheet2 and Sheet3.

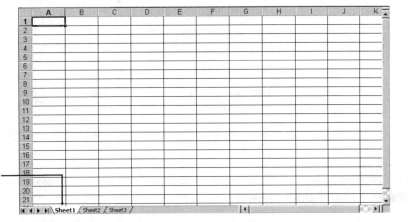

To move from one worksheet to another, click on the tab that displays its name.

An Excel worksheet

If three worksheets are not enough, you can add more to your workbook – up to a maximum of 256. Think of worksheets as pages in a book, and the workbook as the book containing those pages.

Now you will learn the names of the important parts of a worksheet.

Cells

The little boxes that make up a worksheet.

Cells are arranged in (horizontal) rows and (vertical) columns.

Active Cell

The cell in which the cursor is currently located.

Only one cell on a worksheet can be the active cell at any one time. You will always know which cell is the active cell: Excel surrounds it with a thicker border. You can make a cell active by clicking on it with the mouse.

The active cell   **A cell that is *not* the active cell**

A worksheet column

When you open a new workbook, Excel makes the top-left cell of the first worksheet, Sheet1, the active cell.

Column

A vertical line of cells from the top of the worksheet to the bottom.

Each worksheet contains 256 columns. Excel names each column with a letter or group of letters. The first 26 are named A to Z. The remainder are AA to AZ, BA to BZ, and continuing through to IA through to IZ.

Row

A horizontal line of cells that stretches left-to-right across a worksheet.

A worksheet row

Each worksheet contains 65,536 rows. Excel gives each row a number, from 1 to 65536.

The total number of cells in a worksheet is therefore 256 multiplied by 65,536 or 16,777,216!

Cell References and the Name Box

Each cell in a worksheet has a unique address or location known as its cell reference.

Cell Reference

The location or 'address' of a cell on a worksheet.

A cell reference is made up of two parts:

- The column letter (A, B, C, ...)
- The row number (1,2,3, ...)

When you open a new workbook in Excel, the active cell is the one on Sheet1 with the cell reference A1.

    ECDL: Module 4

Remember: column letter first, row number second. For example, B6, C8 and J12.

Column Letters: Upper or Lower Case?

You will always see cell references written with the column letters in upper-case letters (for example, A1, B10 and W90) rather than in lower-case ones (for example, a1, b10 and w90). This is true for Excel's online help – and this book.

However, when you type a cell reference into Excel, as you will in Exercise 4.1, it does not matter whether you type the column letter in upper or lower case. Excel accepts either. You may find it easier to enter column letters in lower case, because you need to type only the letter key, and not the letter key in combination with the SHIFT key.

Name Box

The rectangular area above the top-left corner of a worksheet in which Excel displays the cell reference of the active cell.

Name Box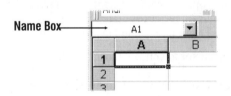

You can use the Name Box to move the cursor to any cell on the worksheet, making that cell the active cell.

To do so, type the cell reference in the Name Box and press ENTER.

Exercise 4.1: Name Box and Cell References

Perform this exercise to learn how to enter a cell reference in the Name Box.

1) Click in the Name Box.

2) Type B2 and press ENTER.

Excel responds by making cell B2 the active cell.

As further practice, repeat these two steps for the following cells: D8, A3, H5 and I19.

Entering Numbers in Cells

When you type something into a cell and press ENTER, Excel looks at your entry and asks:

- Is this a number?
- Is this text?
- Is this a cell reference?
- Is this a calculation?

Excel treats each type of entry in a different way. In this Section, you will deal with entering numbers, text and cell references.

Excel accepts two kinds of calculations: formulas (you will learn about these in Section 4.2) and functions (covered in Section 4.3).

Exercise 4.2: Entering a Number in a Cell

1) Click on B3, making it the active cell.

2) Type the number 1274.   3) Press ENTER.

	A	B
1		
2		
3		1274
4		

	A	B
1		
2		
3		1274
4		

Why Does Excel Right-Align Numbers?

In Exercise 4.2, Excel did two things after you pressed ENTER.

- It moved 1274 from the left of cell B3 to the right.

  This is because Excel assumes that you will want to perform addition or other arithmetical operational on the entered number. When you write a list of numbers on paper to add them, you line up the numbers from the right. Excel right-aligns numbers for the same reason.

- It moved down the cursor to cell B4, the cell under B3.

  Again, this is because of arithmetic. Excel assumes that you will want to enter another number under the previous one.

Entering Text in a Cell

You can enter text in a worksheet as well as numbers. By using text to identify the meaning or source of numbers, you make your worksheet easier to read and understand.

Exercise 4.3: Entering Text in a Cell

1) Click on B2, making it the active cell.

2) Type the word: Add.

3) Press ENTER.

	A	B
1		
2		Add
3		1274
4		

Notice how Excel responded after you pressed ENTER.

- 'Add' remained in the left of the cell B2.
  While Excel right-aligns numbers, it left-aligns text.

- It moved the cursor down to cell B3, the cell under B2.
  Excel assumes that this is the next cell you will want to use.

Text that describes a number on a worksheet is known as a label.

Label
A piece of text in a worksheet cell that provides information about the number in an accompanying cell, usually either below it or to its right.

Entering a Cell Reference in a Cell

The Equal To key is located to the left of the Backspace key.

Another type of entry you can make in a cell is a cell reference – that is, the address of another cell – preceded by the equals sign (=). When you do so, Excel reproduces the content of the other cell to the active cell.

Exercise 4.4: Entering a Cell Reference in a Cell

1)   If B3 does not contain the number 1274 from Exercise 4.2, enter it now.

2)   Click on cell B10, type the following, and press ENTER:

=B3

That is, an 'equal to' sign (=) followed by cell reference B3.

Excel responds by displaying the current content of B3 (that is, number 1274) in B10.

The ARROW Keys

So far you have used the mouse and the Name Box to move the cursor around the worksheet.

Another way of moving the cursor is by pressing the ARROW keys. You may find this method faster than moving and clicking the mouse, because you need not take either hand away from the keyboard.

Editing the Content of a Cell

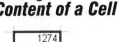

Sometimes, you will want to change the content of a cell. Exercise 4.5 shows how you how.

Exercise 4.5: Editing the Content of a Cell

1)   Double-click on B3.

Excel makes the cell border thinner and displays a blinking cursor in the cell. (The location of the cursor within the cell depends on which part of the cell you double-clicked on.)

2)   Using the ARROW keys, move the blinking cursor to the left of the 4.

3)   Press DELETE once, deleting the 4.

4)   Type 5.

5)   Press ENTER.

This moves the cursor out of B3 and down to B4. Excel has replaced 1274 with 1275. Notice that the number in B10 also changes.

Dependent Cells

Cell B10 is an example of a dependent cell – a cell whose content depends on the content of another cell. In this case, the other cell is B3.

When B3 changed from 1274 to 1275, so too did B10. That is because B10 contains the cell reference of =B3.

As you will learn in later Sections of this Module, cell relationships are the basis of spreadsheets.

	A	B
1		
2		Add
3	**Content**	1275
4	**of B10**	
5	**depends**	
6	**on**	
7	**content**	
8	**of B3**	
9		
10		1275
11		

F2: Excel's EDIT Key

In Exercise 4.5, you double-clicked on cell B3. This made the cell editable – that is, you were able to move the cursor within the cell and change the cell content.

When a cell is already the active cell, you can make it editable by pressing F2. This is Excel's EDIT key. You may find this method faster than double-clicking with the mouse.

Deleting the Content of a Cell

Want to delete a number, text or cell reference from a cell? The following exercise shows you how.

Exercise 4.6: Deleting the Content of a Cell
1) Move the cursor to cell B10. Because of the steps taken in Exercises 4.4 and 4.5, B10 contains the cell reference =B3 and displays the number 1275.

2) Press BACKSPACE or DELETE.

Excel removes the content of the cell. B10 is now empty.

Deleting and the ENTER Key

When you enter something into a cell, you must press ENTER to confirm the new content of the cell. Similarly, when you edit a cell, Excel makes the change only after you press ENTER.

When deleting a cell's content, however, you do not need to press ENTER to confirm the deletion. Just pressing BACKSPACE or DELETE is enough.

Deleting Cell Content – Not the Cell

Another way to delete the content of a cell is to right-click on the cell and choose **Clear Contents** from the pop-up menu.

Do not choose **Delete** from this pop-up menu. This command not only deletes the cell contents – it also removes the cell itself from the worksheet! As a result, other cells must change their position to fill the space left empty.

Standard and Formatting Toolbars

Standard Toolbar

Only two of Excel's toolbars are relevant to this ECDL Module: the Standard Toolbar and the Formatting Toolbar.

The Standard Toolbar includes buttons for managing files and working with numbers in cells.

Formatting Toolbar

The Formatting Toolbar includes buttons for changing the appearance of text and numbers in cells.

Rather than introduce all these buttons at once, we will explain the ones you need to know about as they become relevant through the remainder of this ECDL Spreadsheet Module.

Working with Toolbars

You can display or hide Excel's various toolbars by choosing the **View | Toolbars** command, and then selecting or deselecting the various toolbar options from the drop-down menu displayed.

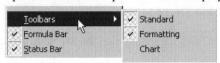

Excel's Undo

Enter the wrong data? Press the wrong key? Don't panic. Excel allows you to undo your most recent cell entry or action if it has produced unwanted results. To undo a cell entry or action:

Choose **Edit | Undo.**
-or-
Click the Undo ↰ button on the Standard Toolbar.

Click the arrow to view actions that you can Undo

Pressing Undo repeatedly reverses your last series of actions. To view a list of recent actions that you can undo, click the arrow at the right of the Undo button. If you undo an action and then change your mind, click the Redo ↱ button (to the right of the Undo button).

Exercise 4.7: Using the Undo Feature
Perform this Exercise to practise using Excel's Undo feature.

1) Click on cell B2, and press DELETE.

2) Click on cell B3, and press DELETE.

Everything that you entered in the worksheet is now deleted! But you can use Undo to get it all back by reversing your two delete actions.

3) Click the Undo button.

    This reverses your most recent action (in step 2 above).
    B3 again contains the number 1275.

4) Click Undo a second time.

    This reverses your second most recent action (step 1 above).
    B2 again contains the word Add.

Working with Excel Workbooks

An Excel workbook is a file containing a collection of worksheets. The file names of Excel workbooks end in .xls. This helps you to distinguish Excel files from other file types, such as Word files (ending in .doc).

Saving Your Workbook

In Excel, as in other applications, always save your work as you go along. Don't wait until you are finished! To save a workbook:

Choose **File | Save**.
-or-
Click the Save 💾 button on the Standard Toolbar.

The first time that you save a workbook file, Excel asks you to give the file a name. Exercise 4.8 shows you how.

Exercise 4.8: Saving and Naming a New Workbook

1) Sheet1 of your workbook should contain the word 'Add' in cell B2 and the number 1275 in cell B3, as entered in this Section's Exercises.

    If not, enter that data now.

2) Choose **File | Save** or click the Save icon on the Standard Toolbar. Excel displays a dialog box with two boxes similar to the ones shown below.

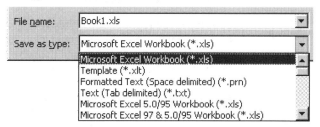

3) By default, Excel names the first workbook file you open and save as Book1.xls. Replace this file name with something that you will find easier to remember and recognise – such as your own name – and click the **Save** button.

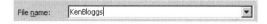

    Excel adds the file name extension of .xls automatically. You need not type it.

Creating a New Workbook

To create a new workbook file:

Choose **File | New**
-or-
Click the New 🗋 button on the Standard Toolbar.

Opening an Existing Workbook

To open an existing workbook file:

Choose **File | Open**
-or-
Click the Open  button on the Standard Toolbar. Select the file you want from the dialog box.

Closing a Workbook

To close a workbook file:

Choose **File | Close**
-or-
Click the Close button on the workbook window.

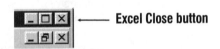 ——— **Workbook Close button**

If you have made changes to your workbook since you last saved it, Excel prompts you to save the changes before it closes the file.

Exercise 4.9: Closing and Reopening a Saved Workbook
In this Exercise you will close and then reopen the workbook you saved in Exercise 4.8.

1) Choose **File | Close** or click the Workbook Close button at the top-right of the workbook window.

2) Choose **File | Open** or click the Open button on the Standard Toolbar to display the File Open dialog box. Locate your workbook and open it.

Quitting Excel

To leave Excel:

Choose **File | Exit**
-or-
Click the Close button on the Excel window.

——— **Excel Close button**

If you have left open any files containing unsaved work, Excel prompts you to save them.

Online Help

Like Word, Access, PowerPoint and other Microsoft Office applications, Excel offers a searchable online help system:

- The 'help' in online help means that the information is there to assist you understand and use Excel.

- The 'online' means that the material is presented on the computer screen rather than as a traditional printed manual.

You can search through and read online help in two ways: from the Help menu, or from dialog boxes.

Using Help Menu Options

Choose **Help | Contents and Index** to display the three tabs of the Help Topics dialog box. These are explained below:

Contents Tab

This offers short descriptions of Excel's main features.

📖 Where you see a heading with a book symbol, double-click to view the related sub-headings.

❓ Double-click on a question mark symbol to read the help text.

🔲 Click a Show me arrow for Excel to demonstrate how to perform a particular action.

⏩ Click a double-arrow to view step-by-step instructions.

Index Tab

Reading the material displayed on this tab is like looking through the index of a printed book.

Just type the first letters of the word or phrase you are interested in.

Excel responds by displaying all matches from the online help in the lower half of the dialog box.

When you find the index entry that you are looking for, click the **Display** button.

Find Tab

Can't find what you are looking for in the Contents or Index tabs? Try this tab.

When you type a word or phrase, Excel performs a deeper search of the online help.

Word also displays some related words to help you narrow your search.

When you find the item you are looking for, double-click on it to display it.

As you search through and read online help topics, you will see the following buttons at the top of the online help window:

- **Help Topics:** Click this to return to the Contents tab.

- **Back:** Click this to return to the previous help topic.

- **Options:** Click this to perform such actions as copying the online help text to a document, or printing it on your printer.

Using Help from Dialog Boxes

You can also access online help directly from a dialog box, as Exercise 4.10 demonstrates.

Exercise 4.10: Using Online Help in a Dialog Box

1) Choose **View | Zoom** to display the Zoom dialog box.

2) Click on the question mark symbol near the top-right of the dialog box. Excel displays a question mark to the right of the cursor.

3) Move the mouse down and left, and click on the Custom option.

4) Excel displays online help text that tells you about the Custom option.

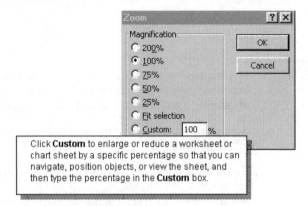

Practise this Exercise with other dialog boxes in Excel.

When finished, you can close your workbook and Excel. You have now completed Section 4.1 of the ECDL Spreadsheet Module.

Section Summary: So Now You Know

An Excel *workbook* is a file containing spreadsheets, which Excel calls *worksheets*. Workbook file names end in *.xls*.

A worksheet is made up of *cells*, arranged in *columns* and *rows*. Each cell has a unique *cell reference*, consisting of its column letter and row number. For example, B3 and G47.

Only one cell is the *active cell* at any one time. You make a cell active by moving the cursor to it, using the mouse, ARROW keys or *Name Box*.

You can enter a number, text (to *label* a number) or a cell reference to any cell. Press ENTER to confirm your entry. Excel *left-aligns text* but *right-aligns numbers*.

To *edit* a cell, first make it editable. You do so by double-clicking it with the mouse. Alternatively, make it the active cell and then press Excel's EDIT key, F2.

You can *delete* the content of the active cell (but not the cell itself) by pressing DELETE or BACKSPACE.

Excel's *Undo* feature, available from a button on the Standard Toolbar, allows you to reverse your recent cell entries or actions if they have produced unwanted results.

You can hide and display Excel's various *toolbars*. The two most commonly used are the Standard and Formatting Toolbars.

Excel's online help system, available from the Help menu and from individual dialog boxes, provides a comprehensive and searchable guide to the program's features and procedures.

Section 4.2: Arithmetic with Excel

In This Section

Prepare to be impressed. In Section 4.1 you learnt the names for the important parts of an Excel worksheet, and practised the simple operations of entering numbers, text and cell references in cells.

Now you have the basics you need to discover the power of spreadsheets in this Section.

You will quickly discover why people who work with numbers – such as accountants, statisticians, engineers and project managers – rely on spreadsheets to perform tedious calculations quickly, easily and accurately.

In the practical Exercises you will use fewer than a dozen numbers. These simple examples differ from the multi-page financial reports of a large corporation in size only. The principles are the same. Learn the principles here in Section 4.2 and you will never meet an amount of data too large or too complex for you to master with your spreadsheet skills.

New Skills

At the end of this Section you should be able to:

- Explain what an Excel formula is, and name its components
- Use Excel formulas to add, subtract, multiply and divide numbers
- Apply the rules of arithmetic to calculations in Excel
- Recognise Excel error messages
- Use Excel's Zoom feature to enlarge and reduce worksheet displays
- Save a workbook to a diskette

New Words

At the end of this Section you should be able to explain the following terms:

- Formula
- Argument
- Calculated cell
- Operator
- Non-adjacent cells
- Constant

Formulas in Excel

In Section 4.1 you learnt how to enter numbers, text and cell references to worksheet cells. Now it's time to discover a fourth type of cell entry, called a calculation.

Calculations are the reason that you enter numbers to cells, because calculations enable you to perform arithmetic – addition, subtraction, multiplication and division – on your entered numbers.

Excel accepts two kinds of calculations: formulas and functions. This Section 4.2 shows you how to perform calculations using formulas. You will learn about functions in Section 4.3.

Exercise 4.11: Adding Two Numbers with an Excel Formula

1) Open the workbook that you saved in Exercise 4.8. If cells B2 and B3 do not contain the word Add and the number 1275, enter that data now.

2) Click on B4, and type the number:

   25

3) Press ENTER.

3) Click on B5, and type:

   =B3+B4

Add	
1275	
25	
=B3+B4	

→

Add	
1275	
25	
1300	

4) Press ENTER.

To type a plus, hold down the SHIFT key and press the Equal To (=) key.

⬆ and ＋＝

Excel displays in B5 the sum of the contents of the two cells B3 and B4.

Congratulations! You have performed your first calculation in Excel.

Formulas and Arguments

Formula and argument are two words you will meet a lot when learning about spreadsheets. So it is important that you understand what they mean.

Formula
An equation that performs operations such as addition, subtraction, multiplication or division on data that is stored in a worksheet.

In Exercise 4.11, the formula you used was =B3+B4. Note the following about formulas:

- Always begin formulas with the equal to (=) sign.

- Always press ENTER to confirm your formula.

The components of a formula are called arguments. In the formula, =B3+B4, the arguments are B3 and B4. Both are cell references. As you will see, you can also use numbers as arguments.

Argument
The inputs to a calculation that generate the result.

Next, let's perform three other arithmetic operations using Excel formulas: subtraction, multiplication and division.

Excel's subtraction key is the Hyphen (-) key, to the left of the Equal To key.

Exercise 4.12: Subtracting with Excel

1) In cell D2, enter the word Subtract.
   (That is, type the word and press ENTER.)

2) In cell D3, enter the number 1275.
   (That is, type the number and press ENTER.)

3) In cell D4, enter the number 25.

4) In cell D5, enter the formula:

   =D3-D4

   (That is, type the formula and press ENTER.)

Excel displays in D5 the result of subtracting the contents of D4 from D3.

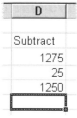

D
Subtract
1275
25
1250

 and

Excel's multiplication key is the Asterisk (*) key, typed by holding down SHIFT and pressing the 8 key.

Exercise 4.13: Multiplying with Excel

1) In cell F2, enter the word Multiply

2) In cell F3, enter the number 1275.

3) In cell F4, enter the number 25.

4) In cell F5, enter the formula:

   =F3*F4

Excel displays in F5 the result of multiplying the contents of F3 by F4.

F
Multiply
1275
25
31875

Excel's division key is the Forward Slash (/) key, to the right of the Full Stop (.) key.

Exercise 4.14: Dividing with Excel

1) In cell H2, enter the word Divide.

2) In cell H3, enter the number 1275.

3) In cell H4, enter the number 25.

4) In cell H5, enter the formula:

   =H3/H4

Excel displays in H5 the result of dividing the contents of H3 by H4.

H
Divide
1275
25
51

Calculated Cells

In Exercises 4.11 to 4.14, the cells B3 and B4, D3 and D4, F3 and F4, and H3 and H4 each:

- Contain a number

- Display a number

In other words, what they contain and what they display are the same.

Cells B5, D5, F5 and H5, however, contain one thing (a formula) but displays another (a number). These are examples of calculated cells.

You can think of a calculated cell as an 'answer cell'.

In addition to arguments, the other type of component in a formula is the operator.

Excel offers other, more complex operators that are beyond the scope of this ECDL Spreadsheet Module.

Adding Down and Across

Two of the most common arithmetic operations in spreadsheets are the addition of numbers that are arranged in vertical or horizontal lists. Exercises 4.15 and 4.16 provide examples of each.

Exercise 4.15: Adding a Vertical List of Numbers

1) In cells B8, B9, B10, B11 and B12, enter the numbers 1234, 4532, 5693, 3512 and 239.

2) In cell A13, enter the word: Total.

3) In cell B13, enter the formula:

=B8+B9+B10+B11+B12

Excel displays in B13 the result of adding the specified cells.

8		1234
9		4532
10		5693
11		3512
12		239
13	Total	15210
14		

Exercise 4.16: Adding a Horizontal List of Numbers

1) In cells B16, C16, D16, E16 and F16, enter the numbers 1234, 4532, 5693, 3512 and 239. (The same numbers as in Exercise 4.15.)

14						
15						Total
16	1234	4532	5693	3512	239	15210
17						
18						

2) In cell G15, enter the word Total.

3) In cell G16, enter the formula:

=B16+C16+D16+E16+F16

Excel displays in G16 the result of adding the specified cells.

Excel can add cells even when they are not arranged in neat, vertical or horizontal lists, as Exercise 4.17 demonstrates. Cells that are not immediately adjoining one another are called 'non-adjacent cells'.

Exercise 4.17: Adding Non-Adjacent Cells
1)   Enter the following numbers:

      1234 in B20, 4532 in C22, 5693 in D21, 3512 in E19 and 239 in F20.

      (The same numbers as in Exercises 4.15 and 4.16.)

2)   In G19, enter the word Total.

3)   In G20, enter the formula:

      =B20+C22+D21+E19+F20

18					
19				3512	Total
20	1234				239	15210
21			5693		
22		4532			

Excel displays in G20 the result of adding the specified cells.

Non-Adjacent Cells

Cells that are not located immediately beside, above or below one another.

Editing Formulas

In Exercise 4.5 of Section 4.1, you learnt how to edit a number in a cell. You can also edit a formula, as Exercise 4.18 demonstrates.

Exercise 4.18: Editing a Formula
1)   Double-click on G20. (Alternatively, move the cursor to it with the ARROW keys, and then press Excel's EDIT key, F2.)

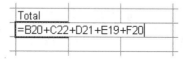

```
Total
=B20+C22+D21+E19+F20|
```

2)   Using the BACKSPACE or DELETE key, delete from the formula the argument F20 and the plus operator (+) in front of it.

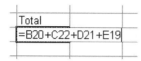

```
Total
=B20+C22+D21+E19|
```

3)   When finished press ENTER.

Excel now displays in G20 the result of adding B20, C22, D21 and E19 only.

Combining Operators

You can enter more than one type of operator in a single formula. In Exercise 4.19, you will enter formulas that contain both the addition and the subtraction operators.

Exercise 4.19: Formulas with Multiple Operators

Your company produces four products. They have fixed costs, variable costs, discounts and prices as set out in the cells shown below.

	B	C	D	E	F	G	H
24							
25	Name	Fixed	Variable	Total	Discount	Price	Profit
26	Product 1	12	2		2	21	
27	Product 2	34	6		8	56	
28	Product 3	56	28		12	112	
29	Product 4	127	92		19	290	
30							

Your task is to enter formulas to calculate the total costs for each product, and determine the profit for each product.

1) Enter the numbers and text in the cells as shown above.

2) Enter the formulas shown on the right in cells E26, E27, E28 and E29.

   When you press ENTER after typing each formula, Excel displays the calculated result.

E
Total
=C26+D26
=C27+D27
=C28+D28
=C29+D29

→

E
Total
14
40
84
219

3) Enter the formulas shown on the right in cells H26, H27, H28 and H29.

   When you press ENTER after typing each formula, Excel displays the calculated result as shown.

   That is, the profit on each product is its price minus the sum of the total cost and the discount.

H
Profit
=G26-(E26+F26)
=G27-(E27+F27)
=G28-(E28+F28)
=G29-(E29+F29)

→

H
Profit
5
8
16
52

Formulas: Using Constants

Excel formulas can contain numbers instead of (or as well as) cell references. Excel calls these numbers 'constants'.

> **Constant**
> An argument in a formula that is a fixed number.

Here are some examples of formulas containing both cell references and constants:

=C26*109   =45*(A12+3)   =B2/100-B3/50

You can even enter formulas that contain only constants and no cell references, as shown in Exercise 4.20.

Exercise 4.20: Entering Constant-Only Formulas

1) Enter the following in cell B32:

   =32/4

Excel displays the result (8) in B32.

Formulas: The Rules of Arithmetic

Excel allows you to combine addition, subtraction, multiplication and division in a single formula. For example:

=C5*(A4+A7) -(C4/C7)

Excel follows the rules of arithmetic in calculating such formulas:

- Multiplication and division are done first, addition and subtraction second.

  For example, the following formula gives a result of 11 because Excel first multiplies 2 by 3 (resulting in 6) and then adds 5.

  =5+2*3

- You can use parentheses (brackets) to force Excel to calculate your formula in a particular order.

  For example, the following formula gives a result of 21 because Excel first adds 5 and 2 (because they are within parentheses) and then multiplies that result by 3 to give 21.

  =(5+2)*3

  Ensure that you follow every opening bracket that you type with a matching closing bracket.

If you have difficulty remembering that:

= (A1+A2)*B1

gives a different result from:

= A1+(A2*B1)

Here's a way to help you remember the order of precedence among arithmetical operators:

My Dear Aunt Sally!

Fixed Factor Calculations

In some calculations, you need to apply the same number or factor several times to different numbers. The fixed factor may be a currency exchange rate, for example, or an employee tax rate or sales commission rate.

It is best to place such a fixed factor in a cell of its own, and enter its cell reference as needed in formulas. Exercise 4.21 provides an example.

Exercise 4.21: Sales Commission and Tax Calculations

Your company employs four sales representatives: Edgar, Sheila, Wallace and Deirdre. In addition to a basic salary, each receives commission of 20% on goods sold. All four are taxed at a rate of 15%.

Given the information displayed below, use Excel formulas to calculate the Net Income of each employee.

	B	C	D	E	F	G	H
34							
35	Comm. Rate		0.2				
36	Tax Rate		0.15				
37							
38							
39	Person	Basic	Sales	Comm.	Gross	Tax	Net Income
40	Edgar	1200	3000				
41	Sheila	1300	3100				
42	Wallace	1600	3500				
43	Deirdre	1700	3800				

1) Enter the numbers and text in the cells as shown above. You enter 20% as .2 and 15% as .15. Excel displays your entered numbers as 0.2 and 0.15.

2) To calculate each employee's sales commission, gross income, tax payment and net income, enter the formulas as shown below.

E	F	G	H
Comm.	Gross	Tax	Net Income
=D40*D35	=C40+E40	=F40*D36	=F40-G40
=D41*D35	=C41+E41	=F41*D36	=F41-G41
=D42*D35	=C42+E42	=F42*D36	=F42-G42
=D43*D35	=C43+E43	=F43*D36	=F43-G43

When you press ENTER after typing each formula, Excel displays the calculated result as shown below.

E	F	G	H
Comm.	Gross	Tax	Net Income
600	1800	270	1530
620	1920	288	1632
700	2300	345	1955
760	2460	369	2091

Exercise 4.22 provides an example of currency conversions, which are another type of fixed-factor type calculations.

Exercise 4.22: Currency Conversion Calculations

Your company sells a range of five products, priced at £100, £150, £200, £250 and £300, to the USA and Japan. The sterling-to-dollar exchange rate is 1.64, and the sterling-to-yen rate is 170.94.

Your task is to create a currency conversion table that shows the prices of your products in sterling, dollars and yen.

1)   Enter the text labels and numbers as shown below.

	B	C	D
45			
46	GBP/USD	1.64	
47	GBP/JPY	170.94	
48			
49	Sterling	Dollars	Yen
50	100		
51	150		
52	200		
53	250		
54	300		

2)   In cells C50 to C54, enter formulas to calculate the price of each product in dollars, obtained by multiplying its price in sterling by the exchange rate in cell C46.

In cells D50 to D54, enter formulas to calculate the price of each product in yen, obtained by multiplying its price in sterling by the exchange rate in cell C47.

Dollars	Yen
=B50*C46	=B50*C47
=B51*C46	=B51*C47
=B52*C46	=B52*C47
=B53*C46	=B53*C47
=B54*C46	=B54*C47

The formulas are as shown on the right.

When you press ENTER after typing each formula, Excel displays the calculated result as shown below.

	B	C	D
45			
46	GBP/USD	1.64	
47	GBP/JPY	170.94	
48			
49	Sterling	Dollars	Yen
50	100	164	17094
51	150	246	25641
52	200	328	34188
53	250	410	42735
54	300	492	51282

Calculations and Recalculations

In Exercises 4.11 to 4.22, you learnt how to use your £1,000 computer as a £10 pocket calculator! You have performed calculations using handfuls of numbers – but you can imagine how you could use the same methods to record and calculate hundreds or even thousands of numbers on a worksheet.

The power – and convenience – of a spreadsheet is not so much the ability to calculate as the ability to *recalculate*. Excel will recalculate the result of an addition (or other type of operation) whenever any of the numbers that make up the operation are changed.

Let's try it and see.

Exercise 4.23: Recalculating an Addition
In Exercise 4.11, you entered the number 25 in cell B4.

1) Click on B4, type 52, and press ENTER.

Notice how Excel recalculates B5 (the 'answer cell'), and displays the new result.

Just two numbers are added in this Exercise, but it could as easily have been hundreds or more.

B	
Add	
	1275
	52
	1300

→

B	
Add	
	1275
	52
	1327

Exercise 4.24: Recalculating a Multiplication
In Exercise 4.22, you entered a sterling-to-dollar exchange rate of 1.64 in cell C46, and a sterling-to-yen rate of 170.94 in cell C47.

1) Click on C46, type 1.68, and press ENTER.

2) Click on C47, type 170.92, and press ENTER.

Notice how Excel recalculates the foreign currency amounts for all five products, as shown below.

	B	C	D
45			
46	GBP/USD	1.68	
47	GBP/JPY	170.92	
48			
49	Sterling	Dollars	Yen
50	100	168	17092
51	150	252	25638
52	200	336	34184
53	250	420	42730
54	300	504	51276

To gain an appreciation of the power of spreadsheets, imagine Excel recalculating the prices for hundreds of products.

As further practice, revisit Exercise 4.21, change the Commission Rate (in D35), the Tax Rate (in D36), and note the effect on the employees' Commission, Gross and Net Income columns.

Error Messages: When Bad Things Happen

If a formula cannot properly calculate a result, Excel displays an error message in the calculated cell indicating the type of error that has taken place.

Here are the main error messages that you are likely to meet when following this ECDL Module.

#####

Your cell contains a number or a calculation result that is too wide for the cell to display. This is not really an error: Excel has the correct information, it just can't display it. You will learn about adjusting column width in Section 4.3.

#VALUE!

Your formula contains text (or a cell reference that points to a cell containing text) instead of a number. Edit the formula or cell to fix the problem.

#DIV./0!

You have tried to divide a number by zero, or by a cell reference that points to a cell containing a zero.

You will see the same error message if you try to divide a number by a cell reference that points to an empty cell. Excel interprets a blank cell as containing a zero.

#REF!

Typically, your formula contains a cell reference that points to a cell that has been deleted.

Excel's Zoom Views

Excel's Zoom feature enables you to magnify or reduce the worksheet display. You can use Zoom in either of two ways:

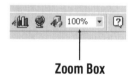

Zoom Box

- Click in the Zoom box on the Standard Toolbar, enter a number between 10 and 400, and press ENTER. (You need not type the percent (%) symbol.)

- Choose the **View | Zoom** command, and select a magnification option from the Zoom dialog box.

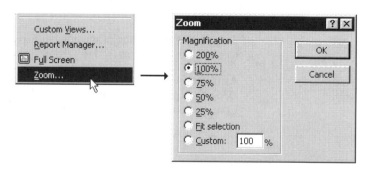

You can choose a preset option (25-200%), or select Custom and enter a number from 10 to 400.

Alternatively, select the Fit Selection option. This magnifies the area surrounding the active cell, or a range of selected cells, so that the cell or cells occupy the full screen. (You will learn about ranges of selected cells in Section 4.3.)

To return from an enlarged or reduced view to normal view, select a magnification of 100% – or click the Undo button on the Standard Toolbar.

Zoom and Printing

The Zoom feature affects only the way that Excel displays a worksheet on-screen – and *not* how Excel prints a worksheet. You will learn how to print a worksheet at a size other than 100% in Section 4.3.

Saving to a Diskette

Have you been saving your workbook as you went along? You should. It is also a good idea to save a copy of your workbook to a diskette. Follow the steps in Exercise 4.25 to learn how.

Exercise 4.25: Saving an Excel Workbook to a Diskette

1) Insert a diskette in the diskette drive of your computer:

   - If it is a new diskette ensure that it is formatted.

   - If it is a previously used one, ensure that there is sufficient space on it to hold the Excel workbook file. Your workbook should be about 16KB in size.

2) Choose **File | Save As**, locate the A: drive, and click **Save** to save the file. Excel suggests the default file name (in this example, KenBloggs.xls) for you to accept or amend.

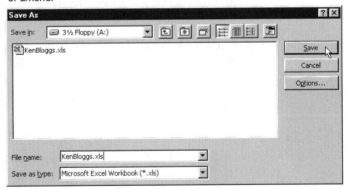

When finished, use **File | Save As** again to resave the workbook to its original location on your computer. (You will be asked if you want to replace the original file: click **OK**.)

If you do not resave your workbook at its original location, saving the file in future (by clicking the Save button on the Standard Toolbar or choosing **File | Save**) will save the workbook to the diskette – and not to your computer's hard disk.

You have now completed this Section 4.2 of the ECDL Spreadsheet Module. You can close your workbook and Excel.

Section Summary: So Now You Know

You can perform *calculations* on worksheet cells in two ways: using formulas and using functions.

A *formula* begins with an 'equal to' symbol (=) and contains one or more *operators* – for example, addition (+), subtraction (-), multiplication (*) or division (/).

The components or *arguments* of a formula can be cell references, numbers or both. A sample formula would be:

=A12+B12+3

A single formula may contain operators of different types – addition and multiplication, for example. Excel follows the rules of arithmetic in calculating formulas: multiplication and division are done first, addition and subtraction second. You can use parentheses (brackets) to force Excel to calculate your formula in a particular order. The following two formulas, for example, give different results:

=(A1+A2)*B1

=A1+(A2*B1)

Excel stores the result of a calculation in a *calculated cell*, which contains the formula but displays the calculation result.

Excel's *Zoom* feature enables you to magnify or reduce the worksheet display. Options range from 10- 400% of normal size. Only screen display and not printing is affected by the zooming.

If a formula cannot properly calculate a result, Excel displays an *error message* in the calculated cell indicating the type of error that has taken place.

Section 4.3: Functions, Formatting and Printing

In This Section

Formulas, as you learnt in Section 4.2, enable you to perform calculations on numbers. In this Section you will discover a second type of calculation method, based on functions. You will also meet the very useful AutoSum button.

When you work with numbers, it's important to get the right answers. But it's also important that your answers look good. Excel provides a wide range of formatting, alignment, border and colour features to help you give your worksheets a professional appearance. You will also learn how to change the width of columns and the height of rows.

Other topics in this Section include adjacent and non-adjacent cell ranges, find-and-replace, headers and footers, and worksheet printing.

New Skills

At the end of this Section you should be able to:

- Use Excel's SUM and AVERAGE functions to perform calculations on cells, and use the AutoSum button on Excel's Standard Toolbar

- Select ranges of adjacent and non-adjacent cells

- Adjust column width and row height

- Change font, font style (bold and italic) and font size

- Align cells horizontally and vertically, and rotate cells

- Apply borders and fills (coloured backgrounds to cells)

- Find, replace and spell-check items on a worksheet

- Change page setup and insert headers and footers

- Print from Excel

New Words

At the end of this Section you should be able to explain the following terms:

- Function

- Adjacent cell range

- Non-adjacent cell range

Excel Functions

You have learnt how Excel's formulas can add, subtract, multiply and divide numbers.

Excel offers a second way to perform calculations: functions.

> **Function**
>
> A predefined formula built-in to Excel and used for a specific purpose.

Most Excel functions are of interest only if you are using a spreadsheet for specialised purposes, such as statistical analysis. But two – SUM and AVERAGE – are useful to almost everyone. The SUM and AVERAGE functions are also part of the ECDL syllabus, so you need to know how to use them.

The SUM Function

In Section 4.2, you learnt how to add numbers by using such formulas as:

=B3+B4+B5

You can imagine that addition formulas can become very awkward – and prone to typing errors – when they contain large numbers of arguments. For example, if there were 100 cells to add rather than just three.

Excel's SUM function allows you to calculate the total of a vertical or horizontal list of numbers by entering just three items:

- The name of the function (in this case, SUM)
- The reference of the first cell
- The reference of the last cell

Upper or Lower Case?

As with row and column letters, you can type function names in upper- or lower-case letters. In the same way that Excel accepts A4 or a4, it accepts SUM or sum, AVERAGE or average.

In Excel's online help (and in this book), function names are written in upper-case. When entering functions on a worksheet, however, you will find it quicker to type their names in lower case, because you need not use the SHIFT key.

The following Exercise shows the SUM function in action.

Exercise 4.26: Using the SUM Function

1) Open the worksheet that you saved in Section 4.2.

2) Click the Sheet2 tab to display the second worksheet of the workbook.

   \ Sheet1 \ **Sheet2** \ Sheet3 /

3) In cells B3, B4 and B5, enter the numbers 2356, 4921 and 2903.

4) In cells A3, A4 and A5, enter the text Conway, Murphy and Smith to label the entered numbers.

5) Type the following function in B6 and press ENTER:

=SUM(B3:B5)

	A	B
1		
2		
3	Conway	2356
4	Murphy	4921
5	Smith	2903
6		=sum(b3:b5)
7		

⟶

	A	B
1		
2		
3	Conway	2356
4	Murphy	4921
5	Smith	2903
6		10180
7		
8		

Well done! You have used Excel's SUM function to add numbers.

The AutoSum Button

Σ

AutoSum button

Because SUM is such a commonly used function, Microsoft gave it a button on the Standard Toolbar.

Exercise 4.27: Using the AutoSum Button

1) Delete the SUM function, entered in Exercise 4.26, from cell B6.

2) With B6 as the active cell, click the AutoSum button on the Standard Toolbar.

3) Excel tries to 'guess' which cells you want to add together. In this example, it assumes (correctly) that the cells start at B3 and end at B5.

	A	B
1		
2		
3	Conway	2356
4	Murphy	4921
5	Smith	2903
6		=SUM(B3:B5)

	A	B
1		
2		
3	Conway	2356
4	Murphy	4921
5	Sullivan	2903
6		10180
7		
8		

4) Press ENTER to confirm that B3, B4 and B5 are the cells for adding.

Excel's SUM is a tolerant function. It ignores:

- Cells containing text
- Empty cells

For example, the function =SUM(W12:W16) adds whatever numbers it finds in the cells W12, W13, W14, W15 and W16.

If any cell contains text instead of a number, or is empty, the SUM function does not display an error message. It just ignores the non-numeric cells and continues on adding up the numeric ones.

In the next Exercise you will enter more numbers and text into your worksheet, Sheet2.

Exercise 4.28: Entering More Numbers and Text

1) On Sheet2, enter two further columns of numbers in columns C and D, as shown below. Across the top of columns B, C, D and E, enter a row of labels (text), also as shown below.

   (The month of March is omitted deliberately. You will insert a new column for March in Exercise 4.45 of Section 4.4.)

	A	B	C	D	E
1					
2		January	February	April	Total
3	Conway	2356	3621	4560	
4	Murphy	4921	4055	3542	
5	Smith	2903	3308	3622	

2) Use the AutoSum button to total the numbers in rows 3, 4 and 5.
   In E3 enter =SUM(B3:D3), in E4 =SUM(B4:D4) and in E5 =SUM(B5:D5).

   When you click on E5 and then click the AutoSum button, Excel will 'guess' which cells you want to total. It assumes (incorrectly) that you want to add the two immediately above it, E3 and E4, as shown on the right.

   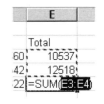

   When this happens, double-click on E5 (or press F2) to make the cell editable. Next, change the arguments of the SUM function to =SUM(B5:D5).

3) Use the AutoSum button to total, in row 6, the numbers in each of the columns C, D and E.
   In C6, enter =SUM(C3:C5), in D6 =SUM(D3:D5) and in E6 =SUM(E3:E5).

   Your worksheet should now look as shown below.

	A	B	C	D	E
1					
2		January	February	April	Total
3	Conway	2356	3621	4560	10537
4	Murphy	4921	4055	3542	12518
5	Smith	2903	3308	3622	9833
6		10180	10984	11724	32888
7					

The AVERAGE Function

This Excel function – you guessed it – finds the average of a group of numbers.

As with the SUM function, the AVERAGE function begins with the = sign. Then follows the function name, and finally the arguments within parentheses. Exercise 4.29 provides an example of the AVERAGE function in use.

Exercise 4.29: Using the AVERAGE Function
1) Click the Sheet1 tab to display the first worksheet in your workbook.

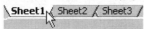

2) In cell B44, enter the label Average.

3) In cell C44, enter the following formula:

   =AVERAGE(C40:C43)

   C44 now displays the average value of the contents of cells C40, C41, C42 and C43.

4) Repeat step 3 for columns D, E, F G and H to average the cells immediately above them.

Row 44 should now look like that shown below.

44	Average	1450	3350	670	2120	318	1802

Formatting and Aligning Single Cells

Formatting refers to the *appearance* of numbers and text in cells. It includes such actions as making cell content bolder (heavier) and putting it in italics.

The *position* of numbers and text within cells is called alignment. Three common options are left, centered and right. The quickest way to apply a formatting or alignment option to a cell is to select it and then click the relevant button on Excel's Formatting Toolbar.

B *I*

Format buttons

You now learn how to format and align cells on a worksheet – in this case, Sheet2 of your workbook.

Alignment buttons

Exercise 4.30: Formatting and Aligning Cells
1) On Sheet2 of your worksheet, click on cell B2.

2) Click the Bold button on the Formatting Toolbar.
   Excel displays the word January in bold.

3) Click the Centre-Align button on the Formatting Toolbar.
   Excel centre-aligns the word January.

4) Click on cell A3, and then click the Italic button on the Formatting Toolbar.
   Excel displays the word Conway in italics.

Formatting and Aligning Cell Groups

You can save time and mouse-clicks by formatting or aligning a group of cells in one, single operation. Before you can do so, you must first select the group of cells.

You can select a group of cells by clicking on the top-left cell in the group, and then dragging the mouse across the other cells. Exercise 4.31 shows you how.

Exercise 4.31: Formatting and Aligning a Cell Range
1) Click cell C2.

2) Drag the mouse across to cell E2.

2		January	February	April	Totals
3	Conway	2356	3621	4560	10537

3) Click the Bold button on the Formatting Toolbar.

2		January	February	April	Totals
3	Conway	2356	3621	4560	10537

4) Click the Centre Align button on the Formatting Toolbar.

5) Select cell A4.

6) Drag the mouse down to cell A5.

7) Click the Italic button on the Formatting Toolbar.

Sheet2 should now look as shown below.

	A	B	C	D	E
1					
2		January	February	April	Total
3	Conway	2356	3621	4560	10537
4	Murphy	4921	4055	3542	12518
5	Smith	2903	3308	3622	9833
6		10180	10984	11724	32888

Click anywhere on the worksheet outside the selected cells A4 and A5 to deselect the two cells.

Cancelling a Selection

Finished formatting your selected cells? Or selected the wrong cells? To cancel a selection, click anywhere outside the selected cell or range.

Cancelling a selection does not delete the cell or range from the worksheet. It just deselects the selected cells.

Cell Ranges

In Excel, a group of cells in a worksheet is known as a cell range.

> **Cell Range**
> *A group of cells on a worksheet.*

Adjacent Cell Range

Cell ranges are of two kinds: adjacent and non-adjacent.

> **Adjacent Cell Range**
> *A group of cells that are directly beside, above or below one another. Adjacent cells are sometimes called contiguous cells.*

You identify an adjacent cell range by:

- The cell reference of the top-left cell

- A colon (:)

- The cell reference of the bottom-right cell

For example, the adjacent cell range A1:B2 includes the following four cells: A1, A2, B1 and B2.

Adjacent cell ranges may also include cells in one column only (for example, B2:B5) or in one row only (for example, D9:F9).

Non-Adjacent Cell Range

Can you select cells that are located on different parts of a worksheet as a single range? Yes. This is what Excel calls a non-adjacent cell range.

> **Non-Adjacent Cell Range**
> *A group of cells that are not directly beside, or above or below, one another. Also called non-contiguous cells.*

A non-adjacent cell range can consist of individual cells dotted around the worksheet. Or, as in Exercise 4.32, it can contain a number of smaller, sub-groups of adjacent cells.

You select a non-adjacent cell range by selecting the first cell (or first sub-group of adjacent cells), holding down the CTRL key, and then selecting further cells (or adjacent ranges).

A non-adjacent cell range is written with commas to separate the individual cells (for example, A2, B3, C4) or the smaller, sub-groups of adjacent cells (for example, A2:A6, H4:H8).

Exercise 4.32: Selecting a Non-Adjacent Cell Range

1) Select the first cell or sub-group of adjacent cells. For example, B2:B6 (that is, cells B2, B3, B4, B5 and B6).

	A	B	C	D	E
1					
2		**January**	**February**	**April**	**Totals**
3	Conway	2356	3621	4560	10537
4	Murphy	4921	4055	3542	12518
5	Smith	2903	3308	3622	9833
6		10180	10984	11724	32888
7					

2) Hold down the CTRL key.

3) Select the next cell or next sub-group of adjacent cells. For example, cell range E2:E6.

	A	B	C	D	E
1					
2		**January**	**February**	**April**	**Totals**
3	Conway	2356	3621	4560	10537
4	Murphy	4921	4055	3542	12518
5	Smith	2903	3308	3622	9833
6		10180	10984	11724	32888
7					

You can continue this process until you have selected all the cells in the non-adjacent range that you want to select.

Click anywhere outside the cell range to cancel the selection.

Selected Cells and the Active Cell

One active cell

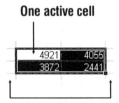

Four selected cells

In Section 4.1 you learnt how to select a single cell – by clicking on it with the mouse, moving the cursor to it with the ARROW keys, or entering its cell reference in the Name Box. That cell is then the active cell.

So, for a single cell, the terms 'active cell' and 'selected cell' mean the same thing. And 'Select a cell' is simply another way of saying 'Make a cell the active cell'.

While you can select any number of cells at one time, only one cell can be the active cell. Excel displays selected cells in reverse (white text on black background). The active cell is shown as black text on a white background.

F8: Excel's SELECT Key

In Exercise 4.31 you selected an adjacent cell range by selecting the first cell, and then dragging the mouse across the other cells in the range. An alternative method is to select the first cell, press F8, and then press the ARROW keys to extend the selected area over the other cells. F8 is Excel's SELECT key. You may find this method faster than using the mouse, but you can use it only for selecting adjacent cell ranges.

Selecting Columns and Rows

Excel offers quick ways of selecting one or more rows or columns.

To select an entire row, click on the row heading.

- To select several adjacent rows, click on the top or bottom one, and hold down the mouse button as you drag down or up.

- To select several non-adjacent rows, click on the first, hold down the CTRL key, and click on the others.

To select an entire column, click on the column heading.

- To select several adjacent columns, click on one and then drag with the mouse to the right or left.

- To select several non-adjacent columns, click on the first, hold down the CTRL key, and click on the others.

Deleting Rows and Column Contents

To delete the contents of one or a selection of rows or columns, select the rows or columns, and press the DELETE key.

This operation removes only the row or column cell contents, leaving behind empty rows or columns. It does *not* delete the actual rows or columns. You will learn how to remove rows and columns from worksheets in Section 4.4.

Selecting the Entire Worksheet

To select the whole worksheet, click on the top-left of the worksheet, where the row heading meets the column heading.

A fast way to delete the contents of all cells on a worksheet is to select the entire worksheet, and then press DELETE.

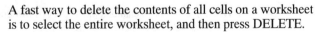

Adjusting Column Width and Row Height

You can change the appearance of your worksheet by adjusting the width of one or more columns, or the height of one or more rows.

- Column Width: To change the width of a column, move the mouse to the column heading, and then drag the boundary on the right side of the column heading until the column is the width you want. See Exercise 4.33.

- Row Height: To change row height, move the mouse to the row heading, and then drag the boundary below the row heading until the row is the height you want. See Exercise 4.34.

Exercise 4.33: Adjusting Column Width

1) In the column heading of Sheet2, click on the boundary line between columns A and B.

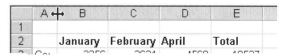

2) Drag the boundary to the left, making column A narrower.

	A ⊹	B	C	D	E
1					
2		January	February	April	Total

3) Reverse the effect of step 2 by dragging the column A boundary to the right, so restoring column A to its original width.

Exercise 4.34: Adjusting Row Height

1) In the row heading, click on the boundary between rows 2 and 3.

2) Drag the line down about one centimetre until it looks like that shown below.

	A	B	C	D	E
1					
2		January	February	April	Total
3	Conway	2356	3621	4560	10537

Well done. You have changed the height of a row on your worksheet. Leave the row at its increased height for Exercise 4.35.

Vertical Alignment

The three alignment buttons (left, centre and right) on the Formatting Toolbar enable you to position cell contents horizontally (left-to-right). Excel also allows you to align cell contents vertically (top-to-bottom). Exercise 4.35 provides an example of vertical alignment.

Exercise 4.35: Changing Vertical Alignment

1) Select cell range B2:E2 in row 2, whose height you increased in Exercise 4.34.

2) Choose **Format | Cells**, select the Alignment tab, select the Centre option from the Vertical: list, and click **OK**.

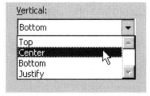

Excel now aligns the cells' content vertically so that it is centred between the top and bottom of the cells' boundaries.

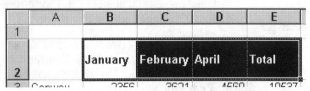

3) Click once on the Undo button on the Standard Toolbar to return the cells to the default vertical alignment of Bottom, and then click a second time to return the row to its original, normal height.

Orientation

Another Excel formatting feature is the ability to rotate or 'orient' the text or numbers at a specified angle within a cell. See Exercise 4.36.

Exercise 4.36: Rotating Cell Content

1) Select cell range B2:E2, choose **Format | Cells**, select the Alignment tab, type 90 in the Degrees box, and click **OK**.

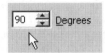

Excel now rotates the cells' content so that it is positioned at ninety degrees to the horizontal, as shown below.

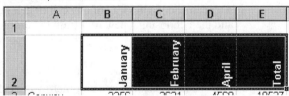

2) Click the Undo button on the Standard Toolbar to return the cells' orientation to the default value of zero degrees.

Entering a positive number in the Degree box rotates the cell content from lower left to upper right. A negative number of degrees rotates the cell content from upper left to lower right.

Fonts

Viewing the fonts on your computer

A font (also called typeface) is a particular style of text. What fonts are installed on your computer? Click the arrow on the drop-down Font box on Excel's Formatting Toolbar to see.

There are really just two kinds (families) of fonts: *serif* and *sans serif*. Sans serif just means without serifs. You can recognise which family a font belongs to by asking: Do its characters have serifs (tails or squiggles) at their edges?

A serif font   **A sans serif font**

Excel's default font is Arial, a sans serif font. The most commonly used serif font is named Times New Roman. Arial and other sans serif fonts are usually better for displaying numbers. You may want to apply a serif font to worksheet labels.

> **Font**
> *A typeface: a particular style of text. The two main font families are serif and sans serif.*

You can change the font of any cell or cell range by first selecting the cells and then choosing a new font from the drop-down list on the Formatting Toolbar.

Font Sizes

Font size is measured in a non-metric unit called the point, with approximately 72 points equal to one inch. Excel's default font is 10 point.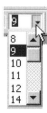

You can change the font size of any cell or cell range by first selecting the cells, and then choosing a new font size from the drop-down list on the Formatting Toolbar.

Font Colours

You can change the colour of cell contents from Excel's default of Automatic. What colour is Automatic? Automatic is black, unless the cell background is black or a dark grey, in which case Automatic switches to white.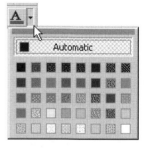

You can change the colour of the text or number displayed in any cell or cell range by first selecting the cells, clicking the arrow on the right of the Font Colour button on the Formatting Toolbar, and then clicking on a colour.

In the next Exercise you will practise changing the fonts, font sizes and colours of the labels in Sheet1 of your workbook.

Exercise 4.37: Changing Fonts, Font Sizes and Colours

1) Click the Sheet1 tab to display the first worksheet of your workbook.

2) Click cell B2. Hold down the CTRL key and click also on the following cells: D2, F2 and H2.

3) From the Formatting Toolbar, change the font to Times New Roman, the font size to 12 point, and the font colour to dark blue. Next, click on the Bold and Centre Align buttons.

Your worksheet should now look as shown below.

Add		Subtract		Multiply		Divide	
1275		1275		1275		1275	
52		25		25		25	
1327		1250		31875		51	

Cell Borders

Excel provides a wide choice of borders that you can use to highlight a particular cell or cell range – such as cells containing sub- and final totals on a worksheet. You can access these options by clicking the arrow on the right of the Borders button on the Formatting Toolbar.

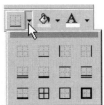

The most commonly used cell border options are the single bottom line (the default), the double and heavier bottom lines, and the outline. The last places a border on all four sides of the selected cells. Exercise 4.38 provides an example.

Exercise 4.38: Placing a Bottom Border on Cells

1) Select the non-adjacent cells B4, D4, F4 and H4.

2) Click the arrow on the right of the Borders button, and, from the list of options displayed, click the heavy, single bottom line.

Your worksheet should now look as shown below.

Add		Subtract		Multiply		Divide	
1275		1275		1275		1275	
52		25		25		25	
1327		1250		31875		51	

Cell Colour Backgrounds

As with cell borders, Excel allows you to change the background colour of a cell – what Excel calls the Fill Colour.

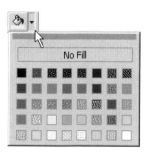

You access this option by clicking the arrow on the right of the Fill Colour button on the Formatting Toolbar.

Exercise 4.39 provides an example.

Exercise 4.39: Changing the Fill Colour
1) Select the adjacent cell range B25:H25.

2) Click the arrow on the right of the Fill Colour button, and click the Yellow button.

Your worksheet should now look as shown.

Name	Fixed	Variable	Total	Discount	Price	Profit
Product 1	12	2	14	2	21	5
Product 2	34	6	40	8	56	8
Product 3	56	28	84	12	112	16
Product 4	127	92	219	19	290	52

In Exercise 4.40 you will further practise your cell border and fill colour skills.

Exercise 4.40: Further Cell Border and Colour Practice
1) Select the adjacent cell range B25:H29.

2) Click the arrow on the right of the Borders button, and click the outline (all four cell edges) border type.

3) Select cell range B35:D36.

4) Click the arrow on the right of the Borders button, and click the hollow outline (edges only) border type.

5) Select cell range D35:D36.

6) Click the arrow on the right of the Borders button, and click the left edge border type.

7) Select cell range B43:H43.

8) Click the arrow on the right of the Borders button, and click the heavy bottom line border type.

9) Select non-adjacent cell range B46:C47, B49:D54.

10) Click the arrow on the right of the Borders button, and click the outline (all four cell edges) border type.

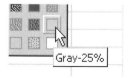

11) With the non-adjacent cell range still selected, click the arrow on the right of the Fill Colours button, and click the Grey (25%) option.

Finding Cell Content

You can search a worksheet for label text, numbers that were entered directly, numbers resulting from calculations, and calculation components (function names, cell references, arithmetic operators and constants) as follows:

- Select the range of cells you want to search. (To search the whole worksheet, click any cell.)
- Choose **Edit | Find**.
- In the Find what: box, enter the item you want to find, and select **Find Next**.

You can cancel a Find operation in progress by pressing the ESC key.

Find Options

Excel's Find feature offers the following options:

- **Search:** Select the direction you want to search in: down through columns, or rightwards across rows.
- **Look in:** The type of cells you want to search through.
- **Match case:** Searches only for characters that match the case of the entered search text. For example, a search for 'smith' does not find 'Smith'.
- **Find entire cells only:** Searches only for complete matches. For example, a search for 'Sm' does not find 'Smith', and 330 does not find 3308.

Replacing Cell Content

Anything that you can search for in a worksheet with **Edit | Find**, you can replace with a specified alternative. For example, you could replace occurrences of cell reference F34 with F36. The procedure is as follows:

- Select the relevant range of cells. (To perform the find-and-replace operation on the whole worksheet, click any cell.)
- Choose **Edit | Replace**.
- In the Find what: box, enter the item you want to replace. In the Replace with box:, enter the replacement item. (You can delete from the selected cells the characters in the Find what: box by leaving the Replace with: box blank.)
- Select **Find Next**. To replace only the highlighted occurrence of the found characters, select **Replace**.
- To replace *all* occurrences of the found characters in the selected cells, click **Replace All**.

Exercise 4.41 provides an example of Excel's find-and-replace feature.

Exercise 4.41: Finding and Replacing Text on a Worksheet

1) Click the Sheet2 tab to display the second worksheet of your workbook.

2) Select the cell range A2:E6.

3) Choose **Edit | Replace**. In the Find what: box, type Smith. In the Replace with: box, type Sullivan.

4) Select the Match case and Find entire cells only options. Select **Replace All**.

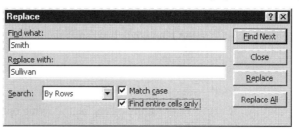

Sheet2 should now look as shown below.

	A	B	C	D	E
1					
2		January	February	April	Total
3	Conway	2356	3621	4560	10537
4	Murphy	4921	4055	3542	12518
5	Sullivan	2903	3308	3622	9833
6		10180	10984	11724	32888
7					

Spell-Checking

Excel can check the spelling of text on all or part of a worksheet.

To check your spelling, follow this procedure:

- Select the range of cells whose spelling you want to check. To check the whole worksheet, click any cell.

- Click the Spelling button ^{ABC}✓ on Excel's Standard Toolbar.

When Excel meets a word that it does not recognise from its spelling dictionary (the same dictionary used by Microsoft Word), it displays the Spelling dialog box, as shown below.

The following are the main options:

- **Ignore:** Leave this occurrence of the word unchanged.

- **Ignore All:** Leave this and all other occurrences of the word in the selected cells unchanged.

- **Change:** Correct this occurrence of the word, but prompt again on further occurrences.

- **Change All:** Correct this occurrence of the word – and all other occurrences without further prompting.

- **Add:** Add the word to the custom (your personal) dictionary. Use this option for the names of people or places, or abbreviations or acronyms, that you type regularly. Excel will recognise such added words during future spell-checks of any worksheet.

Practise by spell-checking Sheet1 and Sheet2 of your workbook.

Page Setup

In the remainder of this Section you will learn about Excel's various printing options, beginning with those available on the four tabs of the **File | Page Setup** dialog box: the Page, Margins, Header/Footer, and Sheet tabs.

Paper Size

Located on the Page tab of the **File | Page Setup** dialog box, this option allows you to select the size of the paper you want to print on. The default is A4, the European standard paper size (21 cm wide and 29.7 cm high).

Orientation

Also on the Page tab, orientation is the direction in which the page is printed. Your options are Portrait ('standing up') and Landscape ('on its side').

Scaling

Two scaling options on the Page tab enable you to reduce or enlarge the worksheet printout:

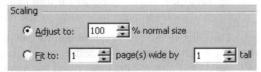

- **Adjust to:** You can enter a number in the range 10-400% of normal size. (You need not type the % symbol.)

- **Fit to:** Reduces the worksheet (or selected cells) so that it fits on the specified number of pages. You can specify the number of pages vertically (tall), horizontally (wide) or both.

Margins

The margins are the distance that the printed worksheet or selected cells are positioned in from the four edges of the printed page. You set this on the Margins tab of the **File | Page Setup** dialog box. You can specify separate margins for headers and footers, which are covered in the next topic.

It is unlikely that you will need to change Excel's default margin values – top and bottom, 2.5 cm, left and right, 1.9 cm.

The Margins tab also allows you to centre your worksheet or selected cells horizontally (positioned evenly between the left and right margins of the printed page), vertically (between the top and bottom margins), or both.

Gridlines and Headings

By default, Excel does not include cell boundary lines or row and column headings on printouts. You can change either or both of these settings on the Sheet tab of the **File | Page Setup** dialog box.

Headers and Footers

These are pieces of text that appear at the top and bottom of every page of a printed worksheet. Typically, they contain such details as file name, author name, date and page number.

With Excel, you need only type in header and/or footer text once, and the program repeats the text on every page. You can apply formatting – font, bold and italics – to text in the headers and footers.

Here are a few facts about headers and footers in Excel:

- You insert them with the Header/Footer tab of the **File | Page Setup** command.

- The Header/Footer tab offers a drop-down list of suggested header and footer texts, from which you can choose the one that best suits your needs.

- You can edit and/or format your chosen header or footer text by clicking the Custom header or Custom footer button on the Header/Footer tab, and then selecting the required options.

- The Custom buttons enable you to format the header or footer text, and insert any or all of the following items: page number, total number of pages, date, time, Excel file name and worksheet name.

- When setting header and footer margins on the Margins tab of the **File | Page Setup** dialog box, ensure that the values are less than the top and bottom page margins – otherwise, the header and footer text may overlap the cells on the printout.

Exercise 4.42 provides an example of Excel's header and footer feature in action.

Exercise 4.42: Inserting a Header and Footer

1) With Sheet1 of your workbook selected, choose **File | Page Setup** and select the Header/Footer tab.

2) On the Header drop-down list, select the Excel workbook file name – in this case, KenBloggs.xls.

3) On the Footer drop-down list, select Page 1 of ?.

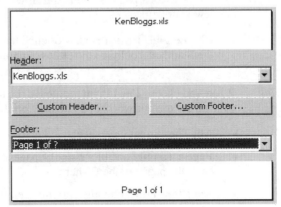

4) Click the Custom Header button, select the file name in the Centre section, click the Text Formatting button, and make the file name bold.

5) In the Left section, type My First Worksheet. In the Right section, type ECDL Module 4.

6) Click **OK** to return to the Header/Footer tab of the Page Setup dialog box.

7) Click the Custom footer button, click in the Left section, and then click the Date button.

8) Click in the Right section, and then click the Time button.

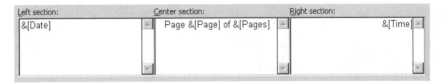

9) Click **OK** to return to the Header/Footer tab of the Page Setup dialog box. Click **OK** again to close the dialog box.

Well done. You have inserted a header and footer in your workbook. You cannot see headers and footers on screen they appear on printouts only.

Printing Options

Excel offers a wide range of printing options. These include the ability to preview a worksheet on your screen before you print it, and the choice of printing all your worksheet, selected cells or pages, or your entire workbook.

Print Preview

This displays each page as it will appear when it is printed on paper. To preview your worksheet:

- Choose **File | Print Preview** or click the Print Preview ⬚ button on the Standard Toolbar. Click **Close** to return to your worksheet.

Print Range Options

When you choose **File | Print**, you have the following options regarding which parts of your workbook you may print:

- **All:** The current worksheet.
- **Pages:** To print one or a range of pages from the current worksheet, enter the page number(s) here.
- **Selection:** Prints only the currently selected cells on the current worksheet.
- **Entire Workbook:** All worksheets that contain data in the workbook.

Other options on the Print dialog box allow you to specify how many copies you want to print, and whether you want the pages collated or not.

Exercise 4.43: Printing a Worksheet

1) Click the Sheet1 tab to select the first worksheet of your workbook.

2) Choose **File | Print**, accept the default options, and click **OK**.

Your printout should look like that shown.

Save and close your workbook and Excel. You have now completed Section 4.3 of the ECDL Spreadsheet Module.

Add	Subtract	Multiply	Subtract
1275	1275	1275	1275
52	25	25	25
1327	1250	31875	51

1234
4532
5693
3512
239

Total 15210

| 1234 | 4532 | 5693 | 3512 | 239 | Total 15210 |

				3512		Total
1234					239	14971
		5693				
	4532					

Name	Fixed	Variable	Total	Discount	Price	Profit
Product 1	12	2	14	2	21	5
Product 2	34	6	40	8	56	8
Product 3	56	28	84	12	112	16
Product 4	127	92	219	19	290	52

8

Comm. Rate	0.2
Tax Rate	0.15

Person	Basic	Sales	Comm.	Gross	Tax	Net Income
Edgar	1200	3000	600	1800	270	1530
Sheila	1300	3100	620	1920	288	1632
Wallace	1600	3500	700	2300	345	1955
Deirdre	1700	3800	760	2460	369	2091
Average	1450	3350	670	2120	318	1802

GBP/USD	1.68
GBP/JPY	170.92

Sterling	Dollars	Yen
100	168	17092
150	252	25638
200	336	34184
250	420	42730
300	504	51276

Section Summary: So Now You Know

Functions are predefined formulas built-in to Excel that allow you to perform specific calculations. As with formulas, functions always begin with an equal to (=) symbol.

With the SUM function, you need enter only two arguments when totalling a vertical or horizontal list of cells: the first and last cell references. An example of a SUM function would be:

=SUM(A2:A6)

A fast way to total a vertical or horizontal list of cells is to select them and click the *AutoSum* button. Excel tries to 'guess' which cells you want to add. If Excel has guessed correctly, just press ENTER to confirm the suggested arguments. If not, edit the arguments of the SUM function.

The AVERAGE function, as its name suggests, calculates the average of a vertical or horizontal list of numbers. For example:

=AVERAGE(D5:F5)

A *cell range* is a group of cells on a worksheet. You can *select* an *adjacent* cell range by dragging the mouse across it. Select a *non-adjacent* cell range by selecting the first cell (or first sub-group of adjacent cells) and then holding down the CTRL key when selecting further cells (or adjacent ranges).

Selected cells can be *formatted* (bold or italic), *aligned* horizontally or vertically) and *rotated*. You can also add *borders* and *fills* (coloured backgrounds), and change *fonts* and *sizes*.

You can adjust *column width* and *row height* by dragging the cell boundaries in the row and column headings.

You can *search* all or part of a worksheet for label text, entered numbers, numbers resulting from calculations, and calculation components (function names, cell references, arithmetic operators and constants). And you can *replace* found items with alternatives. You can also *spell-check* all or part of a worksheet.

The standard page size is *A4*, and pages can be oriented in *portrait* or *landscape*. A *margin* is the distance of the cells from a particular edge of the page.

Headers and footers are small text items that reoccur on every printed page, and typically contain such details as the workbook name, author name and date. Either can also contain the automatically generated *page number*.

Excel's *print options* include a print preview feature and the ability to print selected cells only.

Section 4.4: Inserting, Sorting and Moving Cells

In This Section

Excel users spend only part of their time creating new workbooks and entering and formatting data in the worksheet cells. The remainder is spent reopening existing workbooks and amending previously entered data.

In this Section you will learn how to perform three types of maintenance tasks.

Row and column insertion allow you to position new cells within a worksheet area that already contains cells with data in them. Insertion (or deletion) means that surrounding cells must adjust their position to make way for the new data (or fill the spaces previously occupied by the deleted data).

Copying, cutting and pasting enable you to reproduce or move cells within the same worksheet, between worksheets in the same workbook, or between different workbooks. Copying and cutting of calculations introduce the idea of relative and absolute cell references.

Finally, sorting allows you to rearrange selected cells in a sequence different from that in which they were entered to the worksheet.

New Skills

At the end of this Section you should be able to:

- Insert and delete rows, columns and cells

- Copy, cut and paste the contents of cells

- Explain the difference between relative and absolute cell references, and identify calculations in which absolute cell references are appropriate

- Sort cells according to one or two criteria

- Insert symbols and special characters from Word to Excel

New Words

At the end of this Section you should be able to explain the following terms:

- Marquee
- Sort
- Relative cell reference
- Sort order
- Absolute cell reference

Inserting and Deleting Rows

With over four million cells on a single worksheet, why would you want to add some more? Answer: Sometimes you need to insert a row or column to hold new data *within* a range of cells that already contain text and numbers.

Exercises 4.44 and 4.45 take you through the steps of inserting new rows and columns.

Exercise 4.44: Inserting a New Row

1) Open the second worksheet of your workbook, Sheet2.

2) Select the heading of the row immediately *below* where you want to insert the new row. For example, to insert a new row below row 4, click on the heading of row 5.

	A	B	C	D	E
1					
2		January	February	April	Totals
3	Conway	2356	3621	4560	10537
4	Murphy	4921	4055	3542	12518
5	Sullivan	2903	3308	3622	9833
6		10180	10984	11724	32888

3) Choose **Insert | Rows**. Excel inserts a new row of blank cells.

	A	B	C	D	E
1					
2		January	February	April	Totals
3	Conway	2356	3621	4560	10537
4	Murphy	4921	4055	3542	12518
5					
6	Sullivan	2903	3308	3622	9833
7		10180	10984	11724	32888

4) Enter new text and numbers in cells A5, B5, C5 and D5, as shown below. Excel recalculates the totals on row 7 automatically as you add the new numbers.

5) In cell E5, enter the following SUM function to add the cells of row 5:

=SUM(B5:D5)

Excel recalculates E7, the total of the Totals column, to include E5, the sum of the numbers that you have entered in row 5. Your worksheet should look as shown below.

	A	B	C	D	E
1					
2		January	February	April	Totals
3	Conway	2356	3621	4560	10537
4	Murphy	4921	4055	3542	12518
5	Smith	3872	2441	4949	11262
6	Sullivan	2903	3308	3622	9833
7		14052	13425	16673	44150
8					

6) To make your worksheet more readable, insert a blank row above the column totals, as shown.

	A	B	C	D	E
1					
2		January	February	April	Totals
3	Conway	2356	3621	4560	10537
4	Murphy	4921	4055	3542	12518
5	Smith	3872	2441	4949	11262
6	Sullivan	2903	3308	3622	9833
7					
8		14052	13425	16673	44150

Deleting Rows

To delete a row, select the row heading and choose **Edit | Delete**. The row beneath moves up to fill the space previously occupied by the deleted row.

Inserting and Deleting Columns

Inserting a new column in a worksheet is similar to inserting a new row. Exercise 4.45 shows you how.

Exercise 4.45: Inserting a New Column

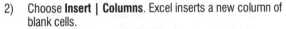

1) Select the heading of the column immediately to the *right* of where you want to insert the new column.

   For example, to insert a new column to the right of column C, click on the heading of column D.

2) Choose **Insert | Columns**. Excel inserts a new column of blank cells.

3) Enter new text and numbers in D2:D6 as shown below.

   Excel recalculates the totals in column F automatically as you add the new numbers in column D.

4) To total the new numbers in column D, enter the following function in cell D8:

   =SUM(D3:D6)

	A	B	C	D	E	F
1						
2		January	February	March	April	Totals
3	Conway	2356	3621	4185	4560	14722
4	Murphy	4921	4055	3814	3542	16332
5	Smith	3872	2441	2888	4949	14150
6	Sullivan	2903	3308	3487	3622	13320
7						
8		14052	13425	14374	16673	58524

5) To make your worksheet more readable, insert a column to the right of the April column.

6) This blank column is wider than it needs to be. In the column heading, click on the boundary between columns F and G, and then drag the boundary to the left.

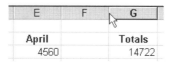 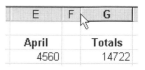

Deleting Columns

To delete a column, select its heading and choose **Edit | Delete**. The column to the right moves left and fills the space previously occupied by the deleted column.

Inserting and Deleting Cells

You can insert individual cells on a worksheet by first selecting a cell immediately below or to the right of where you want to insert the new cell, and then choosing **Insert | Cells**.

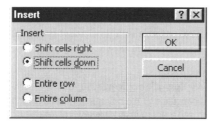

To delete a cell, select it and choose **Edit | Delete**.

Be careful about inserting or deleting a new cell or cell range, because Excel adjusts the position of the surrounding cells accordingly. Excel prompts you to choose whether the surrounding cells should move right or down.

Copying and Pasting Cell Contents

Suppose you have text or a number in one cell, and you want to copy it to another cell. How do you do it?

Of the many ways of copying and pasting a cell or cells on a worksheet, here are the two most convenient:

- Drag-and-drop

- Right-clicking

You will learn about each method in Exercises 4.46 and 4.47.

Exercise 4:46: Copy and Paste with Drag-and-Drop

1) Select the cell you want to copy from.

   For example, click the Sheet1 tab to display your first worksheet. Type 1234 in cell B57 and press ENTER. Next, click B57 to select it.

   See how the cursor is shaped like a plus sign (+).

2) Move the cursor to the bottom edge of the selected cell and hold down the CTRL key. Excel changes the cursor from a plus sign to an arrow with a smaller plus sign.

   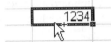

   (You can move the cursor to any edge of the selected cell – it doesn't matter which edge. The cursor still changes shape.)

3) Holding down the CTRL key, drag the cell to the destination cell that you want to paste to – for example, D57.

4) Release the mouse button *first*, and then the CTRL key.

   (If you release CTRL first, Excel cuts rather than copies the cell contents.)

   If there is already something in cell D57, Excel overwrites it with the pasted data.

Well done. You have copied a number from one cell of a worksheet to another – without clicking a toolbar button or choosing a menu command!

Exercise 4:47: Copy and Paste by Right-Clicking

1) Select the cell whose contents you want to copy. As in Exercise 4.46, select B57.

2) Right-click with the mouse.

3) Choose **Copy** from the pop-up menu. Excel places the contents of B57 in the Clipboard.

4) Click cell F57.

5) Right-click with the mouse.

6) Choose **Paste**.

If there is already something in cell F57, Excel overwrites it with the pasted data.

You are not limited to using drag-and-drop and right-clicking with single cells only. You can use both methods with selected ranges of cells.

About the Clipboard

When you copy (or cut) and paste by any means other than drag-and-drop, the copied (or cut) cells are held in a temporary storage area called the Clipboard. Four points you should remember about the Clipboard:

- The Clipboard is temporary. Turn off your computer and the Clipboard contents are deleted.

- The same Clipboard is available to all Windows applications. For example, you can copy from Excel and paste into Word.

- The Clipboard can hold only a single, copied item at a time. If you copy a second item to it, the second overwrites the first.

- An item stays in the Clipboard after you paste from it, so you can paste the same item to as many locations as you need.

The Flashing Marquee

When you copy (or cut) a cell or cell range by any means other than drag-and-drop, Excel surrounds the selected cells with a flashing rectangle called a marquee.

> **Marquee**
>
> *A flashing rectangle that Excel uses to surround a cell, or cell range, that you have copied to the Clipboard.*

You can remove a marquee at any stage by pressing the ESC key at the top-left of your keyboard.

If you remove a marquee, Excel removes the contents of the selected cell or cell range from the Clipboard.

Exercise 4.48: Copy and Paste a Cell Range

In this Exercise you will copy and paste an adjacent cell range. You will use the keyboard shortcuts to perform the copy and paste actions.

1) Type 1234 in cells C57 and E57.

2) Select the cell range B57:F57.

3) Press CTRL+c to copy the cells to the Clipboard.

4) Click cell B59, and press CTRL+v to paste from the Clipboard.

Excel copies the cells to the new cell range B59:F59, as shown below.

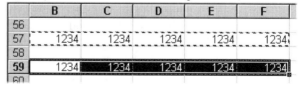

You can paste from the Clipboard to several locations in a single action, as Exercise 4.49 demonstrates.

Exercise 4.49: Copy and Paste to Multiple Locations

1) With cell range B57:F57 still in the Clipboard from Exercise 4.48, select the adjacent cell range B61:F64.

2) Press CTRL+v to paste to the cells. All four adjacent rows of the destination cell range now contain the pasted cells.

3) Select the non-adjacent cell range B66:F66, B68:F68, B70:F70.

4) Press CTRL+v to paste to the cells. The three non-adjacent rows of the destination cell range now contain the pasted cells.

Your worksheet should look as shown below.

	B	C	D	E	F	G
60						
61	1234	1234	1234	1234	1234	
62	1234	1234	1234	1234	1234	
63	1234	1234	1234	1234	1234	
64	1234	1234	1234	1234	1234	
65						
66	1234	1234	1234	1234	1234	
67						
68	1234	1234	1234	1234	1234	
69						
70	1234	1234	1234	1234	1234	
71						

Pasted to an adjacent cell range (rows 61–64)

Pasted to a non-adjacent cell range (rows 66, 68, 70)

Cutting and Pasting Cell Contents

Cut-and-paste differs from copy-and-paste in that Excel removes the content of the original cell contents, whereas the contents of copied cells' remain in their original location. Cutting does not remove the cells, in the way that the **Edit | Delete** command does. It just removes their contents, leaving behind empty cells.

To cut and paste using drag-and-drop, do not hold down the CTRL key while dragging the cell contents to their new location.

To cut and paste using the pop-up menu, choose **Cut** rather than **Copy**. **Cut**, **Copy** and **Paste** commands are also available on Excel's **Edit** menu. The keyboard shortcut for cutting a cell or cell range is CTRL+x.

Yet another cut or copy and paste method is to use the relevant buttons on Excel's Standard Toolbox.

Copy button   **Cut button**   **Paste button**

Copying between Worksheets and Workbooks

You are not limited to copying or cutting and pasting cells within the same worksheet (such as Sheet1). You can also copy or cut and paste between different worksheets of the same workbook (such as Sheet1 and Sheet2 of your workbook), and even between different workbooks.

Exercise 4.50: Copying and Pasting between Workbooks

1) On Sheet2, select cell range A2:G8.

2) Choose **Edit | Copy** to copy the cells to the Clipboard.

3) Click the New ⬜ button on the Standard Toolbox to open a new workbook. The new workbook opens with Sheet1 displayed.

4) In the Name Box of the new workbook, type A100 and press ENTER. This moves the cursor to cell A100, making it the active cell.

5) Choose **Edit | Paste** to paste the cell range from the Clipboard.

You have completed the Exercise. Close the new workbook without saving it.

Moving Calculations

Numbers and text can be copied or cut and pasted without problems. But what about calculations? Can errors arise when moving formulas or functions?

Yes – but only when fixed-factor calculations are involved. As you learnt in Section 4.2, these are calculations where a common cell reference, indicating the fixed factor, is used in formulas or functions on different rows or columns. Common examples of fixed factors are currency exchange rates, and tax and sales commission rates.

Exercise 4.51 demonstrates the problem that can arise when copying fixed factor calculations.

Exercise 4.51: Copying Fixed Factor Calculations

1) On Sheet1, select the cell range B46:D54, and press CTRL+c to copy it to the Clipboard.

2) Click cell F46, and press CTRL+v. Excel copies the cells to their new location without error.

   If you click on any calculated cell, however, you can see that Excel has automatically adjusted the formula arguments to reflect the new cell references.

   For example, C50 contains the formula =B50*D46. The corresponding cell in the pasted data, G50, contains the formula =G50*G46.

3) Select the cell range B49:D54, and press CTRL+c to copy it to the Clipboard.

4) Select cell J49, and press CTRL+v to paste from the Clipboard.

   This time the pasting of the cells does produce calculation errors. Excel has changed the cell references of the two fixed factors (the dollar and yen conversion rates) so that the formula cells now 'point to' the new cell locations K46 and K47 – but these cells are empty.

	J	K	L
46			
47			
48			
49	Sterling	Dollars	Yen
50	100	=J50*K46	=J50*K47
51	150	=J51*K46	=J51*K47
52	200	=J52*K46	=J52*K47
53	250	=J53*K46	=J53*K47
54	300	=J54*K46	=J54*K47
55			

There is a way to remedy this problem. First, select the pasted cell range J49:L54, and delete it with the **Edit | Clear | All** command. This removes *both* the cell content and the cell formatting.

5) Double-click on C50, and change the formula to the following: B50*C46. Similarly, in C51:C54, change all references from C46 to C46.

Next, in cells D50:D54, change all cell references from C47 to the new format of C47. Your worksheet formulas should now look as shown below.

48			
49	Sterling	Dollars	Yen
50	100	=B50*C46	=B50*C47
51	150	=B51*C46	=B51*C47
52	200	=B52*C46	=B52*C47
53	250	=B53*C46	=B53*C47
54	300	=B54*C46	=B54*C47
55			

6) Select cells B49:D54, and press CTRL+c to copy them.

7) Select cell J49, and press CTRL+v to paste from the Clipboard.

No errors! If you click on any of the formula cells, you can see that Excel has not adjusted the cell references that contained the $ symbol. Although pasted to a new location, the calculations continue 'pointing to' the original cell references of the two currency conversion rates.

In this Exercise you have learnt the difference between relative and absolute cell address. The next topic provides further details.

Cell References: The Two Kinds

In Section 4.1, you learnt that each cell on a worksheet has a unique reference, written in the form A1 – column letter first, row number second.

In fact, Excel supports two kinds of cell references: relative (the A1 type you know already) and absolute (the A1 type you met in Exercise 4.51).

Why is one type of cell reference not enough? The answer, as you discovered in Exercise 4.51, lies in the way that Excel copies and pastes calculations that contain cell references.

A cell reference that Excel adjusts automatically when the calculation cell containing it is moved to a new location is called a relative cell reference.

Relative Cell Reference

A reference to a cell or cell range in the format A1. Excel changes a relative cell reference when you copy a formula or function containing such a reference.

An absolute cell reference, however, does not change when the calculation containing it is moved to a new location. Accordingly, you should use absolute cell references when entering fixed-factor type calculations. You can make part of a cell reference absolute and part relative. For example, G$13 or $D17.

Absolute Cell Reference

A reference to a cell or cell range in the format A1. Excel does not adjust an absolute cell reference when you copy a calculation containing such a reference.

Exercise 4.52: Working with Absolute Cell Reference
In this Exercise, you will use the Find and Replace feature to convert relative cell references to absolute ones, and then copy the related calculations to a new location.

1) On Sheet1, select cell range E40:E43.

2) Choose **Edit | Replace**. Type the values shown below, and select **Replace All**.

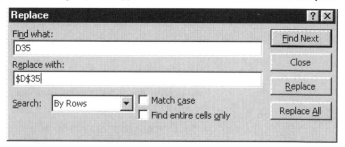

3) Select cell range G40:G43, and repeat step 2. This time, replace all occurrences of D36 with D36.

   You are now ready to copy the cells that 'point to' the two fixed factors, sales commission and taxation rate.

4) Select cell range B39:H44, and press CTRL+c to copy them to the Clipboard.

5) Click cell J39, and press CTRL+v. The calculations copy without error.

Sorting: Reordering Cells by Content

The order in which you typed entries in a worksheet may not be the order in which, later on, you would prefer to display or print that information. Suppose, for example, that you have entered a list of numbers in a column of a worksheet.

By selecting the cell range and choosing the Sort Ascending (or Sort Descending) button, you can rearrange the cells so that Excel displays them in order of increasing (or decreasing) value. The reordered list may now be easier to read than the original, unsorted one.

> **Sorting**
>
> *Rearranging columns of cells based on the values in the cells. Sorting does not change the content of cells, only their location.*

Excel offers a number of sequencing options, called sort orders.

> **Sort Order**
>
> *A particular way of ordering cells based on value. A sort order can be alphabetic or numeric, and can be in ascending (0 to 9, A to Z) or descending (9 to 0, Z to A) sequence.*

Exercise 4.53: A Simple Sort

Sort Ascending button

Sort Descending button

1) On Sheet1, click B73 and enter the label Original.

2) In the six cells immediately below B73, type the following vertical list of numbers: 453, 123, 340, 683, 987 and 213.

3) In cells C73 and D73, enter the labels Ascending and Descending.

4) Select the cell range B74:B79, and press CTRL+c.

5) Select the cell range C74:D79, and press CTRL+v.

6) Select the cell range C74:C79, and click the Sort Ascending button on the Standard Toolbar.

7) Select the cell range D74:D79, and click the Sort Descending button on the Standard Toolbar.

Your worksheet should look as shown below.

	B	C	D
72			
73	Original	Ascending	Decending
74	453	123	987
75	123	213	683
76	340	340	453
77	683	453	340
78	987	683	213
79	213	987	123
80			

The two Sort buttons give you a quick, one-click way of reordering a cell range. As you will discover in Exercise 4.54, Excel's **Data | Sort** menu command provides an additional option: you can sort a cell range based on the values in more than a single column. This is called a 'multiple sort'.

Exercise 4.54: A Complex Sort

The rows of Sheet2 are currently arranged in alphabetic sort order according to surname: Conway first, then Murphy, Smith and, lastly, Sullivan.

	A	B	C	D	E	F	G
1							
2		January	February	March	April		Totals
3	Conway	2356	3621	4185	4560		14722
4	Murphy	4921	4055	3814	3542		16332
5	Smith	3872	2441	2888	4949		14150
6	Sullivan	2903	3308	3487	3622		13320
7							
8		14052	13425	14374	16673		58524
9							

1) Select row 7 by clicking on its row heading, and choose **Insert | Rows**. Next, press CTRL+y twice. This is the keyboard shortcut for Excel's REPEAT command. Excel inserts three new, blank rows under row 6.

7						
8						
9						
10						
11	14052	13425	14374	16673		58524
12						

2) Enter in rows 7, 8 and 9 the text and numbers as shown below.

	A	B	C	D	E	F	G
1							
2		January	February	March	April		Totals
3	Conway	2356	3621	4185	4560		14722
4	Murphy	4921	4055	3814	3542		16332
5	Smith	3872	2441	2888	4949		14150
6	Sullivan	2903	3308	3487	3622		13320
7	Rafferty	2512	2864	3290	3741		12407
8	Higgins	3463	3981	4210	4974		16628
9	Smith	5951	6226	6481	6852		25510
10							
11		25978	26496	28355	32240		113069
12							

In row 11, edit the arguments of the SUM functions to include the three new rows. For example, in B11 enter the function =SUM(B3:B9).

Enter new SUM functions in G7, G8 and G9 to calculate the row totals. For example, in G8 enter =SUM(B8:E8).

3) Select column B by clicking on its column heading, and choose the **Insert | Columns** command. In the new column, enter the first names as shown.

	A	B	C	D	E	F	G	H
1								
2			January	February	March	April		Totals
3	Conway	John	2356	3621	4185	4560		14722
4	Murphy	Robert	4921	4055	3814	3542		16332
5	Smith	Zowie	3872	2441	2888	4949		14150
6	Sullivan	Andrew	2903	3308	3487	3622		13320
7	Rafferty	Aidan	2512	2864	3290	3741		12407
8	Higgins	Tracey	3463	3981	4210	4974		16628
9	Smith	Catherine	5951	6226	6481	6852		25510
10								
11			25978	26496	28355	32240		113069

4) Select cell range A3:H9, and choose **Data | Sort**.

By default, Excel shows the first column in the selected range, column A, in the Sort by drop-down box.

In the Then by drop-down box, select Column B.

Next, select the sort order of Ascending for both columns A and B, and click **OK**.

Your worksheet should now resemble that below.

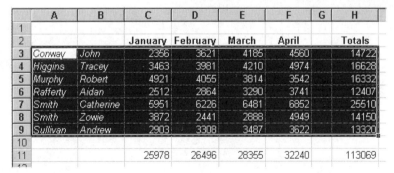

	A	B	C	D	E	F	G	H
1								
2			January	February	March	April		Totals
3	Conway	John	2356	3621	4185	4560		14722
4	Higgins	Tracey	3463	3981	4210	4974		16628
5	Murphy	Robert	4921	4055	3814	3542		16332
6	Rafferty	Aidan	2512	2864	3290	3741		12407
7	Smith	Catherine	5951	6226	6481	6852		25510
8	Smith	Zowie	3872	2441	2888	4949		14150
9	Sullivan	Andrew	2903	3308	3487	3622		13320
10								
11			25978	26496	28355	32240		113069

The multiple-column sort is useful where one column has duplicate entries. In this Exercise, cells A5 and A9 both initially contained the same text entry of 'Smith'.

Symbols and Special Characters

If you have completed the ECDL Word Processing Module, you will know that Microsoft Word allows you to insert symbols and special characters in your documents.

- **Symbols:** Among these are foreign language letters with accents (such as à, è, ä, d ë), fractions, and characters used in science and mathematics.

- **Special Characters:** These include copyright (©), registered (®) and trademark (™), plus typographic characters such as the en (or short) dash, the em (or long) dash, and various types of opening and closing quotes.

Unlike Word, Excel offers no command for inserting symbols or special characters. As Exercise 4.55 shows, however, you can paste symbols and characters from Word to Excel.

Exercise 4.55: Inserting a Special Character and Symbol to a Worksheet

1) On Sheet1 of your workbook, type 100C in B82.

2) Start Microsoft Word. It should open with a new, blank document ready for you to type into.

3) Choose **Insert | Symbol**, select the Symbols tab, and double-click the degree character (°) in the Word document. Click **Close** to close the dialog box.

4) Select the degree (°) character in the Word document, and press CTRL+c . You can now close the Word document and Word itself. You need not save the document.

5) Switch to Excel, double-click cell B82 to make it editable, position the cursor between the 100 and the C, and press CTRL+v. Cell B82 should now look like that shown below.

```
100°C
```

Section Summary: So Now You Know

A common maintenance task in Excel is *row and column insertion*. Insertion results in the surrounding cells adjusting their positions to make way for the new data.

Conversely, *row and column deletion* causes the surrounding cells to move up or to the right, to fill the spaces previously occupied by the deleted data. You can also insert and delete individual cells and cell ranges.

You can reproduce (copy) or move (cut) a selected cell or cell range within the same worksheet, between worksheets in the same workbook, or between different workbooks. A wide variety of *copy, cut and paste* methods are provided by Excel, including drag-and-drop, commands on the pop-up menu activated by right-clicking, menubar commands, keyboard shortcuts, and buttons on the Standard Toolbar.

Excel automatically adjusts the cell references in calculations whenever the calculations are pasted to a new location. To prevent Excel from adjusting a cell reference in this way, specify the cell address as an *absolute cell reference* in the format (A1). Absolute cell references are most commonly used with fixed-factor type calculations.

Sorting allows you to rearrange selected cells on the basis of the values they contain. Sorting changes only the location of cells, and not their content. The *sort order*, the particular way in which cells are arranged by value, can be alphabetic or numeric, and can be in ascending (0-9, A to Z) or descending sequence (9-0, Z-A).

You cannot insert symbols and special characters in Excel directly, but you can can insert them in a Word document, and then copy or cut and paste them from Word to Excel.

Section 4.5: More about Numbers, Text and Calculations

In This Section

In Sections 4.1 and 4.2 you learnt the basics of working with numbers, cell references and text. Now it's time to build on what you know.

Here you will discover that there are really four types of number and two types of cell reference, and that Excel treats the different types in different ways.

You will also learn more about entering text, and meet AutoFill, a convenient, time-saving feature for entering data in cells.

New Activities

At the end of this Section you should be able to:

- Choose the appropriate number format for the type of numbers that you want to enter and store in your worksheet

- Enter text across multiple columns

- Enter numbers as text

- Recognise the type of numbers that should be entered in calculations as absolute rather than relative cell references

- Use AutoFill to copy numbers and text, and to increment number series and special entries (dates, days, months and years)

- Use AutoFill to copy calculations that apply to multiple rows or columns

New Words

At the end of this Section you should be able to explain the following terms:

- Number format
- General format
- Comma style
- Currency style
- Per cent style

- Relative cell reference
- Absolute cell reference
- Increment
- AutoFill

Numbers: The Different Formats

In Section 4.1 you learnt that a number was one of the four kinds of entries you could type in a worksheet cell – the others were text, cell references, and calculations (formulas and functions).

In fact, Excel recognises many types of numbers, and calls each a number format. Do not confuse this term with the use of the word format for stylistic items such as bold and italic.

Number format affects only the way that a number looks on screen and on printouts – and *not* its value. Consider the following example:

- A cell contains the number 1.2345.

- The same cell has a number format of one decimal place.

The number will display as 1.2. But when its cell is used in calculations, the value used will be 1.2345. This can lead to surprising results on occasion!

In the example on the right, cell A1 is multiplied by B1, and cell A2 by B2. The results are shown in C1 and C2. A1 contains the same value as A2, but

	A	B	C
1	1.2345	2	2.469
2	1.2	2	2.469

is formatted with only one number after the decimal point.

> **Number Format**
> The way in which Excel displays a number on screen and on printouts. Number format affects only the appearance and not the value of numbers.

The General Format

Excel's default number format is called the General Format. Unless you change to a different number format, Excel applies this format to every number you enter.

123.4
345.75
9383.5
45

Examples of General Format

Here are some things you need to know about the General Format.

Zeros after the Decimal Point

The General Format does not display zeros after the decimal point. Enter 123.00, for example, and Excel's General Format displays 123.

Trailing Zeros

A zero you enter as the last digit after a decimal point is called a trailing zero.

The General Format does not display trailing zeros. Enter 123.40, for example, and Excel's General Format displays 123.4.

123.0
456.70
45.450

Examples of Trailing Zeros

*Thousands
Separators*

The General Format does not automatically insert the comma symbol (,) to separate thousands.

Enter 2500, for example, and Excel displays it as 2500, not 2,500.

Currency Symbols

If you type a currency symbol (such as £) before a number (such as 123), Excel may treat your entry as text rather than a number. As a result, using the entry of £123 in a calculation may generate Excel's #VALUE! error message.

*Unsuitable for
Financial Amounts*

All the above points make the General Format unsuitable for displaying amounts of money on a worksheet.

The Comma
Style

Change to the comma format for Excel to insert a comma to separate thousands. Excel also displays all numbers to two places of decimals. Exercise 4.56 demonstrates the comma style.

**Comma style
button**

Exercise 4.56: Changing Number Format to the Comma Style

1) Open Sheet2 of your workbook and select cell range C3:C9.

2) Click on the Comma Style button on the Standard Toolbar.

    Excel inserts commas and two places of decimals in the selected cell range, as shown on the right.

    Choose **Edit | Undo Style** (or press CTRL+z) to revert to General Format.

The Currency
Style

Change to the currency format when your numbers represent amounts of money. Exercise 4.57 demonstrates the currency format.

**Currency
style button**

Exercise 4.57: Changing Number Format to the Currency Style

1) On your worksheet select cell range C3:H11.

2) Click on the Currency Style button on the Standard Toolbar.

Excel inserts the currency symbol (£), the thousands separator (,) and trailing zeros.

	C	D	E	F	G	H
1						
2	January	February	March	April		Total
3	£ 2,356.00	£ 3,621.00	£ 4,185.00	£ 4,560.00		£ 14,722.00
4	£ 3,463.00	£ 3,981.00	£ 4,210.00	£ 4,974.00		£ 16,628.00
5	£ 4,921.00	£ 4,055.00	£ 3,814.00	£ 3,542.00		£ 16,332.00
6	£ 2,512.00	£ 2,864.00	£ 3,290.00	£ 3,741.00		£ 12,407.00
7	£ 5,951.00	£ 6,226.00	£ 6,481.00	£ 6,852.00		£ 25,510.00
8	£ 3,872.00	£ 2,441.00	£ 2,888.00	£ 4,949.00		£ 14,150.00
9	£ 2,903.00	£ 3,308.00	£ 3,487.00	£ 3,622.00		£ 13,320.00
10						
11	£25,978.00	£26,496.00	£28,355.00	£32,240.00		£113,069.00

The Percent Style

Percent style button

This number format performs two actions. It:

- Multiplies the selected cell or range by 100.

- Places the percent sign (%) after each selected number.

Use it to display decimal fractions (such as 0.0525) as more readable percentages (such as 5.25%).

In Exercise 4.58, you will generate some decimal fractions suitable for expression as percentages. In Exercise 4.59, you will then change the numbers to the percent style.

Exercise 4.58: Creating Decimal Fractions

In this Exercise you will add two new items to Sheet2:
– A new column to show each person's total as a proportion of the overall total
– A new row to show each month's total as a proportion of the overall

1) Enter the percent symbol (%) in cells I2 and B13, and make the symbols bold and centre align them.

2) In I3, enter the formula =H3/H11 to calculate the percentage of the total contributed by John Conway.

    Enter similar formulas for cells I4:I9.

    For example, in I5 enter = H5/H11 and in I6 enter =H6/H11.

    Column I should look as shown on the right.

I
%
0.130204
0.147061
0.144443
0.109729
0.225614
0.125145
0.117804

3) In C13, enter the formula =C11/H11 to calculate the percentage of the total contributed in January.

    Enter similar formulas for cells D11:F11. For example, to D11 enter = D11/H11. Row 13 should look as shown below.

	B	C	D	E	F
12					
13	%	0.22975351	0.23433479	0.25077607	0.28513563

Exercise 4.59: Applying the Percent Style

Now you will display the calculation results from Exercise 4.58 as percentages, using the percent style. You will also apply a fill (coloured background) to the percentage cells.

1) Select range I3:I9 and click the Percent Style button. Also centre align the cells.

2) With range I3:I9 still selected, click the drop-down arrow to the right of the Fill Colour button on the Formatting Toolbar.

3) From the colour palette, choose Grey 25%. Click **OK**.

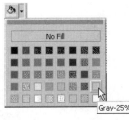

4) Select the range C13:F13 and click the Percent Style button.

5) Repeat steps 2 and 3 for C13:F13, filling the cells' background with 25% grey.

6) With C13:F13 still selected, centre align the cells.

	C	D	E	F	G	H	I
1							
2	January	February	March	April		Total	%
3	£ 2,356.00	£ 3,621.00	£ 4,185.00	£ 4,560.00		£ 14,722.00	13%
4	£ 3,463.00	£ 3,981.00	£ 4,210.00	£ 4,974.00		£ 16,628.00	15%
5	£ 4,921.00	£ 4,055.00	£ 3,814.00	£ 3,542.00		£ 16,332.00	14%
6	£ 2,512.00	£ 2,864.00	£ 3,290.00	£ 3,741.00		£ 12,407.00	11%
7	£ 5,951.00	£ 6,226.00	£ 6,481.00	£ 6,852.00		£ 25,510.00	23%
8	£ 3,872.00	£ 2,441.00	£ 2,888.00	£ 4,949.00		£ 14,150.00	13%
9	£ 2,903.00	£ 3,308.00	£ 3,487.00	£ 3,622.00		£ 13,320.00	12%
10							
11	£25,978.00	£26,496.00	£28,355.00	£32,240.00		£113,069.00	
12							
13	23%	23%	25%	29%			

Well done. You have finished this Exercise. Your worksheet should now look as shown above.

Changing from the General Format

There are two ways that you can change Excel's number format:

- First enter the numbers, and then change the number format.

- Change the number format of the blank cells first, and then enter the numbers.

The second method is better. If you are creating a new worksheet to enter financial amounts, select the whole worksheet and change the number format to currency style before entering any numbers. The currency style will affect only the entered numbers and not any text entries.

The Number Format

Spreadsheets are often used to record physical measurements and the results of laboratory experiments. Such numbers do not represent financial amounts, so the Currency style is inappropriate. Moreover, such numbers typically require a number of decimal places greater than two or three. The number format to apply in such situations is called ... Number Format. Exercise 4.60 provides an example.

Exercise 4.60: Specifying the Number of Decimal Places

Your task is to record the following numbers to four places of decimals: 3.4512, 5.13, 9.59383 and 4.531.

1) Click the Sheet1 tab to display the first worksheet of your workbook.

2) Select cell range B84:B88 and choose **Format | Cells**.

3) On the Number tab, select the Category of Number, and select 4 for Decimal places.

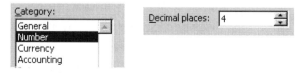

4) Click on B84, and enter the first number. Next, enter the remaining numbers in the other three cells in the range.

As shown on the left, Excel displays your cell entries to the specified number of decimal places:

3.4512
5.1300
9.5938
4.5310

- Where an entered number had more than four decimal places, Excel displayed only the first four

- Where the number has less, Excel added trailing zeros

Also available on the Number tab of the **Format | Cells** dialog box is the option to specify the thousands separator (,).

☐ Use 1000 Separator (,)

You can select this option whether you specify a fixed number of decimal places or not.

Toolbar Buttons

Two buttons on Excel's Formatting Toolbar offer quick ways of increasing or reducing the number of decimal places displayed in a selected cell or range. Each time you click on a button, the number of decimal places in the selected cells is increased or decreased by one.

Increase Decimal button

Decrease Decimal button

The buttons work with numbers in the General, Currency and Number formats.

Excel and Dates

Whether entered with financial transactions or results of experiments, dates can be very important in a worksheet. Excel treats dates as numbers, with the serial number one corresponding to the date January 1, 1900. In this way Excel can add and subtract dates, and include them in other calculations.

Entering Dates

Use a slash or a hyphen to separate the parts of a date. For example:

17/10/00
26-Nov-01
February 9, 1957

If you just type in DD/MM, Excel assumes the current year.

When you type a date that Microsoft Excel recognises, it applies one of its built-in date formats to the cell, and right-aligns it.

If Microsoft Excel cannot recognize the date, the date is recorded as text, and is left-aligned in the cell.

Formatting Dates

The way that Excel displays entered dates depends on the number format applied to the cell containing the dates.

To view a list of possible date options, choose **Format | Cells**, select the Number tab, and select Date in the Category: list. You can then see the date format options in the Type: list.

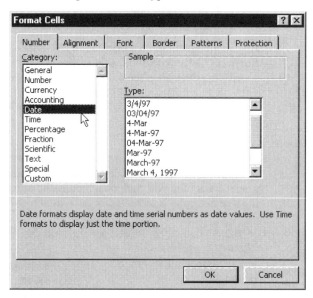

Become familiar with how Excel handles dates by entering a number of dates in different formats in your worksheet. Then, select the cells and apply to your entries some of the formats listed in the **Format | Cells** dialog box.

Regional Settings

Regional
Settings

Options you select in the Regional Settings of the Windows Control Panel affect both the currency and date conventions applied by Excel to your cell entries:

- **Changing Currency:** To use a different currency on your workbooks, choose **Start | Settings | Control Panel**, and double-click on the Regional Settings icon.

  On the Regional Settings tab, select the required country. On the Currency tab, accept or amend the currency conventions such as symbol, number of decimal places and digit grouping symbol.

- **Changing Date:** To use the date conventions of another country on your workbooks, select the required country on the Regional Settings tab, and, on the Date tab, accept or amend the calendar conventions.

Excel and Text

Two further items you need to know about Excel and text: you can enter text that displays across several columns of a worksheet, and you can enter numbers as text.

Text across Multiple Columns

Sometimes you may want to enter a line of text that is longer than the width of a single cell. Excel allows you to do this – provided that the text does not run into any cell which has data in it.

Exercise 4.61 provides an example of entering and displaying text that stretches across several columns.

Exercise 4.61: Entering Text across Multiple Columns
1) Select row 1 of Sheet2 by clicking on the row heading.

2) Choose **Insert | Rows**.

3) Press CTRL+y to repeat the row insertion. You now have two new, blank rows at the top of the worksheet.

4) In C2, enter the following text:

   First Quarter Sales Figures for 2000

5) Select C2, click on the Font Size drop-down box, and select 14 point.

6) With C2 still selected, click on the Bold and Italic buttons on the Formatting Toolbar.

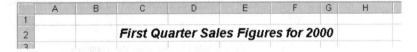

The top rows of Sheet2 should now look as shown.

Entering Numbers as Text

Why would you ever want Excel to treat a number as anything other than a number? The answer is when the number is not an amount but an identifier of some kind. Examples include part and model numbers (such as 010-34 or M5339), ID numbers (such as 99-10837), and telephone and fax numbers.

If you find it hard to think of a telephone number as anything other than a number, imagine how ridiculous it would be to add two telephone numbers together!

To enter a number as text, you must first apply the Text format to the empty cells, and then enter the numbers, as shown in Exercise 4.62. If you enter the numbers first, Excel will not apply the Text format to them – you will need to reenter all the numbers!

Exercise 4.62: Formatting Numbers as Text

1) On Sheet2, select cells B20:B23.

2) Choose **Format | Cells**.

3) On the Number tab, select Text from the Category list, and click **OK**.

4) Enter the numbers in cells B20:B23 as shown on the right.

010-56
M56-47N
091-10000
W1-S9

Excel treats the numbers as text. You can now delete the four entries from the worksheet.

Excel's AutoFill Feature

Excel provides a very convenient feature called AutoFill for copying or incrementing (increasing in a defined sequence) the entries in a cell or range.

Exercise 4.63: Using AutoFill to Copy and Increment Numbers and Text

1) In Sheet1, enter the following in cell range B19:F19, C20.

19		12	12	Hello	Jan	Mon
20			13			

2) Click on cell B19 and position the cursor over the fill handle – the black square at the bottom-right of the selected cell.

The fill handle

3) Drag the fill handle down to cell B24. Excel copies the contents of cell B19 to the other selected cells.

4) Select cell range C19:C20 and drag the fill handle down to C24.

5) Select D19 and drag the fill handle down to D24.

6) Select E19 and drag the fill handle down to E24.

7) Select F19 and drag the fill handle down to F24.

Your worksheet should now look as shown.

19		12	12	Hello	Jan	Mon
20		12	13	Hello	Feb	Tue
21		12	14	Hello	Mar	Wed
22		12	15	Hello	Apr	Thu
23		12	16	Hello	May	Fri
24		12	17	Hello	Jun	Sat

| *AutoFill and Single Numbers, Text* | For cell ranges B19:B24 and D19:D24, you began by selecting a single cell containing a number (12) and text item (Hello). As you dragged the fill handle, Excel copied the number and text into the cells that you dragged over. |

| *AutoFill and Number Series* | For cell range C19:C24, you began by selecting two cells. Excel recognised that they contained two numbers in an increasing series, (12 and 13). As you dragged the fill handle, Excel placed increments of the series (14, 15 and so on) into the cells that you dragged over. |

| *AutoFill and Months, Days, Times and Years* | For cell ranges E19:E24 and F19:F24, Excel recognised that the single cell you selected contained the name of a month and a day. As you dragged the fill handle, Excel placed increments of the series (Feb, Mar ... and Tue, Wed ...). |

Excel also recognises times (such as 9:00 or 12:30), dates (such as 1-May or 10-April) and years (such as 1996 or 2001).

| *AutoFill and Calculations* | Columns or rows of a worksheet often need the same action applied to them; for example, summing or averaging. Use AutoFill in a two-step process to avoid entering calculations (formulas and functions) individually to sum or average each row or column. |

- Enter the calculation for one row or column.
- Use AutoFill to copy the formula or function to the adjacent cells.

| *AutoFill and Cell References* | AutoFill adjusts the cell references as it copies the calculation to the selected cells. |

Where a calculation contains a fixed factor – such as a tax, currency conversion or sales commission rate – you will *not* want Excel to adjust the fixed factor's cell reference as it AutoFills the selected cells. In such cases, first change the fixed factor's cell reference to an absolute cell reference. Exercise 4.64 provides an AutoFill used with relative and absolute cell references.

Exercise 4.64: Using AutoFill to Copy Calculations
1) On Sheet2, select cell range H6:I11, and press DELETE to delete its contents.

Cell I5 now shows 100%, and the total cell H13 shows £14,722.00.

2) Select cell H5 and drag the fill handle down to cell H11.

AutoFill extends the calculation in H5 to the cells in the range H6:H11.

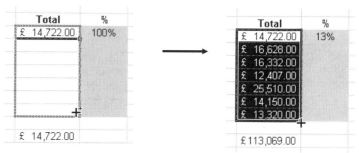

In each case, AutoFill adjusts the cell reference. For example, cell H5 contains the function =SUM(C5:F5) but cell H9 contains the function =SUM(C9:F9).

3) Select cell I5, and edit the function to change relative cell reference H13 to absolute cell reference H13.

4) With I5 still selected, drag the fill handle down to cell I11.

AutoFill extends the calculation in I5 to the cells in the range I6:I11. As it does, AutoFill adjusts the relative cell reference H5 but not the absolute cell reference H13.

Total	%
£ 14,722.00	13%
£ 16,628.00	15%
£ 16,332.00	14%
£ 12,407.00	11%
£ 25,510.00	23%
£ 14,150.00	13%
£ 13,320.00	12%
£ 113,069.00	

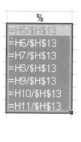

AutoFill works across rows as well as down columns, as you will learn in steps 5 and 6 of this Exercise.

5) Select cell range D13:F13, and press DELETE to delete their contents.

6) Select C13 and drag the fill handle to the right as far as cell F13.

You may find it quicker to apply AutoFill using the keyboard short cuts rather than dragging the fill handle with the mouse. Follow these steps:

- Select the cells you want to fill from.

- Drag the mouse down (or right) to select the cells you want to fill.

- Press CTRL+d to fill down or CTRL+r to fill right.

AutoFill
An Excel tool for quickly copying or incrementing (increasing in a defined sequence) the entries in a cell or range.

You have now finished this Section 4.5 of the ECDL Spreadsheet Module. You may save and close your workbook, and close Excel.

Section Summary: So Now You Know

Excel's default number format, the *general format*, does not display trailing zeros, does not automatically insert commas to separate thousands, and is unsuitable for entering financial amounts.

The *comma style* automatically inserts a comma to separate thousands, and displays all numbers to two places of decimals.

The *currency style* automatically inserts your national currency symbol, and follows your currency's convention for decimal places.

The *percent style* multiplies numbers by 100, and places the percent sign (%) after each one.

When changing to a non-default number format, it is better to do so *before* you enter your numbers. Only numbers and not text are affected by number formatting.

You can enter *multi-column text* (provided the other, over-typed cells are blank) and format *text as numbers*. This can be useful when the numbers are identifiers (part numbers, phone numbers and so on) rather than amounts.

In calculations, cells can have *relative references* or *absolute references*. Excel changes relative cell references when you copy the calculation to another cell; absolute references are unchanged by copying. Use absolute cell references for cells containing fixed factors such as tax rates.

AutoFill copies the contents of a cell to other, selected cells in the same row or column. AutoFill can also increment a series of numbers, times, dates, days, months, and years.

Section 4.6: Charting with Excel

So far you have used Excel to enter, edit, calculate, format and re-position cells on your worksheets.

In this Section you will learn how to present the contents of your worksheet cells in what Excel – an American product – calls a chart. On this side of the Atlantic, we would use the term 'graph' or 'diagram' rather than chart.

New Skills

At the end of this Section you should be able to:

- Use Excel's Chart Wizard to create charts that are based on the numbers, text and calculations in your worksheet

- Choose the appropriate options from the following dialog boxes of Excel's Chart Wizard

- Create column, bar and pie charts

- Format chart text and change chart colours

- Add and edit data labels

- Move and resize charts

- Change the scale of chart axes

New Words

At the end of this Section you should be able to explain the following terms:

- Chart

- Chart area

- Plot area

- Data point

- Data series

- Data label

Charting: The Two Steps

You follow two main steps to creating a chart in Excel:

- Select the cells whose contents you want to chart.
- Select and run Excel's Chart Wizard.

> **Excel Chart**
>
> *A graphic or diagram based on the numbers, text and calculations that are located in the rows and columns of an Excel worksheet.*

The Four Dialog Boxes of an Excel Chart

When you run the Chart Wizard, Excel presents you with a series of four dialog boxes. These are:

Chart Type: Excel offers lots of different chart types. You decide which is best for your data.

Chart Source: What data do you want to chart – all the cells on your worksheet, or just a selected cell range?

Chart Options: How do you want your chart to look? Excel offers a variety of choices.

Chart Location: Where do you want the chart stored – on your current worksheet, on a different worksheet, or in a new workbook? You decide.

Does this seem like a lot of dialog boxes to learn about? Don't worry. All four dialogs offer a default option that in most cases will create an impressive-looking, ECDL-exam-passing chart. So, when in doubt, just click the **Next** button on the first three dialog boxes, and the **Finish** button on the fourth.

Creating Your First Chart in Excel

Perform Exercise 4.65 to make yourself familiar with charting in Excel.

Exercise 4.65: Creating a Simple Excel Chart

1) Open the workbook that you saved in Section 4.5 and click on Sheet2 to display its second worksheet.

2) Select the non-adjacent cell range A4:A11, C4:C11.

   Do this by clicking in A4, dragging the mouse down to A11, and releasing the mouse button. Next, hold down the CTRL key, click in cell C4 and drag down to C11.

Excel's Chart Wizard button

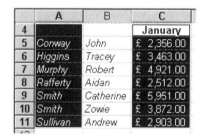

The non-adjacent cell range selected for charting

3) See the ▥ button towards the right on the Standard Toolbar? That's Excel's Chart Wizard button. Click on it.

4) Excel displays a series of four dialog boxes. On the first three, click the **Next** button. On the fourth and last, click **Finish.**

Congratulations. You have drawn your first chart in Excel!

Chart Area:
To move your chart to a different position on your worksheet, click here and drag with the mouse.

Plot Area:
The area of the plotted chart

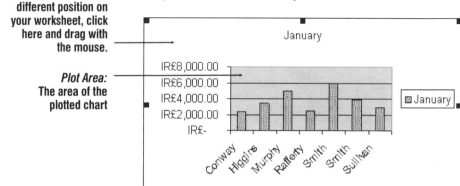

5) Unfortunately, Excel positions your chart on top of your data, so you cannot see both at the same time. Move the chart by clicking on any blank part of the chart margin – Excel calls this the Chart Area – and then dragging the chart down until its top-left corner is positioned over the cell B19.

Chart Area

The margin area inside the chart boundaries but outside the actual plotted chart. It typically holds labels identifying the chart axes.

Plot Area

The area containing the actual plot. It is bounded by the two chart axes and enclosed within the chart area.

Charts: Two Ideas You Need to Know

All charting – in Excel or with pen and paper – is based on two very basic ideas: the *data point* and the *data series*.

You will see these two terms a lot on Excel's charting dialog boxes and online help screens. Understand these two ideas and you will be able to exploit fully Excel's charting possibilities.

About Data Points

Data point: the idea is so simple that you will wonder why anyone bothered even to give it a name. Consider the four examples below.

Item	Value		Item	Value
Apples	4		January	IR£ 1,965.34
Pears	3		February	IR£ 2,451.50
Bananas	6		March	IR£ 8,301.49

Item	Value		Item	Value
Mary	15.00%		Sales	IR£4,954,032.00
Catherine	50.00%		Costs	IR£394,823.00
Margaret	35.00%		Overheads	IR£25,068.00

Each example consists of individual items (or people) being measured. They are types of fruit, months of the year, people and amounts of money.

Each item has a number that is its measured value. A *data point* is a single item and its numerical value.

In the first example, the three data points are: Apples and 4, Pears and 3 and Bananas and 6. Other data points from the above examples are February and IR£2,451.50, Catherine and 50%, and Overheads and IR£25,068.00

A data point always has two parts: the item and the value. On its own, a number is not a data point, nor is it an item. You need both for a data point.

Data Point
An item being measured and its measured value.

About Data Series

A single data point does not tell us very much. A chart is useful only if there is more than one data point. A collection of data points is called a data series.

For instance, you may want to create a chart that shows the company's sales figures for different months. Or a chart that compares one month's sales figures for different departments.

Data Series
A group of related data points. For example, your data series may compare different items measured at the same time, or single items measured at different times.

Single Data Series Charts

We used the word 'simple' to describe the chart that you created in Exercise 4.65. More precisely, it is an example of a single data series chart.

Exercise 4.66: Creating More Single Data Series Charts

Practise your charting skills by selecting the four non-adjacent cell ranges below and creating a chart from them. Drag the first chart down beneath the chart from Exercise 4.65. And drag the other three down Sheet2 so that each is positioned beneath the previous one.

Data Series: A4:A11, F4:F11

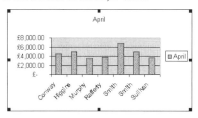

Data Series: A4:A11, I4:I11

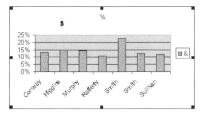

Data Series: C4:F4, C15:F15

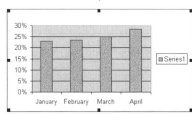

Data Series: B4:B11, H4:H11

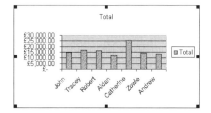

Creating a Multiple Data Series Chart

You can have more than one data series in a collection of related information.

Consider the part of your worksheet shown on the right. How many data series can you see? Answer: two.

There is one data series for January, and a second for February.

	January	February
Conway	IR£ 2,356.00	IR£ 3,621.00
Higgins	IR£ 3,463.00	IR£ 3,981.00
Murphy	IR£ 4,921.00	IR£ 4,055.00
Rafferty	IR£ 2,512.00	IR£ 2,864.00
Smith	IR£ 3,872.00	IR£ 2,441.00
Smith	IR£ 5,951.00	IR£ 6,226.00
Sullivan	IR£ 2,903.00	IR£ 3,308.00

Two data series, one for each of the two months

	January
Conway	IR£ 2,356.00
Higgins	IR£ 3,463.00
Murphy	IR£ 4,921.00
Rafferty	IR£ 2,512.00
Smith	IR£ 3,872.00
Smith	IR£ 5,951.00
Sullivan	IR£ 2,903.00

	February
Conway	IR£ 3,621.00
Higgins	IR£ 3,981.00
Murphy	IR£ 4,055.00
Rafferty	IR£ 2,864.00
Smith	IR£ 2,441.00
Smith	IR£ 6,226.00
Sullivan	IR£ 3,308.00

In Exercises 4.67 and 4.68 you will create a two-data series and a three-data series chart.

Exercise 4.67: Creating a Two-Data Series Chart in Excel

1) Select the cell range A4:A8, C4:D8.

2) Click the Chart Wizard button and accept the default options in the sequence of four dialog boxes. Your chart should look as shown below.

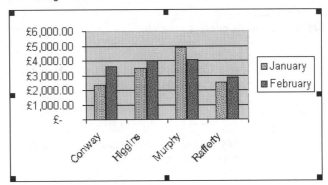

3) Drag your chart down the worksheet to beneath the last of the four charts that you created in Exercise 4.66.

When Excel draws a chart with more than a single data series, it uses a different colour to represent different items.

Exercise 4.68: Creating a Three-Data Series Chart in Excel

1) Select the cell range A4:A8, C4:E8.

2) Click on the Chart Wizard button and accept the default options in the sequence of four dialog boxes. Your chart should look as shown below.

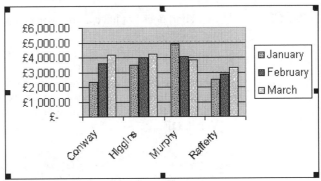

Drag the chart down the worksheet to beneath the chart that you created in Exercise 4.67.

Editing Your Chart

When you create a chart, don't think of it as fixed forever. You can change just about every aspect of a chart.

Changing Chart Data

You can amend the content of worksheet cells on which your chart is based; as soon as you change the cells in your worksheet, Excel updates the chart to reflect your changes.

Resizing the Chart

Changing your chart's size can affect its appearance dramatically. To resize a chart:

- Click once on the chart area. Handles (small black squares) appear around the chart's edges.

- Click on any handle and hold down the mouse button as you drag the chart to a different shape.

If you drag on a corner handle, the chart expands and contracts proportionately to its current size; if you drag on an edge handle, the chart expands or contracts in that direction only. Excel automatically adjusts the font size used in the chart text as you resize.

Changing the Chart Title

To edit the chart title, click anywhere on it, and then click anywhere within the title text. You can now edit the text.

To remove the chart title, click on it once, and press DELETE.

To reformat the chart title, double-click anywhere on it to display the Format Chart Title dialog box. Select the options you require from the three tabs of the dialog box: Borders and Patterns, Font, and Alignment.

Adding a Chart Title

If your chart does not have a title, you can add one as follows:

- Right-click on the chart area.

- From the pop-up menu displayed, choose **Chart Options**, select the Titles tab, type the new title in the Chart title: box, and click **OK**.

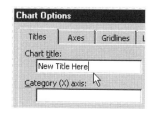

Chart Title

Text describing the chart. By default, Excel centres the chart title in the chart area over the plot area.

Adding Data Labels

In an Excel chart, a data label is an item showing the name (such as Conway) or value (such as £2,356.00) of a data point in a plotted data series. By default, Excel does not display labels.

You can add two kinds of data labels to a chart:

- **Value Labels:** These indicate the numerical values of the individual data points. See Exercise 4.69.

- **Text Labels:** These display the names of the data points. By default, Excel already displays these names on an axis. See Exercise 4.70.

Exercise 4.69: Adding Data Labels

1) On Sheet2, click on chart area of the first chart you created, the one in Exercise 4.65, and press CTRL+c to copy it to the Clipboard.

2) Click the Sheet3 tab to display the third worksheet of your workbook. Click cell B3 and press CTRL+v to paste the chart from the Clipboard.

3) Right-click on the chart area, choose **Chart Options** from the pop-up menu, and select the Data Labels tab of the dialog box.

4) Select the Show value option, and click **OK**.

Adding data labels to your chart provides more information to the reader, but has the disadvantage of making your chart more cluttered. You can remedy this by stretching the chart horizontally.

5) Click the chart, and then click the middle handle on the right edge of the chart area.

6) Drag with the mouse until the chart's right boundary ends in column K. The axes and plot area of your chart should look as shown below.

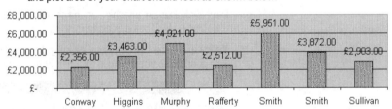

Exercise 4.70: Adding Data Name Labels

1) With the chart from Exercise 4.65 still in the Clipboard, click on a cell beneath the chart pasted in Exercise 4.69, and press CTRL+v. Choose **Chart Options** from the pop-up menu, and select the Data Labels tab of the dialog box.

2) Select the Show label option, and click **OK**.

3) As in Exercise 4.69, drag the chart's right boundary to column K. The axes and plot area of your chart should look as shown below.

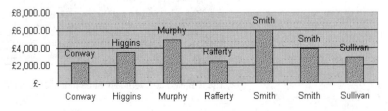

Formatting Data Labels

To format data labels, right-click on a label, choose **Format | Data Labels** from the pop-up menu, and select your required options from the following four dialog box tabs: Patterns, Font, Number, and Alignment.

Data Label
The name or numerical value of a data point in a plotted data series.

Changing the Scale

To change the scale of an axis, double-click anywhere along the axis and choose **Format Axis** from the pop-up menu.

Excel allows you to change the the minimum, maximum and increment values displayed for each axis, and the point at which the two axes cross. In Exercise 4.71 you will change the scale of a chart's vertical (or Y) axis.

Exercise 4.71: Changing the Scale of the Vertical Axis
1) Is the first chart you created, the one in Exercise 4.65, still in the Clipboard? If not copy it to the Clipboard now.

2) Click the Sheet3 tab to display the third worksheet of your workbook. Click on a cell beneath the chart pasted in Exercise 4.70, and press CTRL+v.

3) Click the chart, and then click on the middle handle on its lower edge. Drag down the mouse until the chart is about twice its original height.

4) Double-click anywhere on the chart's vertical axis and, on the Format Axis dialog box, select the Scale tab.

5) Change the Minimum: box from 0 to 2000. And change the value in the Major unit: box from 2000 to 500. Click **OK** to close the dialog box.

6) Double-click again anywhere on the chart's vertical axis, and, on the Format Axis dialog box, reselect the Scale tab.

    Notice that Excel has changed Category (X) axis Crosses at: box from 0 to 2000. This is because you changed the Minimum box: from 0 to 2000.

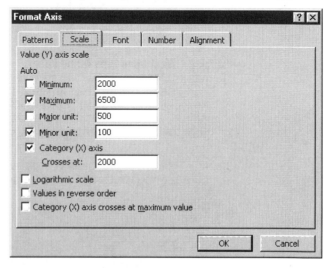

The rescaled and vertically stretched chart should now look as shown.

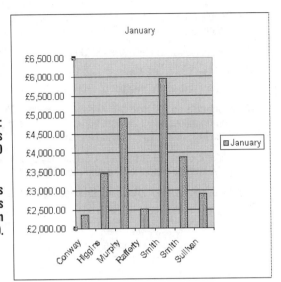

Rescaled chart: Vertical axis values begin at £2,000 rather than £0.

Also, vertical axis is in expressed in units of £500 rather than £2,000.

Changing Chart Colours

Excel enables you to change the colours of three parts of a chart: the chart area, the plot area and the data series. In each case, you right-click on the relevant element, choose the **Format** command from the pop-up menu, and select your required fill colour. See Exercise 4.72.

Exercise 4.72: Changing a Chart's Colours

1) Right-click on the chart area of the chart you created in Exercise 4.71.

   (The chart area is the blank margin surrounding the actual plotted chart.)

2) Choose the **Format Chart Area** command from the pop-up menu, select the Patterns tab, click the colour yellow in the Area section of the dialog box, and click **OK**.

3) Right-click on the plot area of the chart.

   (This is the actual plotted chart, bounded by the two chart axes.)

4) Choose the **Format Plot Area** command from the pop-up menu, click the colour yellow in the Area section of the dialog box, and click **OK**.

5) Right-click on any of the chart columns.

   (The columns represent the data series of the chart.)

6) Choose the **Format Data Series** command from the pop-up menu, select the Patterns tab, click the colour red in the Area section of the dialog box, and click **OK**.

In the second part of this Exercise 4.72, you will reformat the text elements of the chart.

7) Double-click the X-axis, select the Font tab, change the font to Bold and the Font Colour to dark blue, and click **OK**.

8) Repeat step 7 for the Y-axis, but do not close the dialog box.

9) With the Y-axis still selected, select the Number tab on the Format Axis dialog box, and set zero as the number of decimal places. Click **OK**.

10) Right-click on the chart title, choose the **Format Chart Title** command from the pop-up menu, select the Font tab, change the Font to Times New Roman, Font Style to Italic and Font Size to 14 point.

11) With the chart title still selected, select the Patterns tab of the dialog box, select the Automatic Border option, and click **OK**.

Well done. You have completed the Exercise. Your chart should now look as shown below.

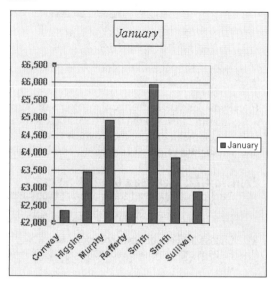

Charts Types

Excel offers over a dozen chart types, but you need only know the following three:

Column Chart:
Items are shown horizontally and values vertically. This is Excel's default chart type, and the only one you have used in your charting exercises so far.

Bar Chart:
A sideways column chart that shows items horizontally and values vertically.

Pie Chart:
Shows the proportion of each item that makes up the total. Unlike column, bar and most other chart types, you can use pie charts for a single data series only.

Setting the Chart Type

When you select a cell range and choose the Chart Wizard, you decide which chart type you want to use in the first of the four dialog boxes displayed by the Wizard, the Chart Type box. As you can see, most chart types offer sub-types or variations.

You can preview how your cell data will look in a particular chart type by selecting a Chart Type option and clicking the Press and Hold to View Sample button.

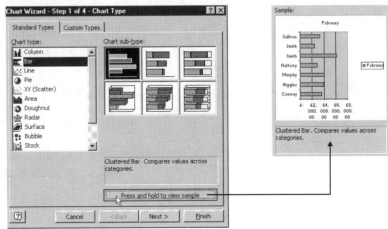

Changing Chart Type

To change the current type of a chart, right-click anywhere within the chart (chart area, plot area or data series – it does not matter), choose the **Chart Type** command from the pop-up menu, and select a different type (or sub-type) from the Chart Type dialog box.

In Exercise 4.73 you will create a new chart of the bar chart type. In Exercise 4.74, you will change a bar chart to a column one.

Exercise 4.73: Creating a Bar Chart

1) On Sheet3, click on a cell beneath the chart you worked with in Exercise 4.72. This will be the location at which the chart you create in this Exercise will begin.

2) Click the Sheet1 tab to display the first worksheet of your workbook.

3) Select non-adjacent cell range C25:D26, F25:G26, and click the Chart Wizard button.

4) Excel now displays the Standard Types tab of the Chart Wizard – Step 1 of 4 – Chart Type dialog box. Select the Bar chart type and click **Next**.

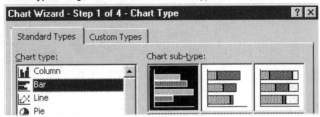

5) Excel now displays the Data Range tab of the Chart Wizard – Step 2 of 4 – Chart Source Data dialog box. Click **Next**.

6) Excel now displays the Data Labels tab of the Chart Wizard – Step 3 of 4 – Chart Options dialog box.

Click the Titles tab, and type a Chart Title of Product 1 and click **Next**.

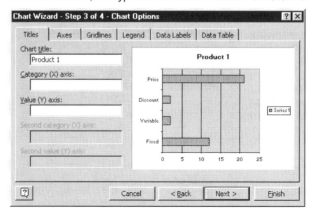

7) Excel now displays the Chart Wizard – Step 4 of 4 – Chart Location dialog box.

Change the As object in: box to Sheet3 and click **Finish**.

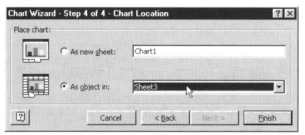

Excel positions the chart on your third worksheet, Sheet3. It positions the chart so that its top-left corner is at the cell you most recently clicked on in that worksheet. Your bar chart should look like that shown.

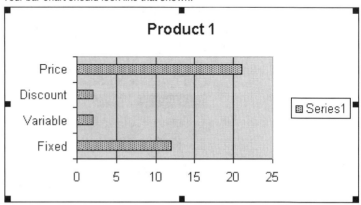

Exercise 4.74: Changing a Column to a Bar Chart

1) On Sheet2, click the third chart you created in Exercise 4.66. It is based on the cell range C4:F4,C15:F15. Copy it to the Clipboard.

2) Click the Sheet3 tab to display your third worksheet. Paste the chart from the Clipboard to a cell beneath the chart from Exercise 4.73.

3) Right-click on the chart area, choose **Chart Type** from the pop-up menu, select bar chart from the dialog box, and click **OK**.

Your bar chart should look like that shown.

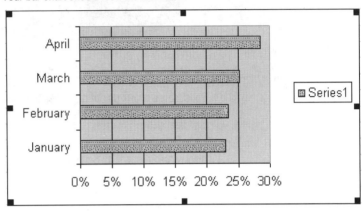

Working with Pie Charts

In Exercise 4.75 you will create a pie chart based on a single data series. You will then format the pie chart, and 'explode' a slice of the pie to draw particular attention to the contribution it represents to the total.

Exercise 4.75: Creating and Formatting a Pie Chart

1) On Sheet2, select the cell range A4:A11, C4:C11.

2) Click the Chart Wizard button.

3) In the Chart Type dialog box, select Pie Chart as the Standard Type, and Pie with a 3D visual effect as the Sub-type. Click **Next**.

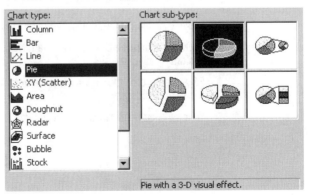

4) On the remaining Chart Wizard dialog boxes, click **Next** and, finally, **Finish**.

Drag the pie chart down Sheet2 to beneath the chart you created in Exercise 4.68. Your chart should look as shown below.

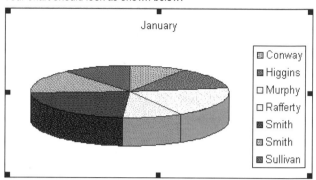

Because pie charts do not have axes to indicate data point names and values, the various slices are typically accompanied by data labels. You will add these in the next step of this Exercise.

5) Double-click on the pie chart plot area (and not the surrounding chart area) to display the Format Data Series dialog box.

6) Select the Data Labels tab, select the option Show percent, and click **OK**. Your pie chart should now look as below. Notice how the plot area shrank in size to make room for the percentage data labels.

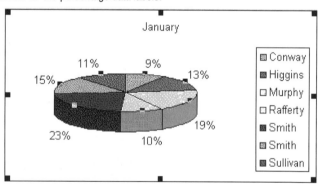

In the final step of this Exercise, you will 'explode' one slice of the pie chart.

7) Click once the plot area of the pie chart. Next, click the slice you want to explode and drag it out of the pie.

For example, click the largest slice, the one with 23% data label, and drag it down and to the left.

Your pie chart should now look as shown.

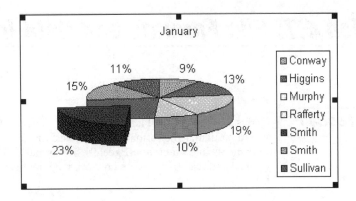

Congratulations. You have now completed Section 4.6 on charting with Excel. You may close and save your workbook, and close Excel.

Section Summary: So Now You Know

To draw a chart in Excel, first select the cells with the numbers and text that you want to chart, and then run Excel's *Chart Wizard*. The Wizard's default options on its four dialog boxes are acceptable in most cases.

If you change any of the data on which a chart is based, Excel updates the chart to reflect the changes.

By default, Excel positions your chart on top of your worksheet data. You can move the chart by clicking on any blank part of the chart margin, and then dragging the chart to a new position.

Charting is based on the ideas of data points and data series. A *data point* is a single item and its related value (for example, the sales figure in January), while a *data series* is a group of related data points (for example, monthly sales figures over a year). You can chart more than one data series at one time.

Excel offers a wide range of *chart types*, with column, bar and pie charts being the most commonly used. You can *format* your chart in a variety of ways by adding data labels, colours and borders.

Section 4.7: File Formats and Data Importing

In This Section

In this Section you will learn how Excel 97, as do all other applications, uses a particular file format. You will also discover how to convert your documents into other, non-Excel 97 file formats, so that they can be opened and read by people who work with applications other than Excel 97.

You will also discover how files containing images, graphs and text may be inserted into Excel worksheets.

New Skills

At the end of this Section you should be able to:

- Save Excel 97 files in the following file formats: Excel 97 template, earlier versions of Excel, other spreadsheets, databases, text-only and HTML, the file format of the World Wide Web.

- Explain the difference between two types of character delimited text files: tab-delimited and column delimited.

- Explain the difference between character delimited and space delimited text files.

- Insert image files in an Excel worksheet, and files containing graphs created in applications other than Excel 97.

- Import text files using Excel's Text Import Wizard.

New Words

At the end of this Section you should be able to explain the following terms:

- File format

- Tab-delimited text file

- Comma separated values (csv) text file

- Column delimited text file

File Formats

In ECDL Module 1, you learnt how all information stored on a computer consists ultimately of just two characters: 1 and 0. This raises two, related questions:

- When you open an Excel workbook file, how are these 1s and 0s translated into the text, numbers and charts you see on your computer screen?

- And, when you save a file, how are the text, numbers and charts converted back to 1s and 0s on your computer?

The answer is that the application developers apply a set of rules that translate between the 1s and 0s and the displayed text, numbers and charts. Such a set of rules is called a file format.

> **File Format**
>
> *A set of rules that translates 1s and 0s into text and graphics on computers screens and printouts, and vice versa.*

An Excel file, for example, is said to be in Excel file format; an Access file in Access file format, and so on.

Different Applications, Different File Formats

Different software companies, however, use different sets of rules for translating 1s and 0s into the text and graphics on screens and printouts.

Moreover, different versions of the one application often use different file formats. The Microsoft Excel 97 file format, for example, is different from the file formats of previous versions of Excel.

These different file formats, as you can imagine, can create problems:

- In one file format, for example, the characters 10101010 might translate as the number '12' positioned in cell A4.

- In another, the same characters of 10101010 might convert to the label 'Annual Profit' in cell Z54.

File Name Extensions

The format of a file is revealed by its three-letter file name extension, which the software application adds to the file name when the user saves the file.

The file name extension of .xls, for example, indicates an Excel workbook, and .mdb an Access database.

The file format used in pages on the Word Wide Web is HTML, which stands for HyperText Markup Language. HTML file names typically end in .htm.

Excel's File Format Options

Excel 97 offers you the ability to save your documents in a format other than its own. This feature is very useful when you want to provide a file you have created to someone who uses an application other than Excel 97.

To view the file formats in which you can save your Excel 97 documents:

- Open a document.

- Choose **File | Save As**.

- Click on the arrow to the right of the Save as type: box.

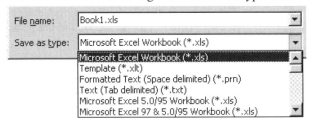

Only some of the listed options are relevant to this ECDL Spreadsheet Module. Note that the features and formatting of a Microsoft Excel 97 workbook might not be available if you save the workbook in the file format of a previous version of Microsoft Excel or of another application.

Excel Template

Excel 97 offers you the ability to save a workbook as a template, and then use the saved template as a basis for quickly creating other, similar workbooks.

For example, you could create a workbook for use as an expense form, enter and format relevant text labels, place borders around certain cells, and enter the function =SUM(C2:C22) in cell C23 so that whatever numbers were typed in the range C2:C22 are totalled and displayed in C23.

By saving such a workbook as a template, you speed up the process of creating further expense forms because the text, formatting and addition calculation need not be reentered.

To save a workbook as a template, choose **File | Save As** and select the Template (*.xlt) option.

Previous Excel Versions

You can save your Excel 97 workbook in the file formats of previous versions of Microsoft Excel. You have two main options:

- **Microsoft Excel 97 & 5.0/95 Workbook:** This saves a workbook in both Excel 97 and Excel 95 file formats in the same .xls file.

- **Any Earlier Format**: If you save a workbook in such earlier Excel file formats as Excel 4.0 or 3.0, features and formatting unique to Microsoft Excel 97 are lost.

dBASE and Quatro Pro Formats	Select from these options to save your work so that it can be opened and read by users with versions of dBASE, a database application, and Lotus 1-2-3 and Quatro Pro, two other spreadsheet applications.	

Only the currently displayed worksheet is converted. To convert other worksheets of a workbook, display and then save each one individually.

Text-Only Format

As its name suggests, this format saves only the text of a file. The word 'text' in this context includes numbers as well as alphabetic characters. All formatting is lost. This format is also called plain-text or ASCII format.

Two of the more commonly used plain-text options are as follows:

- **Text (Tab-delimited):** This saves only the currently displayed worksheet. To convert other worksheets of a workbook, switch to each sheet and save it separately. The file name extension added is .txt.

  In this format, cell entries in different columns but on the same row are separated from each other by the tabs. Different rows are separated by paragraph breaks.

  As you can see in the example below, text in the tab-delimited format does not necessarily line up vertically in neat columns.

Original Data in Excel File

	A	B	C	D	E	F
1						
2		January	February	March	April	May
3		12	45	35	41	56
4		11	42	34	39	47

Excel file saved in tab-delimited format, and viewed in Notepad text editor

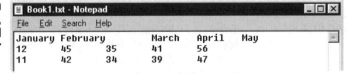

- **CSV (comma delimited):** As tab-delimited above, but with a comma separating cells on the same row. The file name extension added is .csv, meaning comma separated values. As you can see in the example below, text in the tab-delimited format does not necessarily line up vertically in neat columns.

Excel file saved in CSV format, and viewed in Notepad text editor

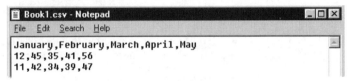

Tab Delimited Text File

A text format file in which data items are separated horizontally by tabs and vertically by paragraph breaks.

> **Comma Separated Values (CSV) Text File**
> *A text format file in which data items are separated horizontally by commas and vertically by paragraph breaks.*

HTML (Web) Format

Web pages are created using the HTML file format. The file name extension of this format is .htm (or, sometimes, .html).

You can save an Excel 97 file in HTML format in either of two ways:

- Choose **File | Save As HTML**

-or-

- Choose **File | Save As**, and select the HTML Document option

The worksheet cells are converted to table cells in the HTML file. You can display and print HTML format files with a Web browser application such as Microsoft Internet Explorer or Netscape Navigator.

Inserting from Other Applications

Microsoft Office applications (and most other Windows applications) allow you to transfer information between them. For this ECDL Spreadsheet Module, you need only know how to insert the following items in Excel:

- Images
- Graphs
- Text

Inserting Images

To insert an image, choose **Insert | Picture**, and then select the relevant option. The range of options available to you depends on whether you have installed the Microsoft Office Clip Art Gallery and whether a scanner is attached to your computer.

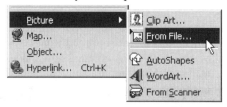

- To *reposition* an inserted image, click it to select it, and then drag the image to a different part of your worksheet.

- To *resize* an inserted image, click on it to select it, then click any handle and drag the image to a different shape.

  If you drag on a corner handle, the image expands and contracts proportionately to its current size; if you drag on an edge handle, the image expands or contracts in that direction only.

Exercise 4.76: Inserting an Image File in Excel

To insert an image in a worksheet, you need an image to work with. If you do not have one to hand, follow steps 1 and 2 of this Exercise to obtain one from the author's website.

1)   Connect to the Internet, start Microsoft Internet Explorer (or Netscape Navigator) and visit the author's website at www.munnelly.com.

2)   Right-click on the image at the top-left of the first page to display a pop-up menu, choose **Save Picture As** (or, in Netscape, **Save Image As**), and save the image file to your computer as munnelly_com.jpg.

3)   Display an Excel worksheet, click on a cell, choose **Insert | Picture | From File**, locate the munnelly_com.jpg image file (or any other image file), and click **Insert**.

   Excel inserts the image as shown below.

Inserting Graphs

Graphs can be created in applications other than Excel – for example, in Microsoft PowerPoint or in non-Microsoft applications.

To insert such a graph, select it in the application in which it was created, copy it to the Clipboard, open the Excel worksheet, and choose the **Edit | Paste** command.

Inserting Text

You may want to insert two types of text into an Excel worksheet:

- Small amounts of text, selected from a text file, for use in Excel as worksheet headings, for example, or labels for individual cells.

   To insert text in a single cell of a worksheet, open the application in which the text was created, copy the text to the Clipboard, switch to Excel, and then use Excel's **Edit | Paste** command to insert it in a selected Excel cell.

- An entire text file, containing numbers as well as text characters, which you want Excel to 'interpret' and arrange correctly across rows and down columns.

   To assist you inserting a text file in this way, Excel provides a Text Import Wizard.

Earlier in this Section you learnt about tab-delimited and comma-separated text files in which the tab and comma characters are positioned within the file to indicate where one column of data ends and the next begins. These are called *character-delimited* files, because a specific character consistently indicates column endings.

In other text files, a column ending may be indicated not by a single occurrence of a specific character but by a series of blank spaces. These are called *column-delimited* files, because the blank spaces cause the data to line up vertically.

In both types of text files, row endings are indicated by paragraph breaks. In Exercise 4.77, you will create a tab-delimited file, and in Exercise 4.78 you will import that file using Excel's Text Import Wizard.

> ### Column Delimited Text File
> *A text format file in which data items are separated horizontally by a series of spaces and vertically by paragraph breaks. The blank spaces cause the data to line up vertically.*

Exercise 4.77: Creating a Tab-Delimited Text File

1) Using Notepad or other text editor, create a new file.

2) Type the following five words, pressing the TAB key after each word except the last (Do not type spaces between the words.):

   January February March April May

3) Press ENTER to move the cursor to a new line.

4) Type the following five numbers, pressing the TAB key after each one except the last. (Do not type spaces between the numbers.):

   12 45 35 41 56

5) Press ENTER to move the cursor to a new line.

6) Type the following five numbers, pressing the TAB key after each one except the last (again, do not type spaces between the numbers):

   11 42 34 39 47

7) Your file should look as shown below. As you can see, the columns do not line up vertically, as is common in tab-delimited files.

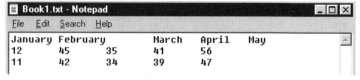

8) Save, name and close the file.

Exercise 4.78: Importing a Tab-Delimited Text File

1) In Excel, choose **File | Open**, and select the text file saved in Exercise 4.77.

2) Excel displays the Text Import Wizard dialog box. As you can see, Excel has correctly interpreted it as a tab-delimited file.

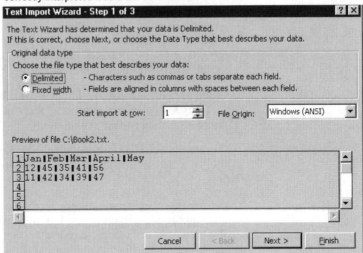

3) Click any **Next** buttons displayed, and finally click **Finish**.

Your worksheet cells should now look as shown below.

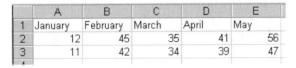

	A	B	C	D	E
1	January	February	March	April	May
2	12	45	35	41	56
3	11	42	34	39	47

You can save and close your workbook, and close Excel.

You have now completed the final Section of the ECDL Spreadsheet Module. Congratulations.

Section Summary: So Now You Know

A *file format* is a set of rules that translates between the 1s and 0s used by the computer to store information and the text and graphics displayed on screens and on printouts. Different applications – even different versions of the same application – can use different and incompatible file formats.

To help you share your files with others, Excel 97 allows you to save your workbooks in a file format other than its own. The options include: earlier versions of Microsoft Excel, Lotus 1-2-3 and Quatro Pro (other spreadsheets), dBASE (a database) and HTML (the Web page file format).

Another option is to save an Excel 97 workbook as an Excel *template*, and reuse any text, numbers, formatting and calculations in the template as a basis for creating further workbooks.

Excel workbooks can also be saved as *text-only* files, with tabs or commas inserted to separate different columns, and paragraph breaks to separate rows.

You can insert image files into an Excel worksheet, and graphs created in other applications. Excel's Text Import Wizard assists you in opening text files because it can recognise characters that have been inserted in the text files to separate different columns and rows.

Module

5 *Databases*

You can never be too rich, too healthy, or too informed. The best kind of information to have is that which is organised in such a way that you can find the facts you need quickly and easily. It's also important to be able to store new items that you come across.

Databases – structured collections of facts about a particular topic – existed long before computers. Address books, card indexes and telephone directories are all examples of databases. But by storing your facts in a database file on a computer, you gain the power to manage and manipulate that information – even very large amounts of information – in a variety of ways.

You will discover how to view information in your database file from different perspectives, sort and select particular pieces you are interested in, and produce printed reports.

Think of this Module as your chance to file rather than be filed. Good luck with it.

Section 5.1: What is a Database?

A database, as you will learn in this Section, is an organised collection of information relating to the same topic or subject matter. By 'organised' we mean that it should easy to find a particular item of information in it, and to add new items to the database.

Microsoft Access is an application that enables you to create and work with databases. To give you an idea of what a computer database looks like, this Section will takes you on a tour of one of the sample databases provided with Access.

And by considering some examples of practical, everyday databases, you will gain an insight into the kind of decisions that designers need to make before they begin constructing their databases.

New Skills

At the end of this Section, you should be able to:

- Explain what a database is

- List some common examples of databases

- State the advantages of computer databases over paper-based ones

- Start and quit Access

- Explore the sample databases provided with Access

- Explain two ways of looking at the information in a computer database

- Decide on a structure for a simple database

New Words

At the end of this Section, you should be able to explain the following terms:

- Database

- Database management system

- Table

- Field

- Record

- Datasheet View

- Form View

An Organised Collection of Information

A database is a collection of information relating to the same topic or subject matter. It is usually organised in such a way that you can easily:

- Find the items of information in which you are interested
- File away the new items that you come across

Database

A database is an organised collection of related information.

A database does not have to be kept on a computer. For example, address books, card indexes, and telephone directories are all databases (even though very few people would call them that!).

Storing a database on a computer, however, enables you to manipulate the information easily and quickly. For example, using a (paper-based) telephone directory, it is relatively easy to find a person's telephone number, but it is very difficult (but not impossible) to find the person's name if you only have their telephone number.

A computer-based directory enables you to find that information quickly and easily. You could also find the names of everyone who lives on a particular road, or everyone whose first name was Paul. Or you could print a report showing the five most common surnames.

Computer-based databases are flexible: they enable you to deal with information – even very large quantities of information – in a variety of ways. Microsoft Access is an example of a database management system – an application that enables you to create and manage a database on a computer.

Database Management System

An application such as Microsoft Access that enables you to collect information on a computer, organise it in different ways, sort and select pieces of information of interest to you, and produce reports.

Records and Fields

Databases use information broken down into its smallest, most divisible parts. Each part goes into its own named *field*. For example, if you were entering names and addresses into a database, you would *not* put all the information into a single field, like this:

James Coogan Sweeney
10744 South Hoyne
Chicago
Illinois 60643
USA

You would normally enter each piece of information into a separate field, as follows:

FirstName:	James
MiddleName:	Coogan
LastName:	Sweeney
FirstAddress:	10744 South Hoyne
SecondAddress:	
City:	Chicago
State:	Illinois
Zipcode:	60643
Country:	USA

Field

A field is a single piece of information about a subject. More precisely, it is the space where that information is held.

In a database, individual pieces of information (such as a telephone number) are called *fields*, and the set of information relating to one individual is called a *record*.

Record

A record is one complete set of fields relating to the same subject.

Tables and Databases

A collection of records is called a *table*. If a database contains just a single table, the table *is* the database. In this ECDL Module, you will be dealing only with single-table databases. All that you need know about multi-table databases is that Access allows you to create them.

When there are thousands or hundreds of thousands of records, a database management system comes into its own. A computer asked to extract and show only records where, for instance, surnames (LastName) begin with 's' and where postcodes (Zipcodes) begin with '60', responds at breathtaking speed, far beyond the capacity of human sorters.

A database management system, however, lacks 'common sense' – it is not able to make judgements. If you did not enter the information in the right field, it will not be retrieved correctly.

Table

A table is a collection of records that contain the same fields.

Two Views: Datasheet and Forms

With Access, and with most database management systems, you can view and manipulate information in two ways: in a datasheet, or in forms.

In *Datasheet View*, you can see the information arranged in columns (one for each field) and rows (one for each record); it is similar in appearance to a spreadsheet. See below.

An example of a *Datasheet View*, where you can see several records at once

Number	Bird Name	Colour	Number Seen	Size	Migratory?	Date Seen	Place Seen
1	Great Northern	Black/White	23	69	Yes		
2	Great Crested (	Grey/White/Brown	21	46	No	3/13/99	Dalkey
3	Little Grebe	Black/Brown	14	24	No	4/9/98	Stephen's Green
4	Gannet	White/Black	5	85	No	12/6/98	Ireland's Eye
5	Fulmar	White/Grey	3	45	No		
6	Great Shearwat	White/Brown	7	42	Yes		
7	Manx Shearwat	Black/White	17	30	No		
8	Storm Petrel	Black/White	1	13	No		
9	Cormorant	Black/White	3	83	No	12/6/98	Ireland's Eye
10	Grey Heron	Grey/White	4	90	No		
11	Mute Swan	White	12	144	No	6/14/99	Malahide
12	Brent Goose	Black/White	34	56	Yes	12/12/98	Dollymount
13	Greylag Goose	Grey	22	76	Yes		
14	Shelduck	White/Brown/Black	16	57	No		
15	Goldeneye	White/Black	9	41	Yes		
16	Teal	Grey/Multicolour	14	34	No	9/28/98	Wexford
17	Mallard	Green/White/Brown	16	55	No	9/28/98	Wexford
18	Sparrowhawk	Blue/White	1	28	Yes	7/6/98	
19	Kestrel	Grey/Brown	2	33	No		
20	Pheasant	Green/Gold	6	0	No	9/27/98	Wexford
21	Dodo	Blue/White/Yellow	0	90	No	8/8/81	Mauritius
22	Blue Tit	Blue/Yellow/Black/White	4	6	No	7/6/99	Ballsbridge
(AutoNumber)			0	0	No		

> ### Datasheet View
> *A view of a database table where you see can information presented in rows and columns, with several records visible at the same time.*

A *Form View* presents all or selected information for a single record at a time. The form can be laid out in a format that is easier to read, perhaps with explanatory text. You can structure the form in such a way that it looks like a paper form, with the fields in the corresponding place on the screen.

An example of a *Form View*, where you can see details from a single record only

Number	11
Bird Name	Mute Swan
Colour	White
Number Seen	12
Size	144
Migratory?	☐
Date Seen	Monday, June 14, 1999
Place Seen	Malahide

> ### Form View
> *A view of a database table that presents all or selected information from a single record only.*

A good way of learning more about computer databases is by examining some sample ones. Access comes with three sample databases: Northwind, Orders, and Solutions. Exercise 5.1 takes you on a tour of the Northwind database. First, you need to start Access.

Starting Access

To start Access, *either*:

- Double-click on the Microsoft Access icon
  -or-

Microsoft
Access

- Choose **Start | Programs | Microsoft Access**

Access starts and displays a dialog box that gives you the choice of opening an existing database, or of creating a new database.

Exploring a Sample Database

Now let's take a tour of a database that Microsoft prepared earlier – the Northwind sample database.

Exercise 5.1: Opening the Northwind Database

1) Select the Open an Existing Database option in the opening dialog box.

2) The sample databases may be listed in the dialog box: if they are, select Northwind.mdb.

```
⌖  ⊙ Open an Existing Database

More Files...
C:\mydocs1\birds
birds2
C:\Program Files\...\Samples\Northwind
C:\Program Files\...\Samples\Solutions
```

If the sample databases are not listed, select the More Files item in the database list. You can then navigate through the directories on your PC to find them. They are most likely in the Samples subdirectory of your Access directory (C:\Program Files\Microsoft Office\Office\Samples). Use Windows Explorer to find them if necessary. When you find Northwind.mdb, select it.

3) Click **OK**.

4) If you are presented with a welcome screen, click **OK** to close it.

Access now displays the Database dialog box.

The Database screen – the 'control centre' of Access

From here you can work with the various database objects

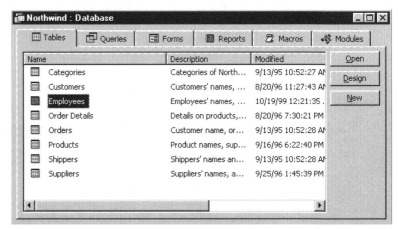

Access File Name Extension

The file names of Access databases end in .mdb (Microsoft database). This helps you to distinguish Access files from other file types such as Excel spreadsheets (.xls) or Word documents (.doc).

The Database Dialog Box

On the Database dialog box you can see six tabs: Tables, Queries, Forms, Reports, Macros and Modules. They are all sets of items – Access calls them *objects* – that are associated with the database in some way. For ECDL, you need learn only about the first four: you don't need to worry about the ones named Macros and Modules.

- **Tables:** You will learn how to create a table in Section 5.2, and modify it in Section 5.3.

- **Queries:** Section 5.4 shows you how to create queries – predefined ways of viewing information from your table on screen.

- **Forms:** Section 5.5 shows you how to create and format the appearance of forms, and how use them to enter and modify records.

- **Reports:** These enable you to extract information from your database as printouts. You will learn about reports in Section 5.6

You will see the Database Dialog box a lot when you are working with Access. From here, you can open any of the database objects – to work with them or to change them – and when you are finished with that object, Access returns you to this Database dialog box, from where you can work with any of the other objects easily.

When you first open a database, the Tables tab is normally on top. If it isn't, simply click the Tables tab, and it comes to the top.

Notice that the Northwind database contains several tables. Open Employees, either by selecting it and clicking **Open**, or by double-clicking on its name or icon. Have a look at the type of information it contains. This will give you a good idea of how databases are actually used. If the table contains more records than can be shown on a single screen, use the vertical scroll bar to move up and down the range of records. If the records are too wide to be displayed on a single screen, use the horizontal scroll bar to move left and right. If you scroll far enough to the right, you will see a Photo column. Double-click any one of these fields to view the employee's photo, then close the photo window.

Maximise button

(If your horizontal scroll bar is not visible, you will have to click the Maximise button, after which the scroll bar becomes visible.)

Database Design Considerations

In Section 5.2, you will create a database of your very own. But before using Access to build *any* database, take some time to think about the kind of information that you want to put into your database, and how you want to use it.

The following four examples demonstrate the kind of decisions that database designers need to make before they begin constructing their databases.

Henry is interested in wine. He reads the wine column in the newspapers and notes the recommendations. When he goes to the supermarket, he brings a list with him, so that he can select wine based on the recommendations. When he buys wine, he might have it in the house for some time before he tastes it, and he likes to record his impressions and compare notes with the original review.

Henry might include the following fields in his database:

- Wine Style (Red / White / Rosé / Sparkling / Sweet)
- Name
- Country/Region
- Grower
- Grape Varieties
- Vintage
- Recommended by
- Review comments
- Available from (shop)
- Price
- Number bought
- Date bought
- Date tasted
- Tasting notes
- Buy again?

With such a database, Henry could print out a separate list for each shop, he could list all the red wines, he could list all the white wines that cost less than £10, he could find where the wines by a particular grower were available, he could view the comments on different vintages of the same wine, and so on.

Michelle plays the piano, and has a large collection of CDs. When she is learning a new piece, she likes to listen to other people playing it. She has built a database with the following fields:

- CD Title
- Artist
- Track Number
- Name of Tune
- Composer
- Date recorded

By sorting the database in the Name of Tune field, she can quickly identify the particular CDs that include the tune she is working on.

Example 3:
The Household
Manager's Database

Oscar started his database for insurance purposes: it enabled him to build up a detailed record of his house contents. It included the following fields:

- Room
- Item
- Category
- Date Purchased
- Price Paid

With this database, he was able to provide an accurate inventory to the insurance company to support a claim. He could provide the original cost, along with the depreciated value, and the replacement value, based on the original cost and the elapsed time since the purchase. He could also quickly give a value for all the paintings in the house, the value of all the clothes in the upstairs rooms, or all the contents of a particular room.

Example 4:
The Bird Spotter's
Database

Every weekend, Clara goes out with her field glasses and notebook, and spends some time watching birds. When she comes home, she puts details of what she has seen into a database. The database has the following fields:

- Bird Name
- Colour
- Size
- Number Seen
- Migratory?
- Place Seen
- Date Seen

Clara has entered into her database the basic information for the first five fields, based on her reference books, and she records her sightings every week. If she sees a bird that she is unable to identify, she can look up all birds of a certain colour and size. (Obviously this is not enough for identification, but it helps her find the right bird in her reference books.) She can then record the date and place of the sighting. After a while, she will be able to identify the best places and times of the year to spot the different species.

Thinking Hard
about Fields

When you are deciding on the fields in the database, think carefully about how they are to be used. If, for example, you want to sort or select wines by country of origin, you should have a column for country: while you might know that Bordeaux is in France, Access doesn't. If you want to find all the albums produced by Nick Lowe, you have to record that information, and preferably in a consistent way (for example, last name followed by first name).

Go back and reread the example of Clara's bird spotting database – this is the database that you will build in Section 5.2.

Closing a Database

To close an Access database:

- Choose **File | Close**,
  -or-

- Click the Close button on the Database dialog box

 ———— **Database Close button**

Quitting Access

To leave Access:

- Choose **File | Exit**
  -or-

- Click the Close button
  on the Access window.

 ———— **Access Close button**

You have now completed Section 5.1 of the ECDL Database Module.

Section Summary: So Now You Know

A *database* is a collection of information, typically held on a computer, and organised in such a way that you can find what you are looking for quickly and easily, and add new data as you need. Computer-based databases enable their users to manipulate large amounts of information more efficiently that paper-based ones.

Microsoft Access is an example of a *database management system* – an application that stores information on a computer, organises it in different ways, sorts and selects pieces of information of interest to you, and produces reports.

A database holds at least one *table* of information; each table has a number of *records*; and each record has a number of *fields*. A field is a single piece of information about a subject. A record is one complete set of fields relating to the same subject. And a table is a collection of records. In single-table databases of the kind covered by this ECDL Module, the table *is* the database.

The *Database dialog box* is the 'control panel' of Access. Using its tabs, you can open and work with any of the application's *objects* including Tables, Queries, Forms and Reports.

Before building any database in Access, consider the information that you want to put into your database, and how you want to use it. Break it down into its smallest (and most useful) divisible parts – each such part should probably be a separate database field.

Section 5.2: Building Your Access Database

Get ready to build your first database in Access! This is not as an intimidating a task as it may sound. Access comes with a number of samples that you can use as a basis for just about any new database that you might want to create. So a lot of the work is already done for you!

The decisions you need to make are: which sample table is closest to the one I want? Which of its fields will I use? And what new names will I give to the fields that I select?

Two new concepts you will meet in this Section are keys and indexes. The first is the unique identifier that makes each record in your database different from all the others; the second is a way of speeding up the sorting and retrieval of records. You will also discover another way of looking at your database, called Design View.

One aspect of database creation that Access cannot help you with is data entry: only you can do that.

New Skills

At the end of this Section, you should be able to:

- Start the Access Database Wizard
- Select a suitable sample table from the list provided
- Select from the sample table the fields you want in your table
- Rename the fields selected from the sample table to suit your needs
- Select a primary key to identify each of your records uniquely
- Enter data to a table in Datasheet View
- Adjust column width in Datasheet View
- Switch to and from Design View
- Create an index

New Words

At the end of this Section, you should be able to explain the following terms:

- Database key
- Design View
- Database index

Overview of Database Creation

In this Section you will create your first Access database. It will be similar to the one that Clara uses to record her bird-watching activities, as outlined in Section 5.1.

Access includes a Database Wizard to simplify the process of creating a database. You will use this automated feature to do some of the work, and you will do some of it the 'hard way', so that you will learn more about how the application works.

Database creation is a nine-step process:

1. Starting the Database Wizard: You begin by starting the Access Database Wizard, and by naming and saving your new database. See Exercise 5.2.

2. Selecting Your Sample Table: Rather than create a new table from scratch, it is easier and faster to base it on one provided by Access. See Exercise 5.3.

3. Selecting Your Fields: You probably won't want every field from the sample table included in your table, so you must specify which ones you need. See Exercise 5.4.

4. Renaming Your Fields: Typically, you will need to rename at least some of the fields that you have selected from the sample table. This is the step at which you also name your table. See Exercise 5.5.

5. Setting Your Primary Key: You need to tell Access which of your fields will act as the key field – the one that uniquely distinguishes each record from all the others. See Exercise 5.6.

6. Entering Your Data: You enter data to your new table in Datasheet View. See Exercise 5.7.

7. Adjusting Column Width: In Datasheet View, some columns may be too narrow; others too wide. You need to know how to change column width. See Exercise 5.8.

8. Switching to Design View: One further step to go, and you can perform it only after you switch from Datasheet View to Design View.

9. Creating Your Index: An index greatly speeds up the sorting and retrieval of data. You create one in Exercise 5.9.

Ready? Let's go build a database.

You begin the creation of your new database by starting the Access Database Wizard.

Exercise 5.2: Starting the Access Database Wizard

1) Start Access, select Database Wizard, and click **OK**.

Blank
Database

**The blank
database icon**

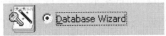

2) In the New dialog box, select the Blank Database icon and click **OK**.

3) In the File New Database dialog, give your new database a name – Birds.mdb – and indicate the directory in which you want to store it.

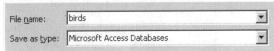

4) Click the **Create** button.

Access then displays the Database dialog box.

5) Normally, when you create a database, the Tables tab is shown on top in the Database dialog box. If it isn't, click on the Tables tab to bring it to the top.

Notice that, unlike the Northwind sample database, each of the tabs in the database you just created is empty. In this Section 5.2 you will create a table object. In Section 5.4, query and form objects. And in Section 5.6, a report object.

It would be impossible for anyone – even Microsoft – to anticipate precisely what you want to do with your database, so the Access Table Wizard offers you a wide range of choices. In the next few Exercises you will pick the options that come closest to matching your needs, and you modify them until they are exactly what you want.

Exercise 5.3: Selecting a Sample Table

1) On the Tables tab of the Database dialog box, click the **New** button at the right. Access displays the New Table dialog box.

2) The New Table dialog box offers five ways to create a new table.

Select the Table Wizard option and click **OK**.

3) Look below the Sample Tables list. Can you see two option buttons – Business and Personal? Depending on which of these options you select, Access displays a different list of sample tables.

4) Select Business and browse through the sample tables. For each table in the first list box, scroll through the sample fields in the second list box. None of the tables seems to be particularly appropriate for your needs.

5) Select the Personal option. Again, look through the sample tables. While there is nothing that relates specifically to bird-watching, one of the tables – Plants – could be modified to suit your bird-watching database.

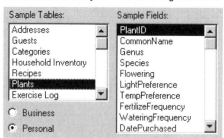

So select the Plant table – you will work with it in Exercise 5.4

Step Three: Selecting Your Fields

The first screen of the Table Wizard shows three list boxes. The first displays Access's sample tables. (You selected the Plants table from this list in Exercise 5.3.) The second list shows all the fields supplied with the selected sample table. And the third list shows the fields that you have decided to include in your new table. Initially, the third list is empty.

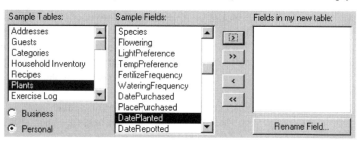

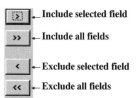

To move a field from the Sample Fields box to the Fields in my new table box, click on it to select it, and then click the > button. If you change your mind about a particular field, select it in the right-hand box and click the < button. You can include all the sample fields by clicking the >> button. Or remove all the fields from the right-hand box by clicking the << button.

Exercise 5.4: Selecting the Fields You Need

1) Move the following fields from the Sample Fields list to Fields in my new table list:

- PlantID
- CommonName
- Genus
- WateringFrequency

- Flowering
- DatePurchased
- PlacePurchased

Fields in my new table:

PlantID
CommonName
Genus
WateringFrequency
Flowering
DatePurchased
PlacePurchased

When finished, the third list box that shows the fields you selected for your table should look as shown on the right.

Step Four: Renaming Your Fields

Now that you have selected the fields you want to use from the Wizard's sample table, your next task is to give them names suitable for your new table. To rename a field, click on it in the Fields in my new table list and click the **Rename Field** button. You then type the new name for the field in the Rename Field dialog box. Rename your fields as shown in Exercise 5.5.

Exercise 5.5: Renaming Your Fields

1) In the Fields in my new table dialog box, select PlantID. Click the **Rename Field** button.

2) In the Rename Field dialog box, type the new name for the field: Number. Click **OK**.

3) Repeat for the other fields in your new table, as follows:

Old Name	New Name
CommonName	Bird Name
Genus	Colour
WateringFrequency	Size
Flowering	Migratory?
DatePurchased	Date Seen
PlacePurchased	Place Seen

4) Click the **Next** button.

Congratulations! You have just created your first Access table.

5) Now you have to give it a name.

Apply all your imagination: call your table Birds – the same name as the database that contains it.

Table Wizard

What do you want to name your table?

Birds

In the same dialog box, Access then asks you whether you want the Wizard to set a primary key, or whether you want to do it yourself. Okay, let's talk about keys.

In the telephone directory, there are many people listed with the surname Murphy; a number of them share the same first name, John. To find the one you want, you need some more information: where do they live? Even that might not be enough – father and son might have the same name – and you might have to ask them some further questions to confirm that you are talking to the right one.

Well, in a computer system, that obviously is not satisfactory. Access needs to know which John Murphy you mean. And you don't want to send a bill, or, worse still, a cheque to the wrong John Murphy. So you give each record an identifier, called a key, which is unique to that record – it is not shared with any other. Exercise 5.6 takes you through the steps.

Database Key

A field (or combination of fields) in a database record that is used to identify that record uniquely.

Exercise 5.6: Setting a Primary Key

1) On the second Table Wizard screen, having specified a name for your new table (in Exercise 5.5), select the option 'No, I'll set the primary key' and click the **Next** button.

2) In answer to the question 'What field will hold data that is unique for each record', select 'Number'.

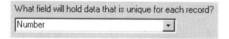

In answer to the question 'What type of data do you want the primary key to contain?', select 'Consecutive Numbers Microsoft Access assigns automatically to new records'.

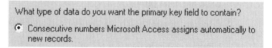

3) Click the **Next** button.

You have now defined your own Primary Key for your table.

4) Access then asks: what do you want to do next: modify the table design, enter data directly into the table, or enter data into a table using a form wizard?

Well, a table with no data is pretty boring, so you probably want to enter data directly into the table without further delay. Choose that option.

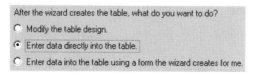

5) Click the **Finish** button.

Step Six: Entering Data into Your Table

When you create a new table, Access displays the table initially in Datasheet View as follows:

- Along the top are column headings that show your field names.

- Underneath the column headings is a single, blank row.

Number	Bird Name	Colour	Size	Migratory?	Date Seen	Place Seen
(AutoNumber)				No		

Click in any field: you can then enter data in that field. You can move from field to field using the TAB key or the arrow keys. There is an exception: the Number field (your primary key) is automatically assigned by Access – you cannot enter a new number or change an existing one. You will learn more about this feature in Section 5.3.

As soon as you start entering data for a record, a new line opens up underneath. So, no matter how many records you enter, there is always a blank record at the end where you can enter the next one.

Exercise 5.7: Entering Data to Your Table

1) In the Birds table, fill in the details of a number of birds, as below.

Number	Bird Name	Colour	Size	Migratory?	Date Seen	Place Seen
1	Great Northern Diver	Black/White	69	Yes		
2	Great Crested Grebe	Grey/White/Brown	46	No		
3	Little Grebe	Black/Brown	24	No		
4	Gannet	White/Black	85	No		
5	Fulmar	White/Grey	45	No		
6	Great Shearwater	White/Brown	42	Yes		
7	Manx Shearwater	Black/White	30	No		
8	Storm Petrel	Black/White	13	No		
9	Cormorant	Black/White	83	No		
10	Grey Heron	Grey/White	90	No		
11	Mute Swan	White	144	No		
12	Brent Goose	Black/White	56	Yes		
13	Greylag Goose	Grey	76	Yes		
14	Shelduck	White/Brown/Black	57	No		
15	Goldeneye	White/Black	41	Yes		
16	Teal	Grey/Multicolour	34	No		
17	Mallard	Green/White/Brown	55	No		
18	Sparrowhawk	Blue/White	28	Yes		
19	Kestrel	Grey/Brown	33	No		
20	Pheasant	Green/Gold	0	No		
21	Dodo	Blue/White/Yellow	90	No		
22	Blue Tit	Blue/Yellow/Black/White	6	No		
(toNumber)			0	No		

At this stage, some fields may be too small to display all the information you enter: don't worry – you'll learn how to adjust column width in Exercise 5.8.

In the case of Migratory?, if the fields contain check boxes, you indicate that a bird is migratory by clicking on the check box. If the fields contain No instead, you indicate that a bird is migratory by typing Yes in the place of No.

Leave the Date Seen and Place Seen fields blank for the moment.

2) When you have entered the descriptive details of the birds into the datasheet, close it by clicking the lower Close button on the top right of the window. You are then returned to the Database screen, this time with one important difference: the new table you created – Birds – is shown on the Tables tab.

That's it. Now you know how to create a table in Access, and how to enter data into it in Datasheet View. (You will learn about entering data in Form View in Section 5.5.)

Step Seven:
Changing the Width
of Your Columns

Changing the width of your columns is easy. By now you will have noticed that Access starts off by making all the columns the same width. Some of them are too narrow for their contents to be displayed in full (as, for example, in some of the birds' names).

And some columns are too wide: the datasheet takes up more space than necessary, with the result that some of your data may be pushed off the right of the screen, and you have to use the left-right scroll bar to see it.

To change the width of a column, click on the dividing line (known as the *field delimiter*) between its title and the one to its right. Notice that the shape of the cursor changes. Then drag the cursor left or right until the column is the right size.

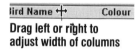

You can make the column width adjust automatically to fit the longest entry in the column by *double-clicking* on the field delimiter.

Exercise 5.8: Adjusting Column Width
1) Change the width of columns in the Birds table to improve the overall appearance of the table.

Before

Bird Name
Great Northern
Great Crested (
Little Grebe
Gannet
Fulmar
Great Shearwat
Manx Shearwat

After

Bird Name
Great Northern Diver
Great Crested Grebe
Little Grebe
Gannet
Fulmar
Great Shearwater
Manx Shearwater

Step Eight:
Switching to Design
View

In Section 5.1, you were introduced to two views of a database: Datasheet View, where you can see several records arranged in rows and columns, and Forms View, where you can see only a single record at a time. In Exercise 5.7, you entered data to your table in Datasheet View.

Now meet a third view: *Design View*. This is the view in which you can change the organisational structure of your table.

**The Design
View button
in Datasheet
View**

**The Table
View button
in Design
View**

If your table is open in Datasheet View, switch to Design View by:

- Choosing **View | Table Design**
  -or-

- Clicking the Design View button on the toolbar

If your table is open in Design View, you can return from Design View to Datasheet View by:

- Choosing **View | Datasheet**
  -or-

- Clicking the Table View button on the toolbar

The toolbar button enables you to switch quickly between the two views, so that when you make any design changes, you can see their effect immediately.

If your table is not open, you can open it in Design View by selecting it at the Database screen, and clicking the **Design** button.

> **Design View**
> *A view in which you can change the organisational structure of your table. You create an index in Design View.*

Step Nine: Creating Your Index

Creating an index from one or more fields can greatly speed up the sorting and retrieval of records, particularly when databases become very large. Looking up a name in the index at the back of a book is easier than scanning hundreds of pages of text looking for it; a more sophisticated index might help differentiate between the 57 Smiths, possibly by including first names or addresses in the index.

Access can use table indexes to avoid time-wasting searches through thousands of records. A multiple field index might, for example, be based on surname, first name and city, since searches are often based on these criteria.

> **Database Index**
> *A list of keys that a database can use to find and sort records. Indexes make such operations faster, as the database only needs to examine the index fields rather than entire records.*

Exercise 5.9 shows you how to build an index for your table.

Exercise 5.9: Creating an Index

**The
Indexes
button**

1) Open the Birds table in Design View.

2) Choose **View | Indexes** or click the Indexes button in the toolbar. You can see the indexes that are already set, each consisting of just one field.

3) Type a unique name in the Index Name field in an empty row. For example, Where & When.

4) In the Field Name column, select Place Seen from the pop-down list, and in the row below that, select Date Seen. If you want, you can select a third value – for example, Bird Name – in the row below that again.

You now set up a multiple field index – the final step in the database creation checklist. You can now save and close your table, and quit Access. You have completed Section 5.2 of the ECDL Database Module.

Section Summary: So Now You Know

Access offers a *Database Wizard* that simplifies the process of creating a new database by providing a number of *sample tables*. Choose one that resembles the table that you want to create. You can customise your chosen sample table by selecting which of its fields you want to use, and then renaming the selected fields as required.

When you create a new table, Access displays it in Datasheet View, with *column headings* that show your selected field names above a single, blank row. You can type record data into the blank row. As soon as you enter one record, Access opens up a new line underneath, so that there is always a blank record at the end where you can enter the next one.

You can *change column width* manually at any stage, or make column width adjust automatically to the longest entry in the field.

A *key* is a field (or combination of fields) in a database record that uniquely identifies that record. An *index*, which you create in *Design View*, speeds up the sorting and retrieval of records. You must *save* and *name* both the database and the table that the database contains.

Section 5.3: Modifying Your Access Database

Now that you have built your first database, you need to learn how to make changes to it. In this Section you will discover how to remove records you no longer need from your database, and reorder existing ones.

Access allows you to add new fields to your records at any time, either at the end of a record or anywhere in the middle. But when you add new fields, you may need to go back and edit all records that you have already entered. So it makes sense to select your fields correctly at database design stage!

As you will also learn in this Section, each field in a table has a particular *data type* that tells Access how to treat the field, how the data is to be stored, and what kind of data is allowed in it. Ideally, you should select the correct data type for each field before you enter data, because changing a field's data type at a later stage may result in data loss.

Access offers a searchable *online help* system that you can access in two ways: from the Help menu, and from the question mark button at the top-right of individual dialog boxes.

New Skills

At the end of this Section, you should be able to:

- Edit the contents of a field
- Delete a record
- Know when to use the following data types: Text, Memo, Number, Date/Time, Currency, AutoNumber and Yes/No
- Change the data type of a field
- Add a new field
- Reorder fields
- Use Access online help

New Words

At the end of this Section, you should be able to explain the following term:

- Data type

Changing and Deleting Database Records

In Section 5.2, you discovered how to create a single-table database in Access. Now it's time to learn how to modify your table in various ways.

To change or delete a record in your Birds database, open Access, open the Birds database, and then open the Birds table. By default, your table opens in Datasheet View.

Changing a Field

To change data in a field, begin by clicking on that field.

- If you click on the extreme left of the field, the entire field is selected and anything you type immediately overwrites the whole field.

- If you click anywhere else in the field, you can use the BACKSPACE or DELETE key to delete characters one by one, or you can insert new characters.

Remember that you cannot change the Number field – it is assigned by Access. Change the Migratory? check box by clicking it. If it is already on, clicking it turns it off; if it is off, clicking it turns it on. (If the Migratory? field contains 'No', you can either leave it alone or change it to 'Yes'; no other input is accepted.)

Deleting a Record

The Delete Record button

To delete a record, select it by clicking anywhere in it: it shows an arrowhead at the extreme left. Then choose **Edit | Delete Record**, or click the Delete Record button on the Toolbar. You can then confirm that you want to delete the record, or change your mind and leave it alone.

▶| **Indicates a selected record**

Number	Date Seen	Place Seen
1		
2	3/13/99	Dalkey
3	4/9/98	Stephen's Green
4	12/6/98	Ireland's Eye
5		
6		
7		
8		
9	12/6/98	Ireland's Eye
10		
11	6/14/99	Malahide
12	12/12/98	Dollymount
13		
14		
15		
16	9/28/98	Wexford
17	9/28/98	Wexford
18	7/6/98	
19		
20	9/27/98	Wexford
21	8/6/81	Mauritius
22	7/6/99	Ballsbridge
*	.toNumber)	

Exercise 5.10: Changing and Deleting Data

1) Open the Birds table in Datasheet View. Change two fields containing incorrect information in record 20 for the Pheasant.

   The Colour should be Red/Black. The Size should be 53.

2) Delete record 21, concerning the Dodo; it is once more extinct!

3) Type the details in the Date Seen and Place Seen fields. Notice that the Date Seen field accepts only valid dates, and forces you to input them in a standard way.

4) When you are finished, close the table. You are then returned to the Database dialog box.

If your database records contain an AutoNumber field, and you delete a record, Access does *not* reassign the number of the deleted record to another record. Access ensures that records keep the number initially assigned to them, and it always assigns higher numbers to later additions than to earlier ones.

The Different Data Types

At this stage, if you've followed the Exercises, you're probably thinking that Access is reading your mind. How does it know that the Date Seen column should only contain dates? And how does it know that the Migratory? column is either ticked for Yes, or left blank for No? (Or that input in that field is limited to Yes and No.) Well, the answer is in the table design, and, to be honest, we cheated a bit.

When you set up a table in Access, there are two things you have to do for each field:

- You have to give the field a *name*, and

- You have to give the field a *data type*.

When you used the Wizard to set up the Birds table, the fields you selected from the Plants sample table had the same characteristics as the corresponding fields in the Birds table. You changed the names of the fields to match the bird-watching application. However, because you chose fields carefully, you didn't have to change the data types.

The data type tells Access how to treat the field, how the data is to be stored, and what kind of data is allowed in it.

Data Type
This determines the kind of data that you can store in a field, and tells Access how to handle it.

Access recognises a number of different data types. The most important ones for our purposes are shown as follows:

Data Type	Used For	Examples
Text	Any sort of alphabetic or numeric data. Typically used where there is a limit on the amount of data. No more than 255 characters may be inputted. (If the data is numeric, it should not be intended for use in calculations.)	Surname, Colour, Zip Code, Telephone Number
Memo	Any sort of alphabetic or numeric data. Typically used for free-form input. Up to 64,000 characters may be inputted. (Again, if the data is numeric, it should not be intended for use in calculations.)	Description, Where Seen, Notes
Number	Numeric data that may be used in calculations.	Quantity in Stock, Number in Flock, Number Sold
Date/Time	Date or time data.	Date Bought, Arrival Time, Planting Date
Currency	Money values or other numeric data used in calculations where the number of decimal places does not exceed four.	Price, Current Value
AutoNumber	A number assigned to each new record automatically. Access assigns the numbers in sequence, starting with 1.	Sequence Number
Yes/No	Fields that can have simple yes/no, true/false, or on/off values only.	Migratory?, Buy Again?, Flowering?

It is easy to change the data type of a field, but ideally you should get it right at the design stage. If you try to change the data type after you have inputted a lot of data, you can confuse Access, and you may lose some of your data.

In Exercise 5.11, you will change some of the data types in the Birds table.

Exercise 5.11: Changing Data Types

1) Open your Birds database.

2) At the Database dialog box, select the Birds table, and click the **Design** button.

3) You then see the Design View of the table: this is divided into two main panes. At the top is the list of field names with their data types.

Field Name	Data Type	
Number	AutoNumber	
Bird Name	Text	
Colour	Text	
Size	Number	
Migratory?	Yes/No	
Date Seen	Date/Time	
Place Seen	Text	

Click on any of the data type fields. A drop-down arrow appears beside the data type. Click on this arrow: you see the list of data types described above (along with a few others that we haven't discussed). To change a data type, you simply select the new one from that list.

Field Name	Data Type
Number	AutoNumber
Bird Name	Text
Colour	Text
Size	Memo
Migratory?	Number
Date Seen	Date/Time
Place Seen	Currency
	AutoNumber
	Yes/No
	OLE Object
	Hyperlink
	Lookup Wizard...

4) Try some experiments.

- Change the Data Type of Migratory? from Yes/No to Number. Close the dialog box, and confirm that you want to save the changes. Then open the table. Notice how the data displayed under Migratory? has changed.

- Go back into Design View. (To do this, click the Table View button in the toolbar, or close the table and then click the **Design** button again.) This time, change the Data Type of Migratory? to Date/Time.

  Then save the change and have a look at the effect of this change on the data displayed in the datasheet. Notice how changing the data type after you have input data can yield surprising results.

  When you have finished experimenting, change the Data Type of Migratory? back to Yes/No.

A check box

5) If the Migratory? field contains Yes or No, change it to a check box, as follows.

- Click on the Migratory? field.

- Then, in the lower pane (Field Properties), choose the Lookup tab, and, in Display Control, choose the option you want: Check Box.

6) In later Exercises, you will want to compare the sizes of different birds. To do this, the Size field must be numeric. So change its Data Type from Text to Number.

7) Finally, save your work.

Adding New Fields to Your Table

Can you add new fields to your database records at any time? Yes. But if you do, you may have to go back and edit all records you have already entered. This applies particularly to numeric fields (where a blank field may be interpreted as 0), and Yes/No fields (where a blank field may be interpreted as No), but it is also important for any field that you use for sorting or filtering data.

So it is better if you think about the fields you want when you are setting up the database, and modify the design as little as possible after that.

Exercise 5.12: Adding New Fields

1) Open your Birds table in Design View.

2) Where do you want to add a new field: at the end of a record or somewhere in the middle?

- To add a new field at the end of the record, click on the next unused Field Name box. For this Exercise, select this option.

- To add the new field between two existing fields, click on the title of the field that will end up *on the right* of the new field and choose **Insert | Field**.

3) Enter the title of the new field: Comments.

4) Specify the Data Type of the new field: Memo.

Field Name	Data Type
Number	AutoNumber
Bird Name	Text
Colour	Text
Size	Number
Migratory?	Yes/No
Date Seen	Date/Time
Place Seen	Text
Comments	Memo
	Text
	Memo
	Number

(A field with Text data type may hold a maximum of 255 characters, whereas a field with Memo data type may hold up to 64,000 characters.)

	Number Seen
▶ 1	23
2	21
3	14
4	5
5	3
6	7
7	17
8	1
9	3
10	4
11	12
12	34
13	22
14	16
15	9
16	14
17	16
18	1
19	2
20	6
21	0
22	4

5) Click the Close button.
-or-

Choose **File | Close**.
-or-

Hold down the CTRL key and type W.
-or-

Click the Table View button.

Access asks you to confirm the change.

You can also insert a new field into a table while you are in Datasheet View: just click on the title of the field that will end up *on the right* of the new field and choose **Insert | Column**. Access assigns this field the Text Data Type. If that is what you want, fine. If it isn't, you will have to go into Design View to specify the Data Type you want.

Try this: input a new field Number Seen to the right of the Colour field, make its Data Type Number, and enter the data shown on the left.

Reordering the Fields in a Table

Reordering fields: cursor

To change the order of fields in the Table, click on the title of the one you want to move. Then click on it *again*, but this time maintain the click (keep pressure on the left button): note that a box appears on the tail of the cursor.

Now drag it to the new location to the left or right. When you arrive at your chosen destination, note how a bold line has appeared, indicating the program's understanding of where you want to place your moving column: if this is correct, release your finger from the mouse button, and the column moves.

Try this a number of times until you are confident about it.

Colour		Number Seen	Migratory?
hite		23	Yes

Saving to a Diskette

Have you been saving your table as you went along? You should. It is also a good idea to save a copy of your database on a diskette. Follow the steps in Exercise 5.13 to learn how to save your database to the A: drive.

Exercise 5.13: Saving Your Access Database to a Diskette
1) Insert a diskette in the diskette drive of your computer:

- If it is a new diskette, ensure that it is formatted.

- If it is a previously used one, ensure that there is sufficient space on it to hold your Birds database.

2) With the Birds table open, choose **File | Save As/Export**.

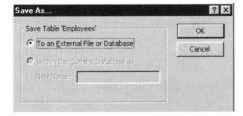

3) Click **OK** to confirm that you want to save the table as an external file.

4) Access displays the Save dialog box, with the file name Birds already entered. You can change this file name if you wish.

5) Locate the A: drive, and click **Save** to save your table. You have successfully saved a copy of Birds on the floppy diskette.

Once a database has been saved, Access does not normally thereafter prompt you to Save Changes when you exit – it assumes, unlike most Microsoft applications, that any changes you make are changes you want to keep.

Online Help

Like Excel, PowerPoint and other Microsoft applications, Access offers a searchable online help system. The word 'help' means that the information is there to assist you understand and use the application. The word 'online' means that the material is presented on the computer screen rather than as a traditional printed manual.

You can search through and read online help in two ways: from the Help menu, or from dialog boxes.

Using Help
Menu Options

Choose **Help | Contents and Index** to display the three tabs of the Help Topics dialog box shown on the next page.

  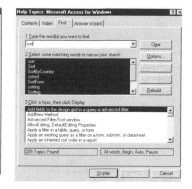

Contents Tab

This offers short descriptions of Access's main features.

Where you see a heading with a book symbol, double-click to view the related sub-headings.

Double-click on a question mark symbol to read the help text.

Click a Show me arrow for Word to demonstrate how to perform a particular action.

Click a double-arrow to view step-by-step instructions.

Index Tab

Reading the material displayed on this tab is like looking through the index of a printed book.

Just type the first letters of the word or phrase you are interested in.

Access responds by displaying all matches from the online help in the lower half of the dialog box.

When you find the index entry that you are looking for, click the **Display** button.

Find Tab

Can't find what you are looking for in the Contents or Index tabs? Try this tab.

When you type a word or phrase, Access performs a deeper search of the online help.

Access also displays some related words to help you narrow your search.

When you find the item you are looking for, double-click on it to display it.

A fourth tab, Answer Wizard, accepts your questions about Access in plain English syntax.

As you search through and read online help topics, you will see the following buttons at the top of the online help window:

- **Help Topics:** Click this to return to the Contents tab.

- **Back:** Click this to return to the previous help topic.

- **Options:** Click this to perform such actions as copying the online help text to a document, or printing it on your printer.

You can also access online help directly from any Access screen, as Exercise 5.14 demonstrates.

Exercise 5.14: Using Online Help from an Access Screen

1) From the Database dialog box, click the Online Help button on the toolbar. Access displays a question mark to the right of the cursor.

2) Click on the Queries tab label.

3) Access displays online help text telling you about the purpose of selected screen elements.

> **Queries tab**
>
> Click to display a list of all queries in the current database. Use the buttons to the right of the list to open the selected query, modify the design of the selected query, or create a new query.

4) Click anywhere on the Access screen to remove the online help text.

Practise this Exercise with various screens in Access.

When finished, you can close your database and quit Access. You have now completed Section 5.3 of the ECDL Database Module.

The most frequently used Access functions are available by clicking a single button on the toolbar.

Normally, Access displays the most suitable toolbar — the one containing the buttons for the functions you are most likely to need.

If you want to turn off the toolbar (and choose all your options from the menus), or if you want to display other toolbars, click **View | Toolbars** and check the toolbars you want displayed.

Section Summary: So Now You Know

A field's *data type* tells Access how to treat the field, how the data is to be stored, and what kind of data is allowed in it. Commonly used data types are: Text, Memo, Number, Date/Time, Currency, AutoNumber and Yes/No.

Try to select the correct data type for each field before you enter data, because changing a field's data type at a later stage may result in data loss.

You can add new fields to the database at any time, but you may need to go back and edit all records that you have already entered, particularly for numeric fields (where a blank field may be interpreted as 0), and Yes/No fields (where a blank may be interpreted as No).

Access offers a searchable *online help* system that you can access in two ways: from the Help menu, and from the question mark button at the top-right of individual dialog boxes.

Section 5.4: Making the Database Work for You

After Sections 5.2 and 5.3, you might still be asking: why bother? You can use a word processor to keep lists of things, and if you want to put them in neat columns, you can use a spreadsheet. Well, Section 5.4 should convince you that a database is a very useful tool for managing your information, and for quickly finding the particular items of interest.

For example, the order in which you entered records originally in your table may not be the order in which, later on, you would prefer to display those records. You could reorder – *sort* – a table of customers, for instance, so that the biggest spenders appear at the top of the list. You can even save *sorts* you use regularly as *queries* so that you can apply them at the click of a button.

Another very useful feature is *filtering* – the ability to reduce the amount of information displayed, either by showing fewer fields in each record, or by showing only those records that match certain criteria.

Finally, as with other Microsoft Office applications, Access includes a *Find* feature that enables you locate a particular item quickly.

New Skills

At the end of this Section, you should be able to:

- Reorder (sort) the database records
- Save a sort as a query and apply it to a database
- Find a particular record or set of records
- Use the Access Find feature

New Words

At the end of this Section, you should be able to explain the following terms:

- Sort
- Sort order
- Find
- Filter
- Query
- Find

Changing the Order of Records in the Table

Open Access and open your Birds table. Notice that the datasheet shows the records in the order you entered them: the Number field reflects that order – records you added later have higher numbers than ones you added earlier.

However, you can choose to display the records in a different order, by *sorting* them.

> **Sort**
>
> *An operation that you carry out on a table to change the order in which the records are displayed. Sorting does not change the content of records, only their location.*

Access offers two sequencing options, called sort orders.

The Sort Ascending button

> **Sort Order**
>
> *A particular way of ordering records based on field values. A sort order can be in alphabetic ascending (A to Z) or descending (Z to A) sequence.*

Suppose you want the records to be displayed alphabetically by bird name, or in order of size (biggest first, smallest last), how would you go about it? Easy. Click on any bird name. Then click the Sort Ascending button on the toolbar. Done!

The Sort Descending button

Click on any size field. Click the Sort Descending button. Again, done! What could be simpler?

Sorted by Name, Ascending

Bird Name
Blue Tit
Brent Goose
Cormorant
Dodo
Fulmar
Gannet
Goldeneye
Great Crested Grebe
Great Northern Diver
Great Shearwater
Grey Heron
Greylag Goose
Kestrel
Little Grebe
Mallard
Manx Shearwater
Mute Swan
Pheasant
Shelduck
Sparrowhawk
Storm Petrel
Teal

Sorted by Size, Descending

Number	Bird Name	Colour	Number Seen	Size
11	Mute Swan	White	12	144
10	Grey Heron	Grey/White	4	90
21	Dodo	Blue/White/Yellow	0	90
4	Gannet	White/Black	5	85
9	Cormorant	Black/White	3	83
13	Greylag Goose	Grey	22	76
1	Great Northern Diver	Black/White	23	69
14	Shelduck	White/Brown/Black	16	57
12	Brent Goose	Black/White	34	56
17	Mallard	Green/White/Brown	16	55
20	Pheasant	Red/Black	6	53
2	Great Crested Grebe	Grey/White/Brown	21	46
5	Fulmar	White/Grey	3	45
6	Great Shearwater	White/Brown	7	42
15	Goldeneye	White/Black	9	41
16	Teal	Grey/Multicolour	14	34
19	Kestrel	Grey/Brown	2	33
7	Manx Shearwater	Black/White	17	30
18	Sparrowhawk	Blue/White	1	28
3	Little Grebe	Black/Brown	14	24
8	Storm Petrel	Black/White	1	13
22	Blue Tit	Blue/Yellow/Black/White	4	6
oNumber)			0	0

These kinds of sorts are called *simple*, or *single criterion sorts*. Now imagine that you have more complex requirements: you want to sort all the birds by colour, and you want to show the biggest birds of any colour before the smaller ones. These are called *multiple criteria sorts*: you cannot use the sort buttons to perform them. Exercise 5.15 shows you how to do them.

Exercise 5.15: Sorting Records Using a Number of Criteria

1) Open the Birds table in Datasheet View. Choose **Records | Filter | Advanced Filter/Sort**.

2) In the lower pane, click on the list button in the first row, first column: a list of all the fields in your table is shown. Select Colour.

3) Click in the second field in the first column. A list button appears. Click on this to choose a sort order. Select Ascending.

4) Click in the first field of the second column: a list button is displayed. Click on it, and choose Size from the list.

5) Click in the field below Size: a list button is displayed. Click on it and choose Descending.

Field:	Colour	Size
Sort:	Ascending	Descending
Criteria:		
or:		

The Apply Filter button

6) Then click the Apply Filter button in the toolbar, and the datasheet is shown, this time listing the birds in order of colour, and with the bigger birds of each colour shown before the smaller ones.

Bird Name	Colour	Number Seen	Size
Little Grebe	Black/Brown	14	24
Cormorant	Black/White	3	83
Great Northern Diver	Black/White	23	69
Brent Goose	Black/White	34	56
Manx Shearwater	Black/White	17	30
Storm Petrel	Black/White	1	13
Sparrowhawk	Blue/White	1	28
Dodo	Blue/White/Yellow	0	90
Blue Tit	Blue/Yellow/Black/White	4	6
Mallard	Green/White/Brown	16	55
Greylag Goose	Grey	22	76
Kestrel	Grey/Brown	2	33
Teal	Grey/Multicolour	14	34
Grey Heron	Grey/White	4	90
Great Crested Grebe	Grey/White/Brown	21	46
Pheasant	Red/Black	6	53
Mute Swan	White	12	144
Gannet	White/Black	5	85
Goldeneye	White/Black	9	41
Great Shearwater	White/Brown	7	42
Shelduck	White/Brown/Black	16	57
Fulmar	White/Grey	3	45
		0	0

7) Close your table.

Why is the button called Apply Filter? Well, Access regards this kind of sort as a particular example of a filter. What's a filter? Don't worry about that for now: we'll be looking at filters a little later.

Saving a Query

If you experiment with sorting, you'll see that you can view the information in your table in many different ways. You can, for example, separate the records into migratory and non-migratory birds; you can quickly identify the smallest bird you saw on a particular date; or you can list the birds you have seen in Wexford.

It's quite likely that you will want to repeat some of these sorts regularly. For example, if you have several hundred birds in your database, sorting them by colour and size would help you identify unusual birds. You can enter the sort criteria each time you want to sort the table in this way, or you can make life easy for yourself, by saving the sort criteria as a query.

> ### Query
> Queries are used to repeatedly view database records in a particular way defined by you.

Exercise 5.16 shows you how to save your sort criteria as a query.

Exercise 5.16: Saving Sort Criteria as a Query

The Save As Query button

1) Set up your sort criteria as in steps 1 to 5 of Exercise 5.15.

2) Choose **File | Save as Query** or click the Save As Query button on the toolbar.

3) Give the query a name: say Colour/Size.

4) Click **OK**, and close the Filter dialog box.

And that's it! Notice that the query shows up on the Query tab on the Database dialog box. From now on, even after you have added more records to the database, or changed the ones that are already there, you simply open this query and the records in the table will be presented in the manner defined by the query.

Note that queries don't make any permanent change to the database; they simply extract information and present it in a certain way.

If you have used a query to view a table in a particular order, you can return to an unsorted view by choosing **Records | Remove Filter/Sort**.

Notice that in this Query, all of the fields were shown. What if we want to view only selected columns?

Exercise 5.17: Creating a Query for Selected Columns Only

1) From the Database dialog box, click the Queries tab then click the **New** button on that tab.

2) Now select Design View and click **OK**.

3) In the Tables tab, select the Birds table. Click the **Add** button, followed by the **Close** button.

4) Now, as in Exercise 5.15, select Colour in the first Field column and choose Sort Ascending then select Size in the second Field column, and choose Sort Descending.

5) Click Bird Name in the third Field column, but this time don't specify a Sort order.

Colour	Size	Bird Name ▾
Birds	Birds	Birds
Ascending	Descending	
☑	☑	☑

The Run button

6) Now, click the Run button in the toolbar.

This time your Query returns only the referenced columns, and cuts out unnecessary or unwanted information in adjacent columns.

Colour	Size	Bird Name
Black/Brown	24	Little Grebe
Black/White	13	Storm Petrel
Black/White	30	Manx Shearwater
Black/White	56	Brent Goose
Black/White	69	Great Northern Diver
Black/White	83	Cormorant
Blue/White	28	Sparrowhawk
Blue/White/Yellow	90	Dodo
Blue/Yellow/Black/White	6	Blue Tit
Green/White/Brown	55	Mallard
Grey	76	Greylag Goose
Grey/Brown	33	Kestrel
Grey/Multicolour	34	Teal
Grey/White	90	Grey Heron
Grey/White/Brown	46	Great Crested Grebe
Red/Black	29	Pheasant
White	144	Mute Swan
White/Black	41	Goldeneye
White/Black	85	Gannet
White/Brown	42	Great Shearwater
White/Brown/Black	57	Shelduck
White/Grey	45	Fulmar

7) Close the dialog box. You are prompted to save the Query – click the **Yes** button. Give the query a name you will remember, such as '3-Column, Colour/Size/Bird Name'. Click **OK**, and it's saved. You can subsequently view the selected fields of the table in the order you specified, simply by opening the query from the Query tab on the Database dialog box.

Restricting the Information Displayed

You can reduce the amount of information displayed, either by showing fewer fields in each record, or by showing only those records that match certain criteria. This is called *filtering*.

Filter

A filter restricts the display of your database information to records and fields that match criteria that you specify.

The Filter by Selection button

Suppose, for example, you want to concentrate on birds that you have seen in Wexford. Simply find any record that matches your criterion – in this case, one with Wexford in the Place Seen column.

Click on the relevant field – Wexford – and then click on the Filter by Selection button in the toolbar.

The display is immediately restricted to records that match your selection – that is, ones that have Wexford in the Place Seen column.

Number	Bird Name	Colour	Number Seen	Size	Migratory?	Date Seen	Place Seen
16	Teal	Grey/Multicolour	14	34	☐	Monday, September 28, 1998	Wexford
17	Mallard	Green/White/Brown	16	55	☐	Monday, September 28, 1998	Wexford
20	Pheasant	Red/Black	6	29	☐	Sunday, September 27, 1998	Wexford

The Remove Filter button

Don't panic: the rest of your records are still in the database. The filter just limits the amount of information in the display. To see all your records again, you remove the filter: click the Remove Filter button in the toolbar.

A word of caution: Recall that you can change the information in the database at any time. And recall that you change a Yes/No check box field by clicking on it: a click turns it on if it was off, and off if it was on. If you are filtering based on a Yes/No check box field, you will *change* the information when you select it. So in the case of a Yes/No check box field, you will have to click on the field *twice* before you click on the Filter by Selection button.

For example, suppose you want to study only migratory birds. As before, find one record of a migratory bird. Click on the Migratory? check box: notice what happens – the box changes from ticked (Yes, migratory) to unticked (No, not migratory). Click it *again*, so that it shows the correct status, and then click the Apply Filter button. The display shows only migratory birds.

Number	Bird Name	Colour	Number Seen	Size	Migratory?	Date Seen
1	Great Northern Diver	Black/White	23	69	☑	
6	Great Shearwater	White/Brown	7	42	☑	
12	Brent Goose	Black/White	34	56	☑	Saturday, December 12, 1998
13	Greylag Goose	Grey	22	76	☑	
15	Goldeneye	White/Black	9	41	☑	
18	Sparrowhawk	Blue/White	1	28	☑	Monday, July 06, 1998

Filtering by Selection

When you select a field, and then filter based on the contents of that field, the process is known as *Filtering by Selection*. Note that you don't have to select the whole field: you might be interested in all the Warblers, or all birds that have Grey somewhere in their colour. No problem.

Selecting part of a field for filtering by selection

As before, find a record that has the characteristic you want – say Grey in its colour. Click and drag the mouse over the *part* of the field that has the word (or part of the word) that you want to match – in this case Grey.

Then click the Filter by Selection button. The display shows the birds that have Grey anywhere in their colour field.

Number	Bird Name	Colour
2	Great Crested Grebe	Grey/White/Brown
10	Grey Heron	Grey/White
13	Greylag Goose	Grey
16	Teal	Grey/Multicolour
19	Kestrel	Grey/Brown

Filtering by Selection includes the ideas 'Beginning with ...' and 'Ending with ...'. If you select the first letter in a field and Filter by Selection, Access displays all records in which the field *begins with* that letter. Similarly, if you select the last letter in the field, Access displays the records in which the field *ends with* that letter.

So if you want to filter based on the first word or the last word in a field, include the first letter or the last letter only if you want to restrict the display to records that begin with or end with the selection. If you want all records that include the word anywhere in the field, select only *part* of the word – a part in the middle of the word, such as 'hit' for White or 'lac' for Black.

Try Filtering by Selection yourself: remove the colour filter, and this time restrict the display to Grebes.

Filtering Filtered Records

If you want to further restrict the records displayed – say to all green-coloured birds spotted in Wexford – you simply repeat the steps above. First, find all the birds spotted in Wexford, then from that list find all the green birds. Alternatively, start by finding all the green birds, then further restrict that list to ones spotted in Wexford.

Bird Name	Colour	Number Seen	Size	Migratory?	Date Seen	Place Seen
Mallard	Green/White/Brown	16	55	☐	Monday, September 28, 1998	Wexford

Find

The Find button

Is there a quick way of finding a *particular* record among hundreds or thousands? Yes. Use the Access Find feature. You can run Find in any of the following ways: choose **Edit | Find**, click the Find button on the toolbar, or use the keyboard shortcut CTRL + f.

Try the following exercise to find a specific record in the Birds table.

Exercise 5.18: Finding a Specific Record

1) Open the Birds table. Click the **Find** button in the toolbar.

2) In the Find What field, enter 'Goldeneye'.

   Ensure that the Search Only Current Field check box is clear. (Click the check box to remove a tick; click again to insert one.) The Search field should contain 'All', and the Match field 'Whole Field'.

3) Click the **Find First** button and Access should highlight the Goldeneye record.

4) Click the **Find Next** button. Access indicates that there are no further records that match the criterion. Click **OK**.

5) In the Find dialog box, click the **Close** button.

6) Now, on your own, and in separate Find operations, find the following data:

- **Malahide** – This should highlight the Mute Swan record.
- **55** – This should highlight the Mallard record.
- **Grey** – This should highlight the Greylag Goose record – this is the only record for which 'grey' is a whole field.

Now change the Match field to read 'Any Part of Field', and find Grey again. This time when you click the **Find Next** button repeatedly, a number of other records should be highlighted – these are records which have 'grey' somewhere in the field.

Section Summary: So Now You Know

A *sort* is an operation that you carry out on a table to change the order in which the records are displayed. Access allows you to perform single criterion and multiple criteria sort operations.

If you perform a particular sort regularly, you can save the sort details as a *query*. You can use queries to repeatedly view database records in a particular way defined by you.

Filtering is the process of reducing the amount of information displayed by Access, either by showing fewer fields in each record, or by showing only those records that match certain criteria. To view all your records again, remove the filter.

You can filter a table by clicking on a particular field, or by dragging the mouse over the word (or part of a word) that you want to match, and then clicking on the Filter by Selection button on the toolbar.

Note that if you are filtering based on a Yes/No field, you need to click on the field twice before you click on the Filter by Selection button. A single click on a Yes/No field will change the information in that field!

You can filter the result of a filter operation to further restrict the information displayed.

Access's *Find* feature provides a quick way of locating a particular record or records based on their field values.

Section 5.5: Working with Forms

Until now, you have been looking at your database records in Datasheet View – they have been shown in rows, with a column for each field. Datasheet View can make reading the information difficult, and it's annoying if the fields and records extend beyond the edges of your screen, so that you have to scroll left and right and up and down to see the items of interest.

Forms are better for those times when all you really want is to see information relating to a single record at one time, laid out in an eye-pleasing manner. Forms have the added advantage of being much easier to read, and you can design different, eye-pleasing forms for different purposes.

As you will learn in this Section, everything you can do in a datasheet, you can also do in a form. You can input new records and change existing records; you can sort the records into a different order; and you can filter the records so that only ones that match your criteria are displayed.

New Skills

At the end of this Section, you should be able to:

- Create a form to display records, in whole or in part, one at a time
- Use a form to create new records
- Use a form to search for and modify a record
- Modify a form that you have previously created
- Import an image or graphic file into a form

New Words

You can relax: there are no new words in this Section.

Forms: What Are They For?

Remember in Section 5.1, you learnt that Access enables you to view and manipulate information in two ways:

- **Datasheet View:** This shows the information for many records, arranged in columns and rows.

- **Form View:** This presents information for one record at a time.

Creating Your Form with the Form Wizard

Forms are based on tables. You can create a form only *after* you have created a table, such as the Birds table created in Section 5.2. In Exercise 5.19, you will use the Access Form Wizard to create a new form.

Exercise 5.19: Creating a Form

1) Open Access, open your Birds database, and click on the Forms tab.

Click the **New** button. As with the Table Wizard, the Form Wizard offers a number of semi-automated options.

2) Select, for example, the AutoForm: Columnar option, select the Birds table, and have a look at (but don't save) the result.

3) Starting again from the Database dialog box, click the **New** button. This time, choose the Form Wizard.

4) Select the table on which the form is based – Birds.

Click **OK**. This starts the Form Wizard.

5) You've seen something like this before, when you used the Table Wizard to design your Birds table in Section 5.2. The screen shows two list boxes. In the one on the left you can see all the fields in the table; in the one on the right, the fields that you have chosen to include in the form. Initially, the one on the right is empty.

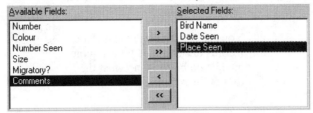

Move the fields you want to use in your form from the Available Fields box to the Selected Fields box by using the arrow buttons. For the exercise, move the fields shown above.

6) Click the **Next** button.

7) The Form Wizard then presents you with three possible layouts for the form. You can get an idea of what each is like by selecting them in turn. The best for your purposes is Columnar. Select this one, and click the **Next** button.

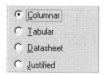

8) The Wizard then offers you a choice of styles for the Form.

   Again, you can preview styles by selecting them in turn.

   For Birds, there can be no contest: the most appropriate style has got to be Clouds.

   Select this one, and click the **Next** button.

9) Access suggests a name for the Form: change this to 'Birds Spotted' to make it easier to identify later.

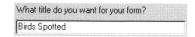

You can then either use the form immediately, or go back and modify it. Select the option to **Open the form**.

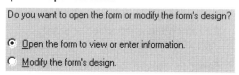

Click the **Finish** button.

You can then use the form to view selected information from the records in your table.

Using Your Form to View Records

When you finish Exercise 5.19, you are immediately presented with a Forms View of the Birds table. At other times, to get to the same point, you start from the Database dialog box, click on the Forms tab, select the form (Birds Spotted), and click the **Open** button.

The form shows the selected fields from the first record in the table.

You can step through the different records one at a time by using the navigation buttons shown at the foot of the screen.

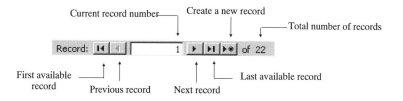

Sorting in Form View

As in Datasheet View, you can sort the records by selection: click on the field that you want to use as the basis for the sort, and click the Sort Ascending or Sort Descending button in the toolbar.

You can also perform a multiple-criteria sort, in exactly the same way as in Datasheet View: choose **Records | Filter | Advanced Filter/Sort**.

Filtering by Selection in Form View

**Filter by
Selection
button**

In Form View, you can filter records by selection, exactly as you did in Datasheet View: find a record that meets your criterion, select the relevant field (or the part of it that is of interest), and click the Filter by Selection button in the toolbar. You will see that the number of records shown beside the navigation buttons reflects the smaller number of records that satisfies your criterion.

As in Datasheet View, you can filter these records again to further refine the search for the records that you are interested in.

Filtering by Form

**Filter by
Form button**

Another option is to Filter by Form. For example, Exercise 5.20 shows you how to restrict the records displayed to those that you have actually spotted.

Exercise 5.20: Using a Form to Filter Records

1) Open the Birds Spotted form. Click the Filter by Form button in the toolbar or choose **Records | Filter | Filter by Form**.

2) Access displays a blank form, into which you can enter your filter criteria. In this case, the date is the criterion of interest.

Number	
Bird Name	
Colour	
Number Seen	
Size	
Migratory?	☐
Date Seen	>0
Place Seen	

3) Click on the Date Seen field. Notice that the drop-down list shows all the dates on which you recorded sightings. If you wanted to find all the birds you spotted on a specific date, you'd simply pick the date from the list.

4) What you want, however, is to find the birds you spotted on *any* date, that is, any record for which the date is not blank (or greater than zero).

So enter the following in the Date Seen field: >0.

**Apply/Remove
Filter button**

5) Click the Apply Filter button in the toolbar: the first record with the date filled in is shown, and the record count shows the number of such records in the table.

6) Click the Remove Filter button in the toolbar (as it is now), and all the records in the table are viewable.

Wildcards in Filters and Queries

You don't have to be precise when you are entering your filter criteria: you can use so-called *wildcards* to tell Access 'Give me everyone whose name includes Donnel', and it will get the Donnellys, McDonnells, MacDonnells, O'Donnells, and so on.

The most important wildcards are an asterisk (*) and a question mark (?). When you specify the criteria for a query or a filter, an asterisk (*) means 'anything or nothing', and a question mark (?) means 'any single character'.

Say, for example, you want to find all the birds that have 'Great' in their names. In the Bird Name field in the form, enter the following:

Great

When you apply the filter, only the three records that include 'Great' will be displayed.

Or, if you want to find birds that are coloured black or brown, you construct a filter with the colour specified as b????. When you apply this filter, you will be presented only with records that have the colour specified as five characters beginning with the letter 'b'. You would not, for example, get blue birds (for the obvious reason that 'blue' has only four characters).

Creating an All Fields Form

The easiest way to enter information into your table is to use a form. However, if you are adding new records to the table, the form you created in the previous exercise is not sufficiently detailed. You need a new form – one that enables you to fill in all the details for each bird (an 'All Fields Form'). Let's make one the quick way.

Exercise 5.21: Creating an All Fields Form
1) From the Database dialog box, select the Forms tab. Click the **New** button.

2) Select AutoForm: Columnar, and specify the Birds table.

3) Click **OK**.

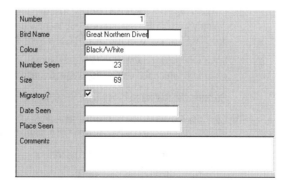

And that's it. Access now presents a new form, ready for use.

Close your form, and save it with the name Allfields.

You can subsequently access this form at any time from the Forms tab on the Database dialog box, and use it to view the records in your table, to change them, or to create new records.

Using a Form to Create New Records

To create new records, click on the Create New Record button in the navigation bar at the bottom of the form. Access presents a new, blank form. Fill it in.

Create New Record button

You can complete the fields in any order by clicking in the field and entering the information. The easiest way to complete the form, however, is to fill in the first field (Access automatically positions the cursor there when you open the form), and then proceed in order through the fields either by pressing TAB or by pressing ENTER. When you have filled in the last field in the form, press TAB or ENTER to open up a new, blank form.

Exercise 5.22: Using a Form to Enter a New Record
1) Open the Allfields form from the Database dialog box. Click the Create New Record button and enter the details of the Golden Eagle as follows:

Bird Name:	Golden Eagle
Colour:	Golden Brown
Size:	120
Date Seen:	6th September 2000
Place Seen:	Colorado

Using a Form to Modify Existing Records

Any changes you make to the information in a form is immediately reflected in the table. Remember that the Datasheet and the Form are just two ways of looking at the same information. To use the form to modify the information in your table, locate the record you are interested in (by paging through the records, one at a time, or by sorting or filtering), click on the field you want to change, and delete, overwrite, or add information.

Exercise 5.23: Using a Form to Modify Records
1) Use the Allfields form to complete all the remaining empty fields in all the records in your table. Make up information – for the exercise, it doesn't have to be accurate, or even truthful!

Modifying Form Layout and Content

For the moment, and for most purposes, the Form Wizard does a fine job. However, Access enables you to design forms from scratch, and to redesign ones that have already been designed. To see some of the possibilities (and there is no need to go into this too deeply), try Exercise 5.24.

Exercise 5.24: Changing the Layout and Content of a Form

1) Open the Birds Spotted form in Design View. (To do this, at the Database dialog box, click the Forms tab then select the Birds Spotted form, and click the **Design** button.)

2) In Design View, you see the different elements in your form set against a grid. Notice how each field has a *title* and a *textbox*.

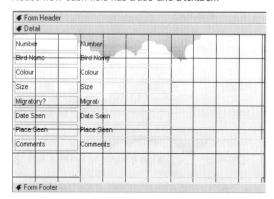

You can change the formatting of both titles and textboxes: select the Bird Name title and click the Bold button in the toolbar. Select the Bird Name text box and click the Italics button in the toolbar.

The toolbar offers a variety of formatting options:

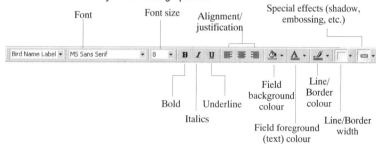

Experiment with these to see the possibilities. Remember, however, that the best forms are simple, laid out clearly, and use colour and other graphic devices sparingly.

3) You can change the shape and size of a field on the form.

- When you select a field, a number of 'sizing handles' are displayed around it. Click on any of these, and use the mouse to drag the border to the new position.

- You can also change the position of a field: click on the border anywhere *except* on one of the handles. The cursor changes to an 'open hand' shape. You can then drag the field to its new location.

- By default, the label and the text box move together, and maintain their position relative to one another. To move the label or text box independently, click on the larger 'move handle' at the top left of the field. The cursor changes to a 'pointing hand'. You can then drag the field to its new location. You might find this tricky to begin with, but it will become easier with practice.

Change the size and position of the fields and labels as shown in the example below.

4) To add a new field to a cut-down form, choose **View | Field List**.

From the list displayed, select the field you want to add and use the mouse to drag it from the list to the approximate location you want it to appear in the form. (You may have to move the Form Footer Bar out of the way. To do this, click on the top line of the footer until the cursor changes, then drag it and drop it in its new position.)

For example, the following screens show the effect:

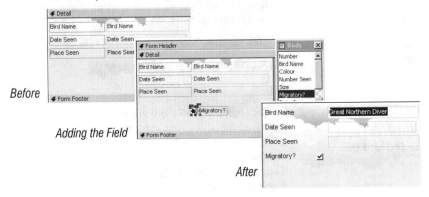

Before

Adding the Field

After

5) To import an image or graphic file into your form, choose **Insert | Picture**.

Access displays a dialog box in which you specify the graphic you want to include in the form. You can navigate around the hard disk, diskette, or CD-ROM to find the picture you want. If you don't have one of your own, a variety is available in C:\Program Files\Microsoft Office\Clipart\Popular.
Select the file named Dove in that subdirectory and then click **OK**.

6) The graphic is now inserted onto your form.

To change the size of the image, right-click it, and then choose **Properties** then, on the Format tab, change Size Mode to Zoom.

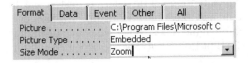

Close the dialog box then click on one of the sizing handles at the corners of the picture, and drag it inwards to the required size.

To move the image to a different location on the form, click on the picture anywhere except on the sizing handles. Hold down the mouse button the cursor changes to hand. Now drag the picture to the right side of the form and release the mouse button.

Moving a graphic image

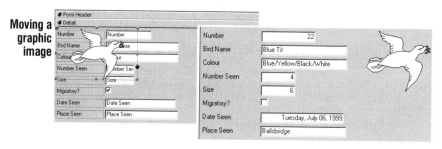

Form View button

Now, click the Form View button on the toolbar and admire your handiwork. Switch back to Design View by clicking the same button again.

7) Click the Close button or choose **File | Close**.

Access prompts you to save your work.

Section Summary: So Now You Know

Forms enable you to view your database records one at a time. As forms are based on tables, you can create a form only *after* you have created a table. Both forms and the datasheet contain the *same information*: any change you make to data in a form is reflected immediately in the datasheet, and any change you make in a datasheet is reflected in the associated forms.

You can create forms quickly and easily with the *Access Form Wizard*. You simply select which fields from the table you want to include on your form, choose from a range of data layouts and decorative styles, and give your form a name.

You can use a form to view existing records in your database. A series of *navigation buttons* along the bottom of the form enable you to step through different records one at a time. Within *Form View* you can sort and filter records, and use *wildcard characters* (* and ?).

An *all fields form* is one that contains every field in your table, and is used typically for entering data. The fastest way to enter data is to fill in the first field and, pressing TAB or ENTER after each one, proceed in order through the fields. When you have filled in the last field in the form, press TAB or ENTER to open up a new, blank form.

To use a form to *modify* the information in your table, locate the record you are interested in (by paging through the records, one at a time, or by sorting or filtering), click on the field you want to change, and delete, overwrite, or add information. You can include graphic images in your forms.

In *Design View* you can change the formatting of both field titles and textboxes, adjust the shape and size of any field, add new fields, and import, resize and reposition graphic images.

Section 5.6: Working with Reports

In This Section

In the earlier Sections of this Module, you learnt how to put information in to your database, and how to manipulate it and view it on screen. In this Section, you will learn how to get information out, and how to present it in a useful and accessible way.

New Activities

At the end of this Section, you should be able to:

- Present information you have extracted from the database on screen
- Print out a report of information from the database
- Create and customise headers and footers

New Words

At the end of this Section, you should be able to explain the following terms:

- Report
- Header
- Footer

Your First Report

Generally speaking, a report is a way of presenting information in printed form. However, the word is increasingly used to describe information in a form *suitable* for printing – even if it is only displayed on screen.

> **Report**
> A document (printed or on screen) that presents information in a structured way.

You have already seen how Access allows you to structure and organise your data, by filtering and sorting records, by using forms to choose the fields you want to display, and so on. You can, of course, print out any of these screens, and this may be quite adequate for your purposes. Simply click the Print button on the toolbar, or choose **File | Print**.

Print button

However, Access gives you a great deal of control over how your information is presented. You can lay it out so that important information is highlighted, data can be grouped into categories, and you can give totals and count information for each category, subcategory, and for the entire report. Some of this is beyond the scope of this book, but you will find that Access provides automated solutions that will satisfy most of your requirements, most of the time. The simplest way to produce a report is to use the AutoReports feature of Access.

Exercise 5.25: Using AutoReports to Produce a Report

1) From the Database screen, select the Reports tab.

2) Click the **New** button.

3) Choose **AutoReport: Columnar**

4) In the drop-down list of tables and queries, specify the **Birds** table.

5) Click **OK** and admire the report on the screen. To view the following pages, click the Next Page button at the bottom left of your screen.

6) If you have a printer, click the Print button on the toolbar, or choose **File | Print**. Then hang your finished report on the wall.

7) Close the Report screen, and (if it is displayed) close the Design screen. You will be prompted to save. Save the report as 'My First Report'.

Now click the Preview button to view it again – then close it. You can store lots of different reports to use and re-use later.

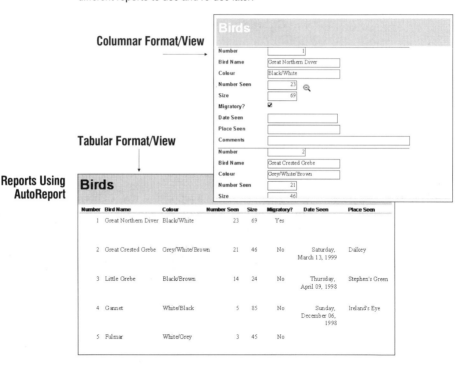

Columnar Format/View

Tabular Format/View

Reports Using AutoReport

While AutoReports make it very easy to produce good-looking reports, you can take full control of the content and layout of your report. But even here, Access makes it easy for you: you can use the Wizard.

Exercise 5.26: Using the Report Wizard

1) From the Database screen, select the Reports tab. Click the **New** button. Select the Report Wizard.

   Specify that you want to produce a report based on the Birds table.

   Click **OK**.

2) You are presented with a familiar-looking screen, similar to the one used to create tables and forms.

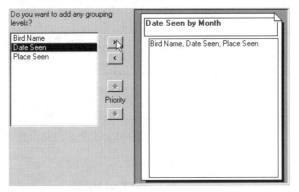

   Choose the fields you want to include in the report from the list on the left and move them into the list on the right. For this exercise, include the fields shown above.

   Click the **Next** button.

3) Specify how you want the records in the report to be grouped. You could, for example, produce a report for each bird, showing when and where you saw it: this would group together all the sightings of a given bird. For this exercise, we'll produce a report by date: this will group together all sightings made on the same date. Select Date Seen and click the > button.

   Click the **Grouping Options** button.

   You can group the sightings by year, quarter, month, week, day, etc.

   Select Month and click **OK**.

   Click the **Next** button.

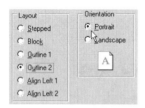

Specifying sort order

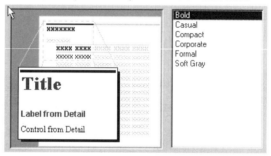

Specifying report layout

4) Next specify the order in which you want the records to be shown in the report. Select Date Seen as the first sort criterion. The Sort button is initially set to sort ascending. To change the order, just click the button: each time you click it, it switches between ascending and descending. Make it descending. This means that the report will show the most recent sightings first.

Select Bird Name as the second sort criterion, and make it ascending. This means that the report will show the most recent sightings first, and on any given day, it will show the birds sighted in alphabetical order. Click the **Next** button.

5) Specify the layout for the report. As in previous Wizard exercises, you can get a good idea of what the final result will look like by selecting each in turn. The best for our purposes is Outline 2, and, because we do not have very many fields in our report, Portrait. Select these options, and click the **Next** button.

6) Specify the typographic style for the report. Again, see what they look like by selecting them in turn.

For the exercise, select Bold, and click the **Next** button.

7) Finally, give the report a title: Spotting Record.

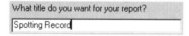

Choose the Preview option.

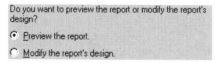

Click the **Finish** button.

You then see the report on screen.

If it is exactly what you want, click the Print button on the toolbar, or choose **File | Print**.

Report produced from Report Wizard

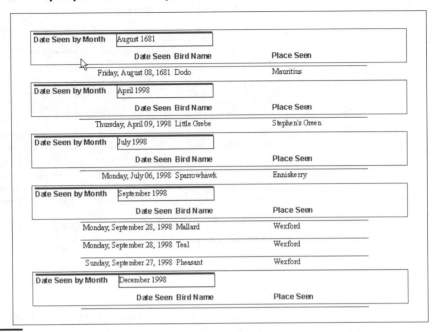

Date Seen by Month	August 1681		
	Date Seen	Bird Name	Place Seen
	Friday, August 08, 1681	Dodo	Mauritius

Date Seen by Month	April 1998		
	Date Seen	Bird Name	Place Seen
	Thursday, April 09, 1998	Little Grebe	Stephen's Green

Date Seen by Month	July 1998		
	Date Seen	Bird Name	Place Seen
	Monday, July 06, 1998	Sparrowhawk	Enniskerry

Date Seen by Month	September 1998		
	Date Seen	Bird Name	Place Seen
	Monday, September 28, 1998	Mallard	Wexford
	Monday, September 28, 1998	Teal	Wexford
	Sunday, September 27, 1998	Pheasant	Wexford

Date Seen by Month	December 1998		
	Date Seen	Bird Name	Place Seen

Modifying the Report Layout

If the report produced by the Report Wizard does not meet your requirements exactly, you may want to fine-tune it. For example, the report you created in Exercise 5.26 needs to be tidied up a little. The range of possibilities in Access is very wide: we'll confine ourselves to a few.

Exercise 5.27: Fine-Tuning Your Report

1) Open in Design View the report you created in Exercise 5.26. (To do this, at the Database dialog box, select the Reports tab, then select the Spotting Record report, and click the **Design** button.)

2) The different elements in your report are shown against a grid. Each field has a title and a text box. You can change the content or formatting of these in the same way as you did when you were designing a form (Exercise 5.24). Double-click in the label boxes listed below, and change them as follows:

Before	After
Date Seen by Month	Month
Date Seen	Date

Make the text box for Month bold.

Then adjust the size of each label box: click on the box. The sizing and move handles are shown around it. (If you have already selected the box for editing, the handles do not appear: first click away from the box, anywhere else on the screen, and then click once on the box.) Use the handles to change the shape and size of the box, or the hand pointer to change the position of the box, just like you did when you were designing forms.

3) The Report Header is text that appears at the beginning of your report. Select the text box, and then click in the text (Spotting Record). You can then modify or delete that header text. Change the header text from Spotting Record to Birdwatching Database. Enlarge the text box to accommodate the text.

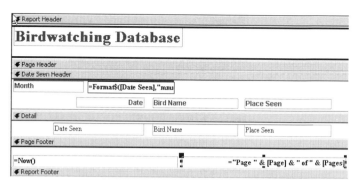

4) The Page Header is text that appears under the Report Header on page 1, and at the top of every other page in your report. Move the mouse pointer slowly over the line dividing Page Header and Date Seen Header – it becomes a moving tool.

Click, hold and drag the Date Seen Header bar down to make room between it and the Page Header.

5) Now, click on the Label button of the Toolbox (if the Toolbox is not displayed, choose **View | Toolbox**) and move it over the Page Header field – it is now a text box drawing tool. In the Page Header field, click the mouse where the top-left corner of the text box should be, hold down the mouse button, drag the pointer to where the bottom-right corner should be, and release the mouse button. Type the following text into the newly created text box: Copyright: Your Name.

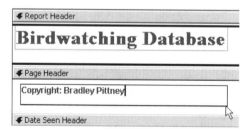

You've now created a Page Header.

6) The Page Footer appears at the end of each page in your report, and the Report Footer appears at the very end of the report. You can create footers in the same way as you created headers. If you do not want a particular header or footer in your report, just reduce the size of the text area to zero (the reverse of what you did in step 4).

7) Close the Report Design dialog box.

Access will prompt you to save your work.

8) From the Database dialog box, click the **Preview** button to open the report again, and critically evaluate the effect of your changes.

Section Summary: So Now You Know

A database *report* is a document (printed or on screen) that presents information in a structured way. Access provides two automated solutions – AutoReports and the Report Wizard – that will satisfy most reporting requirements.

To use the Report Wizard, choose the relevant table, select the fields you want to include, and specify the *grouping*, the *sort order*, the *layout* options and the typographic *styles*.

You can modify a report by changing the content of each field's title and text box, and by adjusting the size of each field's label.

You can insert or amend *headers and footers* to the report as a whole or to each page.

This Module should have given you a glimpse of the power of Access, and enough confidence to explore that power further by yourself. If you want to use more advanced features, the Help features included with Access provide you with plenty of guidance.

6

Presentations

Tomorrow you have two appointments: a visit to the dentist, and a presentation to an audience of strangers and friends. Which one fills you with greater terror?

Whether it's to a group of potential customers, a national conference of fellow workers, or a local community group, delivering an address can be an intimidating prospect.

Faced with these situations, you'll want to learn about any tools that will help you to feel less pressurised and more organised – tools that will make you more confident and help you make your points more effectively. This is where presentation software comes in.

In this Module, you will discover how to create support materials that will reinforce your message, both textually and graphically. You will also find out how to design your materials – both on-screen slides and paper hand-outs – so as to maximise their audience impact.

Software won't turn a bad presentation into a good one. But it can help a good presentation succeed in its aim: better communication of your bright ideas.

Think of this Module as your chance to speak rather than be spoken to. Good luck with it.

Section 6.1: Presentation Basics

This Section deals with the basic concepts of presentation software, introduces you to the terminology you will need, and lets you sample the possibilities on offer.

New Skills

At the end of this Section, you should be able to:

- Explain what presentation software is used for
- Start and quit PowerPoint
- Open and close a presentation
- Show a PowerPoint presentation on your computer
- View the presentation in a variety of ways
- Print out a PowerPoint presentation – as overhead projections (OHPs), handouts, or 35mm slides
- Use PowerPoint's online help facilities
- Modify PowerPoint's toolbar display

New Words

At the end of this Section you should be able to explain the following terms:

- Presentation
- Slide
- Slide View
- Outline View
- Slide Sorter View
- Notes Page View
- Slide Show View
- OHPs

Presentations and Presentation Software

When you demonstrate a new product, describe the results of your research, or announce a new organisational structure, you typically make a speech. To grab your audience's attention, and reinforce your messages, you show them a variety of visual aids while you are talking. To ensure they retain key information, you give them handouts to take away and study afterwards. That's a presentation.

Presentation software helps you to design and produce the visual aids and the handouts. Unfortunately, it doesn't help you with the speech, but it does help you to organise your thoughts, and it helps ensure that questions and comments from the audience don't put you off course. For the ECDL, you have to know how to produce the visual aids and handouts; you don't have to make a speech. Phew!

The visual aids reinforce and complement what you say – they shouldn't *duplicate* it. They should include images wherever possible (pictures, graphs, charts, maps, cartoons, diagrams). Text should be kept to a minimum, using headline style and bullet points.

The visual aids can be printed on paper or on overhead projection foils (OHP), they can be output to 35mm transparencies (slides), they can be displayed directly on the computer screen, or they can be projected from the computer using a directly connected projector. The choice of output depends on the number of people in your audience, the size of the room in which you are making the presentation, and the technology available.

Although 35mm slides are probably the least common form of output, most presentation software packages call the basic element of a presentation a 'slide'.

> **Slide**
>
> A slide is the basic building block of a visual presentation. It is equivalent to a page in a printed document; it can contain both text and graphics.

Starting PowerPoint

Double-click on the PowerPoint icon

-or-

Choose **Start | Programs | PowerPoint**.

Opening an Existing Presentation

The file names of PowerPoint files end in .ppt, .pps, or .pot. (Each of these is used for different purposes, as you will see later.) This helps you to distinguish them from Word documents (.doc), Excel workbooks (.xls), and other file types.

To open an existing presentation, either:

- Select Open an Existing Presentation on the first dialog box displayed when you start PowerPoint.
  -or-
- (If you have already been working in PowerPoint) Choose **File | Open** (or click the Open button on the Standard Toolbar).

Then select the file you want from the dialog box.

Open button

Exercise 6.1: Opening a Presentation

To experiment in this Section, open Dale Carnegie's presentation on presentations:

1) Choose **File | Open**.

2) From the Files of Type drop-down list, choose Presentation Templates.

   (The example we are going to use is this type of file. Most PowerPoint files you will be working with, however, are the default Presentations and Shows).

3) Navigate to the Microsoft Office folder (usually a subfolder in Program Files), and from there to the Templates | Presentations folder.

   You will see a number of files listed. Scroll down to the Presentation Guidelines file, select it, and click **Open**.

Working with PowerPoint Presentations

PowerPoint enables you to look at the same material in a variety of different formats, to view individual slides, and to print out the presentation.

Different Views

The different viewing options are available from the View menu:

Viewing options on the View menu

- **Slide** lets you see one slide at a time. This is the normal viewing mode when you are creating a presentation. You are able to see what the finished product will look like, and you are able to edit the text, add graphics, and so on.

- **Outline** shows the text of all the slides, without formatting or graphics. It is most useful when you are organising your thoughts, or for checking or changing the overall structure of the presentation.

- **Slide Sorter** shows a miniature version of the entire slide show. You can use this to check the consistency of the layout and colour scheme, and also to check, and if necessary change, the order of the slides.

- **Notes Page** shows the slides one at a time, half-sized, with a space below for speaker's notes.

- **Slide Show** shows the slides full-screen (without any menu bars), exactly as they would appear projected. To exit from Slide Show view, press the ESC key.

At the bottom left of the screen (except in Slide Show view), there are five icons, representing the five viewing modes – use these to switch quickly from one mode to another.

Zoom

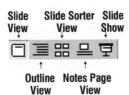

Slide View, **Slide Sorter View**, **Slide Show**, **Outline View**, **Notes Page View**

The View menu also offers a Zoom option: use this to enlarge or reduce the slide shown on the screen.

Finding Your Way Around a Presentation

Certain navigation keys can be used in all PowerPoint views:

To advance to the next slide	Press PAGE DOWN
To return to the previous slide	Press PAGE UP
To go to the first slide in the show	Press HOME
To go to the last slide	Press END

In all views except Slide Show view, you can also use the scroll bar at the right of the screen to move forwards or backwards.

In Slide Show View, a wider range of options is available:

To advance to the next slide	Left mouse click Spacebar N Right arrow Down arrow ENTER Page Down
To return to the previous slide	Backspace P Left arrow Up arrow Page Up
To go to a particular slide	Type the number of the slide, and press ENTER
To go to the first slide in the show	Hold down both mouse buttons for two seconds
To blank out the screen	B (for black) W (for white)
To return to the presentation	B or W again
To end a slide show	ESC

If you forget any of these controls, don't worry: press F1 any time during a presentation and the full list of controls is displayed.

Exercise 6.2: Exercises in Navigation

1) In Slide view, go back and forth through the presentation, one slide at a time, using the keyboard.

2) In Slide Show view, go back and forth through the presentation, one slide at a time, using the mouse wherever possible.

3) Go to slide 4. What Tip is given on that slide?

Printing a Presentation

You can print out a PowerPoint presentation in a variety of ways, depending on your requirements and on the hardware at your disposal. Printing in PowerPoint is similar to printing in other applications.

Print button

First, choose **File | Print**, or click the print button in the button bar.
Then, in the Print What drop-down box, you can choose to print slides, outline, speaker notes, or handouts. If you choose handouts, you can choose the number of slides per handout.

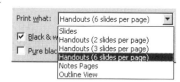

You can then specify, in the Print range area of the dialog box, whether you want to print all slides, the current slide, or a selected range of slides. To print a contiguous range of slides, type the number of the first slide, a hyphen, and the number of the last slide. To print non-contiguous slides, type the individual slide numbers separated by commas.

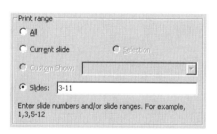

If you want to produce overhead projection foils (OHPs), you need to load your printer with blank foils before clicking **OK** on the Print dialog.

If you want to produce 35mm slides, you need to have a special desktop film recorder connected to your computer.

Exercise 6.3: Exercises in Printing

1) Print a set of handouts for the entire presentation with six slides on each page.

2) Print the first three slides of the presentation.

3) Print the first and fourth slide of the presentation.

Using Online Help

The online help built into PowerPoint provides additional information to help you to use the various features and to get the most from the software. To use it, click **Help | Contents and Index**, choose the Index tab and type the word you are looking for. A list of topics is then shown: click on the one that most closely matches your interest, then click **Display**.

You can also get help by clicking the Office Assistant button on the Standard Toolbar, or (if PowerPoint is set up this way) by pressing the F1 key.

Office Assistant button

You should familiarise yourself with the online help facility: remember, you can use it while you are doing your ECDL test.

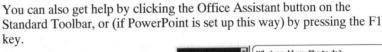

Modifying the Toolbar Display

The options in the Menu Bar give you access to all of PowerPoint's features. However, it is easier and quicker to select a feature by clicking a single button. Buttons may be displayed in a *Button Bar* or *Toolbar*.

In PowerPoint, you can display a number of different Toolbars, each covering a different range of functions. Click **View | Toolbars**. If they are not already displayed, check Standard, Formatting, and Drawing. These will be the most useful for your work in this Module.

Closing a Presentation

To close the presentation, choose **File | Close** or click the Close button on the presentation window.

If you have made changes to the presentation since you last saved it, PowerPoint prompts you to save the changes before it closes the file.

To close the presentation, click here.

Quitting PowerPoint

To quit PowerPoint, click here.

To leave PowerPoint, choose **File | Exit** or click the Close button on the PowerPoint window.

If you have left open any files containing unsaved work, PowerPoint prompts you to save them. You are then returned to the Windows desktop.

Section Summary: So Now You Know

A *presentation* is an address to an audience, accompanied by visual aids, such as slides or overhead projection foils (OHPs), and possibly handouts for the audience.

Presentation software, such as PowerPoint, helps you to prepare all the support materials for a presentation.

The basic building blocks of a presentation are called *slides*.

While you are working with PowerPoint, you can view your slides in five ways – Slide view, Outline view, Slide Sorter view, Notes Page view, and Slide Show view. Slide Show view is what the audience sees when you are making the presentation.

You can move around a presentation using the Page Up and Page Down keys. Other options are available in Slide Show view.

You can print out your presentation materials in a variety of ways.

PowerPoint includes a built-in help facility that contains reference material on all the software's functions, and many helpful tips for creating convincing presentations.

You can modify the toolbar display so that the features you use most often are readily available.

Section 6.2: Creating Your First Slides

In This Section

In this Section, you will learn how to use PowerPoint to create simple text-based slides.

New Skills

At the end of this Section, you should be able to:

- Create a new, text-based slide
- Enter, edit, and delete text in a slide
- Import text and other objects into a PowerPoint slide
- Delete objects from a slide
- Delete a slide
- Save a presentation to hard disk or diskette

New Words

At the end of this Section you should be able to explain the following terms:

- Placeholder
- AutoLayout
- Portrait
- Landscape

Creating a New Presentation

To create a new presentation:

If you have already been using PowerPoint and it is still open:

- Choose **File | New**. Then, in the General tab, select the Blank Presentation icon. Click **OK**.
  Alternatively, click the New button on the Standard Toolbar.

New button

Otherwise:

- Start PowerPoint by double-clicking on the PowerPoint icon or by choosing **Start | Programs | PowerPoint**. Click the Blank Presentation button and click **OK**.

All the exercises in this Section contribute to creating the new presentation.

Exercise 6.4: Using the Placeholders to Enter Text

1) When you create a new presentation, PowerPoint displays a dialog box that offers a choice of ready-made layouts (called AutoLayouts) for your slides. As you click on a layout, PowerPoint shows the name of that layout in an area to the right of the dialog box.

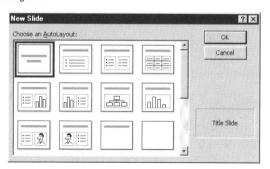

Select the first layout, which PowerPoint calls Title Slide, and click **OK**.

2) You are now shown a screen that contains two boxes surrounded by dotted lines. PowerPoint calls these boxes *placeholders*. Click on the top placeholder.

3) The border of the placeholder changes and a blinking text cursor appears inside it. You can now type text in the placeholder. Enter the following text in the first placeholder:
New Product Launch.

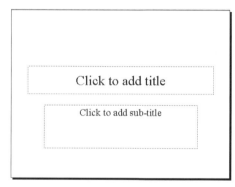

4) Click on the second placeholder and enter the following text:
Round Wheels.

Your screen should now look like that on the right.

Congratulations! You have created the first slide of your first presentation in PowerPoint.

You can add, edit or delete text from a slide in any PowerPoint view, with the exception of Slide Show. Simply position the cursor where you want to make the changes and edit.

> **AutoLayout**
> One of 24 ready-made slide layouts. They typically include placeholders for text and other objects such as images and charts.

> **Placeholder**
> A frame or box within a slide for holding text or graphics.

Remember: click on a placeholder to select it so that you can type or edit text. Click outside the placeholder to deselect it.

Landscape or Portrait?

Most cinema screens, television screens and computer screens are wider than they are tall: so will most of your slide presentations be. This format is known as *landscape*; the alternative (taller) is known as *portrait*. If you ever want to produce a presentation in portrait format, choose **File | Page Setup**, and under Orientation, Slides, click Portrait.

Adding Slides to Your Presentation

After the title slide, you will want to create further slides to hold the main body of your presentation. Do this as follows:

Exercise 6.5: Adding Slides to a Presentation

1) Choose **Insert | New Slide** or click the New Slide button on the Standard Toolbar.

New Slide button

2) Select the slide layout you want to use. This time, select the Bulleted List.

3) Click on the first placeholder and type:
Amazing Features.

Bulleted List layout

4) Click on the second placeholder and type:
Smooth Travelling for Passenger Comfort.

5) Press ENTER. PowerPoint creates a second bullet point on a new line. Type:
Reduced Fuel Consumption.

6) Press ENTER. Continue to enter the features as shown right.

> ### Amazing Features
> • Smooth Travelling for Passenger Comfort
> • Reduced Fuel Consumption
> • Longer Engine Life
> • Multiple Uses in Transport Sector
>   – Cars
>   – Bicycles
>   – Trucks

Promote   Demote

Use the Demote button on the Formatting Toolbar to create the second level of bullet for the different modes of transport. (Use the Promote button to elevate them to the first level.)

Well done! That's two slides created already.

Using Outline View

Perhaps the best way to organise your ideas is to use Outline view. This enables you to see the text of all your slides, arranged like a table of contents. In Outline view, you can add, edit, and delete text. You can also change the order of the slides, and arrange the text so that the more important text is made more prominent.

Outline View

Shows the text of all your slides, so that you can judge how well your ideas and text flow from one slide to the next.

Outline View button

To see your presentation in Outline view, choose **View | Outline**, or click the Outline View button.

You can use the buttons on the Outlining Toolbar to move slides or text, show only slide titles, and change the indent level of titles and text. Try it.

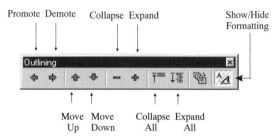

Exercise 6.6: Using Outline View to Add Slides

1) When you open Outline View, you see the text of the slides you have created so far.

   Click at the end of the text and press ENTER.

   1 ☐ New Product Launch
       Round Wheels
   2 ☐ Amazing Features
       • Smooth Travelling for Passenger Comfort
       • Reduced Fuel Consumption
       • Longer Engine Life
       • Multiple Uses in Transport Sector
           – Cars
           – Bicycles
           – Trucks

2) Type the headline for the next slide: Advantages and Disadvantages. Press ENTER. Notice that the text takes on the attributes of the previous line of text: it appears as a minor bullet on slide number 2.

3) Correct the status of the headline by using the Promote button on the toolbar. Notice that when it reaches the top of the hierarchy (that is, when you have promoted it as far as you can), it is automatically assigned a slide number (3).

4) Add the text of the first advantage: Faster. Press ENTER. Notice once again that the new text takes on the attributes of the previous line of text: it appears as a separate slide. Use the Demote button to establish it as a subordinate point. Then add the remaining advantages and disadvantages, as shown right.

   3 ☐ Advantages and Disadvantages
       • Faster
       • Smoother
       • Easier to Start
       • Harder to Control
       • Needs Replacement of Existing Equipment
       • Very Boring

5) Add four more slides, with text as shown right.

   Note that the last three contain only a headline.

6) Click the Slide View button, or choose **View | Slide**. Move forward and back through the slides (using any of the methods described in the previous Section) to see the effect of your work.

Slide View button

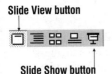

Slide Show button

7) Click the Slide Show button, or choose **View | Slide Show**. Again, move forward and back through the presentation to see how it would look to the audience.

By now you should realise that you can create an acceptable PowerPoint presentation very quickly.

Notice that PowerPoint assumes that some of the slides will have more text added later, and has created placeholders for that text. (The placeholder text ("Click to add text" etc.) is not displayed in Slide Show view.)

Copying Text within PowerPoint

To copy text from one slide to another, or from one part of a slide to another, select the text by clicking and dragging, then choose **Edit | Copy** (or hold down the CTRL key and press C). Then position your cursor where you want the text to appear and choose **Edit | Paste** (or hold down the CTRL key and press V).

Exercise 6.7: Moving Text within PowerPoint

1) Open slide number 3 (Advantages and Disadvantages) in Slide view.

2) Choose **Format | Slide Layout**, and select the 2-Column Text layout.

   Click **Apply**.

2-Column Text layout

3) Select the last three bulleted points.

   Choose **Edit | Cut**.

Advantages and Disadvantages
- Faster
- Smoother
- Easier to Start
- Harder to Control
- Ne...
  Ex...
- Ve...

• Click to add text

4) Click in the right-hand text placeholder.

   Choose **Edit | Paste**.

   The three "disadvantage" points are moved into position.

Advantages and Disadvantages
- Faster
- Smoother
- Easier to Start

- Harder to Control
- Needs Replacement of Existing Equipment
- Very Boring

Importing Text from Another Application

If you have text in another application, such as Microsoft Word, you can use that text in PowerPoint without having to retype it.

The simplest way is to select the text in the other application, choose **Edit | Copy** (or hold down the CTRL key and press C), and then, in PowerPoint, position your cursor where you want the text to appear and choose **Edit | Paste** (or hold down the CTRL key and press V). You can paste the text in any PowerPoint view except Slide Show.

You can also open a Word file in PowerPoint. Choose **File | Open**, select the file you are interested in, and click **Open**. PowerPoint tries to guess how you want the text treated: if you have not done any formatting in Word, it treats each paragraph as a separate slide. If you have used Word paragraph formats or tabs, PowerPoint interprets these as best it can. In any case, you can rearrange and reformat the text, as shown above.

This exercise shows the copy-and-paste technique.

Exercise 6.8: Copying Text from Another Application

1) Choose **Help | Contents and Index**, choose the Index tab and type the word 'import'. A list of topics is then shown. Under Importing data, click on the *text* option. Click **Display**.

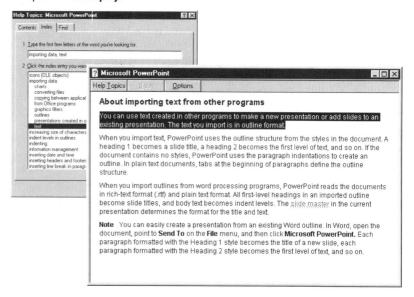

2) Select the first paragraph of text in the help page. Choose **Options | Copy**. Close the Help dialog box.

3) In PowerPoint, select Outline View. Position the cursor at the end of slide number 6 (Sales Projections).

   Press ENTER (to create a new, blank slide).

4) Choose **Edit | Paste**.

   The paragraph from the help text appears as slide number 7.

7 ▢ You can use text created in other programs to make a new
presentation or add slides to an existing presentation. The text
you import is in outline format.

8 ▢ Product Identity Scheme

Demote

5) Use the Demote button in the Outlining Toolbar to make the text part of slide number 6.

6 ▢ Sales Projections
  • You can use text created in other programs to make a new presentation or add slides to
    an existing presentation. The text you import is in outline format.
7 ▢ Product Identity Scheme

Notice how the final slide is renumbered to take account of the change.

You can use the same technique to copy objects from other applications: for example, you can select a range of cells in an Excel worksheet, copy them (as above), and paste them into a PowerPoint slide. Or you can copy a chart created in Excel, or a table created in Word, or a graphic file (such as a scanned image) from a graphics progam.

Deleting a Slide

To delete a slide, position the cursor anywhere in the slide and choose **Edit | Delete Slide**. You can do this in any view except Slide Show view.

Exercise 6.9: Deleting a Slide

1) Delete slide number 5 (Sales & Marketing) from your presentation.

PowerPoint's Undo Feature

Undo   **Redo**
button   **button**

Enter the wrong text? Press the wrong key? Delete something you didn't mean to? PowerPoint allows you to undo your most recent actions if they have produced unwanted results. Choose **Edit | Undo** or click the Undo button on the Standard Toolbar. You can also Redo actions that you have undone: choose **Edit | Redo** or click the Redo button on the Toolbar.

Exercise 6.10: Using Undo

1) Choose **Edit | Undo**. The presentation reverts to the condition it was in before your most recent action.

2) Repeat undoing until the presentation is in the condition it was in before Exercise 6.8.

Saving Your Presentation

Save button

To save your presentation, choose **File | Save** or click the Save button on the Standard Toolbar. As in all programs, you must name your presentation and specify where it is to be saved when you save it for the first time.

Choose **File | Save As** to save a presentation under a different name or in a different location.

Exercise 6.11: Saving Your Presentation to Hard Disk or Diskette

1) Save the presentation that you have created in this Section. Give it a name that you will find easy to remember and recognise. For example, if your initials are KB, call it KBpres1.

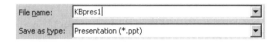

Click **Save**.

Up One Level button

2) Save the presentation again, this time on diskette. To do this, you will need to click the Up One Level button repeatedly until you are at the My Computer level. Then insert a diskette in the diskette drive, click the icon for the A: drive, and click **Save**.

3) Save the presentation again, in its original location on the hard disk. (Otherwise all your subsequent work will be carried out on the diskette.)

Section Summary: So Now You Know

To create a new slide, you choose an *AutoLayout* that most closely matches your needs.

AutoLayouts contain *placeholders* in which you enter the text.

Alternatively, you can import from another source such as a word processor.

You can use Outline view to collect and organise your ideas, without worrying too much about formatting and style.

If you make changes that you don't like, you can Undo them.

And you can save your presentation to hard disk or diskette. PowerPoint presentations have the extension .ppt, .pps, or .pot.

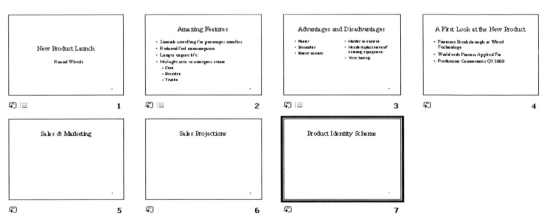

PowerPoint Presentations: The Story So Far

Section 6.3: Adding Graphics and Pictures

In This Section

In this Section, you will learn how to include pictures and other graphics in your slides.

New Skills

At the end of this Section, you should be able to:

- Add simple graphic devices (lines, boxes, etc.) to a slide
- Edit and delete graphic devices
- Create and modify organisation charts, bar charts, and pie charts and include them in a presentation.
- Import a photograph or clip art image to a slide
- Copy and paste images (within the presentation, between different presentations, and between PowerPoint and another application)
- Move, change the size and shape, rotate, and flip objects in a slide

New Words

At the end of this Section you should be able to explain the following terms:

- AutoShapes
- Organisation Chart
- Clip Art

The exercises in this Section further develop the presentation created in Section 6.2. Open the presentation before beginning the exercises in this Section.

Using PowerPoint's Drawing Tools

The Drawing Toolbar includes a number of tools for drawing simple objects, including lines, arrows, rectangles, and ellipses.

The Drawing Toolbar

Line and Arrow *Tools*	To draw a line, click on the Line button, place the cursor where you want the line to begin, click and drag to where you want the line to end, and release the mouse button.
	To draw an arrow, click on the Arrow button and draw it in the same way.
	Change the style of arrowhead, or the direction of the arrow, by clicking the Arrow Style Button.

Rectangle Tool

To draw a rectangle, click on the Rectangle button, place the cursor where you want one corner of the rectangle, click and drag diagonally to where you want the opposite corner of the rectangle, and release the mouse button.

To draw a square, hold down the SHIFT key as you drag with the mouse.

Ellipse Tool

To draw an ellipse, click on the Ellipse button, place the cursor where you want the shape to begin, click and drag until the shape is the size you want, and release the mouse button.

To draw a circle, hold down the SHIFT key as you drag with the mouse.

Line Colour and Style

In the case of straight lines, arrows, rectangles, and ellipses, you can specify the colour and thickness of the line. Click on the Line Colour button and select a colour, either before you draw the line, or, with the line selected, after you have drawn it.

 Change the thickness of the line by clicking the Line Style button.

 Make the line a dashed line (in a choice of dash styles) by clicking the Dash Style button.

Fill Colour

Use this button to choose the colour with which the inside of the rectangle or ellipse should be filled.

A choice of colours pops up when you click the arrow beside the button. Again, you can choose the fill colour before you draw the shape, or you can select an existing shape and then choose a fill colour.

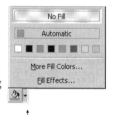

Click here to choose a colour or fill effect

Text Box

A Text Box is an alternative means of adding text to a slide. Use the Text Box tool in the same way as you use the Rectangle tool; then type text into it. Change the format of the text by selecting it and then choosing options from the Format menu (in particular, Font, Bullet, and Alignment). Note, however, that text added to a slide using Text Box does not appear in Outline View.

Editing Drawn Objects

To change the shape or size of any object created with the drawing tools, click on the object to select it. A number of sizing handles are shown around the object. Click on any of these and drag the handle until the object is the required shape and size.

To change the position of any object created with the drawing tools, select the object by clicking on it anywhere except on a sizing handle. The cursor changes to a cross shape. Drag the object to the desired new location.

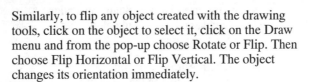

Repositioning Cursor Shape

To move an object between slides, use the Cut and Paste commands on the Edit menu.

To rotate any object created with the drawing tools by 90° in either direction, click on the object to select it. Click Draw on the Drawing Toolbar and, from the pop-up, choose Rotate or Flip. Then choose Rotate Left or Rotate Right. The object changes its orientation immediately.

Options available from the Drawing Toolbar

Similarly, to flip any object created with the drawing tools, click on the object to select it, click on the Draw menu and from the pop-up choose Rotate or Flip. Then choose Flip Horizontal or Flip Vertical. The object changes its orientation immediately.

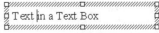

To rotate an object freely, click on the object to select it. Then click on the Free Rotate button. The sizing handles are replaced by rotating handles. Click on any of these (the cursor changes shape), and drag the object to its new orientation. You can limit the object's rotation to 15° steps by holding down the SHIFT key as you drag with the mouse.

Free Rotating Cursor Shape

Rotating handles

To delete any object created with the drawing tools, click on the object to select it and press DELETE.

Exercise 6.12: Drawing Shapes

1) Open slide number 7 (Product Identity Scheme) in Slide View.

2) We do not want the lower placeholder: choose **Format | Slide Layout**, and select the Title Only layout. Click **Apply**.

Title Only layout

3) Draw three circles, as shown right. The two bigger circles have a line thickness of 6 points: the smallest circle has a line thickness of 3 points. All circles are red, with blue fill.

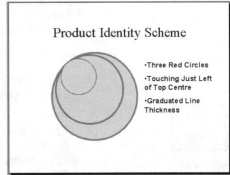

4) Add a text box to the right of the circles. Add text as shown. Make the text Arial bold, 24 point. Make it bulleted.

5) Save the presentation.

Grouping and Ungrouping Objects

You can group objects so that you can work with them as if they were a single object. You can format, move, rotate, flip and resize grouped objects in a single operation.

To group objects, hold down SHIFT and click each of the objects in turn. Next, click the Draw button on the Drawing Toolbar and choose **Group.**

To ungroup a selected group of objects, click the Draw button on the Drawing Toolbar and choose **Ungroup**.

Click the arrow to get at the grouping options

Inserting AutoShapes

AutoShapes are commonly used, ready-made shapes that you can insert in your presentations. They include lines, basic shapes, flowchart elements, stars and banners, and callouts.

When you insert an AutoShape on a slide, you can change its size and colour, and rotate it, as required.

To select an AutoShape, click the AutoShapes button on the Drawing Toolbar and choose from the options offered by the pop-up menu.

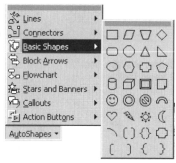

> **AutoShapes**
>
> *Ready-made shapes, including lines, geometric shapes and flowchart elements that you can use in your presentations.*

Inserting Organisation Charts

Organisation charts are used to illustrate hierarchical organisations or structures. People or units in an organisation are represented by boxes, and their relationships are represented by lines. You could draw them using the drawing tools, but they are used so frequently that PowerPoint provides a tool especially for producing them.

> **Organisation Chart**
>
> *A diagram used to illustrate the people or units in an organisation (represented by boxes) and their relationships (represented by lines).*

There are three ways to include an Organisation Chart in a slide:

- Start with a blank slide, or one with only a title, and choose **Insert | Picture | Organisation Chart**.

  -or-

- Choose **Format | Slide Layout**, and select the Organisation Chart layout.
  Click **Apply**.
  Then double-click on the organisation chart icon.

Organisation Chart layout

-or-

Organisation Chart icon

- Choose **Insert | New Slide**, and select the Organisation Chart layout. Click **OK**.
  Then double-click on the organisation chart icon.

PowerPoint opens a new window that displays an Organisation Chart template and offers new menus of commands. The Styles menu, for example, allows you to choose different chart types, while the Text, Boxes and Lines menus each allow you to format the respective chart elements.

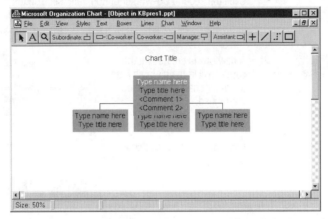

You can alter the template as you wish. Although the boxes have text labels in them, such as 'Type name here', you can enter any type of information in any box – the labels are for your guidance only.

Exercise 6.13: Inserting an Organisation Chart

1) Open slide number 5 (Sales and Marketing) in Slide View.

2) Choose **Format | Slide Layout**, and select the Organisation Chart layout.

   Click **Apply**.

3) Double-click on the organisation chart icon to open the Organisation Chart window.

4) Edit the text in the template as shown right.

5) When you have finished working in the Organisation Chart window, return to your slide by choosing **File | Exit and Return to**, and then clicking **Yes** on the dialog box displayed.

Within PowerPoint, you can move, resize or delete a chart as you would any other object. To make any other changes to the chart, however, you have to double-click on the chart and make your changes in the Organisation Chart window.

Exercise 6.14: Modifying the Structure of an Organisation Chart

1) Open slide number 5 (Sales and Marketing) in Slide View. Double-click on the organisation chart.

2) The chart is opened in the Organisation Chart window. The toolbar provides buttons for adding boxes (Subordinates, Co-workers, Managers, Assistants) and lines.

Click the second Co-worker button, then click on the box containing Graham Horton.

A new box is created, at the same level in the hierarchy, and the other chart elements are rearranged.

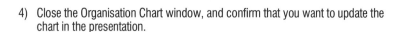

3) Click the new box, and enter text as shown right.

4) Close the Organisation Chart window, and confirm that you want to update the chart in the presentation.

Presenting Quantitative Information

In many circumstances, you will need to present quantitative data. This kind of information is often best presented in the form of graphs, or charts. Luckily, PowerPoint provides a facility for including a variety of chart types in your slides.

To include a graph or a chart in a slide:

Chart layout

Chart icon

- Start with a blank slide, or one with only a title, and choose **Insert | Chart**.

   -or-

- Choose **Format | Slide Layout**, and select the Chart layout (or Text & Chart, or Chart & Text).
   Click **Apply**.
   Then double-click on the chart icon.

   -or-

- Choose **Insert | New Slide**, and select the Chart layout.
   Click **OK**.
   Then double-click on the chart icon.

PowerPoint inserts a model chart into the slide, and, in a separate window, presents a mini-datasheet showing the numbers and titles upon which the chart is based.

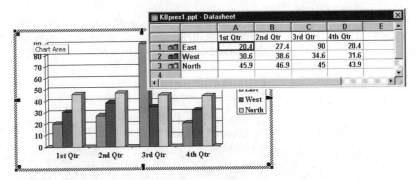

By changing the numbers and titles, you change the underlying chart. You can add new rows and columns by entering data into the datasheet. To delete rows or columns, click on the letter at the top of the column or the number at the left of the row (the column/row changes colour) and press DELETE. When you are finished, close the datasheet window.

To change the colour or format of any element in the chart, double-click on it: you are presented with options that are relevant to that element.

To change the data:

- Choose **View | Datasheet**

  -or-
- Right-click on the plot area (that is, in the chart placeholder, but not on any element of the chart), and choose Datasheet from the pop-up menu.

The datasheet upon which the chart is based is shown, in which you can make your changes.

To change the chart type:

- Choose **Chart | Chart Type**.

  -or-
- Right-click on the plot area, as above, and choose Chart Type.
- Select the chart type and sub-type from the menu.
- Click **OK**.

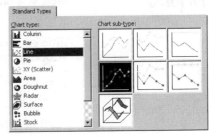

The most commonly used types are Column, Line, and Pie:

- Column charts are typically used to show figures that are measured at a particular time.
- Line charts are typically used to illustrate trends over time.
- Pie charts are typically used to illustrate the breakdown of figures in a total. Note that a pie chart is based on a single column of numbers.

PowerPoint gives you a wide variety of presentation options for charts. Some of them, however, are more decorative than informative: be careful that your message isn't obscured.

Exercise 6.15: Inserting a Chart

1) Open slide number 6 (Sales Projections) in Slide View.

2) Choose **Format | Slide Layout**, and select the Chart layout.

   Click **Apply**.

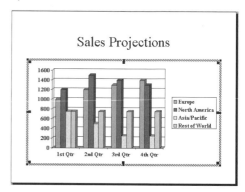

		A	B	C	D	E
		1st Qtr	2nd Qtr	3rd Qtr	4th Qtr	
1	Europe	1000	1200	1300	1400	
2	North America	1200	1500	1400	1300	
3	Asia/Pacific	750	500	250	250	
4	Rest of World	750	750	750	750	
5						

3) Double-click on the chart icon to open the Datasheet window.

4) Edit the text in the datasheet, as shown right.

5) When you have finished working in the datasheet window, close it and you return to your slide.

Within PowerPoint, you can move, resize or delete a chart as you would any other object. To make changes to the data in the chart, however, you have to make your changes in the Datasheet window. Double-click on the chart. If the Datasheet window is not displayed immediately, choose **View | Datasheet**.

Importing Pictures

You can also illustrate your slides by inserting graphic images – drawings created in other software applications, scanned photographs, or clip art.

PowerPoint includes a gallery of clip art images that you can use in different presentations. They are grouped in categories, ranging from Academic to Food and Travel.

Clip Art

Standard or 'stock' images that can be used and reused in presentations and other documents.

To include a picture in a slide:

- Start with a blank slide, or one with only a title, and choose **Insert | Picture | Clip Art**.

  -or-

- Choose **Format | Slide Layout**, and select the Clip Art & Text (or Text & Clip Art) layout. Click **Apply**. Double-click the clip art icon.

Clip Art & Text layout

Clip Art icon

-or-

- Choose **Insert | New Slide**, and select the Clip Art & Text layout. Click **OK**. Double-click the Clip Art icon.

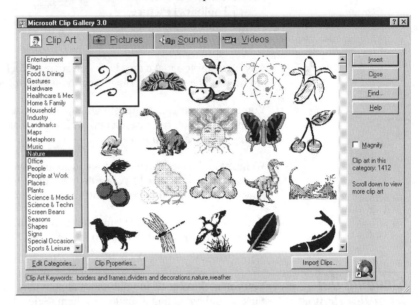

You are then presented with a gallery of images. Select the one you want to use, and click **Insert**.

Exercise 6.16: Inserting a Clip Art Image

1) Open slide number 4 (A First Look at the New Product) in Slide View.

2) Choose **Format | Slide Layout**, and select the Clip Art & Text layout. Click **Apply**.

3) Double-click on the clip art icon to open the Gallery.

4) Search the Gallery for a suitable image.

   Click on the image and click **Insert**.

   The image is inserted into the slide.

5) Choose **View | Slide Show**, or click the Slide Show button. Move forward and back through the presentation to see how it would look to the audience.

6) Save the presentation.

You can move, resize or delete the image as you would any other object.

To change the colours,
brightness, or contrast of the
image, you need the Picture
Toolbar. Either choose
View | Toolbars | Picture,

or right-click on the image and choose Show Picture Toolbar from the
pop-up menu.

Any changes you make are shown on screen. Click on the close box at the
top right of the Picture Toolbar when you are finished.

You are not restricted to inserting images on slides whose layout includes a
graphic icon. You can insert a clip art image on any slide by choosing
Insert | Picture | Clip Art.

To insert an image of your own – your company logo, for example –
choose **Insert | Picture | From File**, and select the required image file.
PowerPoint accepts images in most common image file formats.

You can also copy images from graphic programs and paste them into
PowerPoint slides, as described in the previous Section.

Standing Out from the Crowd

You can make objects in your slides appear to stand out from the
background by adding a shadow to them. Select the object, then click the
Shadow button on the Drawing toolbar. You can choose from a variety of
shadow styles. Be careful, if you are choosing a colour for the shadow, that
you do not interfere with the legibility of your text.

Exercise 6.17: Adding a Shadow to an Object

1) Open slide number 5 (Sales & Marketing) in Slide View.

2) Select the chart by clicking anywhere on it.

3) Click the Shadow button on the Drawing toolbar. Choose Shadow Style 5.

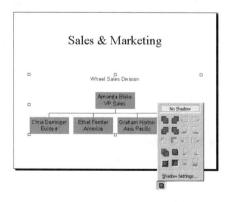

4) Click the Shadow button again.

   Click Shadow Settings, and in the Shadow Settings button bar, click the Shadow Color button, and pick a mid-blue as the shadow colour.

   Close the Shadow Settings button bar.

5) Save the presentation.

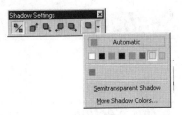

Section Summary: So Now You Know

You can draw simple shapes (lines, arrows, rectangles, ellipses) within PowerPoint. You can also add more complex shapes (AutoShapes) within PowerPoint.

You can change the shape, size, position, and colour of such shapes, rotate them, flip them, and add shadows behind them.

You can create organisation charts, and a range of graphs and charts to illustrate quantitative data.

You can also import graphics created in other applications – charts, worksheets, tables, diagrams, pictures, photographs, maps, etc.

1

2

3

4

5

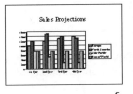

6

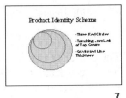

7

PowerPoint Presentations: The Plot Thickens

Section 6.4: Projecting a Consistent Image

In This Section

In this Section, you will learn how to choose an overall style for your presentation, how to pick a colour scheme, and how to establish a coherent typographic style. These are important if your presentation is to convey a strong, confident image. If each of your slides looks entirely different, your message will appear confused and disjointed.

New Skills

At the end of this Section, you should be able to:

- Choose an overall design for your presentation
- Select and modify a colour scheme
- Select and modify a background for your slides
- Use master slides to control the consistency of your slides
- Change the text attributes of individual slides
- Save a presentation as a template for subsequent use

New Words

At the end of this Section you should be able to explain the following terms:

- Presentation design
- Colour scheme
- Slide master
- Presentation template

The exercises in this Section further develop the presentation created in Sections 6.2 and 6.3. Open the presentation before beginning the exercises in this Section.

Using Presentation Designs

PowerPoint is supplied with a variety of presentation designs that you can use in your presentations. You can either use them directly, without any change, or you can adapt them to your particular needs or taste, or to your company's identity scheme.

You can either create a new presentation using one of these designs, or you can apply a design to a presentation that you have already created.

To create a new presentation using a PowerPoint design, choose **File | New**. Then click the Presentation Designs tab, and select one of the designs: a preview of the design is shown on the right. When you have found one you want to use, click **OK**.

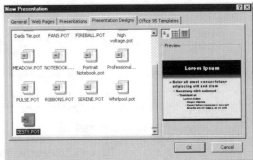

To apply a design to an existing presentation, choose **Format | Apply Design**. Locate the designs folder (usually in c:\Program Files\Microsoft Office\Templates\Presentation Designs: the file names end in .pot). Choose the design you want to use. (To see a preview of the design, click the Preview button.) Click **Apply**.

Preview button ↑

Exercise 6.18: Choosing a Design

1) Apply a new design to the presentation previously created. Use the design called "Contemporary Portrait".

2) Save the presentation.

3) Choose **View | Slide Show**, or click the Slide Show button. Move forward and back through the presentation to see how it would look to the audience.

Making the Design Your Own

The design establishes a typographic framework for the presentation, and uses graphic devices (lines, colours, background images) to create an overall image. You can alter these to make the design your own. Rather than changing each slide individually, you can make global changes – this saves effort and it helps make your slides consistent.

Modifying the Colour Scheme

PowerPoint has a number of built-in colour schemes. Each scheme consists of a set of eight co-ordinated colours.

When you select a scheme, PowerPoint applies the different colours of the scheme to specific slide elements, such as title text (the text in the title placeholder), non-title text, background, graphic fills, and so on.

Exercise 6.19: Applying a Colour Scheme

1) Choose **Format | Slide Colour Scheme**. On the Standard tab, select one of the schemes. For this exercise choose the third colour scheme on the second row – the one with the blue background.

2) On the Custom tab, select Text and lines and click **Change Color**.

   Pick a bright yellow. Click **OK**.

   Select Accents & Hyperlinks, and change its colour to mid blue.

   Click **OK**.

3) Click **Apply to All**. This has the effect of applying the new colour scheme to all the slides in the presentation.

4) Save the presentation.

5) Click the Slide Show button, and move forward and back through the presentation to see how it would look to the audience.

Colour Scheme

A set of eight, preset co-ordinated colours you can use to give your presentation an attractive and consistent appearance.

Modifying the Background

In the colour scheme, you can specify only a single background colour. If, instead of a flat colour, you want to specify gradients, textures, patterns, or pictures as the background to your slides, you can do so as shown below. Again, however, a word of caution: these options are intended to make your slides more exciting and dynamic, but if you do not use them carefully, they can make your slides illegible!

Exercise 6.20: Changing the Background

1) Choose **Format | Background**.

   As in the colour scheme, you can choose a single colour, either from the drop-down palette, or from the More Colors option.

   The more interesting options, however, are found in Fill Effects.

   Click this option.

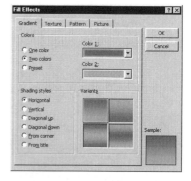

2) The screen shows four tabs – Gradient, Texture, Pattern, and Picture. In each, when you select an option, a sample is displayed on the lower right. Explore the options on offer. Then select the Gradient tab.

3) Click the Two Colors button. Make Color 1 dark blue, and Color 2 light blue. Click the Horizontal shading style, and the first variant. Click **OK**.

4) Click **Apply to All**. This has the effect of applying the new background to all the slides in the presentation.

5) Save the presentation. Once again, take a look at the whole presentation to see how it would appear to the audience.

The Slide Master

Whether you know it or not, every slide you insert in a PowerPoint presentation is based on the style of the *Slide Master*.

It is from the Slide Master that all slides take their default text formatting and positioning. In addition, anything that you insert on the Slide Master appears automatically on every slide of your presentation. This is useful for company logos or for graphic elements such as lines and borders.

To view the Slide Master, choose **View | Master | Slide Master**. It consists of two placeholders:

- **Title Placeholder**: Determines the format and positioning of text in every title placeholder in your presentation.

- **Object Placeholder**: Determines the format and positioning of text in every non-title placeholder.

Notice that the Slide Master includes the yellow "painted" line.

Your audience never sees the Slide Master; they see only its effects on the slides in your presentation.

You can override the defaults supplied by the Slide Master on any individual slide.

Slide Master

The Slide Master stores all the default attributes that you want to apply to new slides, including text formatting and positioning, background, and standard graphics, such as your company logo.

Exercise 6.21: Reformatting Text in the Slide Master

In this Exercise, you change the text format of your presentation by changing the Slide Master.

1) Choose **View | Master | Slide Master** and select all the text in the lower placeholder.

2) Choose **Format | Font,** and change the font of the selected text to Arial Bold. Click OK.

3) Choose **View | Slide**. Notice that the font of the text in all the non-title placeholders of all the slides in your presentation has been changed.

You can use the Slide Master to change other attributes of text in your presentation in exactly the same way: explore the options available in the Format menu, and in particular:

- **Bullet**, which allows you to choose the bullet character that applies to each level of text

- **Alignment**, which allows you to specify whether the text is to be ranged left or right, centred, or justified

- **Line Spacing**, which allows you to determine the amount of space between lines in a paragraph and between different paragraphs

Formatting Text on Individual Slides

The Design, the Colour Scheme, and the Slide Master help you to establish rules that apply to all slides in a presentation. You can also, if you wish, break those rules on individual slides – you can make text bigger or smaller, change its font or style, change its alignment, or change the spacing between it and other text.

To do any of these, first select the text you want to change. Then proceed as follows:

- To change the font, size, style (italics, bold, underline, superscript, subscript, etc.), colour, or effects, choose Format | Font, or click the relevant button in the Formatting toolbar

- To change the case of the text (initial capital, all lowercase, all uppercase, initial capitals on all words, or the opposite of the current selection), choose Format | Change Case and make your choice.

- To change the alignment of the text, choose Format | Alignment, or click the relevant button in the Formatting toolbar.

- To change the spacing between lines or paragraphs, choose Format | Line Spacing, or click the Increase Paragraph Spacing button, or the Decrease Paragraph Spacing button in the Formatting toolbar.

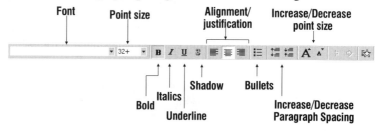

Exercise 6.22: Formatting Text on a Slide

1) Open slide number 1 (New Product Launch) in Slide View.

2) Click anywhere on the second placeholder to select it. Then drag the mouse across the text to select the text.

3) Choose **Format | Font** and change the font to Arial, 72 point, bold.

4) Enlarge the placeholder so that it is big enough to hold the text on a single line.

5) Select the text again, and click on the Center Alignment button in the Formatting toolbar. Click the Shadow button in the Drawing toolbar and choose Shadow Style 5.

6) Save the presentation, and page through it to see the effect of the changes.

Adding Borders to Objects

Any object you draw or include in a slide has a border around it. Most of the time, this border is invisible (it has zero width), but you may want to change its width, colour or style.

Line Style button

- To change the width of the border around an object, select the object, then click the Line Style button in the Drawing toolbar and choose from the pop-up menu.

- To change the border around an object to a dashed or dotted line, select the object, then click the Dash Style button in the Drawing toolbar and choose from the pop-up menu.

Line Color button   Dash Style button

- To change the colour of the border around an object, select the object, then click the Line Color button in the Drawing toolbar, or select from the Line Color pop-up menu.

- To delete a border around an object, select No Line in the Line Color pop-up menu.

Tips for Better Presentations

If you use PowerPoint's built-in designs and colour schemes, your presentation will almost certainly succeed. However, you probably want to personalise it using some of the features described above. But the range of options is so vast that you could end up with a disaster. Here are some guidelines for success.

How Much Should You Put on a Slide?

As little as possible. Write economically, using headlines and bullets. Don't give the audience the opportunity to read ahead: if you do, they won't listen to you, and they won't retain your message. If you are presenting information in bulleted lists, don't have more than eight or nine bullets. If you must have more, divide them into logical groups and split them over several slides.

What Font Size Should You Choose?

It depends on two things: the size of the screen on which the slide will be shown, and the distance from the screen to the back of the audience. Let's say your slides will be viewed on a 4-foot high screen from a maximum distance of 32 feet (that is, eight times the height of the screen). Now measure the height of the slide as it appears on your computer screen: if it is 9 inches high, you can pretend to be in the back row of the audience by looking at it from a distance of 6 feet (9 inches multiplied by 8). Choose your minimum point size by looking at your computer from this distance.

The 'eight times' rule is actually a good guideline for most situations: if the room is larger, it is likely that the screen will be bigger. However, if in doubt, choose a bigger size: nobody ever complained that a slide was too legible, but many people have complained that slides were illegible.

What Font Should You Choose?

In general for projected images, choose a sans serif font, such as Swiss, Helvetica, Arial, or Gill. (However, for large bodies of *printed* text, a serif font is generally recommended.) Typefaces vary in their legibility, and you might have to choose a bigger point size in certain fonts.

What Colours Should You Choose?

Make sure that the colours you choose for text and background are sharply contrasting. You will find that reversed type (text in a light colour, background in a dark colour) is more legible. (The opposite is true of printed documents.) Remember that viewing conditions are often less than ideal, with lights shining onto the screen. A plain slide that can be read easily is much more valuable (to you and to your audience) than a fancy one that nobody can read.

Using the Same Style Again

If you have created a style that you like, or that reflects your corporate colour scheme, you can save it as a template. Then, the next time you want to create a presentation, you can start with that template and all the slides will take on its characteristics. To do this, choose **File | Save As**. From the Save as type drop-down list, choose Presentation Template. You can give it a name other than that suggested, if you wish. PowerPoint Template files have the extension .pot.

Section Summary: So Now You Know

PowerPoint contains a variety of *presentation designs*. These determine the overall look of the presentation. You can use them without change, or you can modify them to your requirements.

You can modify the colour scheme used, the background, or the typography.

The attributes of the design are held in the *Slide Master*. Any changes you make to the Slide Master are applied by default to all the existing slides in the presentation, and to all new slides you create. You can, however, change text attributes on individual slides.

You can also include graphic devices in the Slide Master: these will then be shown on every slide in the presentation.

When you have tailored a design to your needs, you can save it as a *presentation template*. This enables you to use the same design in subsequent presentations.

1

2

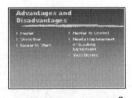

3

4

5

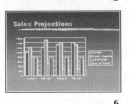

6

7

PowerPoint Presentations: Good Enough

Section 6.5: Building a Presentation

In This Section

In the previous Sections, you learnt how to create slides that will impress your audience. In this Section, you will learn how to assemble those slides into a convincing presentation, how to order and reorder your slides, how to insert and delete slides, how to make slides usable in other applications, and how to import slides from other sources.

New Skills

At the end of this Section, you should be able to:

- Reorder slides in a presentation

- Copy slides between presentations

- Delete slides

- Export PowerPoint slides to other applications

- Save presentations for use in other versions of PowerPoint

Once again, the exercises in this Section are based on the presentation created in Sections 6.2, 6.3, and 6.4. Open the presentation before beginning the exercises in this Section.

Using Slide Sorter to Check Your Slides

Use Slide Sorter view to check that your formatting is consistent and that text placeholders are aligned. This is particularly important if you have made changes to the design or formatting of individual slides.

Choose **View | Slide Sorter**. This shows you all the slides in your presentation on a single screen. (If they don't all fit on your screen, use the scroll bar on the right.)

To see or edit a particular slide in Slide view (full size), double-click it.

Changing the Order of Slides

When you have created all your slides, you might decide that you want to present them in a different order, so that the ideas flow better. The easiest way to do this is in Slide Sorter view.

You can reorder your slides in two ways: by dragging them with the mouse (better for small presentations), or using the cut-and-paste commands on the Edit menu (better for large presentations).

Reordering by Dragging

In Slide Sorter view, select the slide you want to move, drag it with the mouse so that a vertical line appears to the *right* of where you want to position the slide, and release the mouse button.

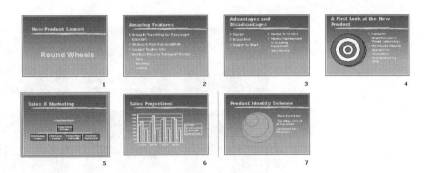

Reordering with Cut and Paste

You can cut, copy, and paste slides in PowerPoint as you would text in a word processor.

In Slide Sorter view, select the slide, choose **Edit | Cut** (or hold down the CTRL key and press X). Click on the slide that will appear *before* the slide you are moving and choose **Edit | Paste** (or hold down the CTRL key and press V).

Exercise 6.23: Re-Ordering Slides

1) In Slide Sorter view, use the dragging technique to reverse the order of slides 5 (Sales & Marketing) and 6 (Sales Projections).

2) Use the cut-and-paste technique to make slide number 7 (Product Identity Scheme) appear after slide number 2 (Amazing Features).

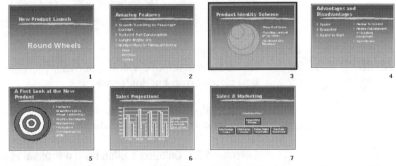

Note that the slides are renumbered to represent their new order: we will refer to them by their new number from now on.

Copying Slides between Presentations

Just as you can cut a slide from one part of a presentation and paste it into another part, you can also cut (or copy) a slide from one presentation and paste it into another. Try it.

Exercise 6.24: Copying a Slide from One Presentation to Another

1) Open Dale Carnegie's presentation on presentations, as in Exercise 6.1.

2) In Slide Sorter view, select slide number 11.

3) Copy the slide by choosing **Edit | Copy** (or hold down the CTRL key and press C).

4) Close Dale Carnegie's presentation.

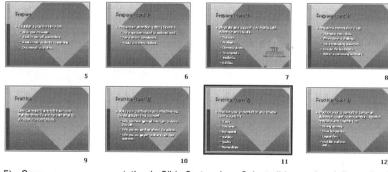

5) Open your own presentation in Slide Sorter view. Select slide number 1 (Launch of New Product), and choose **Edit | Paste** (or hold down the CTRL key and press V).

The copied slide appears as slide number 2 in your presentation. Note that, while the content of the slide is exactly the same, the format has changed to agree with the design and layout of your presentation.

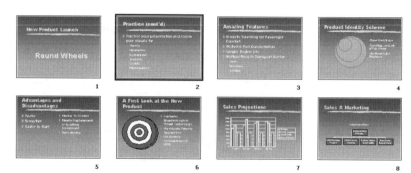

Deleting a Slide

If you want to remove a slide from your presentation, simply cut it, as described above, but don't paste it.

You can also delete a slide in any view, with the exception of Slide Show view, by choosing **Edit | Delete Slide**.

Exercise 6.25: Deleting a Slide from a Presentation
1) Delete the slide that you copied into the presentation in Exercise 6.24.

2) Save the presentation.

Hiding a Slide

If you do not want to show a particular slide during a presentation, choose **Slide Show | Hide Slide**.

Using PowerPoint Slides in Other Applications

In general, you should not have to enter information into one software application and then subsequently enter the same information into another application. For example, when you create your PowerPoint slides and you want to use the same text in a report you are writing in Word, you should not have to type it again.

You don't.

- To use text from a single slide, copy the text in PowerPoint (select it and choose **Edit | Copy**), and paste it in Word (position the cursor and choose **Edit | Paste**).

- To use the text of the whole presentation in Word, choose **File | Save As**.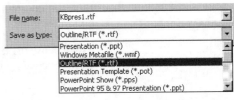
From the Save as type drop-down list, choose Outline/RTF.
If you wish, specify a file name other than the one suggested (the same as the presentation, with the extension .rtf).

Click **Save**.

If you want to use the slides in other graphic programs, or in web pages, you should save them in one of the graphic formats: either JPEG File Interchange Format, or GIF. Try it.

Exercise 6.26: Making Slides Viewable in a Web Browser

1) Choose **File | Save As**. From the Save as type drop-down list, choose GIF. Click **Save**. Note that you can save a single slide or the whole slide show. For the exercise, specify a single slide.

2) Minimise PowerPoint and open the web browser on your computer (typically Microsoft Internet Explorer or Netscape Navigator). There is no need to connect to the Internet: open the program offline.

3) Choose **File | Open** (Microsoft Internet Explorer), or **File | Open Page** (Netscape Navigator). Locate the .gif file you created in step 1 and click **Open**.

4) Check that the slide appears correctly in your browser, and then close the browser.

Working with Earlier Versions of PowerPoint

Each version of the PowerPoint software includes features that were not available in earlier versions. This means that, while you can generally use a later version of the software to open, view, edit, and save a presentation that was created in an earlier version, the reverse is not true.

If, in PowerPoint 97, you save a presentation that was originally created in PowerPoint 95, PowerPoint 4.0, or PowerPoint 3.0, it will be saved in its original format, unless you choose **File | Save As** and specify a different name, a different folder, or a different software version.

If you want a presentation you have created to be viewable with an earlier version of PowerPoint, you must choose **File | Save As** and specify the software version in the Save as Type box. Note that some of the effects that you can specify in PowerPoint 97 will not display properly in earlier versions of the software.

Section Summary: So Now You Know

Once you have created a presentation, you can change the order of slides. The best way to do this is in Slide Sorter view, where you can either drag the slide to its new location, or cut and paste it.

You can copy slides into your presentation from other PowerPoint presentations. When you do, they take on the design and layout of your presentation.

You can use the text of your presentation in another application, such as a word processor, either by cutting and pasting, or by saving the file in .rtf format.

You can save individual slides or the whole presentation in .jpg or .gif format: these formats can be used in graphic programs and in web pages.

And if you want your presentation to be viewable in an earlier version of the software, you have to specify this when you are saving the file.

1

2

3

4

5

6

7

PowerPoint Presentations: Getting the Message?

Section 6.6: Wowing the Audience

In This Section

In this Section, you will learn how to make your presentation more dynamic, by using animations and transitions. You will learn how to prepare handouts for the audience, and notes for the presenter. And you will learn a few tricks that you can use when delivering your presentation.

New Skills

At the end of this Section, you should be able to:

- Specify transition effects
- Create build slides
- Add sound effects to slides
- Prepare handouts for your audience
- Number slides
- Prepare speaker notes
- Check the spellings in your presentation

New Words

At the end of this Section you should be able to explain the following terms:

- Slide transition
- Build slide

The exercises in this Section add professional polish to the presentation created in the earlier Sections of this Module. Open the presentation before beginning the exercises in this Section.

Slide Transitions

A transition is a graphic effect that determines how one slide replaces another – for example, the new slide could appear to drop down from the top of the screen, or the old slide could be made to dissolve, leaving the new slide.

PowerPoint lets you control two aspects of a transition:

- **Effect Type:** The nature of the special effect with which PowerPoint introduces the slide.

- **Effect Timing:** The speed with which PowerPoint runs the visual effect when introducing the slide.

You can also specify that you want a sound to accompany the transition.

**PowerPoint offers a wide
range of Transition Effects**

A visual effect, such as a box-out, dissolve, or fade, that determines how one slide in a presentation is replaced by another.

Exercise 6.27: Applying a Transition to Your Presentation

1) With any slide open in Slide view, choose **Slide Show | Slide Transition**.

2) First explore the options on offer:

   Effect: Each time you click an option from the drop-down list, PowerPoint runs the effect in the sample picture. You can rerun the preview by clicking the picture.

   Timing: The options – Slow, Medium or Fast – set the speed at which the transition effect runs. Click an option and PowerPoint runs the effect with that timing in the sample picture.

   For the exercise, select the Dissolve effect, with Fast Timing.

**Choose the speed of the
transition effect**

3) Click **Apply to All**. Note that you have the option of applying a different transition to each slide (by clicking **Apply**), but be careful: this may have the effect of distracting or unsettling your audience.

4) See how the transitions affect the presentation by choosing **View | Slide Show** and paging through the presentation.

Automatic or Manual Advance

You can choose to have your presentation advance from slide to slide:

- On command (as described in Section 6.1)

- Automatically, based on specified timings

- Either, whichever comes first

This is also specified in the Slide Transitions dialog box. The two effects are independent, however: you can automate the running of your slide show without applying a transition, and you can apply a transition without automating your slide show. You should also note that the timings have nothing to do with one another: the effect timing (Slow, Medium, Fast) relates to the speed of the transition from the previous slide; the automated advance time specifies how long the slide is displayed before being replaced.

Automatic advance is often used in presentations that are left running in public areas, such as trade shows, where they are not accompanied by a speaker.

Build Slides

Build slides allow you to reveal the information on a slide gradually. They are typically used for bulleted text: when you first show the slide, the audience sees only the first bullet. You then reveal the remaining bullets, one-by-one, as you talk to your audience. This has the advantage of keeping your audience engaged with what you are saying, rather than having them read ahead while you are still talking about the first point.

Build Slide

A slide in which different elements are revealed at different times.

With a build slide, you can highlight each point in turn, to focus your audience's attention. When you are talking about your second point, you can leave the first one on the screen, but dim it, so that it still serves as a context and reminder, but doesn't distract.

You can also control how each new element arrives on the screen – for example, bullet points can fly in from the right, left, top, or bottom. Let's try it.

Exercise 6.28: Applying a Build to a Slide

1) Display slide number 2 (Amazing Features) in Slide view.

2) Click anywhere in the lower placeholder, where the bulleted text is.

3) Choose **Slide Show | Preset Animation** and select the Flying option.

4) Choose **View | Slide Show** to see the effect. The contents of your original slide are now revealed one line at a time. You show the second and subsequent lines by clicking the mouse button or pressing a keyboard key, as described in Section 6.1.

5) Choose **Slide Show | Custom Animation**. Click on Text 2.

Select the following settings:

In **Timing**:
Animate,
On Mouse Click

In **Effects**:
Dissolve,
No Sound,
Light blue,
All at Once,
Grouped by 1st level
paragraphs

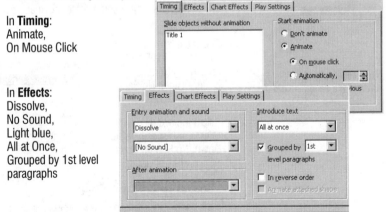

Ignore **Chart Effects** and **Play Settings**.

Click **OK**.

6) Again, choose **View | Slide Show** to see the effect.

Exercise 6.29: More Complex Builds

1) Display slide number 3 (Product Identity Scheme) in Slide view.

2) Choose **Slide Show | Custom Animation** to display the Custom Animation dialog box.

3) In the Timing tab, select Oval 2 (the largest circle). It is highlighted in the preview screen. Click the **Animate** and **Automatically** buttons: specify 1 Second after Previous Event.

   The element (Oval 2) is transferred to the Animation Order box.

4) Repeat Step 3 for each of the other ovals and for the bulleted text.

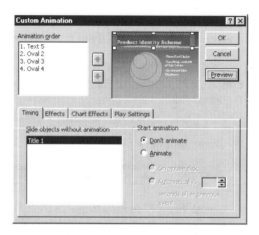

5) Click **Preview** to see how the slide will be presented.

6) Check that the elements in the Animation Order box are in the following order: first the three ovals, biggest first, smallest last, then the text. To change the order, select the name of the object you want to move and use the arrow buttons to move it up or down.

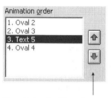

Use these buttons to change the animation order

7) Select each of the ovals in turn and, in the Effects tab, specify Fly from Bottom-Right, No Sound, and Don't Dim.

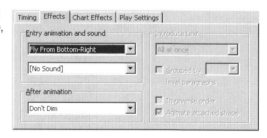

8) Select the text, and in the Effects tab, specify Wipe Down, No Sound, Don't Dim, and All at Once.

   Click **Preview** to see the effect.

9) Click **OK** to close the Custom Animation dialog box.

Exercise 6.30: Grabbing Their Attention

1) Display slide number 1 (New Product Launch) in Slide view and choose **Slide Show | Custom Animation**.

2) Select the text in the lower half of the screen (Round Wheels), and specify that it is to be animated, as in the previous exercise.

3) In the Effects tab, specify Spiral, No Sound, Don't Dim, and All at Once.

Click **Preview** to see the effect.

Experiment with the alternatives to All at Once – By Word and By Letter – and each time click **Preview** to see their effect.

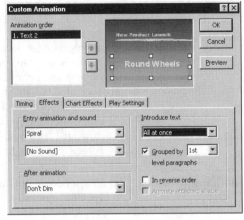

4) Click **OK** to close the Custom Animation dialog box.

Exercise 6.31: Animating a Chart

1) Display slide number 6 (Sales Projections) in Slide view and choose **Slide Show | Custom Animation**.

2) In the Timing tab, specify that the chart is to be animated.

3) In the Chart Effects tab, specify By Series, Animate Grid and Legend, Appear, No Sound, and Don't Dim. It may be difficult to see the effect of this by using the **Preview** button, so click **OK**, then choose **View | Slide Show** and go through the presentation from the beginning.

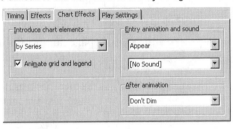

Exercise 6.32: On Your Own

1) Animate slide number 4 (Advantages and Disadvantages) so that the advantages appear one at a time, flying in from the left, and the disadvantages appear one at a time, flying in from the right.

2) Animate slide number 5 (A First Look) so that the features appear one at a time, flying in from the right.

Music and Other Noises

If you followed the exercises above, you specified No Sound each time. If you were adventurous, you probably tried out some of the other options. If you didn't, try them now: you can choose a sound to accompany each transition and each animated effect. There is a wide range of sound effects available: the most commonly used are already listed in the Sound drop-down list. You can find others by choosing **Other Sounds** and selecting any file that has the extension .wav.

Preparing Handouts

You can, if you wish, simply print out your slides and distribute them to your audience. However, this is somewhat inelegant: the size of type that is appropriate for a slide is much too big for normal reading. Instead, PowerPoint gives you the option of producing handouts in which several slides are shown on a page. To do this, choose **File | Print**, and from the Print What drop-down list, choose the handout format you want to use.

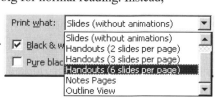

Numbering Your Slides

When people in your audience ask questions, they may want to refer to a specific slide, so it is useful to identify each slide by number.

Exercise 6.33: Adding Slide Numbers

1) Choose **View | Header and Footer**.

2) In the Slide tab, check Slide Number. Leave the other options unchecked.

3) Click **Apply to All**.

Note that this tab also enables you to include the date and time on each slide.

If you choose similar options on the other tab – Notes and Handouts – the page number (or date and time) will be shown only on the handouts and speaker notes, but not on the slides themselves.

Remember that if you want to display a particular slide in Slide Show view, just type the slide number and press ENTER.

Speaker Notes

If you want to write a script to accompany the slides, or simply make notes to remind you of the key points or additional background information, you can use the speaker notes facility. This enables you to create a document with one page for each slide. The slide is shown in the top half; you enter your notes in the bottom half. (PowerPoint does not display the notes on screen as part of your presentation.)

You can enter text on your speaker notes pages at any stage when creating or editing your presentation.

> **Speaker Notes**
> *A document that has one page for each slide in the presentation. Each page is divided into two: the slide is shown at the top, and speaker notes are shown at the bottom.*

Notes View

To enter, edit, or view speaker notes, choose **View | Notes Page**.

To enter or edit text, click on the text placeholder.

By default, PowerPoint displays a notes page at 40% of its full size. You may want to increase this to nearer 100% when typing or editing. Do this by choosing **View | Zoom**.

To print out speaker notes, choose **File | Print**, and from the Print What drop-down list, choose Notes Page.

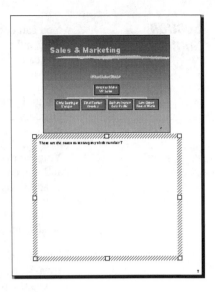

Check Your Spelling!

Spelling mistakes really spoil a presentation: they make you look either careless or ignorant – and your effort to impress the audience may be wasted. While it is dangerous to rely totally on a spell-checker, it is also foolish not to use one at all.

To use the spell-checker, choose **Tools | Spelling**, or press F7. Any words that fail the spell check are shown, with suggested alternatives. You can accept one of the suggestions, edit the word yourself, or leave the original unchanged.

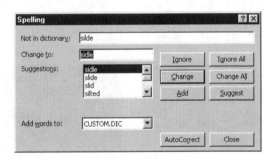

Note that the spell checker will not find incorrect spellings that are themselves valid words (such as "form" instead of "from").

Saving Your Presentation as a Slide Show

You already know how to use Slide Show view to start your presentation. Another option is to save the presentation as a slide show, so that it always opens as a slide show, whether you open it within PowerPoint or directly from the desktop. To do this, choose **File | Save As**, and specify PowerPoint Show. The file will be saved with the extension .pps.

Section Summary: So Now You Know

You can control the way a new slide replaces an old one with *transition effects*; these can be as conservative or as dramatic as you like. In addition, you can add sound effects to the transition, so that the new slide arrives with an explosion or a clash of cymbals.

To hold your audience's attention, you can reveal the material on a slide piece-by-piece, in a *build slide*. Build slides can be animated in a variety of ways.

You can prepare *handouts* for your audience, with several slides to a page, and you can prepare *speaker notes*, with the script that you want to follow, or additional details to support your presentation.

You can number slides for easy reference, and you can check the spelling on all your presentation materials.

Finally, you can save your presentation as a *slide show*, so that it will always open in Slide Show view. If you do this, the file will have the extension .pps.

1

2

3

4

5

6

7

PowerPoint Presentations: Here's One I Prepared Earlier

Module

7

Information and Communication

'The Internet is like a library'. You will hear this kind of statement a lot from people who know little about either.

If the Internet is a library, it's a strange one indeed. For starters, there is no indexing system. At any rate, the books are not arranged on numbered shelves but scattered on the floor. A lot of what is in the books is untrue, even in the non-fiction ones. There is no librarian, and no information desk. Did we mention also that the lights are turned off?

What's more, you can make as much noise as you like when using the Internet, while at the same time collecting facts and figures (and fiction and music and video and sports results and stock prices and weather reports and recipes) from all around the world.

In fact, the principal use of the Internet is for e-mail – a way of sending messages from your computer to someone else's computer, whether they are in the next room or in a different hemisphere.

Think of this Module as your chance to borrow knowledge and skills you won't ever be asked to return, and to become part of an on-line electronic community. Welcoming to the Internet Age!

Section 7.1: Exploring the Web

In This Section

Prepare to take your first steps in exploring the World Wide Web or 'Web' as it is popularly known. In this Section you will visit and explore websites operated by national newspapers based in Australia, France, Germany and Italy, and by a Paris-based art gallery and an American music store.

Also in this Section you will learn the basics of operating Internet Explorer, the Microsoft software application for exploring – otherwise known as browsing or surfing – the Web.

New Skills

At the end of this Section you should be able to:

- Start Internet Explorer and visit a website

- Explore a website by scrolling down pages and clicking on hyperlinks

- Move backwards and forwards through previously visited web pages

- Open several windows at once in Internet Explorer

- Print web pages, and use the main page setup and print options

- Save text, images, and complete pages from the Web

- Access and use Internet Explorer's online help

New Words

At the end of this Section you should be able to explain the following terms:

- Home page

- Address Bar

- Website

- Web server

- Web browser

Starting Internet Explorer

To open Internet Explorer you can:

Internet
Explorer

- Double-click the Internet Explorer icon

  -or-

- Choose **Start | Programs | Internet Explorer**

If your computer has a permanent Internet connection, you are ready to surf the Web with Internet Explorer.

If you have a dial-up connection, you must first dial your Internet Service Provider (ISP). Internet Explorer may be set up to do this automatically. If not, you will need to dial your ISP separately.

Enter your user name and password (if Internet Explorer has not recorded them from the last time that you dialled your ISP), and click **Connect**.

Your Browser's Start Page

Typically, Internet Explorer is set up so that it takes you to a particular web page whenever you start the application.

If you obtained Internet Explorer from your ISP, this start page is probably the front page of the ISP's website. Such a front page is called a home page.

Home pages of two Internet Service Providers (ISPs)

Home Page

The first or front page of a website. Typically, it presents a series of links that you can follow to view the site's other pages.

You will learn how to change Internet Explorer's start page in Section 7.4.

Visiting and Exploring a Website

In Exercise 7.1 you visit and explore the website of *The Age*, a newspaper published in Melbourne, Australia.

Exercise 7.1: Visiting and Exploring a Website

1) Choose **File | Open** or press CTRL+o. (That is, hold down the CTRL key and press the letter 'o' key.)

Press CTRL and 'o' to enter a web address

2) In the Open dialog box displayed, type www.theage.com.au, and click **OK**.

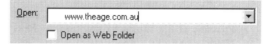

Internet Explorer displays the home page of *The Age* website.

Click here

3)

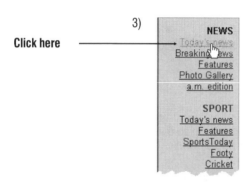

Along the left of *The Age's* home page you can see a list of the newspaper's main sections – Today's News, Breaking News, Photo Gallery, and so on.

Scroll down the page to view the list in full.

Each section name is underlined, indicating that it is a hyperlink.

A hyperlink is an item of text (or a graphic) on a web page that, if clicked, leads to another web page.

Click the Section named Today's News.

4) Internet Explorer now displays a new web page, the Today's News page.

NEWS
Today's news
Breaking news
Features
Photo Gallery
a.m. edition

SPORT
Today's news
Features
SportsToday

TODAY'S NEWS

Yallourn workers return to work

Striking Yallourn Energy workers this evening reluctantly obeyed a return to work order by the State Government, although power restrictions will continue until at least Wednesday. FULL REPORT

Click here

Here you can see summaries of the day's main news stories. Each summary ends with a hyperlink named Full Report.

5) Click on any Full Report hyperlink to display a web page containing an individual news story.

Leave the news story page open on your screen in preparation for Exercise 7.2.

You are now three pages 'deep' inside the *The Age* website.

- First, you visited the front or home page.

- Second, you visited the Today's News page, with its list of news summaries.

- Third, you visited a page containing a particular news story.

Internet Explorer Toolbar

As with Microsoft Office applications such as Word and Excel, Internet Explorer includes a Standard Toolbar that offers fast, one-click access to commonly used actions. Rather than introduce all the Toolbar buttons at once, we will explain each one as it becomes relevant.

Internet Explorer Toolbar

In Exercise 7.2, you will use the Back and Forward buttons on Internet Explorer's Standard Toolbar.

If the Standard Toolbar is not currently shown on your screen, choose **View | Toolbars | Standard Buttons** to display it.

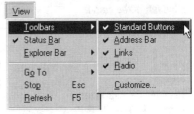

Moving Through a Series of Web Pages

In Exercise 7.2, you learn how to return to web pages that you visited earlier, and then move forward again to the ones you visited most recently.

Exercise 7.2: Moving Backwards and Forwards Through Web Pages

1) With a news story displayed from *The Age* newspaper, click once on the Back button, located on the left of Internet Explorer's Standard Toolbar.

   This returns you to the web page you visited most recently – the Today's News page.

Back button: Returns you to the previously displayed web page

2) With the Today's News page displayed, click a second time on the Back button.

   This returns you to the second-last web page that you visited – the website's home page.

3) With *The Age's* home page displayed, click once on the Forward button. It is located just to the right of the Back button on the Standard Toolbar.

   This button moves you forward, one page at a time, retracing your original movement through the website.

Forward button: Reverses the effect of pressing the Back button

4) With the Today's News page displayed, click a second time on the Forward button.

   This brings you forward to the web page from which you originally began to move backwards – the individual news story page.

Browsing with the Address Bar

When you visit a web page, notice that its web address is displayed in the area immediately above Internet Explorer's main window. This is called the Address Bar.

You can also use the Address Bar to enter a web address. Although the Address Bar always displays 'http://' before a web address, you need not type 'http://' when entering an address in the Bar.

If the Address Bar is not currently shown on your screen, choose **View | Toolbars | Address Bar** to display it.

Exercise 7.3: Entering an Address in the Address Bar

1) Click anywhere in the Address Bar. This selects the currently displayed web address, which is then shown in reverse (white-on-black).

Removes the character to the *left* of the cursor

2) Use the BACKSPACE or DELETE key to remove the currently displayed web address. The Address Bar is now empty.

3) Type the following web address in the Bar, and click Go or press ENTER: www.torontostar.ca

Internet Explorer now displays the front page of Canada's *Toronto Star* newspaper.

Removes the character to the *right* of the cursor

Practise your Web browsing skills by clicking on hyperlinks to display pages within the Toronto newspaper, and by scrolling up and down each displayed web page.

> **Address Bar**
>
> *An area above the main window that shows the address (preceded by a 'http://') of the currently displayed web page. You can also use the Address Bar to enter a web address. (You need not type the 'http://'.)*

Printing a Web Page

You can print out the currently displayed web page by choosing **File | Print** and then clicking **OK** on the Print dialog box.

Print button

Alternatively, click the Print button on the Internet Explorer Standard Toolbar. Clicking this Print button does *not* display the Print dialog box.

Page Setup Options

Internet Explorer's **File | Page Setup** command enables you to control the following:

- **Paper Size:** A4 is the European paper size standard.

- **Orientation:** Portrait ('standing up') or Landscape ('on its side').

- **Print Range:** Your options are: all pages, a specified range of pages, or the part of the page that you have selected.

- **Number of Copies:** If you select any number greater than one, you can specify whether you want the copies collated or not.

- **Margins:** The distance of the page's printed content (text and graphics) from the edge of the paper. You can set each of the four margins (top, bottom left and right) independently.

- **Header and Footer:** You can include or exclude the following in the header and footer areas of the printed web pages:

  – Page title
  – Web page address
  – Page number in printout

– Total number of pages in printout
– Date of printing

Internet Explorer indicates these options by symbols as &P and &d. Do you need to remember all these symbols? No; you can refer to Internet Explorer's online help, even during the ECDL test. You will learn about online help at the end of this Section.

Saving from the Web

If you see something on the Web that you like – such as an image, some text, or even an entire web page – can you copy it from the website to your computer? Yes. This topic shows you how.

Saving an Image

To save an image from the currently displayed web page, right-click on the image to display a pop-up menu. Next, choose **Save Picture As**, select the location on your computer that you want to save to, accept or change the current name of the image, and click **Save**.

Exercise 7.4 provides an example of image-saving from the Web.

Exercise 7.4: Saving an Image from a Web Page

1) Choose **File | Open** or press CTRL+o and enter the following web address: metalab.unc.edu/wm/paint/auth/monet/

   Internet Explorer displays the Claude Monet page from the Paris-based WebMuseum Project.

2) Click on the following hyperlink: Waterlilies

Early works, Sainte-Adresse, near Le Havre 1840-1872
First Impressionist paintings
Later Impressionism
Paris
Rouen Cathedral
- Poplars on the Epte
Click here ⟶ • Waterlilies
- Haystacks
- Houses of Parliament, London
- Last years

3) On the next web page displayed, click the small picture entitled Water Lilies (The Clouds).

Click here ⟶

Water Lilies (The Clouds)
1903 (180 Kb); Oil on canvas, 74.6 x 105.3 cm
(29 3/8 x 41 7/16 in); Private collection

Internet Explorer now displays a larger version of the image.

4) When it has displayed fully, right-click anywhere on the image, and choose the **Save Picture As** command from the pop-up menu.

5) In the Save As dialog box then displayed, accept or change the image's file name (monet_wl-clouds.jpg), select the drive and folder you want to save the file to, and click **OK**.

Image File Formats

Most image files on the Web are in either gif (pronounced with a harsh 'g', as in giraffe) or in jpg (pronounced jay-peg) format.

Selecting and Saving Text

You can save and reuse all or a selected part of the text from the currently displayed web page. This is a two step process:

- **Copy:** You select and then *copy* the text to the Clipboard, a temporary holding area.

- **Paste:** You *paste* the text from the Clipboard into another file such as a Word document or an Excel spreadsheet.

Four points you should remember about the Clipboard:

- The Clipboard is temporary. Turn off your computer and the Clipboard contents are deleted.

- Text stays in the Clipboard after you paste from it, so you can paste the same piece of text into as many different files as you want.

- The Clipboard can hold only a single, copied item at a time. If you copy a second piece of text, the second overwrites the first.

- Text copied from a web page and pasted into Word or other application may lose the formatting that it had on the Web.

Exercise 7.5 takes you through the steps of copying and pasting selected text from a web page.

Exercise 7.5: Saving Text from a Web Page

1) Choose **File | Open** or press CTRL+o, enter the following web address, and press ENTER:
www.well.com/user/smalin/miller.html

Here you will find a copy of George A. Miller's classic essay, *The Magical Number Seven, Plus or Minus Two: Some Limits on Our Capacity for Processing Information.*

Press CTRL and END to move to the bottom of a web page

2) When the web page has loaded fully, scroll down to the end of the page. (A quick way of moving to the bottom of a page is to press CTRL+END.)

Now, press PAGE UP two or three times until Internet Explorer displays the last paragraph of the essay, which begins with the words 'And finally'.

3) Click at the start of the paragraph and drag the mouse down and right until you have selected the entire paragraph. Your screen should look like that shown.

> And finally, what about the magical number seven? What about the seven wonders of the world, the seven seas, the seven deadly sins, the seven daughters of Atlas in the Pleiades, the seven ages of man, the seven levels of hell, the seven primary colors, the seven notes of the musical scale, and the seven days of the week? What about the seven-point rating scale, the seven categories for absolute judgment, the seven objects in the span of attention, and the seven digits in the span of immediate memory? For the present I propose to withhold judgment. Perhaps there is something deep and profound behind all these sevens, something just calling out for us to discover it. But I suspect that it is only a pernicious, Pythagorean coincidence.

When you select text, Internet Explorer displays that text in reverse (white text on black background), rather like the negative of a photograph.

4) Choose **Edit | Copy** or press CTRL+c to copy the text to the Clipboard.

5) Open Microsoft Word, open a new document, and choose **Edit | Paste** or press CTRL+v to paste the selected text into Word.

When finished, you can close the Word document without saving it, and close Word.

Saving All Text

When you want to save *all* the text from a web page, Internet Explorer offers you two options. You can:

- Choose **Edit | Select All**, and then copy the text to the Clipboard.

-or-

- Choose **File | Save As**, select the Text File (.txt) option, select the location on your computer that you want to save to, accept or change the default file name, and click **Save**.

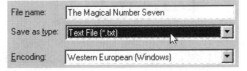

Saving a Web Page

You can save an entire web page – including text, graphics and other components. Exercise 7.6 shows you how.

Exercise 7.6: Saving a Web Page
1) Visit the MP3 music website at www.mp3.com.

2) Choose **File | Save As**, select the Web Page complete option, select the location on your computer to save to, accept or change the default file name, and click **Save**.

The web page is still on the website. You have saved only a *copy* of that page on your computer.

Copyright

As you have learnt, it's not difficult to copy text and images from the Web to your computer. But it may not always be legal. If you intend reproducing copyright material that you obtained from the Web, ask for permission first.

Opening Multiple Web Pages

Internet Explorer allows you to open several web pages at one time. Follow Exercise 7.7 to discover how.

Exercise 7.7: Opening Multiple Web Pages

1) Visit the following website: www.lemonde.fr

    Internet Explorer now displays the home page of the French newspaper, *Le Monde*.

2) Choose **File | New | Window** or press CTRL+n.

    Internet Explorer opens a new, second window. By default, the new window displays whatever web page is shown in the previous one – in this case, the home page of *Le Monde*.

Press CTRL and 'n' to open a new window in Internet Explorer

3) Press CTRL+o and enter www.welt.de, the web address of the German newspaper, *Die Welt*.

4) Open a third window, and enter the following web address: http://www.lastampa.it. This is the home page of the Italian newspaper, *La Stampa*.

LA STAMPA *web*

You can continue to open further windows in Internet Explorer – the only limit on the number of simultaneously open windows is the size of your computer's memory.

Close button

5) Close all windows except one. You close a window by clicking the Close button at the top-right of the Internet Explorer window or by choosing **File | Close**.

Web Words

In this Section we have been using the word 'website'. Let's look at what this and related terms mean.

The Internet or Net is an inter-network – a network of networks. As you may remember from Module 1, a network is a group of computers (and perhaps other devices such as printers and scanners) connected together by some means.

On the Net, the word *site* is used to describe a single network. A Net site becomes a website when it includes a computer that acts as a web server. The Net existed long before web servers, and today not every Net site includes a web server.

> **Website**
>
> *An Internet-connected network that is owned and managed by an individual, company or organization, and that includes a web server.*

Web Servers and Web Browsers

What's a web server? It's a computer that stores files of a particular format, and makes them available ('serves them up') over the Internet to computer users who have a software application called a web browser.

> **Web Server**
>
> *A computer on an Internet-connected network that stores files and delivers them over the Internet in response to requests from web browsers.*

What's a web browser? It's a software application that can send requests to a web server for files, and then display the files on the user's screen. Microsoft Internet Explorer and Netscape Navigator are the two most popular web browser applications.

> **Web Browser**
>
> *An application such as Microsoft Internet Explorer that enables a user to request files from a web server over the Internet, and displays the requested files on the user's computer.*

The term 'Web' is typically written with an initial capital. When it is used as an adjective, however, a lower-case initial is more common. For example, web server and web browser. The term 'website' is typically written as a single word.

Online Help

Like Excel, Access, PowerPoint and other Microsoft applications, Internet Explorer offers a searchable online help system:

- The 'help' in online help means that the information is there to assist you understand and use the application.

- The 'online' means that the material is presented on the computer screen rather than as a traditional printed manual.

You can search through and read online help in two ways: from dialog boxes, or from the Help menu.

Using Help from Dialog Boxes

You can access online help directly from a dialog box, as Exercise 7.8 demonstrates.

Exercise 7.8: Using Online Help in a Dialog Box

1) Choose **File | Page Setup** to display the Page Setup dialog box.

2) Click the question mark symbol near the top-right of the dialog box. Internet Explorer displays a question mark to the right of the cursor.

3) Drag the mouse down and right, and click anywhere in the Header box.

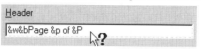

4) Internet Explorer now displays help text telling you about the various header codes.

Practise Exercise 7.8 with other dialog boxes in Internet Explorer.

Using Help Menu Options

You can also access online help from the Help menu. Choose **Help | Contents and Index** to display the three tabs of the Help Topics dialog box.

Contents Tab	**Index Tab**	**Find Tab**

Contents Tab

This offers short descriptions of Internet Explorer's main features.

📖 Where you see a heading with a book symbol, double-click to view the related sub-headings.

❓ Double-click a question mark symbol to read the help text.

Index Tab

Reading the material displayed on this tab is like looking through the index of a printed book.

Just type the first letters of the word or phrase you are interested in.

Internet Explorer responds by displaying all matches from the online help in the right of the dialog box.

When you find the index entry that you are looking for, click the **Display** button.

Find Tab

Can't find what you are looking for in the Contents or Index tab? Try this tab.

When you type a word or phrase and click **List Topics**, Internet Explorer performs a deeper search of the online help.

When you find the item you are looking for, double-click it to display the relevant help text in the right of the dialog box.

As you search through and read online help topics, you will see the following buttons at the top of the online help window:

- **Hide/Show:** Hides or displays the left-hand pane of the online help dialog box.

- **Back/Forward:** Moves you backwards and forwards through previously visited help topics.

- **Options:** Offers a number of display choices, and enables you to print the currently displayed online help text.

- **Web Help:** Takes you to Microsoft's Web-based support site for Internet Explorer.

Take a few minutes to look through Internet Explorer's online help system. Remember that you will be free to use online help during an ECDL test.

When finished, you can close Internet Explorer by clicking the Close button or choosing **File | Close**. You have now completed Section 7.1 of the ECDL Information and Communication Module.

Section Summary: So Now You Know

Internet Explorer is a *web browser* application that enables you to request information from *web servers* over the Internet.

Internet Explorer typically takes you to a particular web page – called the *start page* – whenever you start the application. If you obtained Internet Explorer from your ISP, the start page is probably the *home page* of your ISP's website.

A home page is the first or front page of a website. Typically, it presents a series of *hyperlinks* that you can follow to view the site's other pages.

You can enter a web address in Internet Explorer using the **File | Open** command, pressing CTRL+o, or by typing it in the Address Bar. The *Address Bar*, located above the main window, always shows the address of the currently displayed web page.

Along the top of the Internet Explorer window is the *Standard Toolbar* that gives you one-click access to commonly used browsing actions such as moving back and forwards through previously visited web pages.

You can open *multiple windows* in Internet Explorer at one time, and display different web pages in each one. The application also allows you to *save* web pages on your computer, or selected images and text from web pages.

Section 7.2: Finding Information within Websites

Many websites contain hundreds – even thousands – of pages. The Web-based edition of a daily newspaper, for example, typically consists of a hundred pages or more. If a newspaper offers an online archive of past issues over three years, the total numbers of pages at its website might exceed ten thousand.

Other examples of very large websites include those run by online retailers that stock tens of thousands of music CDs or several million books. Travel and holiday websites can also contain huge numbers of pages offering timetable and destination information.

How do you find particular items of information on such sites? This Section shows you how.

Also in this Section you learn about web address standards, how different countries follow slightly different web addressing conventions.

New Skills

At the end of this Section you should be able to:

- Find a word or phrase on a web page
- Use a site index to locate information within a website
- Use a search engine to find information within a website
- Use an interactive form to find information within a website
- Describe the web address standards used in the US, UK, Italy, France, Germany, Australia and South Africa
- Explain how folder and file names are incorporated within web addresses

New Words

At the end of this Section you should be able to explain the following terms:

- Navigation bar
- Keyword
- Website search engine
- Interactive form
- Web address (URL)

Finding Text within a Web Page

To help you find a particular word or phrase on a web page, Internet Explorer provides the **Edit | Find (on this Page)** command. This command searches only:

- The currently *displayed* web page – not the entire website, and not the whole World Wide Web!

- The currently *loaded* part of the web page. So wait until the page is completely loaded (copied from the website to your computer's memory) before using the command.

Status Bar indicates when the web page has fully loaded →

- The *text* of the page. Words that are displayed within images are ignored.

Exercise 7.9 shows you how to use this command on a lengthy, text-intensive web page.

Exercise 7.9: Finding Information within a Web Page

1) Open Internet Explorer and visit the web page containing George A. Miller's essay, *The Magical Number Seven, Plus or Minus Two*. The address is: www.well.com/user/smalin/miller.html

2) Choose **Edit | Find (on this Page)** or press CTRL+f, enter the word 'variance' in the Find dialog box, and click **Find Next**.

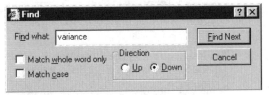

Internet Explorer takes you to the first occurrence of the word on the web page. The dialog box stays open on your screen.

3) To find further occurrences, click **Find Next** again. When finished, click **Cancel**.

Finding Information within a Website

Larger websites can contain many hundreds even thousands of individual web pages. To help you locate particular information, such websites generally offer one or more of the following three features:

- **Site Index:** Sometimes called a Site Map or Site Guide, this is a web page that lists the main contents of the website.

- **Search Engine:** A program that searches for occurrences of text (words, numbers or other keyboard characters) that you enter, and displays a list of all web pages that contain such text, together with a summary description of each listed page.

- **Interactive Forms:** These enable you to request specific information. You will commonly find forms on travel and holiday websites, and on websites that sell highly configurable products (such as computers).

Website Index Pages

Exercises 7.10, 7.11 and 7.12 provide examples of how to display the index pages on three websites – an American software developer (Borland), a German airline (Lufthansa) and a British media organisation (the BBC).

In each Exercise, click on a number of links from the index web page to explore the particular website. And then click the Back button to retrace your steps.

Tech Corner
Books
Site Map

Exercise 7.10: Displaying the Index Page of a Software Developer's Website

1) Visit the website of Borland by entering the following address: www.borland.com

2) Along the left of the home page you will see a number of hyperlinks. Click on the one named Site Map.

This brings you to Borland's index page, where you will find a comprehensive listing of the website's contents.

Accessories

FAQ
My Profile
Index

Exercise 7.11: Displaying the Index Page of an Airline Website

1) Visit the English-language version of the Lufthansa website. The address is: www.lufthansa.de/ehome.htm

2) Along the left of the home page you will find a link named Index. Click it to display the contents of the airline's website.

FIND
Home
A-Z
Search
On TV & Radio
Text Only

Exercise 7.12: Displaying the Index Page of a Media Website

1) Visit the website of the British Broadcasting Corporation at www.bbc.co.uk

2) Near the top-left of the home page you will find a link named A-Z. Click it to display the contents of the BBC's website.

Some websites display their main links across the top of every front page; others list them down one side of the page. A list of the main website links is called a navigation bar or 'navbar'. A navbar may be made up of text or graphics.

Navigation Bar

A horizontal or vertical list of hyperlinks to the main components of a website, such as Home (the front page), Site Index (or Site Map or Guide), Company Profile, Products, Services and Staff Contacts.

Site Index

Also known as a Site Map or Site Guide, this is a web page that lists the main contents of a website.

Website Search Engines

Site indexes can help you to discover the range and depth of information available on a website. To find one or a few specific items, however, search engines are better.

Exercises 7.13, 7.14 and 7.15 provide examples of search engines on three websites – a film information site (Internet Movie Database), a magazine archive (The Scout Report), and an online dictionary of computer terminology (PC Webopedia).

Exercise 7.13: Searching a Film Database

1) Visit the Internet Movie Database by entering the following address: www.imdb.com

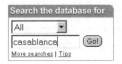

2) In the Search box near the top left of the home page, enter a film title – for example, *Casablanca* – and click the **Go** button.

The IMDB responds by listing pages from its database that relate to your selected film.

Exercise 7.14: Searching a Magazine Archive

1) Visit the Scout Report website. This weekly online publication identifies and reviews Internet resources of interest to researchers and educators. Its address is: scout.cs.wisc.edu/report

2) In the Search box near the top right of the home page, enter a subject in which you are interested – for example, botany – and click **Go!**

The Scout Report responds by listing articles from its archives that relate to your entered topic.

Exercise 7.15: Searching a Computer Dictionary

1) Visit the PC Webopedia website at www.pcwebopedia.com

2) In the Search box near the top of the home page, enter a term you would like explained – for example, modem – and click **Go!**

PC Webopedia responds by displaying a page containing an explanation of your entered word.

In Section 7.3 you will learn about search engines that enable you search the Web and not just an individual website. You will also learn how to perform searches with multiple keywords.

Now is a good time to define some of the terms related to searching a website, and to searching the Web as a whole.

Keyword
Text or other keyboard characters entered in a search engine. The engine then displays or 'returns' a list of documents containing the entered text. Typically, the returned list provides links to the individual pages, and displays a summary description of each page.

Website Search Engine
A program that searches a website for keywords entered by the user. It displays or 'returns' a list of web pages on which it found occurrences of the entered word or words.

Interactive Forms

On the Web, an interactive form is a page containing blank boxes called fields into which you can enter information. Typically, you use forms to specify the particular type of product (for example, a music CD), service (for example, a legal service) or information (for example, train departure times) that you require.

You can also use forms to submit information to a website. When buying a book from an online book shop, for example, you will be presented with a form in which you enter your name and credit card details.

Interactive Form
A series of fields on a web page that you use to request a specific item of information, or a product or service. You can also use a form to submit information, such as your name and credit card number.

Exercises 7.16 and 7.17 provide two examples of interactive forms on websites. The first enables you to request a train timetable, the second to specify a PC configuration and view the corresponding price.

Exercise 7.16: Using a Form to Request a Train Timetable
1) Visit the Irish Rail website at www.irishrail.ie

2) On the home page, click the link named Timetables.

3) On the Timetables page now displayed, click the **Let's Go** button alongside the line that says Waterford to Dublin.

4) On the next web page displayed, make the selections as shown below and click **Let's Go**.

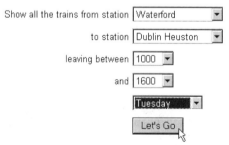

5) The website responds by listing all train services that match your entered requirements. See the following page.

Timetable from Waterford to Dublin Heuston
For departure times 1000 - 1600
Tuesdays, Wednesdays and Thursdays

Waterford	1055	1455
Thomastown	1117	1517
Kilkenny(a)	1135	1535
Kilkenny(d)	1140	1540
Mumie Bheag	1206	1606
Carlow	1221	1621
Athy	1236	1636
Kildare	1255	1654
Newbridge	1303	-
Dublin Heuston	1335	1726

Cars, sandwiches and personal computers are all examples of highly configurable products whose price varies with the combination of 'ingredients' chosen. In Exercise 7.17 you use a form to specify a PC's configuration and display the resulting price.

Almost all PC manufacturers now sell their products online. Note that the links and link names in the website chosen – Dell UK – may change slightly over time.

Exercise 7.17: Using a Form to Price a Customised PC

1) Visit Dell's British website at www.dell.co.uk.

▶ **Home & Home Office**

2) Click the link named Home & Home Office.

3) Click the link for Desktop. You should now see a new page listing a number of PC models. Click any PC model to see a new page that includes a link named Customise.

▶ **Customise**

4) Click the link named Customise. You should now see a form that lists several options for such PC components as Memory, Monitor, Hard Drive and so on.

5) Make and change a number of selections.

Notice that, as you do, the price of the PC, as displayed at the bottom of the web page, changes accordingly.

Example of a form used to specify a PC's configuration.

The form recalculates the PC's price according to the cost of the components that you select.

Memory

128MB SDRAM (1 x 128Mb)

Monitor

Dell 19" Monitor (17.9" viewable area)

Video Adapter

32Mb Diamond Viper V770D nVidia AGP Video Card

Hard Drive

20.4GB Hard Drive

Speakers

Altec Lansing ACS340 speakers

Network Card

3COM 3C900B Combo (+£40)

Price: £1,639 (excl. VAT)

6) When finished experimenting with the form, click the Back button repeatedly to revisit Dell's home page.

About Web Addresses

In this and the previous Section you have been entering web addresses and visiting the associated web pages. A web page is just another type of computer file. Whereas Word files end in .doc, for example, and Excel files in .xls, web pages end in .htm (or, sometimes, .html or shtml). Let's look at web addresses in more detail.

To request a web page with Internet Explorer, you need to know two things:

- The name of the *web server* – the Internet-connected computer on which the particular web page is located
- The name of the *web page* (that is, the file) on the web server

Add these two items together and you get what is called a *web address*. Another, more technical, term for a web address is a URL (Uniform Resource Locator).

URL (Web Address)
The unique address of a web page. It contains the name of the web server and includes (or implies) the name of the particular web page.

Sample URLs

The best way to learn about web addresses is to look at a few examples and discover why they are written the way they are. Here are the URLs of three American web sites:

www.latimes.com   www.princeton.edu   www.cia.gov

In a US web address, the last part of the address – the so-called *suffix* – indicates the type of organisation.

For a commercial business (such as the *Los Angeles Times* newspaper), the suffix is .com; for an educational institution (such as Princeton University), it's .edu; and for a government agency (such as the CIA), it's .gov.

Here are some Italian (.it), French (.fr) and German (.de) URLs:

www.yahoo.it	www.smartweb.fr	www.infoseek.de
www.juventus.it	www.renault.fr	www.bmw.de
www.ferrari.it	www.louvre.fr	www.berlinonline.de

In each case, the suffix indicates only the country. Addresses are not categorised by type.

British web addresses end in .uk, but they also include a component to identify the organisation type: .co for commercial, .ac for the further and higher education sector, and .gov for government. Here are a few examples:

www.cttraining.co.uk	www.mcc.ac.uk
www.landrover.co.uk	www.cam.ac.uk
www.thisislondon.co.uk	www.ox.ac.uk
www.itn.co.uk	www.bcs.org.uk
www.chelseafc.co.uk	www.amnesty.org.uk

A suffix for primary- and second-level schools, .sch.uk, is becoming increasingly popular.

Other countries that use two suffixes – one for organisation type and one for the country itself – are Australia and South Africa. Here are some examples:

www.sym.com.au   www.southafrica.co.za
www.microsoft.com.au   www.icdl.co.za
www.ntu.edu.au   www.unisa.ac.za
www.uwa.edu.au   www.up.ac.za
www.ics.org.au   www.cssa.org.za
www.foe.org.au   www.sarl.org.za
www.deet.gov.au   www.finance.gov.za
www.thesource.gov.au   www.durban.gov.za

Practise your Web surfing skills by visiting some of the URLs listed in this topic.

URLs and Files

A URL specifies *two* things: the name of the web server and the name of a particular web page on that server. So: where is the web page name in this URL?

www.munnelly.com

Answer: when you enter just the web server name, the server displays the default web page. This is the front or main page of the web site, and is usually called index.htm (or index.html).

The web address of www.munnelly.com, therefore, is really:

www.munnelly.com/index.htm

Notice how a forward slash (/) separates the web page name from the web server name.

Here are some other URLs with the name of the default web page included as part of the web address:

www.wit.ie/index.html   www.ucd.ie/index.html   www.ucg.ie/index.html

When you want to view a web page that is *not* the front or main page, enter a URL that includes the page name. For example:

www.ucg.ie/departments.html   www.refdesk.com/paper.html
www.botany.com/narcissi.html   www.surfnetkids.com/pocahontas.htm

URLs and Folders

On web servers, as on other computers, files are organised into folders. In the four examples above, the web pages are in the main folders of the web servers. But web servers can also store pages in sub-folders or sub-sub-folders. Here are some examples of URLs that include sub-folder names:

www.irlgov.ie/aras/hist.htm
www.lastampa.it/rubriche/ultima/rubriche/lst/cinema/cinemahome.htm
www.fieldandstream.com/bookstore/fishbooks.html
www.ozsports.com.au/cricket/commentary.html

A forward slash (/) separates folder names and page names.

Sometimes a URL contains just the web server and folder name – but not the name of the page within the folder. In such cases, your web browser displays the default web page within *that* folder. Again, this is typically called index.html (or index.htm). For example:

www.tcd.ie/drama/

is really:

www.tcd.ie/drama/index.html

Further practise your Web surfing skills by visiting some of the above URLs that contain folder and file names.

When finished, you can close Internet Explorer. You have now completed Section 7.2 of the ECDL Information and Communication Module.

Websites typically display a navigation bar or *navbar* – a horizontal or vertical list of hyperlinks to the main components of a website – along the top or down the left of each page.

Larger websites help users to navigate by providing one, two or all three of the following features:

- A *site index*, sometimes known as a site map or site guide, is a web page that lists the main contents of a website. It is similar in purpose to the contents page of a printed book.

- A website *search engine* is a program that searches a website for *keywords* entered by the user. It displays or 'returns' a list of web pages on which it found occurrences of the entered word or words.

- An *interactive form* is a series of fields on a web page that you use to request a specific item of information, or a product or service. You can also use a form to submit information, such as your name and credit card number.

An *URL* is the unique web address that contains the name of the web server and includes (or implies) the name of the particular web page. Where no page is specified in an URL, the browser displays the default page, usually *index.htm* or *index.html*.

URLs have at least two parts, separated by a dot (.). In the US, the first part is the organisation's name; the second indicates its type. Commercial sites end in *.com*, educational sites in *.edu* and government sites in *.gov*.

Italian, German and French sites are not categorised by type. Their domain names consist of just the organisation name and a suffix indicating their nationality (*.it*, *.fr*, and *.de*).

In the UK, commercial sites end in *.co.uk*, academic sites in *.ac.uk* or *sch.uk*, and government sites in *.gov.uk*. Australia and South Africa also categorise web addresses by organisation type.

Section 7.3: Finding Information on the Web

In This Section

A report published in early 2000 revealed that there were over one billion pages on the Web, stored on almost five million websites. Some 85% of the pages were in English, and just over half (55%) of web addresses ended in .com. Faced with such a phenomenal amount of data, how can Web surfers hope to locate individual items of information which are of interest to them?

It's not as difficult as it may sound – once you know how. In this Section you will discover the techniques for searching and finding information on the Web.

New Skills

At the end of this Section you should be able to:

- Locate information on the Web by navigating through the categories of a directory site

- Locate information on the Web by entering a keyword to search engines and meta search engines

- Perform phrase searches using quotation symbols

- Perform multiple keyword searches using the plus (+) and minus (-) logical operators

New Words

At the end of this Section you should be able to explain the following terms:

- Web directory

- Web search engine

- Web meta search engine

- Logical search

Finding Information on the Web

If you are exploring the Web for information on a particular topic, four types of websites can help you find what you are looking for:

- **Directory Sites:** These are websites that catalogue information on the Web according to subject matter.

- **Search Engines:** These are websites that search the Web for keywords – occurrences of specified words or phrases.

- **Meta Search Engines:** These are websites that submit keywords to several search engines. In effect, they allow you to use multiple search engines at once.

- **Natural Language Search Engines:** These are websites that accept queries in plain English. For example: 'Who is the Prime Minister of New Zealand?'

In this Section you will learn about each type of website, and discover how you can best use them to find the information you need.

Web Directory Sites

A directory website organises information in an easy-to-follow, top-down structure. They tend to be selective, so that only the better sources of information are listed. Unfortunately, the Web changes so quickly that directory sites may not be always up-to-date.

The original and biggest directory site is Yahoo!, where you can browse information by category, sub-category, and, more often than not, sub-sub-category. Exercise 7.18 provides an example.

Exercise 7.18: Finding Information on Yahoo!

1) Open Internet Explorer and visit the Yahoo! website at www.yahoo.com.

2) Click the link named Astronomy, which is located in the right-hand category column under the Science heading.

Science
Animals, Astronomy, Engineering...

3) You are now shown a new web page. It lists astronomy sub-categories in alphabetic order. Click the link named Planetaria.

- Pictures *(86)*
- Planetaria *(63)*
- Radio Astronomy *(77)*

4) You are shown a third web page. This one lists the websites of some fifty planetaria, including Armagh (at www.armagh-planetarium.co.uk). Click on Armagh Planetarium to visit its web page.

- Allentown School District Planetarium
- Armagh Planetarium (United Kingdom)
- Astronaut Memorial Planetarium and Observatory - Brevard Community College

You have now completed the Exercise.

Exercise 7.18 demonstrates both the range and depth of information available on the Web – and the usefulness of directory sites such as Yahoo!

There are country-specific versions of Yahoo! available for a wide range of nations including the UK, Ireland, France, Germany, Italy, Australia and New Zealand. You can link to them from the main site at www.yahoo.com. Other popular web directory sites include About.com and NetGuide.

Web directory sites www.yahoo.com, www.about.com and www.netguide.com.

Most directory sites also offer a search engine facility.

> **Web Directory Site**
> *A website that lists and categorises other sites on the Web according to their subject matter. Typically, it offers several hierarchical layers, with a listing of website addresses at the lowest level.*

Web Search Engines

A search engine allows you to enter a word or phrase, searches for instances of it, and then displays ('returns') a list of websites that match your entered word or phrase, with a summary of each. You can then click on the one that seems most appropriate to you.

Search engines *do not* search the entire Web, but their own smaller, regularly updated list of websites, which typically accounts for about 10-15% of the total number of sites on the Web.

A search on the word 'ECDL' at www.altavista.com returns over 19,000 matching web pages

Web search engines work in a very similar way to the website search engines you met in Section 7.2. The main difference is that they search the Web – and not just an individual website.

Search engines frequently find individual pages from web sites that have nothing to do with what you are looking for. You can often discover unexpected gems of information this way – but be prepared to wade through a lot of irrelevant information too!

Exercises 7.19 and 7.20 provide examples of single keyword searches using search engines. In Exercise 7.19 you use Internet Explorer's default search engine.

Exercise 7.19: Searching with Internet Explorer's Default Search Engine

1) Click the Search button on Internet Explorer's Standard Toolbar.

Search button

This displays the Search bar to the left of the main window.

(Your Search bar may look slightly different, depending on how Internet Explorer is set up.)

2) With the Search Category at its default setting of Find a Web page, enter the keyword 'ecdl'.

3) Click the **Search** button.

You should now see a list of web pages that contain the word 'ecdl'.

You can change Internet Explorer's default search engine by clicking **Customize** at the top-right of the Search bar and selecting a different search engine.

The Web offers dozens of search engines. You should explore the various alternatives and choose the one that best suits your needs.

Here are some of the better search engine websites:

www.google.com
www.altavista.com
www.alltheweb.com
www.northernlight.com
www.excite.com
www.hotbot.com
www.webcrawler.com
www.lycos.com
www.go.com
www.snap.com
www.ibound.com
www.mckinley.com

In Exercise 7.20 you visit the Google search engine and use it to find information on ECDL.

Exercise 7.20: Searching the Web with Google
1) Visit the Google search engine at www.google.com

2) Enter the keyword ECDL and click the **Google Search** button.

Google responds by displaying a list of web pages that contain your entered keyword.

When your query returns more than a single page of results, search engines provide Next and Previous links at the bottom of each page to allow you to move forwards and backwards through the pages of results.

To print the result of a Web search, simply print the results page(s) as you would any other web page.

Web Search Engine Site

A website that enables you to search for material on the Web by entering a word or phrase. The search engine returns a list of sites where the specified words were found.

Phrase Searches

When searching for a phrase – a sequence of words in a particular order – enclose the phrase within quotes. Phrase searches are commonly used to find information on people and organisations – even song lyrics. Here are some examples:

"Manchester United"
"Edgar Allen Poe"
"Ministry of Defence"
"Candle in the Wind"

Why do you need to enclose phrases inside quotes? The answer is that if you search (say) for Manchester United rather than "Manchester United", your results may include pages that refer to Manchester Council or United Biscuits.

By placing quotes around a query your ensure that you find only pages which:

- Contain *all* the words of your query

- Contain the words in the *order* in which you type them

Phrase Search

A query to a search engine that is placed inside quotes. Only web pages containing all the entered words, in the order entered, are found.

Practise your phrase searching skills by entering your full name, within quotes, to the Google search engine.

The Plus Operator

Often you want to search for multiple words that are not necessarily adjacent to one another. In such cases, phrase searches are inappropriate. Instead, use the plus (+) operator.

Suppose, for example, you want to find information about the rules of the card game solitaire. You could enter:

solitaire +rules

Only web pages that contain both words should appear in your results. Note three points about the plus operator:

- You don't need to type the plus operator before the first word that you type in your query.

- Don't leave a blank space between the plus operator and the word following it.

- Leave a blank space after each word

Here are some other examples:

Word +97 +templates
Excel +97 +autosum
ECDL +Cyprus
Recipe +Thai
Shakespeare +Hamlet

You can combine the plus operator with phrases inside quotes, as the following examples show:

algebra +"square roots"
"Excel 97" +"keyboard shortcuts"
Volkswagen +Golf +"metallic blue"
"Manchester United" +"David Beckham"
Shakespeare +"Shall I compare thee"
Bogart +Bacall +"The Big Sleep"

Exercises 7.21, 7.22 and 7.23 provide examples of Web queries that contain the plus operator.

Exercise 7.21: Using the Plus Operator on NorthernLight

1) Visit the Web search engine www.northernlight.com

2) Type the following terms and click **Search**.
   Bizet +Carmen +Domingo

Your results should include web pages that refer to performances of Bizet's opera Carmen which feature singer Placido Domingo.

Exercise 7.22: Using the Plus Operator on AltaVista

1) Visit the Web search engine www.altavista.com

2) Type the following terms and click **Search**.
   "James Bond" +"Sean Connery"

Your results should include web pages about James Bond films that starred actor Sean Connery.

Exercise 7.23: Using the Plus Operator on Excite
1) Visit the Web search engine www.excite.com

2) Type the following terms and click **Search**.
Barcelona +restaurants +vegetarian

Your results should include web pages listing restaurants in Barcelona that cater to vegetarians.

The plus operator is particularly useful when you find yourself overwhelmed with returns from a Web search. By adding one or a few terms, each preceded by the plus operator, you can progressively refine your search so that you receive only the information you need.

The Minus Operator

Sometimes, you want a search engine to find pages that contain one word – but do *not* contain another word. You can do this using the minus (-) operator.

Suppose, for example, you want information about the solo career of singer Geri Haliwell, but don't want to be overwhelmed by pages relating to her former group, the Spice Girls. You could enter:

"Geri Haliwell" -"Spice Girls"

Similarly, to find information on the post-Beatles career of John Lennon, you could enter:

"John Lennon" -Beatles

If you are a fan of the original Star Trek series, but don't want pages relating to various follow-up series, you could enter:

"Star Trek" -Voyager -"Deep Space Nine" -"Next Generation"

In Exercise 7.24 you search the Web for information on Windows 98, and exclude pages that mention the other versions of the Microsoft operating system, Windows 3.1, Windows 95, Windows NT, Windows 2000 or Windows CE.

Exercise 7.24: Using the Minus Operator on Go

1) Visit the Web search engine www.go.com

2) Type the following and click **Find**:

Windows -95 -3.1 -NT -2000 -CE

Your search results should provide information on Windows 98 only.

In Exercise 7.25 you will search the Web for references to Dublin that is not Dublin, Ireland.

Exercise 7.25: Using the Minus Operator on Snap

1) Visit the Web search engine www.snap.com

2) Type the following and click **Find**:

Dublin -Ireland

Your search results should list pages that refer to places named Dublin in the USA. Because not every page that refers to the Dublin in Ireland actually contains the word 'Ireland', however, many of your returned pages will relate to Ireland's capital city.

In general, the minus operator helps you to get better results by allowing you to subtract terms that are not of interest. You can combine the plus and minus operators in a single search query.

Logical Searches

A search of the Web – or of a single website – that contains the plus and/or minus operators is called a logical search.

An alternative way of creating a logical search is to use the so-called Boolean operators instead of the plus and minus symbols. Named after their creator, nineteenth-century mathematician George Boole, these operators include the words AND, OR and NOT, and are typically written in upper-case letters.

The following two logical searches, for example, produce the same results:

"James Bond" AND "Sean Connery"
"James Bond" +"Sean Connery"

Boolean searches have been used traditionally for database searches. On the Web, however, the plus and minus operators are supported by more search engines, and are easier to remember and use.

Logical Search

A Web search that uses logical operators, such as the plus and/or minus symbols, to include and/or exclude specified words or phrases from the results.

Meta Search Engines

A meta search engine is a search engine that searches search engines. Just enter your word or phrase and the meta search engine submits it to a range of individual search engines, and returns the matching results.

Three popular meta search engines are:

www.dogpile.com
www.mamma.com
www.metacrawler.com

Exercise 7.26: Using the Dogpile Metasearch Engine

1) Visit the meta search engine at www.dogpile.com.

2) Enter the following and click **Fetch**:
"access 97" +sort

Your results will include web pages, found by a range of individual search engines, that describe sort operations in the Microsoft Access 97 database application.

Natural Language Search Engines

The Ask Jeeves website at www.aj.com is an example of a search engine that accepts questions in plain English. Here are some sample queries that you could enter:

Who is the secretary general of the UN?
Who invented plastic?
Who wrote Catch 22?
What is the currency in Portugal?
What is the temperature in Florence?

A version of the search engine that returns web pages suitable for younger Web surfers, Ask Jeeves for Kids, is at www.ajkids.com.

Exercise 7.27: Using the Ask Jeeves Natural Language Search Engine

1) Visit the Ask Jeeves website at www.aj.com

2) Type the following question and click **Ask**:
   How do I find an email address?

Your results screen should look like that shown below.

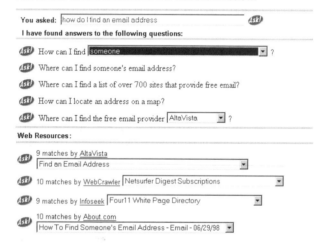

In the top part of the screen Ask Jeeves displays the answers to what it has interpreted as your question. In the lower half it shows the results of entering the words in your question as keywords to various Web search engines.

You may now close Internet Explorer. You have completed Section 7.3 of the ECDL Information and Communication Module.

Directory websites such as Yahoo! catalogue information on the Web according to subject matter. You can locate information on the Web by navigating through the various category levels.

Web search engines trawl the Web for keywords – occurrences of specified words or phrases, and return a list of websites where the specified words were found.

A *phrase search* is a query to a search engine that is placed inside quotes. Only web pages containing all the entered words, in the order entered, are found. Phrase searches are commonly used to find information on people and organisations.

A *logical search* is a Web search that uses logical operators, such as the plus and/or minus symbols, to include and/or exclude specified words or phrases from the results.

If you are overwhelmed with irrelevant returns from a Web search, add one or a few terms, preceded by the *plus operator*, to refine your search so that you receive only the information you need.

The *minus operator* helps you get better Web search results by allowing you subtract terms that are not of interest. You can combine the plus and minus operators in a single search query.

A meta search engine is one that submits keywords to several other search engines, allowing you use of multiple search engines at once.

A *natural language search engine* such as Ask Jeeves accepts queries in plain English syntax.

Section 7.4: Taking Control of Internet Explorer

In This Section

In this Section you will discover how to adjust the appearance and operation of Internet Explorer to suit your working needs and personal taste.

You begin by learning how you can explore the Web more quickly by switching off the display of images on web pages. If there is a particular web page that you visit very frequently, you will discover how to make it display automatically each time you start Internet Explorer.

Another convenient feature of Internet Explorer is its ability to save web addresses, and to group saved addresses into folders for easy reference.

Finally, you will learn how to control the display of Internet Explorer's toolbars and various other screen elements, and specify how the application displays web page text.

New Skills

At the end of this Section you should be able to:

- Switch on and off the display of images on web pages

- Save web addresses as Favorites

- Organise saved addresses into folders

- Revisit saved web addresses

- Change Internet Explorer's start page

- Display and hide Internet Explorer's Standard Toolbar and Address Bar

- Display and hide Internet Explorer's three Explorer Bars: Search, Favorites and History

- Adjust the text size of displayed web pages

New Words

At the end of this Section you should be able to explain the following term:

- Favorites

Switching Web Page Images Off and On

Web pages with lots of images – or a few large ones – can take an unacceptably long time to display on your computer's screen. Often, these images will be advertisements, company logos and decorative elements that you may regard as inessential – especially if you are the one paying the telephone bill!

Internet Explorer icon indicating a non-displayed image on a web page

Internet Explorer allows you to switch off images, so that you can display web pages more quickly. When you switch off images, Internet Explorer displays only the text of visited web pages, together with a small icon indicating the location of each non-displayed image.

When you arrive at a web page that contains images that you want to display, you can then switch images back on again. Don't be afraid to try this feature – it will save you time and, as Exercises 7.28 shows, it's easy to use.

Exercise 7.28: Switching Off Images

1) Open Internet Explorer and choose **Tools | Internet Options**.

2) Click the Advanced tab, scroll down the list until you come to the Multimedia category, and then deselect Show pictures.

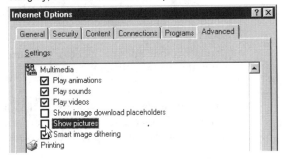

3) Click **OK**.

To display images on all web pages, simply reverse step 2 above.

When images are switched off, you can view an individual image by right-clicking its icon and then choosing **Show Picture**.

Favorites

As you browse the Web, you will discover pages that you would like to return to at a later stage. You can tell Internet Explorer to store a web page's address by using the Favorites feature.

Creating a favorite web page saves you needing to remember (or write down) that page's web address. To revisit such a page, you simply click its name from your list of saved favorites – so much easier than retyping its address each time you want to visit it.

Favorites store just web page addresses on your computer, and *not* the actual pages themselves!

Exercises 7.29 to 7.31 take you through the steps of saving web addresses, organising them into folders, and revisiting them.

Favorites

Favorites button

Exercise 7.29: Saving a Web Address

1) Visit the web page whose web address you want to save. For example: www.yahoo.com

2) Is the Favorites area displayed to the left of Explorer's main window? If not, click the Favorites button on the Standard Toolbar to display it.

3) At the top of the Favorites area, click the **Add** button.

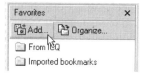

4) You are now shown the Add Favorite dialog box. Accept or change the name of the web page whose address you are saving. (In this case, Yahoo!).

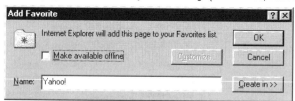

5) Click **OK**.

Internet Explorer adds the name of the currently displayed page as the last item in the Favorites list.

Organising Your Favorites

You can group favorites in folders, so making them easier to find. In Exercise 7.30 you create a folder to store addresses of search engine websites, and then add a number of web addresses to that folder.

Exercise 7.30: Managing Favorites in Folders

1) Is the Favorites area displayed to the left of Internet Explorer's main window? If not, click the Favorites button on the Standard Toolbar to display it.

2) At the top of the Favorites area, click the **Organize** button to display the Organize Favorites dialog box.

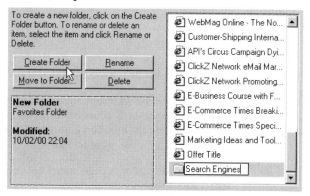

3) Select **Create Folder**, name the new folder Search Engines, and click **Close**.

4) Visit the following website: www.altavista.com

5) At the top of the Favorites area, click the **Add** button.

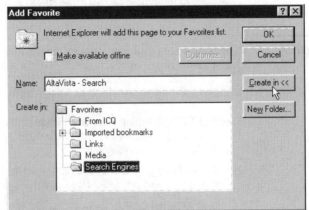

6) In the dialog box displayed, click **Create in << **, select the Search Engines folder, and click **OK**.

7) Repeat steps 3, 4 and 5 for each of the following search engine websites:

    www.northernlight.com
    www.alltheweb.com
    www.hotbot.com
    www.google.com
    www.excite.com

Well done. You now have a folder of saved web addresses.

Revisiting a Saved Web Address

Revisiting a saved web address is easy. In Exercise 7.31, you revisit a web address that you added as a favourite in Exercise 7.30.

Exercise 7.31: Revisiting a Saved Web Address

1) Is the Favorites area displayed to the left of Internet Explorer's main window? If not, click the Favorites button on the Standard Toolbar.

2) Scroll down the list of Favorites until you see the Search Engines folder that you created in Exercise 7.30. Click on it.

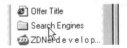

3) Click a saved web address from the Search Engines folder. For example: www.hotbot.com. Internet Explorer displays the associated web page.

Changing Your Start Page

Your start page (which Internet Explorer calls the home page) is the web page that the program visits and displays when you open Internet Explorer.

Exercise 7.32 shows you how to change your start page.

Exercise 7.32: Changing Your Start Page

1)   Go to the page you want to display whenever you start Internet Explorer. For example, www.munnelly.com.

2)   Choose **Tools | Internet Options** and select the General tab. In the Home page area of the dialog box, select **Use Current** and click **OK**.

To display your preferred start page at any stage, click the Home button on Internet Explorer's Standard Toolbar.

Home button

You can restore your original start page – the one set up when Internet Explorer was installed – by selecting the **Use Default** option.

To specify a blank start page – that is, no start page – select the **Use Blank** option.

Screen Elements

Internet Explorer's main window is the area in which the application displays the web pages. Surrounding the main window are various screen elements designed to assist you explore and find information on the Web:

*   Across the top of the main window are the Standard Toolbar and the Address Bar

*   Along the left are the three Explorer Bars: Favorites, History and Search

In this topic you will learn how more about these screen elements.

Standard Toolbar

You have already learnt the purpose of the following buttons on Internet Explorer's Standard Toolbar: Back, Forward, Home, Search, Favorites and Print.

Internet Explorer Toolbar

Two other important buttons are Stop and Refresh. Click the Stop button if the web page you are trying to view is taking too long to display. The Refresh button re-requests the current web page from the web site. Click this button if a web page displays incorrectly or incompletely.

To hide the Standard Toolbar, choose **View | Toolbars** and deselect the Standard Buttons option. To redisplay the Toolbar, choose **View | Toolbars** again and reselect Standard Buttons.

Address Bar

Beneath the Standard Toolbar is the Address Bar. As you learnt in Section 7.1, this area shows the web address of the currently displayed web page. You can also use it to enter a web address: you type in the required address and then click the Go button or press the ENTER key.

To hide the Address Bar, choose **View | Toolbars** and deselect the Address Bar option. To redisplay the Address Bar, choose **View | Toolbars** again and reselect Address Bar.

Explorer Bars

This is the name that Internet Explorer gives to the three screen elements that you can display to the left of the main window. You can display only one at a time:

Internet Explorer History Bar

- To view the Favorites Bar, click the Favorites button on the Standard toolbar, or choose **View | Explorer Bar** and select the Favorites option. You can then view your list of saved web addresses.

- To view the Search Bar, click the Search button on the Standard Toolbar, or choose **View | Explorer Bar** and select the Search option.

- To view the History Bar, click the History button on the Standard Toolbar, or choose **View | Explorer Bar** and select the History option.

The History Bar shows the web addresses that you visited in previous days and weeks. To revisit a web page in the History bar, click a week or day, click a website folder to display individual pages, and then click the page icon to display the web page.

You can sort or search the History Bar by clicking the relevant arrow next to the View button at the top of the History Bar.

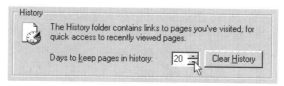

To change the number of days that Internet Explorer keeps track of your visited pages, or to delete the list completely, choose **Tools | Internet Options**, select the General tab, make the required change, and click **OK**.

Text Size Display

You can change the default size in which Internet Explorer displays text – a very useful feature if you have low or limited vision.

Choose **View | Text Size**, and select the size of text that you want.

You can revert to the default text size of Medium at any stage.

Finally, you can maximise the size of Internet Explorer's main window by choosing **View | Full Screen**.

To revert to normal display, click the Restore button at the top-right of the screen.

Some web pages – such as home pages at www.adobe.com and www.zdnet.com – are designed with fixed-sized fonts, so that using the **View | Text Size** options does not change how they display.

Congratulations. You have now completed the first half of ECDL Module 7, Information and Communication.

Section Summary: So Now You Know

You can adjust the appearance and operation of Internet Explorer to suit your working needs and personal taste.

To display web pages more quickly, switch off the display of images. Internet Explorer displays only the text of visited web pages, together with a small icon indicating the location of each non-displayed image.

You can store web addresses, and organise them into folders for easy reference, using Internet Explorer *Favorites*. If there is a particular web page you visit very frequently, you can make it the default *start page*.

Internet Explorer's *Standard Toolbar* offers quick access to commonly used browsing actions. At the left of the main window you can display any one of the following: the *History Bar*, *Search Bar* or the *Favorites Bar*. Explorer allows you to adjust the size in which text is displayed on-screen.

Section 7.5: E-Mail with Outlook Express

In This Section

Question: what do most people use the Internet for? Answer: e-mail. It's fast becoming the preferred method of communication in business, and – because it is so inexpensive to use – it is also used by friends and family as a way of staying in contact.

This Section introduces you Outlook Express, the Microsoft e-mail application. You will explore the application's main screen elements and discover how to arrange them to suit your personal taste.

You will also learn how to address, compose and send an e-mail over the Internet, and how to collect and read incoming e-mails addressed to you.

New Skills

At the end of this Section you should be able to:

- Start and quit Microsoft Outlook Express
- Display the following four screen elements: Folders List, Message List, Preview Pane and Toolbar
- Select an e-mail from a Message List and display it in the Preview Pane
- Select an e-mail from a Message List and display it in a separate window
- Compose and send e-mails
- Collect and read incoming e-mails
- Print and delete an e-mail

New Words

At the end of this Section you should be able to explain the following terms:

- Folders List
- Message List
- Preview Pane
- E-mail collection

Starting Outlook Express

To open Outlook Express you can:

Outlook
Express

- Double-click on the Outlook Express icon.

  -or-

- Choose **Start | Programs | Outlook Express**.

If your computer has a permanent Internet connection, you are ready to send and receive e-mail messages with Outlook Express.

If you have a dial-up connection, you must dial your Internet Service Provider (ISP). Outlook Express may be set up to do this automatically. If not, you will need to dial your ISP separately.

Enter your user name and password (if Outlook Express has not recorded them from the last time that you dialled your ISP), and click **Connect**.

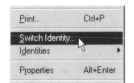

If your computer is used by a number of people, you may have to identify yourself, so that you get your own mail, and not someone else's. To do this, choose **File | Switch Identity**, select your name from the list, and click **OK**.

Changing Outlook Layout

You can change the layout of the Outlook Express screen so that the features you use most often are shown, and those you use very seldom are hidden. This means that two people using Outlook Express might have screens that look very different.

For the purpose of the Exercises in this Module, change the screen layout as directed in Exercise 7.33.

Exercise 7.33: Choosing the Display Elements

1) Choose **View | Layout** for Outlook Express to present a list of layout options, with a checkbox beside each one.

2) In the upper area of the dialog box, select the Folder List, Status Bar and Toolbar options, and deselect all the others.

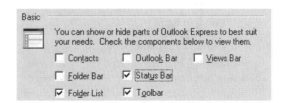

3) In the lower area of the dialog box, select the Show preview pane, Below messages, and Show preview pane header options, and deselect all others.

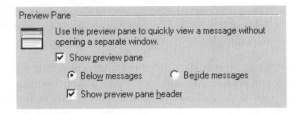

4) Click **OK**.

Your Outlook Express screen should now look like that shown below.

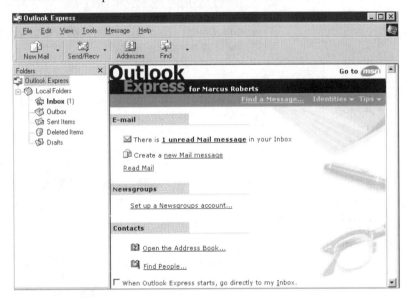

The Four Layout Elements

Let's take a look at the four main screen elements of Outlook Express: Folders List, Message List, Preview Pane and Toolbar.

Folders List

The Folders List, on the left, shows five folders:

Bold type indicates that a folder contains unread e-mails

- **Inbox:** This is where all your incoming e-mails – those sent to you by other people – are held.

- **Outbox:** This can hold all your outgoing e-mails – those you have composed yourself – until you send them.

- **Sent Items:** This can hold copies of all the e-mails you have sent to other people.

- **Deleted Items:** This is where you put all e-mails – both incoming and outgoing – that you no longer want to keep.

- **Drafts:** This is where you store any e-mails that you have not finished composing.

When a folder contains an unread e-mail, Outlook Express displays the folder name in bold, and shows, in brackets, the number of unread e-mails in that folder.

In addition to the five e-mail folders provided with Outlook Express, you can create folders and subfolders of your own, and move e-mails in and out of them. You will learn how to do this in Section 7.7.

Message List

When you click any folder in the Folders List, Outlook Express displays the folder's contents in an area on the right of the screen called the Message List. This is called 'opening the folder'.

Click on a folder to display its contents in the Message List

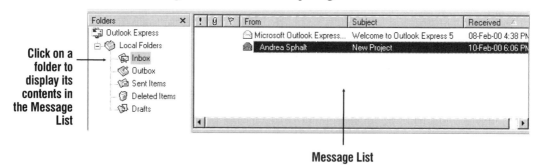

Message List

Outlook Express displays some basic details about each e-mail – the sender or recipient, the subject, and the date and time it was sent or received – and uses the following symbols to provide you with more information:

 A *read* e-mail, displayed in light type.

 An *unread* e-mail, displayed in bold type.

📎 An e-mail, whether read or unread, with one or more *files attached*. (You will learn about e-mail file attachments in Sections 7.6 and 7.7.)

❗ An e-mail marked as *high-priority*. (You will learn about e-mail priority in Section 7.6.)

When you click on an e-mail in your the Message List, Outlook Express displays the e-mail's contents in an area beneath the Message List called the Preview Pane.

Click on an e-mail in the Message List to display its contents in the Preview Pane.

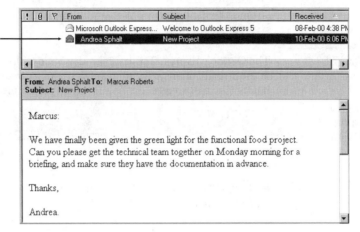

To display a different e-mail in the Preview Pane, simply click on a different e-mail in the Message List.

You can resize the Preview Pane and the Message List by clicking on the border between them, holding down the mouse button, and dragging the border up or down.

Resizing the Message List and Preview Pane by dragging with the mouse

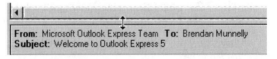

Preview Pane

An area of the Outlook Express screen that shows the contents of the e-mail that is currently selected in the Message List.

If you receive a long e-mail, you may prefer to read it in a separate window. To do this, double-click the e-mail in the Message List.

Reading an e-mail in a separate window

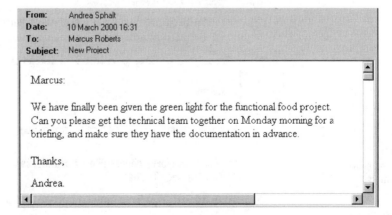

You can then minimise the e-mail's separate window (so that you can come back directly to it at any time), or maximise it (so that it fills the screen). When you are finished with it, close it by clicking the Close button at the top right of the window. This closes only the e-mail's separate window – and not Outlook Express.

Outlook Express Toolbar

The Outlook Express Toolbar provides buttons that offer one-click access to the e-mail actions you will want to use most frequently. Different buttons are displayed according to which part of the Outlook Express

Outlook Express Toolbar

screen you are working in.

Rather than introduce all these buttons at once, we will explain each one as it becomes relevant through this Module.

You now know enough about Outlook Express to compose and send an e-mail (Exercise 7.34) and to read an e-mail sent to you.

Composing and Sending an E-Mail

Exercise 7.34 leads you through the steps of composing and sending an e-mail in Outlook Express.

New Mail

Compose new e-mail button

Exercise 7.34: Composing and Sending an E-mail

1) Choose **File | New | Mail Message** or click the New Mail button on the Toolbar.

   Notice how your e-mail address (for example, marcus@redact.ie) is displayed in the From: box.

2) Click in the To: box, and type the address of the person to whom you are sending the e-mail.

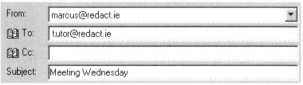

3) Click in the Subject: box, and type a brief description of your e-mail.

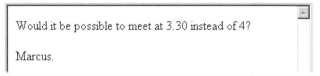

Send

Send e-mail button

4) Click in the main text box, and type the text of your e-mail.

5) When finished typing, choose **File | Send Message**, or click the Send button on the New Message Toolbar.

Congratulations! You have now composed and sent your first e-mail.

What happens to your outgoing e-mail? The answer depends on:

- Your type of Internet connection – permanent or dial-up.
- Your selected e-mail sending option – immediate or in a group with other outgoing e-mails.

Outgoing E-mail: Permanent Internet Connection

When you send an e-mail, Outlook Express can transfer it directly to the Internet. To set up this option, choose **Tools | Internet Options**, select the Send tab, select the Send messages immediately option, and click **OK**.

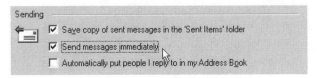

Send and Receive e-mail button

If you do not select this option, your e-mail goes only as far as your Outbox folder. It remains there, along with any other outgoing e-mails, until you choose **Tools | Send and Receive | Send All** or click the Send/Recv button on the Outlook Express Toolbar.

Don't confuse the Send button on the New Message Toolbar with the Send/Recv button on the Outlook Express Toolbar.

- **Send button:** This sends the current e-mail to the Internet or to your Outbox folder, depending on how Outlook Express is set up.
- **Send/Recv button:** This sends all e-mails in your Outbox folder to the Internet.

Outgoing E-mail: Dial-up Connection

As with a permanent Internet connection, you can choose to send each e-mail immediately – or store them in your Outbox for sending later.

You would generally choose to hold all your outgoing messages in your Outbox until you were ready. That way, you can view and type e-mail messages without being connected to the Internet. You need only dial-up your ISP when you are actually sending or receiving the mail, so that you can exchange all your messages (even hundreds of them, to all over the world) in a single local phone call.

Outgoing E-Mail and the Sent Items Folder

Outlook Express can place a copy of all outgoing e-mails in your Sent Items folder, so that you have a copy of them for future reference.

To set this option, choose **Tools | Options**, select the Send tab, select the Save copy of sent messages in the 'Sent Items' folder, and click **OK**.

Collecting and Reading Your E-mail

Just as you can send your outgoing e-mails one-at-a-time or all together, you can collect your incoming e-mail as often as you like, either automatically or manually.

E-mail Collection: Permanent Internet Connection

You can collect e-mail from the Internet in two ways:

- Automatically at specified time intervals. Choose **Tools | Options**, select the General tab, select Check for new messages every 30 minutes, and click **OK**. You can change the timing to suit your needs.

- Manually, by choosing **Tools | Send and Receive | Receive All** or by clicking the Send/Recv button on the Standard Toolbar.

  Even if you have set up the automatic, timed e-mail collection, you can click Send/Recv at any stage to check if any new e-mails have been sent to you.

E-mail Collection: Dial-up Connection

If you are using a dial-up connection, you will generally use the same phone call to send your outgoing messages and collect any incoming messages. When you choose **Tools | Send and Receive | Send and Receive All** or click the Send/Recv button, that's what happens.

Don't confuse the action of collecting e-mail with the action of reading it. If you have a dial-up Internet connection, you can read your e-mail whether you are online or not. You need only go online to collect your e-mail from the Internet.

> **E-mail Collection**
>
> *The action of transferring e-mails from the Internet to your computer. You must be connected to the Internet to collect e-mail, but you can read your collected messages whether you are online or not.*

E-mail Collection at Startup

You can set up Outlook Express so that it automatically collects your e-mails from the Internet when you start the application. To do so, choose **Tools | Options**, select the General tab, select the Send and Receive messages at startup option, and click **OK**.

If you have a dial-up connection to the Internet, you may prefer not to select this option. Otherwise, Outlook Express will attempt to dial-up your ISP every time that you start the application.

Reading an E-mail

Outlook Express places incoming e-mails in your Inbox folder. When you click on your Inbox folder, your Message List shows all your received e-mails, with the one e-mail highlighted. The text of that e-mail is shown in the Preview Pane.

Click once on any other e-mail in the Message List to display its text in the Preview Pane. Double-click on any e-mail in the Message List to display its text in a separate window.

The same technique applies irrespective of which folder the message is in: open the folder; select the message; read.

Printing an E-mail

To print an e-mail, choose **File | Print** or click the Print button on the Toolbar.

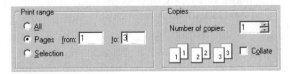

The Print dialog box (which is displayed only if you choose the **File | Print** command and not when you click the Print Toolbar button) gives you the options:

- **All:** Prints every page of the e-mail.

- **Selection:** Prints only the currently selected text of the e-mail.

- **Pages:** To print a range of pages from an e-mail, enter the first and last page number of interest.

Other options on the Print dialog box allow you to specify how many copies you want to print of your selected pages, and indicate whether you want the multiple copies collated.

Deleting an E-mail

To delete an e-mail, irrespective of whether it is in your Inbox, Outbox, Sent Items, or Drafts folder, just click on it in the Message List and choose **Edit | Delete** or click the Delete button on the Toolbar.

Is the e-mail really deleted? No. Outlook Express places it in the Deleted Items folder. To retrieve the e-mail:

- Click on the Deleted Items folder in the Folders List. Your Message List now displays all deleted e-mails.

- Click on the e-mail in the Message List, and hold down the mouse button.

- Drag the e-mail from the Message List to the Inbox or other folder in the Folders List.

| Manual E-mail Deletion | You can permanently remove all deleted e-mails from Outlook Express by emptying the Deleted Items folder. To do so, select the Deleted Items folder in the Folders List, choose **Edit | Empty Deleted Items Folder**, and click **OK**. |

| Automatic E-mail Deletion | If you don't want e-mails to be saved in the Deleted Items folder when you quit Outlook Express, choose **Tools | Options**, select the Maintenance tab, select the Empty messages from the 'Deleted Items' folder on exit option, and click **OK**. |

Quitting Outlook Express

To leave Outlook Express:

Choose **File | Exit**, or click the Close button at the top right of the Outlook Express Window.

Using Online Help

Like Internet Explorer and other Microsoft applications, Outlook Express offers a searchable online help system:

You can search through and read online help in two ways: from dialog boxes, or from the Help menu.

| Using Help from Dialog Boxes | Exercise 7.35 provides an example of accessing online help from a dialog box. |

Exercise 7.35: Accessing Online Help from a Dialog Box

1) Choose **Tools | Options**, and click the General tab.

2) Click the question mark symbol near the top-right of the dialog box. Outlook Express displays a question mark to the right of the cursor.

3) Drag the mouse down to the option named Play sound when new messages arrive.

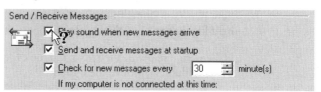

4) Click anywhere on the option checkbox or name.

Specifies whether your computer plays a sound when new messages arrive. If you clear this check box, you do not hear any sound, but the Outlook Express status bar and message list will indicate that you have unread messages.

Outlook Express now displays help text telling you about the option.

Practise Exercise 7.35 with other dialog boxes in Outlook Express.

You can also access online help from the Help menu. Choose **Help | Contents and Index** to display the three tabs of the Help Topics dialog box.

Contents Tab

This offers short descriptions of main features of Outlook Express.

📖 Where you see a heading with a book symbol, double-click to view the related sub-headings.

[?] Double-click a question mark symbol to read the help text.

Index Tab

Reading the material displayed on this tab is like looking through the index of a printed book.

Just type the first letters of the word or phrase you are interested in.

Outlook Express responds by displaying all matches from the online help in the right of the dialog box.

When you find the index entry that you are looking for, click the **Display** button.

Find Tab

Can't find what you are looking for in the Contents or Index tab? Try this tab.

When you type a word or phrase and click **List Topics**, Outlook Express performs a deeper search of the online help.

When you find the item you are looking for, double-click it to display the relevant help text in the right of the dialog box.

As you search through and read online help topics, you will see the following buttons at the top of the online help window:

- **Hide/Show:** Hides or displays the left-hand pane of the online help dialog box.

- **Back/Forward:** Moves you backwards and forwards through previously visited help topics.

- **Options:** Offers a number of display choices, and enables you to print the currently displayed online help text.

- **Web Help:** Takes you to Microsoft's Web-based support site for Outlook Express.

Take a few minutes to look through the Outlook Express online help system. Remember that you will be free to use online help during an ECDL test.

When finished, you can close Outlook Express by clicking the Close button or choosing **File | Close**. You have now completed Section 7.5 of the ECDL Information and Communication Module.

Section Summary: So Now You Know

Microsoft Outlook Express is an *e-mail application* that enables you to *compose* (address, write and edit) new e-mails, *send* e-mails (from your computer to the Internet), *collect* incoming e-mails (from the Internet to your computer), and *read* collected e-mails.

To help you organize your e-mails, Outlook Express contains a built-in *Folders List* in which messages are stored and grouped by type: received (*Inbox*), waiting to be sent (*Outbox*), already sent (*Sent Items*), marked for deletion (*Deleted Items*), and held for later editing (*Drafts*). Users can create additional folders for further organising their e-mails.

You can collect your incoming e-mails *manually* from the Internet, or you can set up Outlook Express to collect them *automatically* each time you start the application and/or at preset time intervals.

You can also tell the application to send each outgoing e-mail as soon as you have finished composing it – or to store outgoing e-mails in your Outbox folder for sending in a group later.

If you have a dial-up Internet connection, you can read and compose your e-mail whether you are online or not. You need only go online to send and collect your e-mail. You can keep copies of all outgoing e-mail in your Sent Items folder.

When you open a folder, Outlook Express displays the e-mails that it contains in a *Message List*, together with a summary of information about each one.

Clicking once on an e-mail in a Message List displays that e-mail's contents in a *Preview Pane* under the Message List. Clicking twice displays the e-mail in a separate window.

When you delete an e-mail, Outlook Express places it in the Deleted Items folder. You can empty the Deleted Items folder manually or set up Outlook Express to empty it automatically each time that you close the application.

Section 7.6: More about Outgoing Mail

In This Section

In this Section you will discover some of the options available for composing and sending e-mails.

You will learn how to copy text into an e-mail from another application, how to check the spelling in your e-mails, how to mark an e-mail as high-priority, and how to send the same e-mail to several people – there are several ways of doing this.

You will also learn how to create a signature and to append it to your outgoing e-mails, and how to attach files to outgoing e-mails – word processed documents, spreadsheets, or photographs of your dog.

New Skills

At the end of this Section you should be able to:

- Copy text into an e-mail
- Check the spelling in an e-mail
- Send the same e-mail to several recipients
- Send a blind copy of an e-mail
- Set the priority of an outgoing e-mail
- Add a signature to outgoing e-mails
- Attach a file to an outgoing e-mail
- Explain why an e-mail may 'bounce', and know what to do about it
- Manage your outgoing e-mail queue

New Words

At the end of this Section you should be able to explain the following terms:

- Cc (Carbon copy)
- Bcc (Blind copy)
- E-mail file attachment
- Signature (sig) file
- Message priority
- Bounced e-mail
- Drafts folder

Copying Text into E-mails

Typing text directly into Outlook Express is just one way of composing an e-mail. Another is to reuse previously typed text by copying it from another e-mail (whether received or sent), and then pasting it into the new one.

As Exercise 7.36 shows, you can also copy text into an outgoing e-mail from another application such as a Microsoft Word document. (You should be familiar with Microsoft Word and have a Word document ready to use before attempting Exercise 7.36. Otherwise, you'll just have to take our word for it!)

Exercise 7.36: Copying Text from Word to Outlook Express

1) Open Microsoft Word and open the document that contains the text you want to copy into your e-mail.

2) Select the text for copying, by clicking at the start and dragging the cursor to the end.

Text selected from Microsoft Word

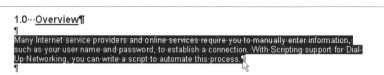

(To select all the text in a Word document, hold down the CTRL key and click anywhere in the left margin.)

3) Choose **Edit | Copy** or press CTRL+c to copy the select text to the Clipboard.

4) Open Outlook Express, and either open the e-mail you want to paste the text into, or compose a new e-mail.

5) Position the cursor where you want the copied text to appear in your e-mail, and choose **Edit | Paste** or press CTRL+v.

Text from Word pasted into an outgoing e-mail

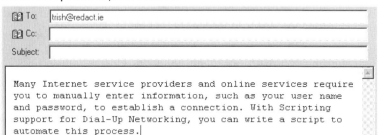

Checking Your Spelling

Check e-mail spelling button

How's your spelling? Outlook Express can check your spelling and suggest corrections to errors in two ways:

- When you send the e-mail (the automatic option)

- When you choose the **Tools | Spelling** command or click the Spelling button on the New Message Toolbar (the on-request option).

If automatic spell-checking is switched on, Outlook Express checks your e-mail after you choose **File | Send Message** or click the Send button on the New Message Toolbar.

It uses the same spelling dictionary as Word and other Microsoft Office applications. If you do not have any of these installed on your computer, spell-checking in Outlook Express is not available.

Exercise 7.37: Switching On the Spell Checker

1) Choose **Tools | Options** and click the Spelling tab.

2) Select the following two options, and click **OK**: Always check spelling before sending, and Suggest replacements for misspelled words.

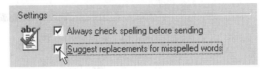

Subsequently, when you send an e-mail, you will be alerted to any word in your e-mail that Outlook Express does not recognise, and offered some alternatives. (Not all unusual spellings are wrong, however, and not all usual spellings are right.)

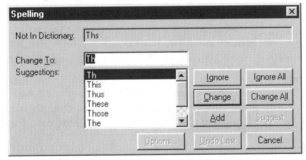

You can **Ignore** the alert, **Change** the problem word to the alternative highlighted, or **Add** the word that caused the problem to the dictionary, so that it does not cause any further alerts.

Finding an E-mail Address

You've seen that sending an e-mail is easy, provided you know the e-mail address of the person you are writing to. Where do you find these addresses? There are five main sources: business cards, incoming e-mails, websites, the Find People option, and the Internet Explorer Address Book:

Business cards: Most people in business today include their e-mail address on the business cards. (Some include *only* their e-mail address – they don't want to be contacted any other way!)

Incoming e-mails: Many of the people you want to send e-mail to have already been in contact with you. Simply go to your Inbox, find an e-mail from the right person, copy their address to the Clipboard and paste it into your e-mail.

Websites: If you know the organisation to which the person belongs, find its website. Many of them (particularly colleges and government agencies) include e-mail directories.

Find People option: Outlook Express provides an option that lets you quickly locate e-mail addresses from Web-based directories.

- Choose **Tools | Address Book** and select the **Edit | Find People** button.

- From the Look in: drop-down list, select a directory service.

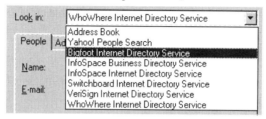

- Type the name of the person you are looking for, and click **Find Now**.

This feature works only when you are connected to the Internet. (And it's not guaranteed to find the person you want.)

Address book: An Outlook Express feature that enables you to record e-mail addresses for easy reference. (You will learn about the address book in Section 7.8.)

E-mailing Multiple Recipients

You can send an e-mail to more than one person. There are three ways of doing this: several equal recipients, one main recipient with copies to others, and blind carbon copy. You use each for different purposes.

Several Equal Recipients

If you want to send the e-mail to several people, enter each of their e-mail addresses in the To: box, separated by a comma or semi-colon. To make a string of multiple addresses easier to read, include a space after each comma or semi-colon.

Multiple To: recipients

One Main Recipient, with Copy to Another

To send a copy of the e-mail to another person, enter their e-mail address in the Cc: (Carbon copy) box. Generally, you use the Cc: box to enter the e-mail address of other recipients you think should see this e-mail as a matter of courtesy or organisational procedure.

Multiple Cc: recipients

🔳 To:	joe@bloggs.com
🔳 Cc:	wallace@preston.com.au, lauren@porridge.ca

Cc is like that: it conveys those kinds of subtle but powerful messages that make office life exciting.

You can enter as many e-mail addresses as you want in the To: box and in the Cc: box.

<table>
<tr><td>Cc: (E-mail Carbon Copy)</td></tr>
<tr><td>A field in an e-mail header where you can enter the addresses of people to whom you want to send a copy of the e-mail.</td></tr>
</table>

Blind Carbon Copying

With blind copying, you send a copy of the e-mail to the second person, *without* the main recipient knowing about it. Before doing this, you need to reveal the Bcc: box by choosing **View | All Headers**. The Bcc: box is shown on all e-mail you subsequently compose, until you turn it off (by choosing **View | All Headers** again).

You simply enter in the Bcc: box the e-mail addresses of anyone you want to blind-copy the e-mail to:

- Bcc: recipients know the names of the To: and Cc: recipients.

- The To: and Cc: recipients do not know the names of the Bcc: recipients.

- The Bcc: recipients do not know each other's names.

To: and Bcc: recipients

Bcc: sends even more subtle messages than Cc:. Let's say you send an e-mail to Trish and Bcc Peter. This has the following effects:

- Trish (To recipient) gets the e-mail.

- Peter (Bcc: recipient) learns that Trish got the e-mail (and sees what the e-mail was).

- Trish is not aware that Peter knows that she got the e-mail, or what was in it.

- Peter knows that Trish *doesn't* know that he knows.

- Peter knows that you don't want Trish to know that he knows.

Fun, isn't it?

Again, you can enter as many e-mail addresses as you wish in the To: box and in the Bcc: box, and you can include both Cc: and Bcc: recipients in the same e-mail.

<table>
<tr><td>Bcc: (E-mail Blind Carbon Copy)</td></tr>
<tr><td>A field in an e-mail header that enables you to copy an e-mail to other recipients. Bcc: recipients can view addresses in the To: and Cc: fields, but not addresses in the Bcc: field. To: and Cc: recipients cannot view any addresses in the Bcc: field.</td></tr>
</table>

*Mass E-mail
and Blind Carbon
Copying*

A common use (abuse?) of the Bcc: field is for the sending of mass e-mails that advertise products or services.

The sender places *all* the recipients' addresses in the Bcc: field, so that no one recipient knows who else also received the e-mail. Should the e-mail fall into the hands of a competing company, they are unable to view the sender's list of clients and prospects. In the To: field, the sender types his or her own e-mail address.

Every e-mail you send must have at least one address in the To: box; otherwise, it will 'bounce' back to you. (Bounced e-mails are explained later in this Section.)

Attaching Files to E-Mails

E-mails are generally short text messages. But suppose you want to send a family photograph to your uncle, a spreadsheet to your accountant, a PowerPoint presentation to head office, or a beautifully formatted word-processed document to your tutor? Easy. You send it as an *attachment* to your e-mail message.

To learn how to attach a file to an e-mail, follow the steps in Exercise 7.38.

Exercise 7.38: Sending an Attachment

1) Compose your e-mail in the normal way.

**Attach file to
e-mail button**

2) Choose **Insert | File Attachment** or click the Attach button on the New Message Toolbar.

3) In the Insert Attachment dialog box, locate the file you want to attach to your e-mail, and click **Attach**.

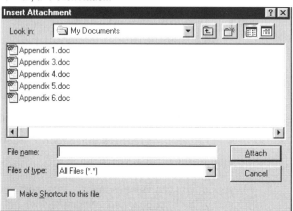

Outlook Express adds a line in the e-mail header to show the attachment file name and file size. To attach multiple files, repeat steps 2 and 3 above.

4) Click **Send** to send the e-mail with its attachment.

Remember that the person who receives your attached file can work with it only if they have the appropriate software application.

E-mail File Attachment
A file, typically a formatted file such as a Word document, that is appended to and sent with an e-mail.

E-mail Priority

All the e-mail you send is important, right? But some of it is more important than others, and you want to make sure that the recipient knows it. Exercise 7.39 shows you how to mark an outgoing e-mail as high-priority.

Exercise 7.39: Sending a High-Priority E-mail
1) Compose the e-mail in the usual way.

2) Choose **Message | Set Priority | High**.

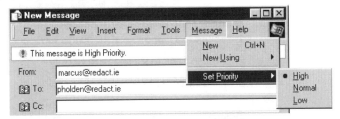

3) Choose **File | Send Message** or click the Send button.

High-priority e-mails (incoming or outgoing) are identified by a red exclamation mark. Use the high-priority setting sparingly. If every e-mail you send is high priority, they will all be treated in the same way.

You can also send e-mails with a Low Priority setting in exactly the same way. But who wants to do that? (Low priority e-mails are identified by a blue down arrow.) The priority of an e-mail *does not* affect the speed with which it is transmitted over the Internet or an internal e-mail network.

E-mail priority indicators

You can also change the priority of e-mails you have received. This is a useful way of highlighting e-mails that you want to come back to at a later stage.

E-mail Message Priority
An indication to an e-mail recipient of a message's urgency, typically represented by a coloured symbol. The priority of an e-mail has no impact on the speed with which it travels over the Internet or private network.

Bounced Messages

If you send an e-mail to someone and, for whatever reason, it cannot be delivered, you usually receive a message to that effect. Such e-mails are said to 'bounce' – you send them out; they bounce right back.

The most likely reason for an e-mail bouncing is that you have typed an incorrect address: did you spell it right? Did you put in all the right punctuation? Did you put in a hyphen (-) instead of an underscore (_)?

> **Bounced E-mail**
>
> *An e-mail that, for whatever reason, fails to reach its recipient, and is returned to its sender with a message to that effect.*

Occasionally, your e-mail fails to get through and you *don't* get any message to that effect. While this is rare, it does happen. Don't assume that because you sent the e-mail, the recipient definitely received it. If it's that important, ask them to acknowledge receipt, either in your e-mail, or automatically. Exercise 7.40 shows you how.

Exercise 7.40: Requesting a Receipt

1) Compose a new e-mail in the normal way.

2) Choose **Tools | Request Read Receipt**.

3) Send the e-mail as normal.

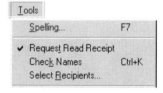

When the e-mail is received and opened by its recipients, they are informed that you have requested confirmation. They can choose to send the confirmation or not, but they don't have to do any work – they just click **Yes**.

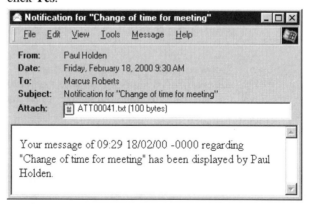

You then get a message like the one above.

Your E-mail Signature

When you compose an e-mail, you may want to finish it off with a small block of text as a signature. The easiest and most efficient way to do this is to create a *signature* (sometimes known as a signature file or a sig file). Outlook Express will append this to your outgoing e-mails – either automatically to all e-mails or only to ones that you select.

Most people include their name and contact details. Some add an advertising slogan, a short message, or a link to their website. You can also create different signature files for different purposes.

Creating a Signature

Follow Exercise 7.41 to learn how to create an e-mail signature file.

Exercise 7.41: Creating Your Signature

1) Choose **Tools | Options**, select the Signatures tab and click **New**.

2) Click the Text button, and in the text box, enter your name, address, telephone number and other contact details.

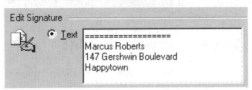

3) Select the Add signatures to all outgoing messages checkbox, but do not select the Don't add signatures to Replies and Forwards checkbox.

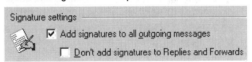

4) Click **OK**.

Outlook Express automatically appends your signature to all subsequent e-mails you compose and send.

If you want to be more selective, do not select the Add signatures to all outgoing messages checkbox, as in step 2 of Exercise 7.41 above. Instead, when you have composed the e-mail, position the cursor at the point in the e-mail where you want the signature to appear and choose **Insert | Signature**.

Alternative Signature Files

To create a second (or a third ...) signature file, choose **Tools | Options**, and select the Signatures tab. Then click **New**, and proceed exactly as when you created your first signature file.

Choose which of your signatures you want to be the default by clicking it and selecting **Set as Default**. Finally, click **OK**.

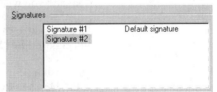

If you have created more than one signature file, and you subsequently choose **Insert | Signature**, you are offered a choice from those available.

Renaming Your
Signature File

You can rename your signature files, so that it is easier to identify the right one for the circumstances. You might have a signature file called Business, one called Personal, and one called Family, for example. Or one for your team and another for head office.

To do this, choose **Tools | Options**, and select the Signatures tab. Next, click the signature file you want to rename, and select **Rename**. Then enter the new name for the file. Do the same for the other files you want to rename. When finished, click **OK**.

Editing a
Signature File

To edit your signature file, choose **Tools | Options**, and select the Signatures tab.

Your signature files are listed. Select the one you want to change by clicking it. Then make whatever changes you want, by adding, deleting, or overwriting the existing information. When finished, click **OK**.

> **Signature (Sig) File**
>
> *An appendage at the end of e-mails. Typical contents include full name, occupation or position, phone and fax numbers, and e-mail and website addresses. Some people also include a favourite quote, company slogan or short personal statement.*

The Drafts Folder

If your e-mails are held in your Outbox folder until you click the Send/Recv button, you have the luxury of being able to change your mind.

You can delete an e-mail in the Outbox in the same way as any other e-mail. You select it in the Message List, and do any of the following: click the Delete button on the Toolbar, choose **Edit | Delete**, or press the DELETE key.

Alternatively, you might want to move the e-mail into the Drafts folder while you think about it some more.

Saving E-mail to
the Drafts Folder

The Drafts folder is where you keep your half-finished thoughts, your letters of resignation, your job applications, until you are sure that they are right and you want to send them.

To put a new e-mail into the Drafts folder, compose the e-mail as normal and choose **File | Save**.

To revisit an e-mail in the Drafts folder, open the folder, select the e-mail in the Message List, and double-click it to open it. You can then make any changes or additions, and either save it again to the Drafts folder, or send it.

You can also move an e-mail directly from the Drafts folder to the Outbox by dragging it from the Message List to the Outbox in the folder list.

Text Size Display

You can change the default size in which Outlook Express displays text – a very useful feature if you have low or limited vision.

Choose **View | Text Size**, and select the size of text that you want.

You can revert to the default text size of Medium at any stage.

When finished, you can close Outlook Express. You have now completed Section 7.6 of the ECDL Information and Communication Module.

Section Summary: So Now You Know

You can *copy text* from a word processor or other application to an e-mail in Outlook Express, and *spell-check* your e-mail messages as you would a document in Microsoft Word.

You can address an outgoing e-mail to *multiple recipients* – as equal addresseés (To:), as *carbon copied* addressees (Cc:), or as *blind carbon copy addresses* (Bcc:). Bcc: recipients can view addresses in the To: and Cc: fields, but not addresses in the Bcc: field. To: and Cc: recipients also cannot view the addresses in the Bcc: field.

When sending an e-mail to several people, separate each e-mail address by a comma or semi-colon. You can optionally include a space after each comma or semi-colon, to make the addresses easier to read.

You can flag your messages as *high* or *low priority*. This indicates the message's urgency to the recipient, but has no impact on the speed with which it is sent over the Internet or private network.

You can append a *signature file* to your outgoing messages, and choose a different signature file for different audiences. Typical signature contents include full name, occupation or position, phone and fax numbers, e-mail and web site addresses. Some people also include a favourite quote, company slogan or short personal statement.

You can *attach formatted files* – such as pictures, spreadsheets and word-processor documents – to your e-mails. A *bounced e-mail* is an e-mail that, for whatever reason, fails to reach its recipient, and is returned to its sender with a message to that effect. The *Drafts folder* of Outlook is where you can store messages that you are not yet ready to send.

Section 7.7: More about Incoming Mail

In this Section you will explore some of the options available with incoming mail.

You will learn how to forward received e-mails to other people, how to send replies to the sender or to everyone who received the original e-mail, and how to copy text between e-mails or from an e-mail to a word processor or other application.

You will also discover how to open any file attachments that you receive, and how to save or delete them.

Another topic covered is mail folders – how to create new ones of your own, how to sort the e-mails they contain in different ways, and how to search through your mail folders for specific e-mails.

New Skills

At the end of this Section you should be able to:

- Forward a received e-mail to another person
- Reply only to the sender of an e-mail
- Reply to all the recipients of the original e-mail
- Copy text between e-mails, and from an e-mail to another application
- Open, save, and delete file attachments
- Create and delete mail folders
- Transfer e-mails between mail folders
- Search in your mail folders for a particular e-mail.

New Words

At the end of this Section you should be able to explain the following terms:

- E-mail forwarding
- E-mail reply to sender only
- E-mail reply all

Actions with Your Incoming Mail

In Section 7.5, you learnt how to display a received e-mail from your Message List by clicking on it once (to view it in the Preview Pane) or twice (to view it in a separate window).

In this Section, you will discover the various actions that you can perform on a received e-mail. In summary, these are:

- Forward it to someone else

- Reply only to the person who sent it

- Reply to the sender – and to any other people who also received the message

- Copy text from it to an outgoing e-mail, to Microsoft Word or to another application

- Open, save or delete any files it may have attached to it

Forwarding an E-mail

If you receive an e-mail that you want to pass on to someone else, the simplest way is to *forward* it. Follow Exercise 7.42 to discover how.

Exercise 7.42: Forwarding an E-mail

1) Select the e-mail you want to forward from your Message List by clicking on it once or twice.

Forward

E-mail forwarding button

2) Choose **Message | Forward** or click the Forward button on the Toolbar.

Outlook Express opens a window that looks like a window for creating a new e-mail, with two differences:

- The Subject: box shows the subject of the original e-mail, preceded by the abbreviation Fw:

- The original e-mail is shown and identified

Area for entering your comments with the forwarded e-mail

Text of received e-mail for forwarding

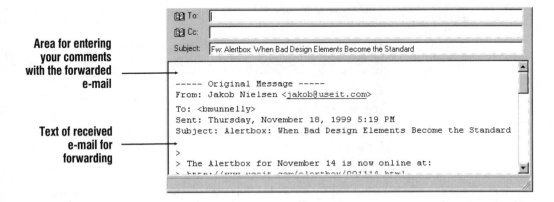

3) In the To: box, type the address of the person to whom you want to forward the e-mail.

4) In the message area, add text of your own. (It is helpful to the recipient if you clearly distinguish your own comments from the original message.)

5) Click **Send**.

Replying to Sender Only

When you receive an e-mail message, you can send a reply *either* to the person who sent it to you (only), *or* to all the people who received the original e-mail.

Most often, you will want to reply to the person who sent you the-mail. Exercise 7.43 shows you how.

Exercise 7.43: Replying to the E-mail Sender Only

Reply to e-mail sender only button

1) Select the e-mail you want to reply to from your Message List by clicking on it once or twice.

2) Chose Message Reply to Sender or click the **Reply** button on the Toolbar. The window that opens up looks like a the window for creating a new e-mail, with two differences:

- The To: box and the Subject: box are already completed

- The original e-mail message is shown and identified

Area for entering your reply ——→

Text of received e-mail you are replying to ——→

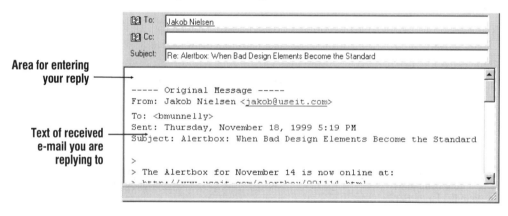

You can edit the Subject: box if you wish. You can also remove all or part of the original e-mail to which you are replying.

3) Enter the text of your reply in the message box, above the words 'Original Message'.

4) Click **Send**.

Remember, it's not very helpful to get a single word reply to an e-mail ("yes", or "4.30"). The person who reads it could have sent hundreds of e-mails, and could be reading your reply several days later. That's why including the original message with your reply is a good idea.

However, if the original message is very long, and your answer is "yes", it is helpful to cut out those parts of the original message that do not require a response, so that it becomes very obvious what you are agreeing to.

Replying to All Recipients

The Reply All option enables you to reply to an e-mail, with your reply going to *everyone* who received the original message. You use it in exactly the same way as the Reply (to sender only) function.

Reply to all e-mail recipients button

You will find this feature particularly useful when working with a number of people on a project (drawing up a contract, for example), or discussing something that requires unanimous agreement (to schedule a meeting, for example).

To use this option with a received e-mail, choose **Message | Reply to All** or click the Reply All button on the Toolbar.

Copying and Moving the Text of a Message

You can reuse the text of one e-mail in another e-mail, or in another application such as Microsoft Word. And you can move text around within the same message. Practice your text-moving skills with Exercises 7.44 and 7.45.

Exercise 7.44: Copying E-mail Text within Outlook Express

1) Open an e-mail, or compose a new one.

2) Select the text you want to copy, by clicking at the start of the text and dragging the cursor to the end.

3) Choose **Edit | Copy** or press CTRL+c.

4) Go to where you want to insert the copied text, either within the same e-mail or in another e-mail.

5) Choose **Edit | Paste**, or press CTRL+v.

Exercise 7.45: Copying E-mail Text into Another Application

1) As in Exercise 7.44, select the text you want to copy, and press CTRL+c.

2) Open the second application (such as Microsoft Word), position the cursor where you want the copied text to appear, and press CTRL+v.

In each case, you can move the text in question (that is, delete it in its original location and insert it in its new location), by choosing **Edit | Cut** instead of **Edit | Copy**, or pressing CTRL+x instead of CTRL+c.

Deleting Text

To delete text, select the text you want to delete, and do any of the following: choose **Edit | Cut**, press CTRL+x, or press the DELETE key.

Receiving File Attachments

Most e-mails are simple, self-contained text messages. Some, however, come with files attached – spreadsheets, formatted documents, presentations, graphics, or audio files, for example.

You can identify an e-mail with a file attachment as follows:

- In the Message List, it is shown with a paper clip icon.

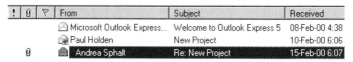

- In the Preview Pane, the e-mail header shows a paper clip icon.

- If displayed in a separate window, the e-mail header shows an Attach: box, with the name and size of the file.

Opening Attachments

You can open a file attachment only if you have an application that is capable of opening it. If someone sends you an attachment that was created in an application that is not installed on your computer (or even a different version of a program that *is* installed), you may be unable to open it.

You can open an attached file in either of two ways:

- If viewing the e-mail in the Preview Pane, click the paper clip icon in the e-mail header to display the file name, and then select the file name from the pop-up menu.

- If viewing the e-mail in a separate window, double-click the file name in the Attach: box.

Saving Attachments

You can save an attached file in any of the following ways:

- Choose **File | Save Attachments**. (This command is available whether you are viewing the e-mail in the Preview Pane or in a separate window.)

  -or-

- In the Preview Pane, click the paper clip icon in the e-mail header and choose **Save Attachments**.

  -or-

- In a separate e-mail window, right-click the file name in the Attach: box, and choose **Save As** from the pop-up window.

In each case, you specify where on your computer you want to save the file, accept or change the file name, and click **Save**.

If you open an attachment and do not save it, you can subsequently open it only from within Outlook Express. If you save it, you can subsequently open it from within Outlook Express *and* from the relevant application.

If you save an attachment and subsequently delete it, you will not be able to open it *either* from within Outlook Express or from within the application. And if you delete the e-mail *without* first saving the attachment, the attachment is also deleted.

Careful: Attachments Can Be Dangerous

Files attached to e-mail messages are among the most common ways of spreading computer viruses. For this reason, you should install a virus protection application on your computer that scans incoming e-mail attachments.

Using E-mail Folders

Once you start using e-mail, you'll probably get a lot of it. Some of it is important at the time, but has a short shelf-life ("Meet you for lunch" "OK"). Some of it you need to keep for reference (the minutes of the project meetings). Some of it is simply junk mail. How do you keep it organised so that you can find what you want, when you want it? You create *mail folders*, that's how!

Exercise 7.46: Creating a New Mail Folder

1) Choose **File | New | Folder**.

2) Type the name you want to give the new folder.

3) Click on the name of the folder in which you want your new folder to be located.

- If you want it to be at the same level as the Inbox, Outbox and other main folders of Outlook Express, click Local Folders.

- If you want it to be a subfolder of an existing folder such as your Inbox, click that folder.

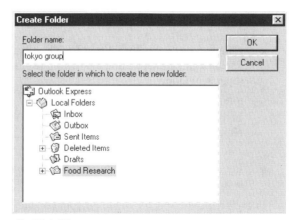

4) Click **OK**.

Transferring E-mails between Folders

As Exercise 7.47 demonstrates, you can transfer an e-mail from one folder to another.

Exercise 7.47: Moving an E-mail from Your Inbox to Another Folder

1) Open your Inbox folder and, in the Message List, select the e-mail you want to move.

2) Choose **Edit | Move to Folder**.

3) Click the folder into which you want to move the message.

4) Click **OK**.

Alternatively, click the e-mail in the Message List, and drag it to the folder in the Folder List on the left of the screen.

What folder do you use for the junk mail and last week's invitations to lunch? Deleted Items, of course!

If you choose **Edit | Copy to Folder** in Exercise 7.47 above, the e-mail will be copied to the second folder – it will appear in both folders.

Deleting a Mail Folder

Be careful. It *is* possible to delete a mail folder, but you can't change your mind. The folder and all its contents will disappear forever. Follow the steps in Exercise 7.48 to discover how.

Exercise 7.48: Deleting a Folder

1) In the Folders List, click to select the folder you want to delete.

2) Choose **File | Folder | Delete** or click the Delete button on the Toolbar.

3) You are asked to confirm that you really do want to delete it.

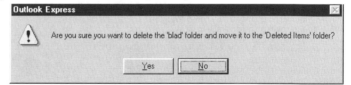

4) Think about it.

Then click **Yes**.

Searching for Specific E-mails

You know that someone – you can't remember who – sent you details of the new MP3 music player. Your friend in Australia sent you a message sometime around Christmas. You need to see all the replies you received to your mail on the subject of Tomorrow's meeting. How do you find what you want?

The quickest way of finding these needles in your e-mail haystack is to use the Find Message function. Exercise 7.49 provides an example.

Exercise 7.49: Finding a Particular E-mail

1) Choose **Edit | Find | Message** or click the Find button on the Toolbar.

2) If you know which folder the message is in, click **Browse** and select that folder for the Look in: box.

   If you're not sure where it is, choose Local Folders and select the Include subfolders checkbox.

3) Fill in whatever you know about the message – who it was from (or, if you sent it, who it was to), the subject, or some word or phrase in the text of the message. You don't have to use full words: even a single letter is enough. You can also specify a range of dates.

4) Click **Find Now**. Outlook Express displays a list of messages that satisfy your criteria.

   When you see the one you want, double-click it to open it.

Sorting Messages in a Folder

An alternative way of finding a particular message is to sort the items in the folder. If you sort your Inbox alphabetically by the name of the sender (the From field), you can find all the messages from a particular person, for example. Or you can find your most recently received messages by sorting it on the Received field.

Exercise 7.50: Sorting the Contents of a Mail Folder

1) Click your Inbox in the Folders List.

2) In the Message List, click the word From in the header. Outlook Express sorts your messages alphabetically by the name of the sender.

3) Click on the word From again. Outlook Express re-sorts the messages into reverse alphabetic order.

4) Click the Received field in the header. Outlook Express sorts your messages into the order in which they were received. As before, you can reverse the order by clicking Received again.

When finished, you can close Outlook Express. You have now completed Section 7.7 of the ECDL Information and Communication Module.

Section Summary: So Now You Know

Outlook Express allows you to perform various actions on e-mails that you receive from others.

You can *forward* an e-mail to someone else, typically accompanied by some comments of your own which you enter in the text area above the original e-mail. You can *reply to the sender only*, so that just the originator of the e-mail sees your reply. Or you can *reply to all recipients* of the original e-mail.

Another option you have is, by using *copy and paste*, to insert the text of a received e-mail in an outgoing e-mail or in another application such as Microsoft Word.

Outlook Express indicates whether an incoming e-mail has a *file attachment*. You can open, save and delete attachments. File attachments may contain viruses, and you should use a reliable virus protection application to scan them.

You can create *mail folders* to keep your e-mails organised, you can *sort* the e-mails in any folder, and you can use the *Find* function to search for a particular e-mail by sender, receiver, subject, or date.

Section 7.8: Address Book and Contact Groups

In This Section

By now, you probably noticed that e-mail addresses can be difficult to remember. Some are cryptic (bill@xyz.com); others are complex (bs_p.sales@xy.pqrcorp.co.uk). Even within the one organisation, different people use different conventions (billsmith, bsmith, bill.smith, bill_smith, bsmth ...). How do you remember all these addresses?

You don't – you keep them in your *address book*.

In this Section you will learn how to organise your contacts in your address book, so that you don't have to remember their e-mail addresses and enter them each time you want to send them a message.

You will also discover how to set up contact groups (also called mailing lists), so that you can send the same message to large groups of people in a single operation.

New Skills

At the end of this Section you should be able to:

- Add, change, and delete contacts in your address book
- Create contact groups that can be e-mailed all at once

New Words

At the end of this Section you should be able to explain the following terms:

- E-mail contact
- Address book
- Nickname (alias)
- Mailing list (contact group)

Your Address Book

Outlook Express contains an area called an *address book* where you can keep information about the people you communicate with.

You can record all sorts of details about your contacts – obvious things, like their name, address, and phone number (and e-mail address!), and less obvious things, like their birthday, and the names of their children.

> **E-mail Contact**
>
> *A person or organisation whose details (such as name and e-mail address) you have recorded in the address book of your e-mail application.*

Address Book button

To explore the variety of information that you can record about your contacts, open Outlook Express, choose **Tools | Address Book** or click the Addresses button on the Outlook Express Toolbar. Next, click the **New** button on the Address Book Toolbar, and then choose **New Contact**.

Click successively on the seven tabs of the dialog box, view the various fields available, and, when finished, click **Cancel**.

> **Address Book**
>
> *A feature of an e-mail application that enables you to record details about your e-mail contacts for easy reference.*

Entering Contacts

In Exercise 7.51 you will practise entering a new contact to your Outlook Express address book.

Exercise 7.51: Adding a Contact to Your Address Book

1) Open your Outlook Express address book by choosing **Tools | Address Book**.

2) Click the **New** button on the Address Book Toolbar, and then select New Contact.

3) In the Name tab, type the First name, Last name and E-mail Address of one of your contacts.

4) In the Nickname field, type a short, easy-to-remember version of their name (even a single letter). Do not enter any spaces within the Nickname.

   You can subsequently enter the Nickname in the To: field of an e-mail. (It is often called an *alias*.)

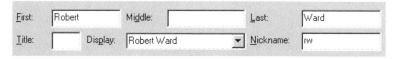

5) Click **OK**.

To create several new contacts in one operation, click **Add** after you type the details of each one. The **Add** button adds new contacts without closing the dialog box. The **OK** button adds the most recently entered contact – and closes the dialog box.

E-mail Nickname (Alias)
A shortened form of an e-mail address that you can enter in the To: field of a message as an alternative to typing the contact's e-mail address in full.

Contacts: The Minimum Details

At a minimum, each contact in your address book must contain a First name, a Last name and a Display name. All other contact details are optional. The first two, you enter; the third is supplied, by default, by Outlook Express.

The Display Name is the name that appears in the To: field of e-mails that you send, and in the From: field of e-mails received from you.

You can change the default Display name by typing in a different name or by selecting an alternative from the drop-down list. The drop-down list contains variations of the First/Middle/Last name, as well as anything you typed in the Nickname box or the Company box of the Business tab.

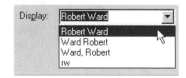

Editing Contacts

At any time, you can change the details of a contact or add further details, simply by:

- Choosing **Tools | Address Book** to open your address book

- Double-clicking to select the relevant contact

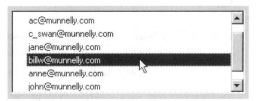

- Overtyping, deleting, or adding the new information

Deleting Contacts

To delete a contact, open your Address Book, select the relevant contact, and do any of the following: click the **Delete** button, press the DELETE key, or choose **File | Delete**.

Adding Contact Details from E-Mail Messages

In Exercise 7.51 you learnt how to add a new contact by opening your address book, and entering and saving the relevant details. You can add a new contact in two other ways:

- Display the Inbox or Outbox message list, right-click on an e-mail, and choose **Add Sender to Address Book** from the pop-up menu.

- When replying to an e-mail, right-click on the name in the To: field, and choose **Add to Address Book** from the pop-up menu.

You can also get Outlook Express to add all reply recipients to your address book automatically as follows:

- Choose **Tools | Options**.

- On the Send tab, select the Automatically put people I reply to in my Address Book option, and click **OK**.

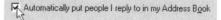

Sorting Your Contacts

You remember her first name but not her last name? You know the telephone number but not the name of the company? With a normal telephone directory, you'd have a problem. With Outlook Express – no problem. Exercise 7.52 and 7.53 take you through the steps.

Exercise 7.52: Sorting by First Name (Method 1)

1) Choose **Tools | Address Book** to open your address book.

2) Choose **View | Sort By**.

3) Select the Name, First Name, and Ascending options.

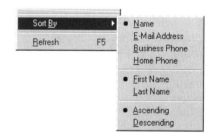

You may have to repeat step 2 to achieve this.

You can then easily find a person by their first name by scrolling through the list.

Exercise 7.53: Sorting by Telephone Number (Method 2)

1) If your address book is not open, choose **Tools | Address Book** to open it.

2) Click the words Business Phone in the header row. Click on the same words a second time.

Note that the order changes with each click, from ascending to descending to ascending again.

You can now find the name you want by scrolling to the telephone number you recognise.

Mailing Lists (Contact Groups)

If you regularly use e-mail to stay in touch with your football team, your research group, or your extended family, you already know that you can send the same message to them by including all their names in the To: or Cc: box. (Remember to separate them with semi-colons!)

However, after a while, all that typing can get a bit tedious. What do you do? You set up what is generally known as a mailing list but which Outlook Express calls a *contact group*. Exercise 7.54 shows you how to create a contact group and add members to it.

Exercise 7.54: Setting Up a Contact Group

1) If your address book is not open, choose **Tools | Address Book** to open it.

2) Click the **New** button and select New Group.

3) Give the new group a name – preferably a short, easy-to-remember name.

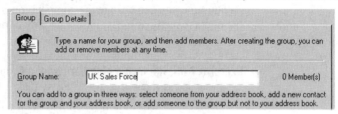

4) Two situations are now possible:

   ■ The people you want to include in your new contact group are in your address book.

   ■ The people you want to include in your new contact group are *not* in your address book.

   If a person is already in your address book, click **Select Members** to view a new dialog box that lists your e-mail contacts. For each contact you want to include, click their name and then click **Select->**.

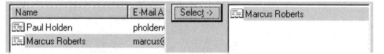

   When finished, click **OK** to return to the main contact group dialog box. Now, go to step 5.

   If the people you want to include are *not* in your address book, and you don't want them to be (because you never want to address them as individuals), type their name and e-mail address and click **Add**.

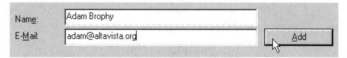

   Continue typing names, e-mail addresses and clicking the **Add** button until you have entered the persons who are not in your address book.

5) When you have finished, click **OK**.

Once you have set up the group, you simply insert its name in the To: field of the message. Outlook Express sends the message to everyone in the group.

Mailing List/Contact Group

A list of e-mail addresses to which you can send a message in a single operation by entering the list's name in the To: field of the message.

A contact group may contain the names of other contact groups. For example, your Global Sales group might consist of three groups – the Europe Sales group, the US Sales group, and the ROW Sales group. An individual may be a member of more than one group.

At any time you can change the composition of your group by adding new members (exactly as in Exercise 7.54 above) or removing members (as in Exercise 7.55 below).

Exercise 7.55: Removing Members from a Group

1) If your address book is not open, choose **Tools | Address Book** to open it.

2) Double-click on the name of the contact group.

3) Click the name of the person you want to remove, and click **Remove**.

4) Click **OK**.

If you remove a name from a group, they still remain in your address book, and in any other group of which they are a member. However, if you delete (or change) a name in your address book, it is deleted (or changed) in every group of which it is a member.

Congratulations! You have now completed Module 7 of ECDL, Information and Communication.

Section Summary: So Now You Know

An *e-mail contact* is a person or organisation whose details (such as name and e-mail address) you have recorded on e-mail application software. Outlook Express allows you to record a wide variety of information about your contacts, spread over seven tabs of a dialog box.

At a minimum, each contact must contain a first name, a last name and a display name. The first two, you enter; the third is supplied, by default, by Outlook Express. An e-mail *nickname* or *alias* is a shortened form of an e-mail address that you can enter in the To: field of a message as an alternative to typing the contact's e-mail address in full.

An *address book* is that part of your e-mail application where your contacts are stored for easy reference. You can type contact information to your address book directly, or you can add contact details to the address book from outgoing or incoming messages.

Outlook Express allows you to *edit* contact details, and to *sort* contacts according to such headings as last name and phone number.

A *mailing list* or a *contact group* is a list of e-mail addresses to which you can send a message in a single operation by entering the list's name in the To: field of the message. A contact group may contain the names of other contact groups. You can change the composition of a contact group by adding or removing members. An individual may be a member of more than one group.